The

Charm of Bombay

The
Charm of Bombay
An Anthology
of writings in praise of
the First City in India

Edited with Notes,

by

R. P. Karkaria

GYAN

Published by

Gyan Publishing House
5, Ansari Road
Daryaganj, New Delhi-110002
Phone: 011-47034999, 9811692060
E-mail: books@gyanbooks.com

Distribution Network
gyanbooks.com
India, USA, Canada, UK, Australia, France

ISBN : 978-81-212-9232-0 (PB)
First Published, 1915

2nd Impression 2023

Printed at: Gyan Press, Delhi.

The Charm of Bombay
Editor: R. P. Karkaria

THE
CHARM OF BOMBAY.

URBS · PRIMA · IN · INDIS

The Charm of Bombay

An Anthology

of Writings in praise of

the First City in India

Edited, with Notes,
by
R. P. Karkaria

Bombay
D. B. Taraporevala, Sons & Co.
103, Medows Street, Fort.

1915.

Preface.

The idea of an anthology of Bombay has steadily grown during these twenty-five years spent in reading off and on about our city and in collecting materials for, as youthful ambition once fondly hoped, a 'big book' about its past history and present proud position. But as years rolled on avocations increased whilst materials multiplied, and the book remained still unwritten. The materials may yet, under Providence, be utilised one day for the purposes for which they were collected. But I thought that meanwhile a good purpose would be served by utilising a part of them in the shape of an anthology of writings about our beautiful city, and I set about the present book which has outgrown its original limits and has been hampered by other work; but now that it is done, I hope it will be thought to have been worth doing.

Nobody can be better aware than myself of its defects and drawbacks, of its sins of commission and still more of omission. But I hope its critics will kindly remember that it is the first and therefore necessarily a tentative edition of the first book of its kind. In the next edition and still more in the succeeding ones, should the book be so fortunate as to go through them, these defects could be easily remedied, especially if other lovers of Bombay will co-operate by their suggestions and criticisms in making it worthier of our great city, emphatically the first in India.

We have unfortunately no Historical Society such as have grown up of late in some other cities of India, for the furtherance of the study of the history and antiquities of our city. If such a Society had existed in our midst—and there was always plenty of work for it—a book like the present and also a much better one, would have appeared long ago under its auspices. A book that casts its nets wide into the voluminous literature of its subject can be better done through the co-operation of such a Society than by a solitary worker however well equipped he may be for the task.

As the book was progressing, the idea struck me, as it will strike many who will read it, that it affords the best justification of the proud motto very happily chosen by James Maclean, as enthusiastic a lover as this city ever had. In its pages will be found arrayed a cloud of witnesses, men, and women too, of all sorts and conditions, testifying to its manifold charms, its great gifts of nature enhanced by art. I do not think any other city in India can adduce equally high estimony from so many people whose testimony is really worth having.

They are very fond of late in Calcutta of usurping our motto, and of calling their city the first in India on the strength of the last Census, as if our claim rested on that basis alone. A few thousand inhabitants more or less does not matter in the least, and we know well that by the proverbial jugglery of figures anything can be proved. Our claims are manifold, and to him who enquires what these are we can only recommend this book and say *circumspice*. We can well afford to smile unconcernedly at the vain efforts of Calcutta to dethrone our city from its rightful place, especially as we know we must make allowances for the mood it is in ever since it was dethroned in reality as the capital of India.

They had for some years a Historical Society there—one of the few points of superiority over us that they really possessed; but I do not think it could have collected testimony as good as ours. It was all along a matter of surprise to me that in the course of its rather brief existence it never set its hands to prepare a book like the present about their city, a really great city with charms and attractions of its own. I should not be surprised if an anthology of Calcutta were to be published now, nay we should be glad, for then we would have the proper means of comparison. But comparisons are odious, and in this case they are certainly not of our seeking and have rather been thrust upon us.

But apart from this, the present book will surely gladden the hearts of all true lovers of

Bombay and justify the faith that is in them. We feel as we read on that we are citizens of no mean city. The eulogists include persons of all shades of opinion, who most probably are at one on this point alone. Great statesmen and famous travellers, visitors and permanent residents, all unite in praising our splendid natural situation and magnificent scenery, the vast achievements of our citizens in the past and the glorious possibilities of the future. We know well, for instance, and have enjoyed often the grand panorama from the Hanging Gardens on Malabar Hill; but we shall enjoy it with greater zest now when we read that a traveller and explorer of world-wide reputation, the late Sir Samuel Baker, rates it so highly that he could find 'no scene throughout the world more beautiful or more impressive than this landscape and sea-view' (p. 101). The same traveller's aphoristic remark that the general aspect of Bombay is a test of British administration ought also to make us feel proud.

It is exactly two hundred and fifty years since Bombay was delivered by the Portuguese to the British in 1665, not ungrudgingly, but with a heavy heart and after raising many difficulties about carrying out the clause in the famous treaty of 1661 relating to the cession of the Island, for the Viceroy of Goa and his advisers well knew that they were parting with a possession which though wilfully neglected by themselves, had great possibilities in the hands of their rivals. During these two centuries and a half of British possession these possibilities became actualities beyond their wildest dreams and Bombay has prospered exceedingly. That prosperity it owes more than any other city in India, entirely to the English. I am glad this book appears in the present year in which falls the two hundred and fiftieth anniversary of that auspicious event. But for the War we would have celebrated it with all the honour due to the great significance of such an historic occasion. It was really the second birth of Bombay when Humphrey Cooke received the keys from its Portuguese Mayor Almeida on that glorious February morning of 1665.

Of the book and its arrangement little need be said. The principle that has generally guided me in the selection of the extracts in all the sections except that of accounts, has been, a good thought well expressed; and I have been somewhat particular in admitting only such passages as are marked by striking language in any form. I have been rather surprised that really fine passages have been so numerous. Our noble city seems to have among its other gifts that of inspiring some very fine writing indeed. This anthology of Bombay will be seen to be marked not only by the distinction of its contributors but also by the generally high level of the contributions. I regret much the absence of two authors of great distinction, Mr. Rudyard Kipling and Pierre Loti; but I could find little in their prose writings which I could ask their permission to include. This is particularly to be regretted in the case, of Mr. Kipling, who is a distinguished son of Bombay. Calcutta is deservedly proud of being the birthplace of Thackeray and the house in which he was born has lately been marked by a memorial tablet. We ought to have done the same to the house on the Esplanade 'between the palms and the sea'* where Mr. Kipling was born; but unfortunately the thatched bungalow in the compound of the School of Arts has been long ago pulled down.

It has been thought advisable to group the passages under certain heads, so that there may be some sort of unity in the great variety of the selections. Hence the arrangement in sections. Within the sections themselves it was at first intended to give the passages in chronological or alphabetical order, but that would have been rather meaningless in a work of this nature. An anthology is not meant for continuous reading or study. Those who want to have passages on kindred subjects brought together may do so by means of the contents.

In one section alone chronological order has been followed for obvious reasons. In the historical accounts of Bombay, given in the last section, it was thought necessary to give them according to the dates when they were written,

* These words are from Mr. Kipling's dedicatory poem in *the Seven Seas*, from which some lines are quoted on p. 538A.

chiefly to show the progress of our city at different periods as evinced in them. Some would doubt the wisdom of including such an historical section in a book like the present meant more for enjoyment than study or use. But *utile dulci;* while the enjoyment of the other sections need not be disturbed by the solid usefulness of this which may moreover be skipped with ease if so preferred. I know there will be some to whom this section will appeal the most. I myself first thought of publishing it with some additions and modifications separately; and this may yet be done, for a collection of such historical accounts is a long-felt want.

Some of the sections, like 'Life and Society' and 'Notable Events' might be enlarged, and some new sections might be added in future editions. I particularly regret that it has not been found possible to add a section on notable persons who flit across the pages of our island story, like Aungier, and Elphinstone and Wilson. The Abbé Raynal's eulogy of Sterne's Eliza is a representative of this class, which has been given out of its place, as it is a *locus classicus* of our literature which many would like to have in a book like the present. In a future edition it may find its proper place with other passages in the section on 'Notable Persons.'

I offer my grateful thanks to the living authors and their publishers for passages from their books quoted in this work. I must not omit to express my cordial obligations to Mr. S. T.

Sheppard, of Trinity College, Oxford, Assistant Editor of the *Times of India,* for suggesting several books and passages. I specially owe to him the extract from the *Description of the Port and Island of Bombay,* published in 1724, an exceedingly rare book, not to be found anywhere else in Bombay, which he kindly lent me from his rich collection of old *Bombayana.* He may be said to continue the literary traditions of Buist and Maclean, past Bombay journalists who have done so much for the literature of our city, and great things are to be expected from him in the future.

Finally, I cannot close without expressing my sense of the great courtesy shown by H. E. Lord Willingdon in writing the Foreword to this book. I take it as his contribution to the anthology and my readers also, I am sure, will be glad to have in addition to the commendations of some of his illustrious predecessors contained in the present volume, His Excellency's appreciation of our city which he very happily calls 'one of the fairest jewels of the Empire's crown.'

R. P. KARKARIA.

CONTENTS.

Scenery and Views.

Burst of the Monsoon.

Approach and Arrival.

First Impressions.

Importance.

Scenes In Bombay.

Life and Society.

Bazaars and Streets.

Notable Events.

Round About Bombay.

Accounts of Bombay.

Supplement.

SCENERY & VIEWS.

SCENERY & VIEWS.

" Ambrosial Ocean Isle."

SIR JOHN REES.

It is impossible to imagine any greater contrast than is afforded by the scenery of Bombay and its unrivalled harbour, to that which we have left behind in Sind. Here everything speaks of an abundant rainfall, hills rise upon hills from the sea-coast to the top of the Ghauts, and every hill is clothed with grass and covered with forest. When all the landscape glowed in the crimson hues of the setting sun, it seemed as if the isle of Bombay itself was the place the Laureate had in his mind which charmed the wanderer out in ocean:

> " Where some refulgent sunset of India
> Streams over a rich ambrosial ocean isle,
> And crimson-hued the stately palmwoods
> Whisper in odorous heights of even."

Tours in India of Lord Connemara, 1892, page 247.

Panorama of Bombay from Bhandarwada Hill.

SIR JAMES M. CAMPBELL.

The high flat ledge to the east of the reservoir plateau on Bhandarwada hill commands one of the completest and most central views of Bombay and its surroundings. To the north a sprinkling of trees and patches of green garden and orchard freshen the foreground of brown roofs and yellow house fronts. Across the muddy Tank Bandar foreshore and the coal heaps of Frere Bandar stand the quarried face of Brae hill, and the Jubilee, Indo-Chinese, and National Mills clustered at the foot of the woody slopes of Golangi or Flagstaff hill. To the right the bare sides of Rowli and Antop rise beyond the fishing village and rock-fort of Sewri. In the distance behind Sewri hill, looms the dim table-land of Tungar. Closer at hand stretching east are the woody slopes and waving outline of Salsette its central hills gathered in three main points above Vehar, Tulsi, and Yeur. Further east, across the north bay and mud flat of the harbour, behind the green swamps and the gray salt lands of Mahul or north-west Trombay, rise the knolls of the Parshik hills, and over them, thirty miles inland, seen only in the clearest air, the lofty deep-cleft crest of Mahuli the guardian of Tansa Lake. At the east foot of Bhandarwada hill the half-mile belt that stretches eastwards to the harbour, with a fair scattering of plantains, cocoa palms, tamarinds, mangoes, and pipals is thick with brown-roofed yellow-faced dwellings, from which stand out the picturesque pale-gray west fronts of two Portuguese churches, Notre Senhora De Rozario at the hill-foot and De Gloria a few hundred yards to the south-east. Fringing the foreshore are the Peninsular and Oriental dockyard, the Mazagon landing-pier, and the British India dockyard.

Further south, close to the hill-foot, are the network of sidings and the long lines of low gray sheds that form the Wadi Bandar terminus. On the left, out from acres of shed roofs, rises the Port Trust Clock Tower and between the tower and the harbour are the rectangular pit of the Merewether dry dock and the broad basins of the Prince's and Victoria wet docks a thicket of lofty masts. South, over the Wadi Bandar sheds and sidings for more than two miles, stretch in strange close-packed confusion piles of many-storeyed dwellings, their white and yellow ends and fronts crowned with peaked gables and brown tiled hummocky roofs topped here and there by a flat view-terrace. Beyond these miles of thick-packed dwellings, on the left, at the harbour side, stand the tower of the Port Trust Moody Bay offices and the Castle Flag-Staff. To the right, from the rough sea of roofs, rises Venice-like, a notable cluster of public buildings, the light pinnacles of the Cathedral, the lofty crocket-ribbed dome of the Victoria Terminus, the peak-roofed finials of the Elphinstone College and the Secretariat, the rounded summit and tiny side minarets of the huge Municipal buildings, the tall square shaft statued-drum and plumed pinnacle of the Rajabai Clock-tower over-topping a confusion of lofty roofs, the steep railtipped roof of the short High Court tower and the turrets of the Public Works Secretariat, of the Post, and the Telegraph Offices. To the right of the Rajabai tower, out of the distant low green line of Colaba, rise the spire of the Memorial Church and the column of the Prongs Light-house In the middle distance, to the right of the High Court, the high pitched roof of the Police Court, the clock tower of the Crawford Market, the finial of the Gokaldas Hospital, and the lantern of St. Xavier's College show like islands in the sea of roofs and tree-tops.

To the west, close at hand, are the reservoir filter-beds and gardens of the lower western top of Bhandarwada hill. Beyond Bhandarwada hill to the south-west, behind the line of the Great Indian Peninsula Railway, stretches the scarped cliff of Nowroji hill, its top and western slopes thick with houses. Further west from the broken mass of roofs that stretch to the palms of Girgaum stand out the wide enclosure and the lofty turrets and pinnacles of the Jamsetji and Motlibai Hospitals. Still more to the right, among the brown roofs that spread to the factories of Tardeo and the foot of Cumbala hill, rise the cupola of the Synagogue, the obelisk of Byculla Church, and the smooth slender twin spires of St. Mary's College. To the north-west, between the Bhandarwada reservoir and the gray of the Flats, the crowd of brown roofs is hidden and broken by the gardens and mango orchards of Mazagon, and adorned by the golden-spiked gleaming white dome and minarets of the Aga Khan's Tomb, and the peak-roofed tower of the Technical Institute. Further to the right, across the middle distance, as far as the green belt of the Mahim palm groves, stretch the Flats bristling with forty lofty chimney stalks and laden with the mighty masses of the Leopold, David, Petit, Imperial, Sun, Jacob, New Sassoon, and other huge factories. Round this great city, to the north-east east and south, stretch the broad waters of the harbour, according to the hour and the season, blue golden tawny or steel gray, with its flocks of small white-winged harbour craft, and, at their moorings, lines and clusters of lading and discharging steamers, fleets of peak-prowed lofty-pooped sea-faring baglas dhingis and kotias, and a sprinkling of stately square-rigged ships. Among the shipping, opposite the Carnac Bandar, lies the bare rocky mound of Cross Island, and about two miles south off the Apollo Bandar, the small flat circle of the Middle Ground Shoal.

Across the harbour the north-east is filled by

the long brown back of Trombay sloping south to the point of Pir Pav. In the east lies the low greenery of Hog Island. In midwater is the flat rocky line of Butcher's Island, and, behind it, the woody hills of Elephanta and to the south-east the separate sharp-cut crests of Little and of Great Karanja. Inland, beyond the low broken line of the Parshik hills, the shivered cliffs and the flat-topped bluffs of the Tavli-Matheran range fill the whole eastern view. In this range from north to south are the bastions of Tavli, the Cathedral Rocks of Bhav Malang the smaller buttresses of Mhas-Mala, the pillar of Navra-Navri, the castle crest of Chanderi, the low fortified head of Peb, the long walls of Matheran and Prabhal, the broken pillars of Isalgadh the False Funnel and of Karnala the True Funnel, and the comb of Manikgad. In the extreme east, through breaks in the Matheran range, looms the dim wall of the Sahyadris. Behind the comb of Manikgad to the left are the gap of the Bor Ghat and the heights round Khandala and, in the clearest air, the more distant forts of Visapur and Lohogad To the right the knuckle tip of Nagphani or the Duke's Nose stands in front of the long plateau of Sakarpathar and the saw-teeth of Jambulni, with, in clear air, more distant peaks, perhaps Tung and Tikona in Bhor. South of Jambulni the line of the Sahyadris rises in a group of noble hills of which Devgad, Morva, Visakar, Koarigad, Masagaum, and part of Saltar in south Poona are visible, and the rest of Saltar and Tel Baili also in south Poona and Bhorap in Bhor are hid by the slope of north Karanja. In the gap between the two Karanjas stands the wooded western top of Mira Dongar the Pen hill.

Further south, between the west point of Great Karanja and the Bluff in nort-east Alibag, the long hill-flanked valley of the Amba river or Nagotha creek winds twenty-six miles south into the heart of the Bhor hills. About ten miles south of the Alibag Bluff, from a sharp cliff overhanging the Amba creek, the main range of the Alibag hills stretches west till, near the fortified top of Sagargadh, it is hid by the beacon-bearing slope of the Alibag Bluff. To the right the crest of the Bluff sweeps south and west rising to the sacred wooded head of Kankeshwar, which falls westward to the sea and the faint outlying circle of Kenery island. Behind the western spurs of Kankeshwar stands the bare block of the western Sagargadh range centering in the point of Parhur. Fifteen miles south over the low lines of the Alibag palms, the land ends in the dim level crest of the Roha and Janjira hills. From the palm groves of Alibag, past the low line of Henery (Underi) and the rocky knoll of Kenery (Khanderi), the sea spreads round the points and reefs of Colaba across the palm-fringed curve of Back Bay, till it is hid by the woody bluff of Malabar Point which rises gently northwards to the house-and palmyra-rcowned crest of the Malabar and Cumbala ridges. North-west, across the palm-dotted curve of the Great Vellard, is a second stretch of open sail-brightened sea, hid for a time by the woody hillock of Love Grove and again opening on either side of the rock of Martand, till it is once more lost behind the woody crest of Varli which, in a broken line, leads north, till the circle is completed in the plam groves of Mahim and the leafy gardens and rice lands of Parel and Matunga overtopped by the casuarinas of Bandra hill, and the long ridge of Pali.

Administration Report, Bombay, 1891-2, pp. 43-44.

View From The Ridge

THE IMPERIAL GAZETTEER.

The views obtainable from the ridge of Malabar Hill and the summit of the Altamont Road, which winds up Cumballa Hill, are magnificent. Standing by night upon the ridge, one looks down upon the palm-groves of Chaupati, and across the sweep of Back Bay to the Rajabai tower, the Secretariat, and the Light-house at Colaba point, the whole curve of land being jewelled with an unbroken chain of lights, which have earned the appropriate title of "The Queen's Necklace." From Cumballa Hill the view to the east includes the whole native city, the hill of Mazagaon, upon which, in early days, a white-washed house stood as a guide for vessels entering the harbour, and beyond them the harbour, islands, and mainland of the north Konkan. To the left lies the industrial area, with its high chimney-stacks and mill roofs, and the coast section of Sewri, in which may still be seen relics of the old fortress built upon a projecting spit of land. Sewri in these days contains the European cemetery, which was originally the garden of the Horticultural Society of Bombay. On the west side Cumballa Hill slopes down to the shore, where, close to the Hornby Vellard, the Mahalakshmi temples command attention. The present shrines are comparatively modern; but they are stated to stand upon the site of three very old temples which were destroyed during the period of Mohamadan domination. The temples form the northern limit of another suburb, known as Breach Candy, where the houses are built close down upon the seashore within the refreshing sound of the waves. The ruined fortress of Warli can be visited from this point; while a good road leads through the great cocoa-nut woods of Mahim to the Lady Jamsetji Causeway and the neighbouring Island of Salsette.

Third edition, 1908 Vol. VIII pages 401-402.

View from The Ridge, Malabar Hill.

JAMES MACLEAN.

From the Ridge we get a magnificent view of the island and harbour of Bombay. Perhaps the best point of view is the Cliff, the late Dr. Wilson's residence, or the Ladies' Gymkhana, a favourite evening rendezvous now for families living on Malabar Hill, and the best time is just before sunset. A poet might well say that "earth hath not anything to show more fair" than the glorious panorama of water, wood, hill, shipping and the stately edifices of a great city which here strikes and fascinates the eye. "This dings Dumbarton" is said to have been the remark of a Scotchman on first seeing Gibraltar; and perhaps even Scott, had he seen Bombay from the Ridge, would have confessed that this is a lovelier scene than that which he describes in such glowing verse, when his hero Marmion looks down upon Edinburgh from the brow of Braid Hill. A double bay lies below, intersected by the island city, which buried at its base in plantations of palm trees, emerges midway into a succession of noble buildings, whose faults of detail are lost in the distance, while the harmonious grandeur of the whole mass is enhanced by the parting rays of the sun shining full upon them. From this culminating point of splendour, the city tapers away towards Colaba in a gently curving promontory just broad enough to mark and complete the perfect outline of Back Bay. Beyond stretches the broad harbour with its islands, and the mountains of the Koncan, with their battlemented summits form the background of the picture. Perhaps, although Bombay does not, like England, appeal to the imagination by the charm of great and holy memories, it might not be esteemed sacrilegious to apply to her, thus seen at sunset, or, still better, in the tropical radiance of the moonlight, the words of the poet—" A precious stone set in the silver sea."

Guide to Bombay, ed. for 1899, Pages 305–6.

" The World Cannot Produce a Finer View "

BALCARRES RAMSAY.

Ride along Back Bay, ascend Malabar Hill: the world cannot produce a finer view. You stand on a lovely wooded hill; beneath you are the rich and fertile islands of Bombay and Salsette, the deep blue sea, the noble shipping in the harbour, and afar the fantastically shaped and picturesque Deccan hills, all forming a wondrously attractive picture. Turn from this lovely scene, ascend one of the narrow paths up the hill, and you will find yourself close to the Parsee burial-ground. On extreme point of this hill is one of the Governor's residences, called Malabar

Point, occupied [1845] by the Commander-in-Chief, Sir Thomas M'Mahon, and his family. As you descend the hill on the other side, the sea alone greets your eye. The road winds along the foot of this hill, and affords a charming drive: this is still a favourite resort of the Bombay people during the evening. Not far from this, and round the Point, is a large portion of waste land called the Flats, about two miles in extent. This, in former years, during the monsoon, was regularly flooded, but a handsome breakwater had been made by Governor Jonathan Duncan. Across these Flats my brother aide-de camp, Captain D'Arcy, made capital bridlepaths.

Ride across these Flats and you come upon the highroad to Thana, and close to Government House, Parell. The grounds at Parell are laid out quite in the English style. The house itself is a fine building,—formerly, under the Portuguese rule, a Jesuit convent, and afterwards the residence of Sir James Mackintosh during the time he was Recorder of Bombay: it has since been much enlarged and beautified. You drive up under a handsome portico, and are received by a host of servants (chobdars). On the ground-floor there is a magnificent room, capable of dining a hundred people ; beyond, a billiard-room ; off these are several bedrooms opening on to spacious verandahs. Up-stairs there is a magnificent drawing-room and reception-room ; at one end a fine portrait of the Marquis of Wellesley. A ball or a reception here is always a pretty sight. In the first place, the ladies are almost always well dressed and the officers in full uniform: and a tulip-bed cannot show more variety than the various uniforms of the British and Indian services. Noble rooms delightfully cool and airy, picturesque costumes, and plenty of room to show them off, are the distinguishing features of an Indian reception.

Rough Recollections, 1882, Vol. I, pages 82-84.

Malabar Point

MRS. POSTANS.

It is difficult to select and particularise, where so many beautiful views, so many fresh combinations of scenery, attract the eye as from the curving and numerous roads winding about this lovely island; amongst the most charming spots, however, is the bold promontory, known as Malabar Point, and crowned with a mansion, originally the residence of Sir John Malcolm, now [1838] set apart for the accommodation of the Governor, when the heat becomes oppressive at Parell. This agreeable resort, pitched upon the tall and rocky headland, like an eiry above the waves, commands a varied and extensive view, lovely at all times, but more peculiarly so when the sun's broad golden disc is half obscured below the azure waters, and the feathery tips of the cocoa-nut woods retain their amber-tinted hues. Then appear the undulating and varied roads, studded with groups of animated figures; the bright bay, bearing numerous pleasure boats, whose oars lie on the glassy medium which reflects the tasselled palms fringing its immediate shores; inland, the wooded knolls look richer as the foliage takes a deeper hue, the bamboos lose their paly green, and the jutting rocks borrow partial shades from the gathering twilight; while below, along the shores, fires brightly burning, mark the funeral pyres of the Hindoo dead; and far from these, solitary figures, in white and flowing raiment, bend their foreheads to the earth, or slowly pace the strand, to catch the gorgeous sun's last ray upon the wave, and "Hail their Creator's dwelling-place among the living lights of heaven."

Western India, 1739, Vol. I pages 36-38.

"Queen of Asiatic Cities."

SIR RICHARD TEMPLE.

For a few days at my beautiful capital, in the finest season of the year, (1880) I had a halcyon time, and a restful feeling which had been long unknown to me. I imprinted on the tablets of my memory the features of this city, doubtless the Queen of Asiatic cities—the highlands and islands, the bays and creeks, the forest of masts in the wide spreading harbour, the horizon on one side bounded by the Western Ghat mountains and on the other side extended far out to the Indian Ocean. As a foreground to this scenery of sea and land was the ornate and palatial line of Government edifices.

Story of my life, 1895, Vol. II, pages 49-50.

Bombay from the Towers of Silence.

BARON VON HÜBNER.

Bombay is at our feet,—the city, the bay and the sea! To the south-west a forest of masts, the tops of which only are discernible, indicates the harbour. Beyond it, on the horizon, are rocks and islets of fantastic outline, some bare, some carpeted with fern, and all of them gilded by the sun. Right beneath us is one of the native quarters, buried in a sea of cocoa-nut palms, and above their waving tufts, through the open fanlike tracery of their leaves, and behind the transparent mists of the distance, the imposing buildings on the Esplanade and Colaba. Farther eastward stands a confused mass of houses, broken here and there by a spire—the actual city of Bombay. At your right, bathing the foot of the heights on which you stand, is the Arabian Sea. The panorama is one of the loveliest, and, from the variety of its constituent parts, one of the richest that can be seen; it might even be called unique. But the contrast offered by the Towers of Silence prevents you from thoroughly enjoying it. Perhaps, without noticing it, you feel upset, and you leave the spot with mingled feelings of pleasure and regret.

Through the British Empire, 1886, Vol. II, pages 18-19.

View From the Fort

VISCOUNT VALENTIA.

The view from the fort is extremely beautiful towards the bay, whose smooth expanse is here and there broken by the islands that are, many of them, covered with wood, while the lofty and whimsically shaped hills of the table land, form a striking back-ground to the landscape. The sea is on three sides of it, and on the fourth an esplanade, at the extremity of which is the black town, embosomed in a grove of cocoa-nut trees.

Voyages and Travels, 1811, Vol. II, page 168.

"The Isle of Palms"

MRS. POSTANS.

The Harbour scenery of Bombay is justly considered the most lovely in the world, the fairest of all

'the Isles that gem
Old Ocean's purple diadem'

To detail the particular features which compcse its beauty, were impossible. The deep smooth waters, the bright blue cloudless sky, the clustering islands, gleaming in still dreamy indistinctness, fringed with the dark feathers of the palm trees, which seem so jealously to conceal the line where the fair elements unite: the pale purple Ghauts, towering, higher and higher, in piles of varied form, their lofty summits dim in the misty distance, blending with the soft haze of a tropic sky, form a picture, which fascinates the eye, and spell-binds the imagination, as completely as it baffles the power of language to pourtray.

To afford to those who may not look upon this glorious scene, a bird's-eye glimpse of its general *coupd'œil,* is all that can be attempted, and the elegant pen of Bishop Heber has well performed that task; objections have been made to his descriptions, as too Italianized and florid, but critics of taste, whom opportunity may have enabled to study the various combinations of pictorial effect among these lovely scenes, must acknowledge, that neither poetry, nor painting, can possibly do justice to the peculliar and exquisite beauty of the "Isle of Palms."

Where the inducements which the fair face of nature presents, are so great, it is not remarkable that yachting should be, as it is, a very favourite recreation; or that the gay streamers of the "Lovely Lucy," and the "Lalla Rookh," should be seen so frequently floating in bright relief against the dark masses of rich foliage which clothe, to the water's edge, the time-hallowed island of Elephanta, and the beautifully wooded scenery of Salsette.

The *modern* town of Bombay, however (for to such a distinction the march of progress entitles it) deserves description; and however charming may be the bright and sparkling bay, the palm-tasselled islets, the varied craft, and the pretty latteen sails which swell in the fresh breeze, a stranger yet desires to step firmly upon land, and mix in the bustling interests of his fellow-men.

The general appearance of Bombay from the harbour, is certainly not attractive. Little can be seen of it but the walls of the fort, flanking the water's edge, the tents of the esplanade rising in white and gleaming clusters, and the island of Colaba, stretching out towards the west, covered with palm trees, and crowned at its extreme end by the Bombay Light-house.

The bundars, or landing-places, are commonly surrounded by singular-looking boats, whose crews ply among the shipping with passengers or cargo. Moored in a busy knot, may be observed the crazy little canoe, laden with cocoanuts and plantains ; the miniature barge, covered with the gay purdah (awning), to screen the fat Parsee, who sits cross-legged in her stern ; and the more important bundah boat, with its comfortable cabin lined with soft cushions, and surrounded with smart green venetians, awaiting an engagement to convey a party to the spot selected for a picnic, or to stretch down the coast to the various beautiful and sea-girt stations of the southern Koncan.

Western India, 1839, Vol. I, pages 4-7.

Bombay and Naples

CAPT. ROBERT GRINDLAY.

The derivation of the name of Bombay is generally considered to be from Buon Bahia, a name given to it by the Portuguese, the first European settlers, and indicating its peculiar excellence as a harbour, in which it is equalled by few others in the world, whether for security to shipping or the picturesque beauty of its scenery.

The far-famed Bay of Naples can scarcely, be placed in comparison with Bombay, from the very different description of beauty which characterizes each. If the former can boast of its Vesuvius, its castellated heights of St. Elmo, and semicircular sweep of shore, fringed with imposing groups of buildings, the latter possesses beauties of a grander description and of more rare combination. While the back-ground is composed of that stupendous range of mountains, the Ghauts, raising their rugged summits in every possible variety of shape, assuming frequently the appearance of vast fortresses, the harbour is studded with numerous groups of islands, of various size and form, and some of them richly wooded to the water's edge.

Scenery in Western India, 1830, page 39.

By Land and Sea.

CAPT. JOHN SEELY.

Nothing can be more delightful than the rides and drives in this island: they extend twenty-one miles, and communicate to the neighbouring island of Salsette by means of a causeway. The prospect is as grand and as beautiful as can be imagined: the mighty range of the Ghats towering in the clouds and extending as far as the eye can reach; the bold views on the continent; the diversified objects on the island; old ruinous convents and monasteries erected by its former conquerors, the Portugueze; the noble country-houses of the Europeans;

Hindoo pagodas, Mahometan mosques; the remains of Mahratta forts and buildings: these, with the rural appearance of Hindoo villages, where every patch of ground is richly cultivated or ornamented, and interspersed with groves of date and cocoa-nut trees, afford a prospect of luxuriance and beauty to be met with nowhere but in the Koncan. As we turn our eyes towards the sea, we are presented with a fine hard beach running on the high and romantic spot called Malabar Point, which promontory is studded with neat villas; while the city and fort are seen in the back-ground, with the ships securely at anchor in the harbour. Nor must we forget the isthmus called Colaba (probably Calab, or black water), running for about two miles in a straight line from Bombay, from which it is separated at high water. On this small island, which scarcely exceeds a quarter of mile in breadth, are several good houses and a range of barracks. At its farthest or western end stands a noble signal and light-house, from the top of which is a very fine view of the Island and adjacent country.

Nor is it on land alone that Bombay possesses the advantages of situation. Its harbour, from its great size, smoothness of the water, and, for the greater part of the day, having a fine sea-breeze blowing, affords almost constant opportunity for aquatic excursions; so open, indeed, and, at the same time, so secure is the bay, that for miles, in various directions, the smallest boats may proceed with safety and by means of the tide, return at almost a fixed hour. These excursions may be extended seaward, inward, or over to the Mahratta continent, for several miles, embracing in the journey a variety of beautiful, picturesque, and grand scenery. How widely different from the boasted river-parties on the Ganges about Calcutta; where you have a muddy and often a very dangerous, stream to sail on, with light and hot sultry air, impregnated with all the poisonous effects of miasma, the wind hardly sufficiently strong to impel the boat; or else tracking, by means of a dozen poor wretches slowly struggling through the low, marshy, and swampy banks of the Ganges, where the eye is unrelieved by the smallest change of scenery, and not a hill is to be seen in any direction: in short where an uninterrupted view of jungle, flat land, water, and mud presents itself. At Madras the scene on the water is widely different from what we see either at Calcutta or Bombay; and a journey on it, whether for amusement or business, is any thing but agreeable, for you are often in danger of your life, and always in dread, in passing to and fro through the tremendously high and long surfs that incessantly roll on the Coromandal shores, and which commence about a mile inside the roadstead, where the ships lie at anchor.

The climate of Bombay is preferable to most parts of India, having a refreshing sea-breeze, commonly called, from its healthful effects, the Doctor. There is now very little wood on the island, no marshes, and but few large pools of stagnant water. To these causes much of the sickness that prevails in other parts of India must be attributed; and the salubrity of Bombay causes it to be resorted to by invalids from the other Presidencies and the interior.

Wonders of Elora, 1824, pages 4-6.

Bombay: Site and Scenery.

PHILIP ANDERSON.

Where is there a site more calculated not only to strike the eye of a casual observer, but to grow in the estimation of a well-informed and scientific resident, than Bombay? Two centuries ago its distinguishing features must have been the same as they are at present; for they could only be altered by the disturbances and revolution of a geological era. The deep capacious harbour, with its channel so narrow, yet safe for careful and well-trained pilots; false harbour of Back Bay, offering to inexperienced mariners or threatenin ginvaders a tempting and dangercus lure; the Eastern hills which rise in rugged and fantastical shapes one behind another, until at noonday they are lost in misty heat; their feet fringed with palm trees, their summits crowned with primeval forests, or here and there with the ruins of ancient fortresses—all form a scene which promises strength and security to the inhabitants; and if it had but the exquisite associations of classic antiquity, or the decorations of Italian taste, might be thought by a lover of the picturesque to rival even the place where Virgil sleeps and the Siren sang—beautiful Parthenope.

But although the outlines of the distant scenery are bold, the appearance of the island when approched from the sea is somewhat insignificant. Flat plains, in some places below the level of high-water mark, are slightly relieved by low ridges of trappean rock, the highest point of which is called Malabar Hill, and that does not exceed a hundred and eighty feet. The whole area of the island is about sixteen square miles. Its shape approaches a trapezoid, with its shorter side, six miles in length, towards the sea, and its longer side extending eleven miles parallel to the mainland. Between the two hilly ridges, which form these sides, there is a level plain, about two miles in width, now called the Flats. The greatest breadth of the Island is little more than three miles. Malabar Point is the name of that extremity which, to the south, faces the open sea, and at the northern extremity are the Hill and Fort of Warli. The line which is parallel to the harbour and mainland has for its southern extremity the Light House and Burial-ground of Colaba, and for its northern the tower called Riva Fort.

Colaba was a separate Island, until joined a few years ago by a causeway to Bombay. Between it and Malabar Hill is the Back Bay, to which we have already alluded. On the Colaba side the Bay is shallow and filled with dangerous rocks; but under the opposite cliff is a channel, sufficiently deep for ships of considerable tonnage. To the north of Bombay is another Bay, with a beach called Mahim Sands, and on that side the island is separated from the mountainous island of Salsette by a small arm of the sea, which at one part is only a hundred and twenty five yards wide, Salsette itself being separated from the mainland by another channel. To the south and east is the harbour, which contains several lofty, interesting islands, and is in one place six miles broad. It extends a considerable distance inland, and, as it narrows, the shores on either side present various scenes of extraordinary beauty.

English in Western India, 1854, pages 51-52.

The Harbour.

DR. BUIST.

As the great bulk of visitors reach us by sea and from Europe, in approaching Bombay will be noticed the beautiful little islands of Henery and Kenery at the mouth of the harbour, fortified in the time of the Mahrathas; long favourite places of resort, for rovers watching to make prizes of merchant ships, when this was known as the pirate coast. The shore all along is here thickly dotted with ruined strongholds, and the remains of the fortifications are still tolerably entire on the two islands just named. Advancing up the harbour the vessels thread their way through the fishing stakes, often to be found thirty and forty miles out at sea,—wherever indeed, a bank within half a day's sail of land presents itself; the fishermen are quite enterprizing enough to extend their operations to any distance, but there is no use in their going further off than they can return with their fish to the market, fresh.

Proceeding up the harbour by and by he passes the Outer Light Ship, a vessel permanently anchored on one of the extremities of the reef called the Prongs. Shortly after this he comes opposite the Light House and the Observatory. He is now opposite the island of Colaba, and Old Woman's island.

The high grounds to the east or right hand as he approaches the harbour form the hill and Angrias Colaba, which are divided from those of Caranja and the other islands by the estuary or creek opening into the Nagotna river. Before him he has now one of the finest open roadsteads in the world, where from fifty to a hundred square-rigged ships are generally to be found at anchor—native vessels of the most picturesque and singular forms are to be seen in thousands all round, carrying betwixt them annually from eight to ten millions worth of commodities. Straight onward will be seen the picturesque hills of Salsette and the far famed island of Elephanta. The vessel has hardly dropped her anchor when she is surrounded on all sides by bunder boats, a clumsy and grotesque species of craft, but safe and withal commodious.

Guide to Bombay, 1856, pages 247-249.

Bombay and Its Surroundings.

SIR WILLIAM HUNTER.

In the beauty of its scenery, as well as in the commercial advantages of its position, Bombay is unsurpassed by any of the cities of the East. Bombay Island is connected with the mainland on the north by two railway embankments and as many causeways. The entrance into the harbour from the sea discloses a magnificent panorama. The background is shut in by the barrier range of the Western Ghats. In front opens the wide harbour, studded with islands, dotted with the white sails of innumerable native crafts, and affording a secure shelter to fleets of steam-propelled merchantmen. The city itself consists of well-built houses and broad streets ennobled by public buildings. The seashore is formed by docks, warehouses, and a long line of artificial embankments extending continuously for nearly five miles. On approaching Bombay from the west, there is little to strike the eye: the coast is low, the highest point, Malabar Hill being only about 180 feet above the sea. But on entering the harbour a stranger is impressed with the picturesqueness of the scene. To the west the shore is crowded with buildings, some of them, as Colaba Church and the Rajabai Clock-tower of the University, very lofty and well-proportioned. To the north and east are numerous islands, and pre-eminent amongst the hills, the remarkable one of Bava Malang, otherwise called Malanggarh, on the top of which is an enormous mass of perpendicular rock, crowned with a ruined fort.

The harbour is an animated and picturesque scene. There are usually a troopship and a man-of-war of H. M's East India Squadron, together with numerous large passenger or merchant steamers, among which may be mentioned those of the Peninsular and Oriental Company, the Italian Rubattino, the British India Steam Navigation Company, the Messageries Maritimes, the Austrian Lloyd, the 'Clan,' 'Anchor,' and 'Hall' lines. Many other steamers, and an occasional sailing vessel, are to be seen riding at anchor, swinging with the swiftly-flowing tide, and discharging or receiving cargo. All kinds of boats, ship's dingies, steam-launches, native baghlas and padaos, incessantly ply in the harbour. At the southernmost point of the "Prongs," a dangerous reef jutting from Colaba point, stands the lighthouse, built in 1874, and containing a first class dioptric light, which is visible for eighteen miles.

The island consists of a low-lying plain about $11\frac{1}{2}$ miles long by 3 to 4 broad, flanked by two parallel ridges of low hills. Point Colaba, the headland formed by the longer of these ridges, protects the harbour lying on its eastern side from the force of the open sea; the other ridge terminates in Malabar Hill; and between the two lies the shallow expanse of Back Bay. The island is in shape a trapezoid. It is popularly likened to a hand laid palm upwards, with the fingers stretching southwards into the sea and the thumb representing Malabar Hill, with Back Bay between the thumb and forefinger: others see in it a resemblance to a withered leg, with a very high heel and pointed toe, the heel being Malabar Hill and the toe Colaba. On a slightly raised strip of land between the head of Back Bay and the harbour is situated the Fort, the original nucleus round which the town grew up, but now chiefly occupied by stately public buildings and commercial offices. From this point the land slopes westward to the central plain, which, before the construction of the embankment known as the Hornby Vellard, was liable to be submerged at high tide. To the north and east recent schemes of reclamation have similarly shut out the sea, and partly redeemed the foreshore for the use of commerce. In the extreme north of the island a large tract of salt marsh still remains unreclaimed.

Imperial Gazetter (revised from Hunter's 1885 ed.) 1908, Vol. VIII, pages 398-399.

View from the Hanging Gardens.

L. R. W. FORREST.

Take an October morning and from the hanging gardens of Malabar Hill look over the city. The sun is lighting up the harbour, fleecy clouds still hang about the nearer hill sides, while over them range after range of mountains appear, and fill up the background of the picture. The air is so clear that everything looks quite close, and the trees on Karanja can be distinctly seen, though seven or eight miles away. It is a wonderful panorama of great beauty. In the evening, the lights round the graceful curve of Back Bay, seen from the same place, make a fairy scene, and Mrs. Kipling, mother of the well-known author, well called it "Bombay's golden necklace."

In the afternoon on driving down from Malabar Hill, one sees, especially on one of the numerous festivals, crowds of people on the sands, circle of women standing in the water around some Brahmin, offering flowers to the sea; the Kennedy sea face thronged with natives taking the air, carriages without number rolling along the Queen's Road, now fringed with trees, and further on fine buildings on the Esplanade with Gilbert Scott's graceful Rajabai Tower rising above them all.

Paper on Bombay, before the Society of Arts, (Journal of the Society, 1901, page 584).

Our Poetic Environment.

THE BOMBAY GAZETTE.

The view from Bombay harbour of the hills and mountains on the opposite mainland of the Konkan is always very fine on a clear morning and evening; but it is never so grand and picturesque as during one of the Elephant storms in October. Sometimes these storms are very weird to witness especially from a coign of vantage like the high hill tops of Matheran or Bava Malang in the Konkan or the Duke's Nose on the Ghauts. Ruskin alone could do justice to these wonderful phenomena of nature in Western India and describe those storms worthily as they roll from hill to hill, and fill the valleys and ravines with fleecy mists accompanied by vivid flashes of lightning that fitfully illumine the sombre scene, and peals of thunder that seem almost to dissolve the foundations of the hills and mountains.

Our prosaic city is set amidst very poetic surroundings; and this sea-girt isle has for its back-ground a very picturesque panorama of hills of various shapes standing out against a blue sky. The top of Malabar or Bhandarwada hills commands an excellent view of the whole city and its poetical surroundings,--the giant horse-shoe of Back Bay studded with noble buildings rising almost from its margin, the extensive grove of palms underneath which the mighty heart of the city seems to lie still, the vast Arabian Sea stretching away to the west and shining a copper hue under the rays of the afternoon sun, and to the east the serrated line of the Sahyadries, the jagged fantastic peaks of the Cathedral Range and other hills of Thana and Kolaba. The late Sir Samuel Baker who was, to use Homer's favourite epithet for Ulysses, a much-travelled man, declared that he had never seen anything during his world-wide tours to match such a scene from Malabar Hill. How many of us pass by almost daily this glorious opportunity of feasting their eyes with such a scene of Nature's beauty and of God's glory which lies around them, without so much as being even aware of it.

The whole panorama of Bombay and its poetic environment of sea and mountain is of course best seen from a height. But the beautiful background of the hills of the mainland is best observed from the harbour especially in a boat moving eastward towards them. Immediately after the rains our atmosphere becomes beautifully clear and translucent and the views are very soft and refreshing. But just before the burst of such storms at the end of the monsoon, the view becomes for a brief while wonderfully clearer still, letting the eye penetrate to a great distance and revealing in a marvellous manner, in bold clear cut outline, all the elements of the scene.

The distant hills appear clothed in deep dark blue, the nearer ones in the harbour itself assume a light gold tint, while the sky wears a somewhat lowering aspect with thick clouds that throw a lurid effect on the whole scene. While the east was in this state, in the opposite quarter of the heavens the sun shone amid an almost clear azure sky with only fleecy specks of clouds swimming across the surface. The effect of light and shade was hence very impressive. Often the rays of the sun striking the hills opposite poured suddenly a flood of light upon the green slopes, and their dark blue momentarily gave way to a bright greenish gold. The fleecy clouds floating across the sun cast weird moving shadows on the hills and heightened the chiaroscuro. As we advance in the boat there appears a vast extended amphitheatre of hills, a long line in the front curving on either hand. The most prominent feature of the scene opposite are the triple hills rising wave-like one behind the other, the low Panwell hills nearest, the long line of the Cathedral Range extending from Karjat to Kallian in the middle, and behind these in the dim distance the top of the Sahyadris the famous Ghauts, which bear aloft on their shoulders the vast plateau of the Deccan.

Matheran is never so strikingly and clearly seen from Bombay as at the close of the rains. From Chowk Point south, to Panorama Point north, the whole flat top is visible, whilst through glasses its thick woods can be easily seen even to the famous "One-tree" knoll at Chowk Point. Usually the neighbouring hill of Prabal hides from us the central part of Matheran; but in October it stands out distinct and bold, while the gap between formed by the Varosha Valley, is rendered visible by the effects of light and shade which gave different tints to these hill sides. On the left of Matheran to the north, are visible the other peaks of the Cathedral Range in a long line,-the steep point of Peb or Vikatghad, the rounded Nakhinda, the massive blade of Chanderi, the finger-like pinnacles of Mhas-Mahra and Navara-Navari, and the hog-backed Tavli. The most famous of this range from whence it derives its name, the lofty top of Bava Malang, which indeed stands quite like a Cathedral in the wilderness with tower and belfrey sharp chiselled as if by human hands—does not Ruskin call all mountains cathedrals of nature?—is partly hid from view behind Tavli and only the line of its summit is visible against the eastern sky. In apparent continuation of these, are visible the Persik hills in Thana, through one of which the G. I. P. Railway has carved a way for itself; while the Tullenje hills of Panwell, which appear between the sea and the Cathedral hills, also extend to the left. In the north-east, quite in the left hand corner, rise the hills of Salsette running from Thana almost to Bassein creek, and containing the famous monastary of Kanheri and the Vehar and Tulsi lakes, fit emblems side by side of ancient and modern civilization.

To the south of Matheran on our right appear the low broken pillar of Ishalghad, and in a line with it the singular top of Karnala with its noted funnel-like rock, which is the well-known land mark of Bombay harbour to all sailors entering it. Some of the Kolaba hills, especially the pyramidal dome of Manikghad, are hidden from our view by the twin islands in the harbour, great and little Karanja. But from behind the gap between the two and over the causeway connecting them, we have a fine glimpse of the Sahyadris of which we see the famous peaks of the double-topped Rajmachi, the 'royal terrace' of the Mahrathas, and the Cobra's Hood better known to us as Duke's Nose at Khandala. Further away to the right appear the hills that skirt Dharamtar creek, those behind Mandwa, among which the flat wooded top of the sacred Kankeshwar is prominent, though owing to clouds not so clear as the hills to our left. As we proceed, the hills running from Mandwa to Alibag rise in view to the south of Kankeshwar, and we see in the distance the famous Sagarghad from the top of which fort the Angriah Chief used to throw his victims.

The islands in the harbour also appear to great advantage: to the left the high triangular Trombay with the village of Mahval and Pirpao at its foot; near them, one behind the other, lie Hog Island and the famous Elephanta, and in front the twin Karanjas which may well be called the Adelphi hills. The effect of light and shade on them is very pretty in their colours, which change every now and then from bright green to sombre dark and blue. Such is our poetic environment in the midst of which we live and move and have our being, if we only have eyes to see and enjoy it on occasions when it reveals itself in its full glory.

December 1906.

BURST OF THE MONSOON.

Burst Of The Monsoon

HENRY MOSES

The day at length arrives when the windows of heaven are to be opened, and man's anxious doubts and fears are to be dispelled by this gracious provision for his wants. Dark clouds, towards noon, gather in the south-west, and gradually steal over the azure firmament, casting a gloomy shadow upon the earth, and obscuring the intensity of the sun's rays as they flit over his surface in their onward progress. A current of cool, strange air now denotes some remarkable atmospheric change. The ocean is unusually agitated; the waves are lifted up—hurried onwards as the breeze increases—the angry waters come foaming and roaring towards the shore, and are broken with violence upon the rock; receding but to break again with redoubled force.—Distant peals of thunder echo among the lofty Ghauts far down the coast, and vivid streams of forked lightning illumine their peaked summits. The dry leaves of the lofty palms rattle overhead, and the forests are agitated and shaken as the hurricane roars through their solemn vistas, and breaks in upon their profound stillness. The soaring kite flaps his outstretched wings, as he rises alarmed from his lone perch, and is hurried away upon the storm. The cattle on the plains congregate together, as if driven by some irresistible impulse to seek the shelter and protection of each other, and lie down with their heads close to the earth, as if conscious of approaching danger; and the poor Hindoo wraps his muslin *kummerband* tighter around him, as the cool air expands its many folds, and exposes his delicately formed limbs to the chilly blast. The skies become darkened, and sheets of blazing lightning, followed up by the roar of deafening thunder, succeed each other with fearful rapidity; and, though in broad day, the eye can scarcely bear to look upon the flaming heavens, so intense is their brightness.

The elements are indeed at war. Large drops of rain begin to fall; and falling, raise up, in consequence of their weight, a cloud of dust; and then, within a brief space, the mighty floods descend upon the thirsty land. The tempest is terrific to behold, and man trembles beneath the storm. He seeks in haste the shelter of his mud-built cabin, and mutters a hurried prayer to the stone idol which he has set up. The high houses in the Fort of Bombay vibrate with every clap of thunder; doors and windows, and walls and floors are shaken by the loud artillery of heaven. Torrents of water pour down from every roof, and bound over, in broken streams, the sounding verandahs below them, sweeping the various streets as the flood rushes onward, laden with mud and rubbish, towards the sea.

To those persons who have but just arrived in the country, and who, having never experienced the setting in of this remarkable season, have formed from description but an imperfect idea of that change, the scene is pregnant with horror of every kind. The newly-arrived Englishwoman in particular suffers exceedingly at this period, being scarcely able to divest herself of the impression, that everything around her is about to be destroyed or washed away; yet it is very seldom that accidents occur or that property is seriously injured. Occasionally we hear of exposed houses being struck by lightning on the Island, of old palm trees blown down, and of leaf roofs being dispersed to the four winds of heaven; for woe be unto him who lives in a bungalow with a bad roof, or in one whose spouts are out of order; but with these exceptions, Europeans on shore have but little to be alarmed about for their personal safety.

Myriads of mosquitoes, now driven in by the rains, fill your apartments; and your lamps at night, if not properly covered over with a glass shade, are liable to be suddenly extinguished by the large green beetles that have sought shelter from the storm without. Flying bugs almost poison you with their fetid effluvia, and contaminate every article of food upon which they may chance to alight. The musk weasels dart in under your China matting, and find their way into your wine-cellars, and every cork they touch, every bottle they spoil. That nimble and really useful reptile, the house lizard, climbs your walls in all directions, and comes out so regularly from under your table after dinner, to feed upon the flies attracted thither, that you quite look for the active little creature as a matter of course, to amuse you during dessert time; and if he fail to appear, express regret, as I have heard an old gentleman do, at its non-arrival. The loathsome centipede gets into your cooking-houses, and hideous spiders, with hairy bodies and long legs, take up their quarters in every available corner and door-way. They are not content with staying at home quietly like our own respectable, though small species, and of taking their chance of what may be sent them; but they must make daily tours all over the establishment, as if it were expected, that they should pay visits to one another, now that the season had brought them into town. In fact, all the entomological tormentors of India appear to have a design upon your house and happiness. A continual buzzing is kept up around you day and night. Ants creep up your legs, while fleas irritate your body; and farewell to sleep, if your gauze curtains display any rents at bed-time. The punkahs or swinging fans suspended in your rooms, now have rest from their labours, for the atmosphere is sufficiently cool without any artificial currents of air. The sweet-scented cuscus mats, or tatties, hung outside between the pillars that support your verandah, and kept wet, in order to lower the temperature of the heated breeze before it enters your house, are now taken down and laid aside; and quite a change takes place in all your little plans within doors.

Sketches of India, 1850, pages 84-88.

Storms Heralding the Monsoon.

SIR GEORGE-BIRDWOOD.

In the afternoon sullen thunder began in the North-west, where clouds had all day been gathering in towering piles. As they thundered the clouds moved slowly down across the North Konkan, and about four o'clock gathered against the jagged crest of Bava Malang. To the North, and all along the Bava Malang range the sky and land were filled with lurid clouds, thunder lightning, and rain, the Kalyan river flowing back as ink through a scene of the most striking desolation and gloom, South of this abrupt line of storm, the country from Bombay to Khandala was full of pure calm light. Every village, every hut, every road and forest-track, even the bridge over the river at Chauk, came clearly into view. The trees and groves looked magically green; and the light picked out the most hidden streams and burnished them into threads of molten silver. The Panvel and Nagothna rivers shone like mirrors, and the sea was scored with bars of vivid sunshine. Suddenly at about five, the storm-rack poured over Bava Malang like a tumultuous sea, and swept into the deep valley between Matheran and Prabal with furious blasts and torrents, awful thunder, and flashes of forked lightning. When the clouds had filled the valley, the rain and wind ceased and the storm stood still, and, in dead stillness, the thunder and lightning raged without ceasing for an hour. The thunder mostly rolled from end to end of the valley, but it sometimes burst with a crash fit to loosen the bonds of the hills. At six o'clock the storm again moved and passed slowly south over Prabal towards Nagothna. Another enchanting scene opened in the South. Every hut, tree and stream grew strangely clear, the rain-filled rice fields and rivers flashed like steel, while fleecy clouds lay on every hillock and slowly crept up every ravine. As the sun set behind Bombay the air was filled with soft golden light. Westwards towards Thana the hill-tops were bright with every hue from golden light to deep purple shadow, while, among them, the winding Ulhas shone like links of burnished gold. Then, the moon rose, brightened the mists which had gathered out of the ravines and off the hills, and cleared a way across the calm heavens, while far in the south the black embattled storm-rack belched flame and thander the whole night long.

The next day (Tuesday) passed without a storm. On Wednesday, the 8th, eastwards towards Khandala vast electric cloud banks began to gather. At two in the afternoon, with mutterings of thunder, the sky grew suddenly black and lurid. At half-past two the storm passed west moving straight on Matheran. A mist went before the storm, thickening as it came, first into trailing clouds and then into dripping rain, with muttering thunder all the while. At three the valley between Matheran and Prabal was filled with storm. Thunder rolled in long echoing peals, and flashes lightened the dense fog with extraordinary splendour. The fog lasted with heavy rain till 3-45, when a light wind swept it west towards Bombay, where about four the monsoon burst.

These appalling electric outbursts end serenely. The storm clouds retreat like a drove of bellowing bulls and their last echoes die beyond the distant hills. The sun shines again in majesty, in every dell the delicious sound of running water wakens life, and the woods are vocal with the glad song of birds.

London Times,
Jan. 1880

Apud Bombay Gazetteer Vol. XIV pp. 247-249.

The Setting in of the Monsoon.

SIR ERSKINE PERRY.

The setting in of the monsoon, as it is called, or the commencement of the annual rains, is a grand meteorological phenomenon in Western India. In Bombay towards the end of May, when the sun is nearly vertical, the sea-breeze from the west, which up to that time had blown strongly throughout the day, ceases, and either a languid air from the south, or more frequently a complete lull, prevails. The earth unrefreshed by a single shower for eight long months is bare of all vegetation, and even the palms which hug the sea-shore in dense profusion, present an adust drooping appearance affording no relief to the brown amber tint of the landscape. Towards sunset masses of clouds of gigantic and most varied forms are seen rolling up from the south in an upper current of the air, and settling themselves on the crest of the mountains. Some of them fleecy, sparkling, diaphanous, speak of deepest summer; others highly charged with electricity, present the lurid hues so often precursors of a hurricane; while mixed with these, gradually overwhelming and enveloping them all is the storm-cloud, black, heavy, and portentous. Vivid flashes of lightning, legible as the writing on the wall, play from one mountain summit to another; and an inexperienced observer thinks that the long-looked for storm is imminent. But an hour or two clears the whole heavens, and one of those beautiful tropical nights succeeds, which, whether with the moon culminating straight over head, or with the brilliant constellations visible near the equator, offer visions of loveliness that I never see equalled in more northern latitudes. Evenings such as these occur for days and days together, affording at every sunset views of the mountain range, and of the neighbouring sea and land-locked harbour, unequalled at any other period of the year, and which, with their highest qualities of glowing tint and sharpness of outline, do not last more than ten minutes at a time in all the intensity of their beauty. At length the atmosphere becomes so completely charged with vapour that the catastrophe can no longer be delayed, and the burst commences. Sometimes, perhaps generally, with a violent thunder-storm ; sometimes, for I have observed many varieties of the commencement of the monsoon, with a gentle shower, which gradually increases until it assumes the character of a steady continuous down pour, such as may be seen occasionally in southern Europe, but of which we have no experience in England. In a few days the whole face of nature assumes a different hue ; the brown parched appearance so characteristic of the East during a great portion of the year, yields to tints of the tenderest green, and vegetation shoots forth in every form, and in most unexpected localities.

Bird's Eye View of India, 1855, pages 19-20.

The Opening Monsoon

SIR JOSEPH CROWE.

We had been visited on the 11th of June by the opening monsoon. No one who has once witnessed this phenomenon can forget the grandeur of the scene presented by the heavens on that occasion. Clouds suddenly gathered in the south-west and rapidly filled the sky, darkening the atmosphere portentously. Out of the black masses there came volleys of fire-works, peal after peal of thunder rent the air, and the rain poured down in such torrents as one only witnesses in countries as warm as India. The monsoon at Bombay is expected with pleasure by all classes of inhabitants. It fills the tanks and furnishes water for all purposes; without it life would have been impossible for half a million of people as late as 1858, when a gigantic system of storage brought water for the first time artificially from the hills. The monsoon also cools the air and makes the hot months of June, July, and August tolerable. But it has other curious effects. On the eve of its coming the glacis at Bombay was bare of all vegetation; twenty-four hours later it was covered with an inch or two of tender grasses. Weeds begin to grow on the double-tiled roofs of the bungalows; damp invades the houses, and fungus spreads over everything. Gloves, leather shoes, woollen clothes are soon covered with mushroom growths, and charcoal fires are required to keep everything dry. The force of the wind which drives the rain is amazing, and I recollect going out to dinner in a shigram, or native carriage, of which the windows received the rain and wind pressure at right angles, and the waters welled over in a few second, and flooded the bottom of the carriage to the height of three or four inches.

Reminiscences. 1895, Pages 249 to 250.

A Grand Phenomenon.

ELIZABETH GRANT.

The opening of the monsoon is one of the grandest phenomena of nature. About a week or two before the outbreak clouds began to gather over a sky that had been hitherto without relief; each day the gloom thickened; at last the storm broke. We were sitting down to luncheon when a feeling of suffocation, a distant rumbling, a sudden darkness, made us all sensible of some unusual change. The servants rushed to the venetians and closed one side of the hall, the side next the storm. The wind suddenly rising burst with a violence which overwhelmed every opposing object, and while the gust lasted we could hear nothing else, not a step, nor a voice, nor a sound of any kind. It brought with it a shower, a tempest rather, of sand, so fine, so impalpable, that it entered through every crevice, covered the floor, the seats, the tables with a red dust that nearly chocked us. This was succeeded by a lull almost awful in its intensity. Then the thunder growled ; at a vast distance it seemed to rumble, then strengthening, it broke suddenly right over the house with a power that was overwhelming; then flash after flash of lighting; then rain such as is known only in the tropics, poured down in flakes with the din of a cataract. On came the thunder ; again and again it shook the house, rolling round in its fearful might as if the annihilation of the world were its dreadful aim.

My mother and I were as pale as two spectres ; in my life, neither before nor after, did I feel so thoroughly appalled. It lasted about two hours, after which a heavy rain set in, falling dully and equally hour upon hour until about tiffin time the following day, when we had a second thunderstorm, less terrific, however, than the first. After this the heavy rain continued unceasingly for forty-eight hours, making a deafening noise and creating darkness and a chill damp equally oppressive. The roads were soon like streams, the plain a lake, the tanks overflowing.

Lady Strachey's " Memoirs of a Highland Lady,"
(1828, pub. 1897) pages 427-428.

The Monsoon

"SLEEPY SKETCHES."

May brings thirty-one days of close, oppressive heat, and thirty-one nights of close, oppressive heat; the thermometer lazily ebbing and flowing from 88° to 92° or even 95°.

As the days grow old, and the heat more and more unbearable, we are all seized with intense anxiety as to the monsoon. Has it burst at Ceylon? Has it reached Goa? Will it break to-morrow or a week hence in Bombay? And each day the newspapers tell us of like anxiety in other far-off towns. Correspondents give minute accounts of the heat of the places from whence they write, and record gravely the weakest rumours and most ill-based statements, as to whether the advent of the monsoon will be early or late.

At last, when all possibility of sound sleep is gone, and we wake each hour or minute wet with perspiration; when even the crows have lost every power but that of crowing,—a power, confound them, that they never lose,—and stand desolate, with their hot wings held comically apart from their hot bodies; then, at last, over the mountains landward of Bombay rise up, in thick black masses, vast clouds, gloomy and terrible against the blue sky; clinging round and blotting out the strange forms and flat tops of the Ghaut Mountains; full of great thunders and lightnings that roll up and flash from the distance into our glad ears and eyes. But still in Bombay we go to bed with the thermometer at 89°.

At last comes a day when the black clouds rise up still higher and blot out the hot blue sky even to the zenith; and, gathering darker each moment, crowd out the light and stifle the air, till darkness is on us, our skins run with perspiration and our lungs labour for breath. And then, beaten about with a mighty wind, down come the clouds in a deluge of rain, and instantly—and this, reader, is the moral—down comes the thermometer to 84°, 83°, 82°, 81°, even 80°! Oh! how intense is the relief! Though the rain beats into our rooms so madly and persistently, and soaks through the walls so irresistibly that our boots, books, glasses, and tables are each morning covered with mildew, and no clothes can be worn till thoroughly dried; though it brings creeping and crawling and flying and croaking things innumerable, of diverse shape and form, as many and horrible as the devilish things that tempted St. Anthony, and a mighty wind that tosses our buggies in the roads as though at sea;—notwithstanding all this, we look on the monsoon as a friend—it brings down the thermometer: Quality as great as Charity.

And for four months the deluge of rain and wind keeps on. And nearly all that time the walls are clammy with dampness, and the paper we write on greasy with dampness, and our shirts limp with dampness ; but the thermometer is below 82° from dampness,—morning, noon, and night seldom or never falling below 80° : morning, noon, and night seldom or never rising above 82°. Seldom or never I write, for sometimes the rain stops for a week, and the blue sky comes back, and all the face of the land looks bright and cool in its green freshness, but the thermometer jumps up to 88° or even 90°.

And at last, about the end of September, the rain and the wind moderate, and in October cease altogether, ending their reign as they began,—with masses of vast clouds full of lightnings and thunders piled up over the Ghauts. And then the sky is again clear, and the earth quickly dries up ; the greenness of nature passes away, and the grass is brown and scorched till the monsoon of the next year comes.

1877, pages 18-22.

Beneficial Effects of the Monsoon.

HENRY MOSES.

We will now steal out from our bungalow, caring little for the pelting storm, for we shall keep under the magnificent plantain leaves that hang over the foot-path, and take a peep at the face of nature—at the fields and woods ; and see the wondrous change which a few days' rain has produced in the vegetable world.

The dry and burnt up plain that crackled under our feet like the stubble of harvest, is now covered with fine grass a foot deep, and of that rich emerald green, which is so refreshing to the eye, and so novel in its appearance, that you feel transplanted, as it were, to some strange land, or to the waving meadows of England's Spring. The united influence of heat and moisture is at work. Every tree and shrub has sent forth some new leaves or tender shoots, and the gums which so long protected them are now dissolved, and diffuse a delicious perfume around you. The cool rains and mild temperature at this season, produce a luxuriance of vegetation unknown, perhaps, in any other country on the face of the earth. The extraordinary and rapid growth of all seeds now planted, appears more like the work of enchantment, than the usual slow progress of nature familiar to us in our northern latitudes. The gourd, melon and cucumber, have now gained the roof of the peasant's hut, and promise by their shining blossoms a plentiful supply of their cooling fruits when the hot season shall arrive. Trees and plants, that during the dry months, had shut up all their pores so as not to be robbed of their juices by evaporation ; and roots, that lay buried in the deep sands or strong clay districts, now spring suddenly into life and beauty, in places that were before barren to the eye.

Creeping plants, that run along the ground, now embrace the trunks of trees, and ascend them with astonishing rapidity, running out upon their branches, and so travelling from one to another, till the forests in the neighbourhood of Bombay appear to be bound together, and canopied over, by the thousand lovely climbers that cast an almost night-like gloom on all things below them. From some of these branches may be seen the charming blossoms of the convolvulus, and other flowering parasitical plants, floating between heaven and earth in graceful festoons, uninjured by the floods of rain, and affording support to all those delicate birds and insects that would perish without this beautiful provision of the great Author of Nature. The woods are now alive with the feathered tribes, and the soft cooing of the turtle-dove, a bird held sacred in India, is repeated for miles around you. The golden oriole, and the azure jay, descending from the lofty trees, now feast upon the luscious fruits; and our own English barn-door bird, the stately jungle cock, makes the coverts ring again with his loud and familiar note, as he sweeps through the sounding woods, and is lost in their deep shadows.

We must now turn aside from these pleasing pictures of the Indian forest, at which we but glanced hurriedly. Memory fails me in recalling the many beauties that surround us here on all sides, and the abundant supply of food that the fields promise to man. The sea, formerly so transparent and serene, is now discoloured by the large rivers, that carry down enormous quantities of earth in their swift and destructive progress. All coasting traffic ceases; and the cocoa-nut sewn Pattemars, and fishing dingis have sought the shelter of some friedly creek or landlocked bay, for three months at least. The Company's steamers change the time of their going to Aden, and the Persian Gulf with the overland mails; and whereas a very brief delay would, at any other time, cause alarm, a week's detention now beyond their time, is scarcely spoken of with surprise, as every one is aware that the monsoons are the cause. Internal communication is now almost laid aside and no person, who can possibly avoid it, travels either by land or water. The mail bags, usually forwarded by runners, each a stage of three coss, or six miles, are often detained for weeks, before an opportunity occurs to ford or swim over the swollen rivers and nullahs! a work often of much difficulty and danger. Weekly reports of heart-rending shipwrecks fill the native papers, and a catalogue of flooded districts, and other disaterss from the country, too often give a painful interest to the rainy season. Yet we must not lose sight of the goodness of the Almighty, in sending these blessed showers at stated periods; for were they but once withheld, the most dreadful consequences must ensue, and thousands upon thousands of human creatures would perish for want of water.

Sketches of India, 1850, pages 90-93.

After the Rains.

DAVID PRICE.

Of the verdant and beautiful months which immediately succeed to the rainy season, particularly in this, our favourite island, the remembrance will readily occur to any one, whom the chances of life may have ever brought to reside upon it. For although the morbid exhalation from the steaming rice grounds, may sometimes be productive of bilious complaints, the healthful air, and picturesque, and varied scenery, of Malabar hill, and its celebrated Point, if they do not amply compensate for this temporary evil, certainly do form a most agreeable contrast, of many a convivial party to the Point, and the secluded shades and pagodas round the noble tank on the northern slope of the hill, I still bear in mind the most pleasing impressions, blended with tints of melancholy, when I reflect that most of those associates who shared with me in those delightful recreations are long since become denizens of another and better world.

At Seu, or Sion, on the opposite or eastern extremity of the island, and at the distance of nine or ten miles, we posssessed another resort for recreation; as the miniature downs, and park-like scenery through which we passed to the eastward of the Governor's country residence, Parell, brought to mind, in a lively degree, the woodland beauties of "the land in the ocean."

Memoirs of A Field Officer. 1839, pp. 176 to 177.

The Monsoon, the True Indian Spring.

E. H. A.

[E. A. ATKINS.]

Of our three seasons, my favourite is, and always has been, the monsoon. It is time of refreshing, and all nature rejoices in it, and I rejoice with nature. What the spring is to northern latitudes, the monsoon is to us. I do not mean that spring has no place in Indian calendar. That mysterious influence which comes with the returning sun, and, undiscerned by eye or ear, awakens the earth, visits us too. Then

> " The wanton lapwing gets himself
> another crest,"

and if a fuller crimson does not come upon the robin's breast, it is because in this country that is not the region in which his crimson is situated; but he and the other birds break out into and begin to build their nests, the trees bud, and many gay butterflies awaken to life. So I say our true spring, the begining of our year, the birthday of our nature, is not in March, but in June. Let it be ushered in with salvoes of artillery and a carnival of the elements, or let it sneak in silently during the night and greet us in the morning, the effect is the same. The leaves of the trees are washed, the dust on the roads is laid, and the spirits of man and beast participate in the baptism.

This is par excellence the season for rambling abroad. At every turn there is something new to see. Out of earth and rock and leafless bough the magic touch of the monsoon has brought life and greenness. You can almost see the broad-leaved vines grow and the twining creepers work their snaky way, linking tree to tree and binding branch to branch.

There is another feature of the monsoon which has a wonderful charm for me, I mean the clouds. Many Englishmen never throw off the bondage of their old English feelings, and a cloudy day depresses them to the last. Such conservatism is not in me. After the monotony of a fierce sun and a blue sky and dusky landscape quivering in the dim distance, I cry welcome to the days of mild light and green earth and purple hills coming near in the clear and transparent air. And later on, when the monsoon begins to break up and the hills are dappled with light and shade, and dark islands move across the bright green sea, the effect on my spirits is strangely exhilarating. Why is it that so few of our Indian painters have given us monsoon scenes?

A Naturalist on the Prowl, 1892, pages 70-77.

APPROACH & ARRIVAL.

APPROACH & ARRIVAL.

Smell Bombay from Afar

FLORA A. STEEL.

So, as we sit, this last evening on board ship, on the forward anchor, catching the breeze of our own making, the question rises, " How far out in the Indian Ocean may we count India ?"

I knew a man once, returning reluctantly to a jungle station after a really fancy furlough, who said that he could smell the Bombay bazzar in longitude 68 ; which is absurd, since, pungent as a bazzar is, even assafœtida cannot travel three hundred miles.

And yet the real edge of India does lie somewhere about there if not in the charts, still in the map of the mind. For, look down into the water through which the black keel is slipping so oily that the little nautilus boats take no harm, but ride away on the long smooth ripple which parts the sea, leaving place for our huge vessel. Look down, I say, and through the milky, almost opalescent depths, what are those snake-like restless brown forms seen, half seen, twining, intertwining ? To the practical scientific botanical eye, it is the zone of sea-weed which, so I am told, drifts within certain limits all round India. But to the old navigators-and to the eye of faith nowadays—it is the zone of sea-serpents, the zone of sea-guardians between the outside world and enchanted India.

This is the true line dividing those who can see behind the veil, from those to whom a spade must ever be a spade, and not the unit of man's civilisation, the means by which he first forced Mother Earth to yield him—not what was to be found ready to his sight and hand—but those things that his heart desired.

India by Mortimer Menpes. Pages, 1 to 3.

Imposing Entrance

SILK BUCKINGHAM.

The entrance to Bombay is very imposing. On the right or south side of the passage, is the continent of India; and in the background, trending away to the north-east, rise the noble hills called the Ghauts, which form the buttresses or bulwarks of the higher land beyond them. On the left is the small low island of Colabah, with its light-house, closely connected with the nearly level island of Bombay, and this again joined by a causeway to the larger and more hilly island of Salsette. The ample expanse of water between these islands on the left, and the Mahratta coast on the right, presents a harbour capacious enough to shelter the whole navy of England, while the several smaller islands dotting its surface, including that of Elephanta with its celebrated Cave Temple, form objects of picturesque beauty, and afford good shelter as breakwaters against the strongest gales. The soundings are of convenient depths, the holding ground good; and the strong ebb and flood tides, rising eighteen and twenty feet perpendicular, facilitate the entrance and exit of ships in all winds and all weathers. No harbour in the world, perhaps, is better entitled than this to the original name given it by its first European possessors, the Portuguese, of "Bon Baia," or Good Bay, from whence the present name of Bombay is formed.

Autobiography, Vol. II. 1855, pages 337-338.

Approaching Bombay.

PRINCE KARAGECORGEWITCH.

The air is heavy with indefinable perfume. We are already coasting the Indian shore, but it remains invisible, and gives no sign but by these gusts of warmer air laden with that inscrutable aroma of musk and pepper. A lighthouse to port, which we have for some time taken for a star, vanishes in the light mist that hangs over the coast, and then again there is nothing but the immensity of waters under the clear night, blue with moonlight.

All the day long a quantity of medusae have surrounded the ship; white, as large as an ostrich's egg, with a pink or lilac heart, like a flower; others of enormous size, of a paler blue than the sea, fringed with intense and luminous green—a splash of light on the dusk of the deep. Others, again, white, blossoming with every shade of rose and violet. Then, towards evening, myriads of very small ones, thickening the water, give it a yellowish tinge, clinging to the ship's side rolling in the furrow of its wake, a compact swarm, for hours constantly renewed; but they have at last disappeared, leaving the sea clear, transparent, twinkling with large flecks of phosphorescence that rise slowly from the depths, flash on the surface, and die out at once under the light of the sky.

Before day break, in the doubtful light of waning night, dim masses are visible—grey and purple mountains—mountains shaped like temples, of which two indeed seem to be crowned with low squat towers as if unfinished.

The morning mist shrouds everything; the scene insensibly passes through a series of pale tints, to reappear ere long in the clear rosy light, which sheds a powdering of glowing gold on the broad roadstead of Bombay.

But the enchantment of this rose-tinted land, vibrating in the sunshine, is evanescent. The city comes into view in huge white masses—docks, and factories with tall chimneys; and coco-palms in long lines of monotonous growth, overshadow square houses devoid of style.

As we go nearer, gothic towers are distinguishable among the buildings—faint reminiscences of Chester, clumsily revived under the burning light of white Asia.

In the spacious harbour, where a whole fleet of steamships lies at anchor, a swarm of decked boats are moving about, sober in colour, with the bows raised very high in a long peak, and immense narrow sails crossed like a pair of scissors, and resembling a seagull's wings.

Enchanted India, 1898, pages 1-3.

A Vision of Gorgeous Ind.

BAYARD TAYLOR.

On the morning of the 27th of December—precisely a month after I embarked at Gibralter—the cessation of the monsoon, the sultriness of the air, the appearance of the clouds, and the arrival of a dove on board, denoted the proximity of land. I have rarely approached any country with a keener interest. Scarce Vasco de Gama himself, after weathering the Cape of Storms, could have watched for the shores of India with more excited anticipation. That vision of gorgeous Ind, the Empress far away in the empurpled East, throned on the best grandeurs of History and canopied by sublime tradition, was about to be confirmed, or displaced for ever. Near at hand, close behind the blue sea-horizon, lay that which would either heighten the fascination of her name, or make it thenceforth but an empty sound to the ear of Fancy.

Therefore, in spite of the breathless heat, I keep watch from one of the paddle-boxes. At noon there is a cry of "Land!" from the foremast, and in a short time the tops of mountains are faintly discernible on the horizon. These are the Western Ghauts which extend along the Malabar Coast, from Cape Comorin to Surat. The island of Salsette, north of Bombay, next rises, and ere long we distinguish the light-house at the entrance of the harbour. A considerable extent of coast, north and south, is visible—the mountains picturesque and beautiful in their forms, and exhibiting, in their drapery of forests, a marked contrast to the desert hills of Arabia, which we have last seen. We are now near enough to distinguish the city, the dwellings of the residents on Malabar Hill, and the groves of cocoa-nut and date trees which cover the island. The sea swarms with fishing-boats, and our native pilot is already on board.

The Bay opens magnificently as we advance. It lies between the islands of Bombay and Salsette and the mainland, and must be fifteen or twenty miles in length. Both shores are mountainous and thickly covered with the palmy growths of the tropics. All is confusion on board and I also must prepare to set foot on the land of Brahma, Vishnu and Shiva.

Visit to India and China, 1856, pages 32-33.

Stately Approach.

SIR FREDERICK TREVES.

It was a fine sunny morning-as all had been-but ahead was a haze along the horizon which hid the land. There were sea birds in the air, and on the water a boat with a white lateen sail. The life seemed to have gone out of the sea, for the waves had become dull and of a sluggish green. Every eye was turned in the direction of the ship's bow, and soon there emerged from the mist a low hill, alone like an island, grey and indistinct. This was India.

As the ship drew near, other high ground came into view, rising above a ghostly coast. In due course a lighthouse, gaudy in stripes of red, white and black, appeared. Behind the light-house were a narrow spit of land with soft rounded trees on it and the tower of a disused pharos. Here, too, were white houses with red roofs, dotting the green, and below them a sandy beach by a fortified wall.

Beyond this narrow spur of land—called, as I came to know, Colaba—was the city of Bombay, shrouded by the mist. Through the haze it was possible to make out the steeples and towers, the domes and pinnacles of a great city.

The approach is stately, for the harbour is magnificent, but there is no particular character about the scene. One is conscious of entering a wide sound and of a city on a bright inlet; but the sound might be in Italy and the city in England. This is not the India one has dreamed about. There is no suggestion of "India's coral strand," no hot beach peopled by turbaned heathen, no line of cocoanut palms by the water's edge. One looks in vain for buildings that follow in some way the architecture of the "willow pattern plate," and, above all, one looks for elephants with howdahs on their backs.

There is, in place of the palms, a line of factory chimneys: while a quite common row of quays meets the sea in place of the coral strand. There are no heathen recognisable as such, and certainly none in the act of bowing down to stocks and stones. There are people in turbans, but they are evidently mere loungers about harbour sides, and the buildings appear, at the distance, to differ but little from those at Limehouse. Of elephants there are none.

The Other Side of the Lantern. 1905, pages 29-30.

2.

The charm of Bombay to those who land for the first time upon its "spacious quays" is bound up in the fact that it is one of the cities of India, that the soil and the people are Indian, and that it is part of that continent which has entered with so much romance into the history of the world.

There is interest in everything that one sees, in the railway trains, the shops, the boats on the beach, the policemen, the street sweepers, the unfamiliar trees and shrubs, and the fragmentary demonstrations of how the people live. Kites and crows, vultures and squirrels are all elements new to city life; while the first time that a parrakeet is sighted, perched on a house top, there arises the conviction that it must have escaped from a cage.

Beyond all this it may be claimed that the chief things, which in tourist language will "well repay a visit" in Bombay, are the native quarter and Malabar Hill.

The Malabar Hill is a modest mound behind the city, brave with gardens and bright villas, from whose summit is to be obtained a view of the sea and of the gleaming harbour. It is a matter of interest that all large bays, viewed from a height, are supposed to resemble the Bay of Naples. The harbour of Bombay comes into this classification of bays, and is therefore regarded as a local Bay of Naples; but the very stones of Malabar Hill must turn when each inspired tourist after another discovers and reveals this stale resemblance, for the sweeping Sound of Bombay shows scarcely a feature which has any parallel in the great Italian inlet.

The Other Side of the Lantern, 1905, pages 31–32.

The City from the Sea.

WALTER DEL MAR.

Bombay from the sea is fair to look upon, and is always a welcome sight after the monotonous voyage of 1660 miles from Aden. The sea front of the Back Bay extends, in a graceful, palm-fringed crescent, from Malabar Point to Kolaba Point. On the latter is the old Kolaba lighthouse, and south of it the Prong lighthouse, which the steamer passes to enter the commodious harbour, where it casts anchor opposite the eastern front of "the Fort," corresponding to "the City" in London or "down-town" in New York. From the anchorage the view of the domes and pinnacles of Bombay is dominated by Tata's Taj Mahal Hotel, one of the most imposing modern buildings in India. In the opposite direction the cliffs of Bawa Malang (or Mallangadh) stand out from the terraced trap peaks of the Western Ghats. To the north-east, in the middle distance, is Butcher's Island and Elephanta, while close at hand are the fortified islands in the beautiful harbour, which is alive with ocean steamers, yachts, and country boats. You barely have time to take in the scene before the launch comes alongside, and in a few minutes you are landed on Ballard's Pier.

Bombay makes a favourable first impression with its broad. well-kept streets, sprinkled with oil to lay the dust, and its handsome buildings, some of which are due to private munificence, but most of them to the public spirit which aims to make Bombay "the first city in India."

India of To-day, 1905, pages 12-13.

Islands in the Harbour.

NORMAN MACLEOD.

With very peculiar emotions did I ascend the deck to look for the first time on that great country, associated with so much to stir the imagination of every British subject, and most of all of every Christian minister. The scene which meets the eye when entering the harbour is most striking and lovely. Every other thought is for the moment lost in a sense of its beauty. The forests of palm-trees which, in the hot and motionless air, repose on the lower hills, along the margin of the shore, at once attract attention as being thoroughly characteristic of Eastern climes. The islands as they unfold themselves, with their masses of verdure, and the bays, and vanishings of the sea into distant river-like reaches, lost in a soft bright haze, above which singular hills—rounded, obelisk terraced—lift themselves, all combine to form a complete picture, framed by the gleaming blue sea below, and by the cloudless sky above, full of intense heat and light of burnished brightness. Looking nearer, one notices the ships from every clime, and of every size and kind, fixed in a sunny mist on a molten sea—ships at anchor—ships crowding their masts near the wharves, and boats without number, with their large matting sails and covered poop, dipping their oars in silver light, all going on their several errands, and a goodly number making for our steamer. Beyond the ships and masts, white houses among trees, and here and there a steeple, indicating the long land line of the Colaba Point, tell us where the famous city of Bombay lies, with its worshippers of fire and of fine gold.

Far East. 1868, Page 11.

"Beautiful Indeed It Is!"

"Life In Bombay."

Beautiful indeed it is! studded with numerous small islands and comprising in a single "*coup d'œil*" every variety of landscape scenery, from the fertile Elephanta covered with the rich vegetation of the tropics, and sparkling like an emerald on the bosom of the waters, to the barren shores of Caranjah, with its rocky headlands projecting boldly, as if in defiance of the softer beauties which surround it. Smaller isles rise, like specks upon a surface, scattered around; whilst in the midst, clearly indicated by its encircling belt of ships and countless buildings, stands the far-famed Island of Bombay. Small as are its dimensions, and although for so long a period after its cession to the English in the year 1661 considered as so utterly unimportant, or rather troublesome an appendage to our territories, perhaps at this moment there is not one spot throughout our wide-spread colonial possessions, to which so great an interest is attached.

In a commercial point of view, the advantages afforded by the situation, and almost unequalled harbour of Bombay, are too manifest, and too generally known to require repetition. Easy of access at every season of the year, and affording a safe anchoring ground for the largest of ships, the haven is at all times thronged by an almost indescribable variety of vessels, descending through every gradation from the statety London-built East-India man, with its well-appointed crew, and costly cargo, to the primitive native canoe, formed from the bark of a single tree, and contributing, with its modest freight of fruits and vegetables, to supply the markets and bazaars of Bombay.

Upon first landing, the immediate impression which strikes every mind, is not only the immense population of the island, but the unceasing variety of costumes and complexions, betokening the natives of the Asiatic, and of several European nations. Parsees, Mussulmans, Hindoos of every caste, Persians, Armenians, Portuguese, and Indo-Britons, literally swarm under the horses' feet as you drive through the bazaars; and it requires no small portion of nerve, as well as dexterity, to steer one's course in safety through streets and roads absolutely alive with human beings, to say nothing of the numerous vehicles, horses, buffaloes, and bullocks which impede one's progress on all sides; invariably bewildering a stranger with the apparently interminable difficulties and dangers to be encountered.

1852: pages 3-6.

A Handsome City Seated on Two Bays.

SIR EDWIN ARNOLD.

The transformation effected in this great and populous capital of Western India during the past twenty years does not very plainly manifest itself until the traveller has landed. From the new lighthouse at Colaba Point, Bombay looks what it always was, a handsome city seated on two bays, of which one is richly diversified by islands, rising, green and picturesque, from the quiet water, and the other has for its background the crescent of the Esplanade and the bungalow-dotted heights of Malabar Hill. He who has been long absent from India and returns here to visit her, sees strange and beautiful buildings towering above the well-remembered yellow and white houses, but misses the old line of ramparts, and the wide expanse of the Maidan behind Back Bay which we used to call "Aceldama, the place to bury strangers in." And the first drive which he takes from the Apollo Bunder—now styled the Wellington Pier—reveals a series of really splendid edifices, which have completely altered the previous aspect of Bombay.

Close to the landing-place the pretty facade of the Yacht Club—one of the latest additions to the city—is the first to attract attention, designed in a pleasing mixture of Swiss and Hindu styles. In the cool corridors and chambers of that waterside resort we found a kindly welcome to the Indian shores, and afterwards, on our way to a temporary home, passed, with admiring eyes, the Secretariat, the University, the Courts of Justice, the magnificent new Railway station, the Town Hall, and the General Post Office, all very remarkable structures, conceived for the most part with a happy inspiration, which blends the Gothic and the Indian schools of architecture. It is impossible here to describe the features of these very splendid edifices in detail, or the extraordinary changes which have rendered the Bombay of to-day hardly recognisable to one who knew the place in the time of the Mutiny and in those years which followed it. Augustus said of Rome, "I found it mud; I leave it marble," and the visitor to India who traverses the Fort and the Esplanade-road after so long an absence as mine might justly exclaim, "I left Bombay a town of warehouses and offices; I find her a city of parks and palaces."

Even the main native streets of business and traffic are considerably developed and improved, with almost more colour and animation than of old. A tide of seething Asiatic humanity ebbs and flows up and down the Bhendi bazaar, and through the chief mercantile thoroughfares. Nowhere could be seen a play of livelier hues, a busier and brighter city life! Besides the endless crowds of Hindu, Gujarati, and Mahratta people coming and going—some in gay dresses, but most with next to none at all—between the rows of grotesquely painted houses and temples, there are to be studied here specimens of every race and nation of the East. Arabs from Muscat, Persians from the Gulf, Afghans from the Northern frontier, black shaggy Biluchis, negroes of Zanzibar, islanders from the Maldives and Laccadives, Malagashes, Malays, and Chinese throng and jostle with Parsees in their sloping hats, with Jews, Lascars, fishermen, Rajpoots, Fakirs, Europeans, Sepoys, and Sahibs. Innumerable carts, drawn by patient, sleepy-eyed oxen, thread their creaking way amid tram-cars, buggies, victorias, palanquins, and handsome English carriages. Familiar to me, but absolutely bewildering to my two companions, under the fierce, scorching, blinding sunlight of midday, is this play of keen colours, and this tide of ceaseless clamorous existence.

But the background of Hindu fashions and manners remains unchanged and unchangeable. Still, as ever, the motley population lives its accustomed life in the public gaze, doing a thousand things in the roadway, in the gutter, or in the little open shop, which the European performs inside his closed abode. The unclad merchant posts up his account of pice and annas with a reed upon long rolls of paper under the eyes of all the world. The barber shaves his customer, and sets right his ears, nostrils, and fingers, on the side-walk. The shampooer cracks the joints and grinds the muscles of his clients wherever they happen to meet together. The Guru drones out his Sanskrit shlokes to the little class of brown-eyed Brahman boys; the bansula-player pipes; the sitar-singer twangs his wires; worshippers stand with clasped palms before the images of Rama and Parvati, or deck the Lingam with votive flowers; the beggars squat in the sun, rocking themselves to and fro to the monotonous cry of "Dhurrum;" the bheesties go about with water-skins sprinkling the dust; the bangy-coolies trot with balanced bamboos; the slim, bare-limbed Indian girls glide along with baskets full of chupatties or "bratties" of cow-dung on their heads, and with small naked babies astride upon their hips.

Everywhere, behind and amid the vast commercial bustle of modern Bombay, abides ancient, placid, conservative India, with her immutable customs and deeply-rooted popular habits derived unbroken from immemorial days. And overhead, in every open space, or vista of quaint roof-tops, and avenues of red, blue, or saffron-hued houses, the feathered crowns of the date trees wave, the sacred fig swings its aerial roots and shelters the squirrel and the parrot, while the air is peopled with hordes of ubiquitous, clamorous grey-necked crows, and full of the "Kites of Govinda," wheeling and screaming under a cloudless canopy of sunlight. The abundance of animal life even in the suburbs of this great capital appears once more wonderful, albeit so well known and remembered of old. You cannot drop a morsel of bread or fruit but forty keen-beaked, sleek, desperately audacious crows crowd to snatch at the spoil; and in the tamarind tree which overhangs our verandah may at this moment be counted more than a hundred red-throated parrokeets, chattering and darting, like live fruit, among the dark-green branches. India does not change!

India Revisited, 1886, pages 54–58.

A Unique City—a Diluvies Gentium.

SIDNEY LOW.

His first few days in the city, if the visitor has never set foot on the soil of India before, are likely to be a period of delighted amazement and most enjoyable confusion. He wanders about, drinking in the fulness of the new experience, perplexed and absorbed by all he sees, trying to wind his way through the jumble of novel human types and unfamiliar customs and costumes borne before him. Bombay is different from any other town outside India; the tourist will presently discover that India itself has nowhere anything quite like it. The Island City is unique—a *diluvies gentium*, a well into which the races of Asia have poured themselves, or, perhaps one should say, a reservoir out of which they pass as fast as they flow in. It is full of the wealth of the East and the wealth of the West, and of the poverty and vice of both. It has its palaces fit for a prince, and its human kennels unfit for a dog. The hand of Vishnu the Preserver, and of Siva the Destroyer, are felt in their might daily. A splendid industrial and commercial activity makes Bombay rich and great, and a canker is working at its vitals. Every tenth person you meet is doomed to swift and painful death by a disease for which science has no remedy. It is the city of the Parsi millionaire. It is the city of the Plague.

When you have begun to disentangle your first impressions, you can appreciate the force of the contrasts which Bombay presents. The East and the West, the Old and the New, are here in curious and piquant juxta-position. A great deal of that part of Bombay which is called the Fort, and is the centre of the

European business life, is very modern indeed. There are enormous ranges of huge public buildings, designed with a fine official disregard for all local associations, great blocks of flats, and flourishing shops, some of which might have been transported from Bond Street and others brought from the Edgware Road; and a life, essentially English and only touching the East at the fringes, is in being here. But a few hundred yards away are the bazaars and the native streets, and you are in the heart of Asia. This is true, more or less, of many Indian towns; but it is specially felt to be the case in Bombay, because there the Europeans are not shepherded apart in cantonments, or in any separate quarter of their own, but are physically, at least, in pretty close contact with the natives. The lines touch at many points, but they do not merge.

A Vision of India 1906, pages 9-10.

All India in Miniature

G. W. STEEVENS.

In the drive from the Apollo Bunder to Malabar Point, all India is unfolded in one panorama. First the business houses and the great buildings—those the richest, these the stateliest in India, and challenging comparison with almost any city in the world. Every variation of design is theirs, but they find a link of uniformity in the red-brown colours common to most, and in the oriental profusion of ornament. First comes the Venetian Secretariat, then the Gothic University Library, and the French University Hall; between them the great Clock Tower, which peals forth hymn-tunes on Sunday and on week-days "God Save the Queen!" and "Home, Sweet Home." The white pinnacled Law Courts follow in Early English, then the Post and Telegraph Offices in Miscellaneous Gothic. But the jewel of Bombay is the Victoria Railway Station, a vast domed mass of stone fretted with point and column and statuary. Between them all you catch vistas of green mead and shrubbery, purple-belled creepers, scarlet-starred shrubs. The whole has its feet in bowers of succulent green and its elbows on shining-leaved banyan-trees. A proud and comely city, you say; the Briton feels himself a greater man for his first sight of Bombay.

Then suddenly the magician turns his ring and new has become old, plain is coloured, solid is tumbled down, the West has been swallowed up utterly by the East. Cross but one street and you are plunged in the native town. In your nostrils is the smell of the East, dear and never to be forgotten; rapturously you snuff that blending of incense and spices and garlic, and sugar and goats and dung. The jutting houses close in over you. The decoration of

Bombay henceforth is its people. The windows are frames for woman, the streets become wedges of men. Under the quaint wooden sun-hoods that push out over the serried windows of the lodging-houses, along the rickety paintless balconies and verandahs, all over the tottering roofs—only the shabbiness of the dust and dirty plaster relieves the gorgeousness of one of the most astounding collections of human animals in the world. Forty languages, it is said, are habitually spoken in its bazaars. That, to him who understands no word of any of them, is more curious than interesting. But then every race has its own costume; so that the streets of Bombay are a tulip-garden of vermilion turbans and crimson, orange and flame colour, of men in blue and brown and emerald waistcoats, women in cherry-coloured satin-drawers, or mantles, drawn from the head, across the bosom to the hip, of blazing purple or green that shines like a grass-hopper. You must go to India to see such dyes. They are the very children of the sun, and seem to shine with an unreflected radiance of their own. If you check your eye and ask your mind for the master-colour in the crowd, it is white—white bordered with brown or fawn or amber legs. But when you forget that and let the eye go again, the scarlets and yellows and shining greens—each hue alive and quivering passionately like the tropical sun at midday—fill and dazzle it anew; in the gilding light the very arms and legs show like bronze or amber or the bloom on ripe damsons. You are walking in a flaring sunset, and come out of it blinking.

Look under the turbans. At first all natives look alike, but soon you begin to mark distinctions of dress and even of type. The first you will pick out is the Arab horse-dealer. His long robe and hood, bound round with cords and tufts of camel's hair, mark him off from the wisp-clothed native of India. The Arab gives you the others in focus. He is not much accounted by those who know him; yet, compared with the Indian, his mien is high, his movements free and dignified, his features strongly cut and resolute. The Bagdad Jew is hardly a type of lofty manhood, but under his figured turban and full-tasselled fez his face looks gravely wise. The blue-bloused Afghan is a savage frankly, but a strong man also. By the side of any one of them the down-country native of Bombay is poor and weak and insignificant. He looks as if you could break him across ycur knee. His formless features express nothing; his eyes have the shining meekness, but not the benevolence, of the cow's; he moves slowly and without snap, like a sick man. He seldom speaks, and when he does his voice is small. Sometimes he smiles faintly—laughs never.

In India, 1899, pages 17–20.

A City of Vast Contrasts.

G. W. STEEVENS.

When things begin to come sorted and sifted, Bombay reveals itself as a city of monstrous contrasts. Along the sea-front one splendid public building follows another-variegated stone facades with arch and colonnade, cupola and pinnacle and statuary. At their feet huddle flimsy huts of matting, thatched with leaves, which a day's rain would reduce to mud and pulp. You sit in a marble-paved club, vast and airy as a Roman atrium, and look out over gardens of heavy red and violet flowers towards choking alleys where half-naked idolaters herd by families together in open-fronted rooms, and filth runs down gullies to fester in the sunken street. In this quarter you may see the weaver twirling his green and amber wool on a hand-loom—a skeleton so simple and fragile that a kick would make sticks of it; go to the street corner, and you see black smoke belch from a hundred roaring mills, whose competition cuts the throat of all the world.

Yet, for all its incongruities, Bombay never will have you forget that it is a great city. If it had no mills it would be renowned for its port; if it had neither it would be famous for its beauty.

In India, page 16.

The Fascination of Bombay For A German.

COUNT VON KOENIGSMARCK.

Even the reek of Bombay makes me feel at home—a blend of musk, of spices, and of the smouldering sandal-wood they burn at prayer and festivals. As then, the fantastic traffic of this city, half Indian, half European, fascinated me to-day with the garish ebb and flow of its population, perhaps the most variegated in hue of the world. The human skin reveals itself here in every shade and tint, and the variety of its garb beggars every colour of the palette.

The fascination of Bombay lies in its diversity—the diversity of its landscape, of its street scenes, of its population. One would like to have a hundred eyes to be able to take in its exotic, kaleiodoscopic *va-et-vient*. Talk of scenes from the Thousand and One Nights! The Orient, in entire fairy-like splendour, and alongside of it sober business-like Europe; the drab commonplaceness of the West rubbing shoulders with these teeming crowds drunk with colour and adventure. Bombay is at one and the same time pan-Asiatic and cosmopolitan—a melting pot of races and religions.

You can tell at the outset that this metropolis is a daughter of Old England. The features of Bombay bewray her history—a history that is part and parcel of those title-deeds to fame which Britain's constructive work claims on Indian soil. Bombay is no mushroom growth of yesterday; her growth comprises more than two centuries—a gauge of the expansion of Anglo-Indian world empire.

In Bombay the wealth and luxury of the East flourish side by side with that of the West, nor have the misery and the vices of either hemisphere spared this commercial metropolis. On every hand the power of Vishnu, the preserver, and of Siva, the destroyer, struggle for mastery. If brilliant industrial enterprise and keen business development promote the prosperity of Bombay, abuses of the most divergent kinds jeopardise the very conditions of its continuity. About every tenth native is condemned to death by plague, against which medical science hitherto fights in vain; Bombay, the city of Parsee millionaires, is at the same time the city of the plague.

The face of Bombay changes with its distance from the roadstead. First seaport, then commercial city, then the hub of politicals and officialdom. Further out the city becomes a garden. At our feet the glassy bay of the Arabian Sea. Along the beach in (so it seems) endless vistas, stretch green lawns, shady gardens, playgrounds for recreation and pastimes. An avenue of glorious palm trees intersects the idyllic landscape and further on climbs the Malabar hill on the further shore of the gulf. On the topmost summit here flies the standard cf the King ; on Malabar Point his representative, the Governor of Bombay, is in residence.

At the foot of the palace lies a town of villas, Malabar Hill. Pretty houses, large and small, simple and splendid, half hidden under the wealth of foliage of the prodigal Nature cf the tropics, earmark the quarter of exalted officialdom. The judges and consuls, the commercial magnates of the Presidency of Bombay have established their household gods here. Everyone who is any one lives on Malabar Hill.

How radiant is the earth here, steeped with the inexhaustible sap of supernormal propagative forces! You can enjoy God's glorious world in full draughts here--if indeed not without a sense of gentle melancholy.

How shall we be able to endure our autumn with the fall of the leaf after the springtide rcses of Bombay ?

A German Staff Officer in India, 1910, pages 45-48.

The Fascination of Bombay a Century Ago.

BASIL HALL.

I was thrown into a high fever of wonder and enjoyment; and assuredly, as long as I have a trace of memory left, must retain the recollection of that happy period carved brightly and distinctly on my mind.

When the day broke, and the sun rose upon us over the flat—topped Ghauts or mountains of the Mahratta country, I remember feeling almost at a loss whether I had been sleeping and dreaming during the night, or whether the gay reality, with its boundless vista of promises, was still before my eyes. But the actual sight of the coast gave reality to pictures which, for many a long year before, I had busied my fancy with painting, in colours drawn partly from the Arabian Nights and Persian Tales, and partly, if not chiefly, from those brilliant clusters of oriental images which crowd and adorn the pages of Scripture.

Of all places in the noble range of countries so happily called the Eastern world, from the pitch of the Cape to the islands of Japan, from Bengal to Batavia, nearly every hole and corner of which I have visited in the course of my peregrinations, there are few which can compare with Bombay. If, indeed, I were consulted by any one who wished as expeditiously and economically as possible to see all that was essentially characteristic of the Oriental world, I would say, without hesitation, "Take a run to Bombay; remain there a week or two; and having also visited the scenes in the immediate neighbourhood, Elephanta, Carli, and Poonah, you will have examined good specimens of most things that are curious or interesting in the East."

For this remarkable distinction, quite peculiar, as far as I know, to that one spot on the earth's surface, this Presidency is indebted to a variety of interesting circumstances. Bombay, as perhaps many people may never have heard before, is an island, and by no means a large one, being only between six and seven miles long by one or two broad. It is not, however, by geographical dimensions that the wealth of towns, any more than the power and wealth of nations, is determined. The harbour unites every posible desideratum of a great sea-port; it is easy of access and egress; affords excellent anchoring ground; is capacious beyond the utmost probable demands of commerce; and, owing to the great rise and fall of the tides, is admirably adapted for docks of every description. The climate is healthy; and the country, being diversified by numerous small ridges and hills, furnishes an endless choice of situations for forts, towns, bazaars, and villages, not to say bungalows or villas, and all sorts of country-houses, and some very splendid retreats from the bustle of business. The roads which intersect this charming island were beautifully Macadamised, as I well remember, long before that grand improvement was heard of in England; and as the soil of the island is made up of that rich kind of mould resulting from decomposed basalt or lava, the whole surface affords a good sample of the perennial verdure of tropical scenery, which dazzles and surprises the new-comer, while its interest seldom, if ever, fails to rise still higher upon a more prolonged and intimate acquaintance.

Such are among the eminent physical advantages enjoyed by Bombay; but even these, had they been many times greater, would have been light in the balance compared to those of a moral, or rather of a political nature, which conspired in 1812 to render it one of the most imporant spots in that quarter of the globe. At the time I speak of, it was almost the only possession exclusively British within several hundred miles in any direction. The enormous territory of the Mahrattas lay close to Bcmbay on the east: and I mention this one district because the name is more or less familiar to English ears, chiefly, perhaps, from its having been the scene of the Duke of Wellington's earliest campaign in command of an army. The brilliant course of that service was wound up by the well-known battle of Assye, not the least hard fought of his hundred fields. Assaye is about twice as far from Bombay as Waterloo from London. To any person familiar with modern Indian history, the name of Bassein, where one of the most celebrated treaties that ever statesmen agreed upon was signed, will be well remembered. Then who is there that has not heard of the caves of Elephanta, those singular temples of the old Hindoos excavated on the side of a hill on an island in the very harbour, and within one hour's row from the fort?

These, and many other circumstances, some military, some historical, give a very peculiar degree of liveliness to the interest we feel in that spot; and I certainly have as yet seen very few places on the globe which fasten themselves with more tenacity on the memory. I allude chiefly to matters of taste, association, and other refinements, with which the natives of the countries surrounding Bombay have no concern. To them it possesses, or did then possess, exclusively, an interest of a different and far more important character. At that time it was almost the only spot in that range of country where persons and property were perfectly secure and in which all men might safely display and enjoy their wealth to the utmost limits of their taste for ostentatious parade, or hoard it as parsimoniously as they pleased, without the slightest chance of arbitrary interference. In addition to this, every form of religious worship was not merely tolerated, but allowed to exercise itself with the most ample and equal freedom. Every native of Asia, or of any other country in the world, so long as he infringed none of the established laws of the Presidency, was allowed equal privileges; and as the advantages of security and freedom, in the most genuine senses of these words, were enjoyed under none of the native governments adjacent, but, on the contrary, were almost entirely unknown in them all, Bombay became the natural place of resort for the wealthy from all parts of India lying on that side of the Peninsula, and indeed from many other regions much more remote.

The population of Bombay is about two hundred thousand; and I think it may be said with truth, that we can see nothing in China, or Java, or the Philippine Islands, or along the Malay Peninsula, or even in the interior parts of India, any single caste, or dress, or custom, or form of superstition, or anything else, belonging peculiarly to Eastern manners, which we may not witness at Bombay in as genuine and apparently unsophisticated a condition as on the spot to which it properly belongs. In twenty minutes' walk through the bazaar of Bombay, my ear has been struck by the sounds of every language that I have heard in any other part of the world, uttered not in corners and by chance, as it were, but in a tone and manner which implied that the speakers felt quite at home. In the same short space of time I have counted several dozens of temples, pagodas, joss-houses, and churches; and have beheld the Parsees, the lineal religious descendants of Zoroaster, worshipping fire; the Hindoos, with equal earnestness, bowing their heads to Baal in the shape of a well-oiled black stone, covered with chaplets of flowers and patches of rice; while in the next street the Mahomedan ceremonies of the grand Moharam were in full display; and in the midst of all a Portuguese procession bearing an immense cross, and other Roman Catholic emblems, as large as life.

I have no language competent to give expression to the feelings produced by the first contemplation of so strange a spectacle. I was startled, amused, deeply interested, and sometimes not a little shocked. The novelty of the scene was scarcely diminished by a further inspection; which may appear a contradiction in terms, but is not so in reality. The multitude of ideas caused by the first view of such an astonishing crowd of new and curious objects, obscures and confuses the observation, in a certain sense, and prevents us from distinguishing one part from another. So I found it in India, especially at that most curious of places, Bombay, where the more I saw of the natives, the more there seemed still to discover that was new. It would be absurd to pretend that all this pedantic kind of reasoning process took place at the moment, for in truth, I was too much enchanted to speculate deeply on the causes of the enjoyment.

Fragments of Voyages, II series, 1832, pp. 108-109.

The Panorama which Greets the Eye.

"ADVENTURES OF THOMAS BROWN."

The splendour of the rising sun was crimsoning the edges of the sea, as the good ship slowly steamed into the magnificent harbour of Bombay. The panorama which greets the eye of the outward-bound on entering the finest harbour in the world, defies all the power of language. It is the lot of most of us to see that gorgeous display many and many a time before we turn our backs for the last time on the golden East and set our faces towards the little sea-girt island; but who can say that he is competent to paint in words the varied beauties of the sunrise over those purple hills and richly-freighted waves?

Yet few, perhaps, have welcomed Bombay apparelled in more perfect harmonies of Nature's robing than on that morning when I drank in the beauties of the swelling hills, the palm tops waving featherly in the liquid blue of the morning sky, and the rich red shoots of the sun's gold splendour across the rippling waves as they lapped, rainbow-hued, the dark sides of many a war ship, many a merchant argosy lying stately in the majesty of dangers overcome and the haven reached.

1891. pp. 80 to 81.

Ascending the Pier Head, 1782.

DAVID PRICE.

On the 22nd of April, 1782, in company with my Bengal friends, I first ascended the steps of that projecting part of the extensive fortifications of Bombay, near the dockyard, called the Pier Head. Any one who had recently taken leave of the slim and fragile figures on the beach at Madras, would scarcely fail to perceive the striking contrast presented by the robust and athletic forms of the Parsee, Marwary, and Bhandary, population of the town and island of Bombay. Of the sea line of works, there are few but will acknowledge that the aspect is truly formidable; and well, and honourably defended, might bid defiance to any attack that could be brought to bear upon it: particularly when provided with furnaces for hot shot.

We were glad to escape from the amalgama of savoury smells, arising from the vast variety of rancid, oily commodities, heaped together on our way to the Bunder: the then residence of the junior civil servants; and to find ourselves at last securely housed in the Bombay hotel, at this period kept by Mr. Macfarlane.

Memoirs of A Field Officer. 1839. Page 59.

The Sea at Bombay.

MEADOWS TAYLOR.

I saw the sea! Day after day I went to its edge, and gazed on its magnificence. I used to lie on the grass of the plain before the fort, and pass hours of a sort of dreamy ecstasy, looking on its varying aspect,—like that of a beautiful woman, now all smiles, again agitated by the passion of love,—or listening to its monotonous and sullen roar, as wave after wave bowed its crest, and broke into sparkling foam on the white sand.

Confessions of a Thug.
1839. Chap 39, p. 334.

A Magnificent Scene.

JAMES TOD.

We pursued our course with a moderate breeze and an unclouded sky, making good progress until the shades of darkness began to close around us, when the wind rather lulled. The night was serene and beautiful: "Orion with all his bands" rode triumphant over our heads, and the deep silence was undisturbed, save by the gentle ripple of my bark as she glided slowly through the water. It was a night for meditation, and I gave myself up to the sweet influences of the past and the future.

Sleep had sealed the eyes of all about us, save Ibrahim, the Nakhoda, and another of the crew, having a like patriarchal appellation, Ayoub, or Job.

Nothing occured in our smooth navigation during the five days of lovely weather, as we approached that magnificent scene, the entrance to Bombay, possessing in every diversity and the grandest forms, all the accessories, mountain, wood, islands and water.

Travels in Western India, 1839, pp. 495-8.

Not One That Can Touch Bombay.

LORD HARRIS.

Imagine a great city, of over 800,000 souls, lying on the shores of a beautiful sea, sparkling in the sunshine, glorious in the monsoon, backed by grand mountains, with many a castellated peak nestling in palm groves, hundreds of sea-going vessels anchored in its harbour; broad thoroughfares and grand buildings, with a most active and intelligent community; lawns crowded day and night with pleasure seekers, and its brightness added to by the most brilliantly dressed ladies in the world, I mean, the Parsees. Imagine it if you can! I have seen many great cities of the East, but I have not seen one that can touch Bombay.

Journal of the Society of Arts, 1901, page 571.

"In the Land of the Arabian Nights"

LEOPOLD VON ORLICH.

We described in the hazy distance the coast of Bombay; from this time we met many fishing-boats, which often go out as far as twenty miles to sea. In joyful expectation, we all stood on deck with our eyes riveted on the rocks and light-house of Bombay; but before we could clearly discern them, total darkness set in. The captain sent up blue lights from time to time, which were answered from the pilot-boats, and by which such a magic brightness was spread around, that the ocean was illumined to a great distance, and our vessel seemed to swim in a sea of light. Towards 8 o'clock, we approached the harbour which was full of vessels, saluting them as we entered with the thunder of our guns, and ere long the loud clank of the ponderous anchor chain, announced the happy termination of our voyage.

You may imagine that I was all impatience to set my foot on shore. Lieutenant Bowen and myself accordingly engaged the first boat; our luggage was speedily stowed in it, and in less than an hour, I trod the soil of India. But how shall I describe the impression which almost overpowered me at this moment! To find myself in the land which was the cradle of the human race, the land of poetry, and of the Arabian Nights!. I could scarcely conceive that the dreams of my youth were realised. Though it was dark, the naked forms that flitted before me, the style of the architecture of the houses, and the foreign character of the scenery, told me that I was indeed in a new world.

Travels in India. 1845 Vol. I. pp. 29-30.

"No Scene Throughout the World More Beautiful."

SIR SAMUEL BAKER.

Upon a first arrival in Bombay the stranger is amazed at the architectural importance of a city which his imagination had pictured simply as the great commercial port of India. He is surprised at the extent of the native bazars and streets, and bewildered by the crowds which stream like the sluggish current of a river slowly but unceasingly through every artery of the city's frame. All these crowds are peaceable; there is no jostling, no angry clamour among the masses, which include every shade of caste and creed; the police well accoutred and organised are always at their posts, but their presence appears unnecessary in the orderly streets of Bombay. The public buildings are superbly arranged, and exhibit the great advantage of a preconceived plan which has enabled the various architects to select designs that harmonise with those of their predecessors. Thus we see at one *coup d'œil* a grand area of magnificent buildings extending along the race-course and sea-front with Back Bay and the palm-covered heights of Malabar Hill terminating the view at a distance of four miles.

There is no scene throughout the world more beautiful or more impressive to an Englishman, than the landscape and sea-view from the new public gardens opposite the reservoir, upon the basalt heights which command the entire circuit of Bombay, including the vast harbour, the numerous islands and the blue sea, backed by the lofty mountains in the distance. The beauty of the scene is full of contrast, and from this one point I have counted forty-eight tall chimneys denoting the manufacturing industry of the people, who, secure under a British administration, have embarked their capital in factories instead of hoarding it in secret places, and are now competing with the mills of Lancashire in producing cotton goods. The general aspect of Bombay is a test of British administration.

When standing upon the heights of Malabar Hill we look down upon the panorama of Bombay, we feel that although this grand picture is due to England, we English are yet a mere handful among those countless natives who are subjects of our Queen.

"Reflections in India." Fortnightly Review, August 1888, pp. 210-211.

FIRST IMPRESSIONS.

FIRST IMPRESSIONS.

" If this be exile, it is splendid exile!"

ELIZABETH GRANT.

We landed on the 8th of February 1828 in Bombay. We entered that magnificent harbour at sunset, a circular basin of enormous size, filled with islands, high, rocky, wooded, surrounded by a range of mountains beautifully irregular; and to the north on the low shore spread the city, protected by the fort, screened by half the shipping of the world. We were standing on the deck. "If this be exile," said my father musingly, "it is splendid exile." "Who are those bowing men ?" said my mother, touching his arm and pointing to a group of natives with coloured high-crowned caps on some heads, and small red turbans on others, all in white dresses, and all with shoeless feet, who had approached us with extraordinary deference. One of the high-caps held out a letter. It was from uncle Edward, who had turned the corner round Sir Griffin Wilson's wall so many years ago with his hat pulled down over such tearful eyes, and these were his servants come to conduct us to his country house. All was confusion around us, friends arriving, departing, luggage shifting (each passenger being allowed to carry a bag on shore with necessaries), and it grew dark in a moment, increasing our perplexity.

At last we were ready, descended the side of our poor old ship, entered the bunder-boat, moved, swung round to the steps of the ghaut, mounted them, found carriages waiting, and away we drove some three miles through part of the town, and then through a wooded plain, till we stopped at a shabby gate which opened on a narrow road and led us to the wide steps of a portico, reached by a good long flight, edged with two lines of turbaned servants glittering with gold adornments, reflected by the torch each third man held. A blaze of light flashed from the long building beyond, in front of the entrance to which stood a tall figure all in white, queen-like as a stage heroine, who gave a sign, and from her sides moved four persons in scarlet robes trimmed with gold and bearing in their hands gold sticks the height of themselves; they opened our carriage doors and out we stepped; and thus we were received by my uncle's wife.

They had come down from Surat, partly to meet us, and partly for my uncle's health, which repeated attacks of gout had much weakened. He was at this moment on the couch, incapable of leaving it, and still in pain, yet he had made every possible arrangement for our comfort. The large house of Camballa, which he had hired to receive us in, was of the usual Indian construction, the long, large centre hall with broad verandahs round it; but *such* a hall, eighty feet long, eighty feet wide, verandahs twenty feet wide. It stood on a platform in the middle of the descent of a rocky hill, round which swept the sea, with a plain of rice fields, and a tank, a handsome tank, between the foot of it and the beach. From the hill end of the hall rose a wide staircase in stages; each stage led off on either hand to a terrace, each terrace on the one hand was a flower-garden, on the other a covered gallery leading to offices. At top of all, and very high it was, the terraces were covered in as bedrooms, catching all the air that blew and commanding from their latticed balconies such a view as was alone worth almost the voyage from Europe.

Dinner was served in one of the verandahs to the great hall with such a display of plate, so brilliant a light, and such an array of attendants as were startling after our cuddy reminiscences. I thought of the Arabian Nights. There was light, vastness, beauty, pomp, and true affection. All was not gold, however; a better acquaintance with our palace disturbed much of our admiration. Our bedrooms were really merely barns, no ceilings, the bare rafters, bare walls, no fastenings to the doors, the bathrooms very like sculleries, the flowery terraces suspected of concealing snakes, and most certainly harbouring myriads of insects most supremely troublesome, and the tank a nuisance; beautiful as it seemed, with its graduated sides descending to the water, interesting from the groups of natives resorting there at all times with those pyramids of Etruscan-shaped pots upon their heads, and their draperied clothing, swinging on with such a graceful step, the tank at night became horrible from the multitude of frogs—the large bull-frog with such a dreadful croak as deafened us. Still those were minor evils. It was all a stage-play life, and we were enchanted with it.

Lady Strachey's "Memoirs of a Highland Lady", 1898, pages 415-416.

2.

I wish I had preserved a more minute recollection of my first Bombay impressions; they were very vivid at the time, and I remember being struck with surprise that all accounts of India that had fallen in my way were so meagre, when materials new and strange were in such abundance.

The youth of women, and the beauty of the majority, was one distinguishing feature of the society; the cheerful spirits of all, ladies and gentlemen, was remarkable, to be accounted for, probably, by the easy circumstances of almost all, and the occupation of their time. There are no idlers in India, every man has his employment; he may do it well or ill, but he has it there to do, a business hour recurring with every day, releasing him every afternoon, and well and regularly paid the first of every month. The women must attend to their households and their nurseries with watchful care, or they will rue it, and though some may neglect their duties more or less, none can avoid them. Then it is the most sociable country in the world, truly hospitable; everybody is acquainted, every door is open, literally as well as figuratively, there is an ease, a welcome, a sort of family feeling among these colonists in a strange land that knits them together pleasantly. There are gradations in the scale of course, and very rigidly observed too, the ladies in particular preserving carefully their proper position. The Governor does for king, his suite for court, the Commander-in-Chief, almost as grand; then the three members of council and their three wives very grand indeed; an admiral, or rather head of the Navy; all the civilians according to seniority, all the military according to their rank; the Judges of the Supreme Court, officials pertaining thereto, barristers, merchants—rather below par, with one or two exceptions; attorneys thought little of; Indian Navy ditto; Royal Navy in great repute when a stray vessel came in. A few French and Americans admitted, and several of the natives quite in fashion; rich Parsees, and one or two Hindus. All these elements shook up together

cordially, and there was an under-grouping of lower caste, native and foreign, all in their peculiar costumes, which, with the singular vehicles, the strange scenery, the ocean, and the cloudless sky, made a succession of bright pictures.

Lady Strachey's "Memoirs of a Highland Lady," pages 417-418.

A Viceroy on his Landing.

THE MARQUIS OF DUFFERIN.

Our landing in Bombay (December 1884) was really a beautiful sight. We were asked to remain on board the ship until half-past four in order that the troops and the spectators might not be inconvenienced by the sun. The fleet has been collected to add dignity to our 'Avatar,' and filled the bay with smoke and thunder. The town is situated on an island, or rather on a peninsula, with some picturesque heights and hills standing up round it. The temperature was exquisite, the atmosphere full of light, while balmy breezes prevented it being too hot. You can easily imagine the scene upon the quay, bright with guards of honour, cavalry escorts, and military and civil dignitaries in uniform; but what it would be impossible for you to conceive was the extraordinary strangeness and beauty of the streets. We had to drive six miles from the landing-stage to Government House, and the road on either side was lined by crowds of men in every sort of costume, interspersed with others with scarcely any clothes at all. Indeed, there were a good many ladies who were by no means profusely clad. But what was unimaginable was the colouring of the whole. A bed of flowers gives you no conception of its brilliancy. Nor indeed was brillincy its chief characteristic, but rather the most delicious harmony—subdued reds and blues and yellows intermingled with a confused mass of dusky limbs and faces, and eyes that sparkled like jewels. They cheered vociferously, with almost as full an intonation as an English crowd. At the same time they clapped their hands or bowed low, touching their foreheads or putting their palms together. As we passed from the richer quarters of the town into the streets where the mechanics dwelt, the spectacle was still more startling, as not only the streets but the windows of the houses were lined with a mass of human beings with scarcely a stitch on their bodies. In fact, there is nothing strikes the new-comer so much as the summery appearance of everybody.

Nothing surprised me more than to find the European portion of Bombay having so much the appearance of a university town. It is crammed with handsome buildings in blue and white stone in the collegiate Gothic style. Many of these have been erected at the cost of rich Parsees One school was filled with

Parsee ladies and girls, dressed in every kind of lovely silk and satin.

I opened an Institution for sick cattle. Having pulled the doors of a cowshed asunder amidst the cheers of the people, a gentleman advanced, bearing in his hand a tray filled with fruits and vegetables; cocoa-nuts and eggs, and bottles of variously coloured unguents. The eggs he dashed upon the ground, to the great detriment of the ladies' dresses. He broke the cocoa-nuts and sprinkled the milk around. He then smeared the lintels of the door-post with his red and yellow coloured ointments, and finally strewed the rest of the contents of his basket on the ground. It was like seeing a chapter of Leviticus in action.

This house is an enormous building, like a body with four legs sprawling out from it. The body consists of a single hall floored with marble, and with a double row of marble columns running from one end of it to the other. The legs constitute four wings, in one of which my wife and I have pitched our tent, two of the remaining wings being devoted to guests.

I liked Bombay much better than Calcutta, the air being far pleasanter. In Calcutta it is damp and muggy and more or less depressing, though not so much so, at all events at present, as the Bosphorus.

Letter to Lady Dartrey in Life by Lyall, Vol. II, 1905, pages 73-75.

A Viceroys First Impressions.

THE EARL OF LYTTON.

Our reception (April 1876) by the population of Bombay appeared to me very enthusiastic. The streets were densely crowded, and we were loudly cheered, nearly the whole way to Government House. I think I never in my life saw a town so picturesque as Bombay—I do not even except Venice; and its very mixed population is clad in an almost infinite variety of costumes except those who are not clad at all. The Parsee ladies seem to wear no petticoats; but the Parsee gentlemen make up for the deficiency by wearing a great many petticoats. These Parsees are, I think, among the very best of your Majesty's Indian subjects; and I wish that your Majesty had more of them. They are a wonderfully thriving community wherever you find them. They have a genius for business, and rarely fail in it. I have not yet seen a thin Parsee, and I doubt if I have seen a poor one. They seem to be all fat, rich, and happy. A population engaged in successful industry, and making money rapidly, is always conservative and loyal to the power which protects its purse. We stayed only one day in Bombay; but during our short sojourn there I was able to visit the principal institutions and one of the cotton-mills, besides receiving many of the local notables.

Letter to Queen Victoria, in Personal and Literary Letters. 1906, Vol. II, pp. 6-7.

An Orientalist's Impressions.

SIR M. MONIER-WILLIAMS.

We need not quote a Western poet in support of the trite truism that impressions on the mind, to be deep, must be made by scenes actually witnessed.

There is an Eastern saying that the distance between the ear and the eye is very small, but the difference between hearing and seeing is very great.

Much information can be gained about India from books and newspapers, and much by asking questions of old Indians who have spent their lives in the country, but, after all, India must be seen to be understood.

The instant I set foot on the landing-place at Bombay, I became absorbed in the interest of every object that met my sight—the magnificent harbour with its beautiful islands, secluded creeks, and grand background of hills; the picturesque native boats gliding hither and thither; the array of ships from every quarter of the globe riding at anchor—every feature in the surrounding landscape, every rock and stone under my feet, every animal and plant around me on the shore, every man, woman, and child in the motley throng passing and repassing on the quay, from the Bhisti, or water-carrier, who laid the dust by means of a skin slung on his back, o the boy who importuned me for *bakhshish* to exhibit a fight between a snake held in his hand and a mongoose concealed in a basket.

Though I was born in India, and had lived as a child in India, and had been educated for India, and had read, thought, spoken, and dreamt about India all my life, I had entered a new world.

On the esplanade, in front of the chief public buildings of Bombay, an extraordinary spectacle presented itself. An immense concourse of people was collected, waiting for the Prince of Wales, who was expected at the Secretariat to hold his first levee—no dingy crowd of Londoners hustling each other in a foggy, smoky atmosphere, but at least a hundred thousand turbaned Asiatics, in bright coloured dresses of every hue, moving sedately about in orderly groups under a glittering sky. The whole plain seemed to glow and flash with kaleidoscopic combinations of dazzling variegated colours. Rows of well-appointed carriages belonging to rich Bombay merchants, some containing Parsi ladies and children in gorgeous costumes, with coachmen in brilliant liveries, line the esplanade. Gem-bespangled Rajas, Maharajas, and Nawabs dashed by in four-horsed equipages, with troops of outriders before and behind.

Modern India and the Indians, 1878, pp. 27–28.

A Lady's Impressions Seventy Four Years Ago

EMMA ROBERTS.

The bunder, or pier, where passengers disembark upon their arrival in Bombay, though well-built and convenient, offers a strong contrast to the splendours of Chandpaul Ghaut in Calcutta; neither are the bunder-boats at all equal in elegance to the budgerows, bohlias, and other small craft, which we find upon the Hooghley. There is nothing to indicate the wealth or the importance of the Presidency to be seen at a glance; the Scottish church, a white-washed building of no pretensions, being the most striking object from the sea. Landward, a range of handsome houses flank so dense a mass of buildings, occupying the interior of the Fort, as to make the whole appear more like a fortified town than a place of arms, as the name would denote. The tower of the Cathedral, rising in the centre, is the only feature in the scene which boasts any architectural charm; and the Esplanade, a wide plain, stretching from the ramparts to the sea, is totally destitute of picturesque beauty.

The first feelings, therefore, are those of disappointment, and it is not until the eye has been accustomed to the view, that it becomes pleased with many of the details; the interest increasing with the development of other and more agreeable features, either not seen at all, or seen through an unfavourable medium. The aspect of the place improved, as, after crossing the Esplanade or plain, the carriage drove along roads cut through palm-tree woods, and at length, when I reached my place of destination, I thought that I had never seen any thing half so beautiful.

The apartments which, through the kindness of hospitable friends, I called my own, commanded an infinite variety of the most magnificent scenery imaginable. To the left, through a wide vista between two hills, which seemed cleft for the purpose of admitting the view, lay the placid waters of the ocean, land-locked, as it were, by the bold bluff of distant islands, and dotted by a fairy fleet of fishing-boats, with their white sails glittering in the sun. In front, over a beautifully-planted fore-ground, I looked down upon a perfect sea of palms, the tall palmyras lifting their proud heads above the rest, and all so intermingled with other foliage, as to produce the richest variety of hues. This fine wood, a spur of what may be termed a forest further to the right, skirted a broad plain which stretched out to the beach, the bright waters beyond expanding and melting into the horizon, while to the right it was bounded by a hilly ridge feathered with palm-trees, the whole bathed in sunshine, and forming altogether a perfect Paradise.

Every period of the day, and every variation in the state of the atmosphere, serve to bring out new beauties in this enchanting scene; and the freshness and delicious balm of the morning, the gorgeous splendour of mid-day, the crimson and amber pomps of evening, and the pale moonlight, tipping every palm-tree top with silver, produce an endless succession of magical effects. In walking about the garden and grounds of this delightful residence, we are continually finding some new point from which the view appears to be more beautiful than before. Upon arriving at tha verge of the cleft between the two hills, we look down from a considerable elevation over rocky precipitous ground, with a village (Mazagong) skirting the beach, while the prospect, widening, shows the whole of the harbour, with the high Ghauts forming the back-ground.

Turning to the other side, behind the hill which shuts out the sea, the landscape is of the richest description—roads winding through thick plantations, houses peeping from embowering, trees, and an umbrageous forest beyond. The whole of Bombay abounds with landscapes which, if not equal to that from Chinchpooglee Hill, which I have, vainly I fear, attempted to describe, boast beauties peculiarly their own, the distinguishing feature being the palm-tree. It is impossible to imagine the luxuriance and elegance of this truly regal family as it grows in Bombay, each separate stage, from the first appearance of the different species, tufting the earth with those stately crowns which afterwards shoot up so grandly, being marked with beauty. The variety of the foliage of the cocoa-nut, the brab, and others, the manner of their growth, differing according to the different directions taken, and the exquisite grouping which continually occurs, prevent the monotony which their profusion might otherwise create, the general effect being, under all circumstances, absolutely perfect. Though the principal, the palm is far from being the only tree, and while frequently forming whole groves, it is as frequently blended with two species of cypress, the peepul, mango, wild cinnamon, and several others.

Overland Journey to Bombay. 1841, pp. 213-217.

A Russian Lady's Impressions

MADAME BLAVATSKY.

Late in the evening of the sixteenth of February, 1879, after a rough voyage which lasted thirty-two days, joyful exclamations were heard everywhere on deck. " Have you seen the lighthouse?" "There it is at last, the Bombay lighthouse."

Cards, books, music, everything was forgotten. Everyone rushed on deck. The moon had not risen as yet, and, in spite of the starry tropical sky, it was quite dark. The stars were so bright that, at first, it seemed hardly possible to distinguish, far away amongst them, a small fiery point lit by earthly hands. The stars winked at us like so many huge eyes in the black sky, on one side of which shone the Southern Cross. At last we distinguished the lighthouse on the distant horizon. It was nothing but a tiny fiery point diving in the phosphorescent waves. The tired travellers greeted it warmly. The rejoicing was general.

What a glorious daybreak followed this dark night! The sea no longer tossed our ship. Under the skilled guidance of the pilot, who had just arrived, and whose bronze form was so sharply defined against the pale sky, our steamer, breathing heavily with its broken machinery, slipped over the quiet, transparent waters of the Indian Ocean straight to the harbour. We were only four miles from Bombay, and, to us, who had trembled with cold only a few weeks ago in the Bay of Biscay, which has been so glorified by many poets and so heartily cursed by all sailors, our surroundings simply seemed a magical dream.

After the tropical nights of the Red Sea and the scorching hot days that had tortured us since Aden, we, people of the distant North, now experienced something strange and unwonted, as if the very fresh soft air had cast its spell over us. There was not a cloud in the sky, thickly strewn with dying stars. Even the moonlight, which till then had covered the sky with its silvery garb, was gradually vanishing;

and the brighter grew the rosiness of dawn over the small island that lay before us in the East, the paler in the West grew the scattered rays of the moon that sprinkled with bright flakes of light the dark wake our ship left behind her, as if the glory of the West was bidding good-bye to us, while the light of the East welcomed the new-comers from far-off lands. Brighter and bluer grew the sky, swiftly absorbing the remaining pale stars one after the other, and we felt something touching in the sweet dignity with which the Queen of Night resigned her rights to the powerful usurper. At last, descending lower and lower, she disappeared completely.

And suddenly, almost without interval between darkness and light, the red-hot globe, emerging on the opposite side from under the cape, leant his golden chin on the lower rocks of the Island and seemed to stop for a while, as if examining us. Then, with one powerful effort, the torch of day rose high over the sea and gloriously proceeded on its path, including in one mighty fiery embrace the blue waters of the bay, the shore and the islands with their rocks and cocoanut forests. His golden rays fell upon a crowd of Parsees, his rightful worshippers, who stood on shore raising their arms towards the mighty "Eye of Ormuzd." The sight was so impressive that everyone on deck became silent for a moment, even a red-nosed old sailor, who was busy quite close to us over the cable, stopped working, and clearing his throat, nodded at the sun.

Moving slowly and cautiously along the charming but treacherous bay, we had plenty of time to admire the picture around us. On the right was a group of islands with Gharipuri or Elephanta, with its ancient temple, at their head. *Gharipuri* translated means "the town of caves" according to the Orientalists, and "the town of purification" according to the native Sanskrit scholars. This temple, cut by an unknown hand in the very heart of a rock resembling porphyry, is a true apple of discord amongst the archœologists, of whom none can as yet fix, even approximately, its antiquity. Elephanta raises high its rockly brow, all overgrown with secular cactus, and right under it, at the foot of the rock, are hollowed cut the chief temple and the two lateral ones. Like the serpent of our Russian fairy tales, it seems to be opening its fierce black mouth to swallow the daring mortal who comes to take possession of the secret mystery of Titan. Its two remaining teeth, dark with time, are formed by two huge pillars at the entrance, sustaining the palate of the monster.

How many generations of Hindus, how many races, have knelt in the dust before the Trimurti, your three-fold deity, O Elephanta? How many centuries were spent by weak man in digging out in your stone bosom this town of temples and carving your gigantic idols? Who can say? Many years have elapsed since I saw you last, ancient, mysterious temple, and still the same restless thoughts, the same recurrent questions vex me now as they did then, and still remain unanswered. In a few days we shall see each other again. Once more I shall gaze upon your stern image, upon your three huge granite faces, and shall feel as hopeless as ever of piercing the mystery of your being.

On the left side of the bay, exctly opposite Elephanta, and as if in contrast with all its antiquity and greatness, spreads Malabar Hill, the residence of the modern Europeans and rich natives. Their brightly painted bungalows are bathed in the greenery of banyan, Indian fig, and various other trees, and the tall and straight trunks of cocoanut palms cover with the fringe of their leaves the whole ridge of the hilly headland. There, on the south-western end of the rock, you see the almost transparent, lace-like Government House surrounded on three sides by the ocean. This is the coolest and the most comfortable part of Bombay, fanned by three different sea breezes.

Bombay is part of a considerable group of islands, the most remarkable of which are Salsette, joined to Bombay by a mole, Elephanta, so named by the Portuguese because of a huge rock cut in the shape of an elephant thirteen feet long, and Trombay, whose lovely rock rises nine hundred feet above the surface of the sea.

Bombay looks, on the maps, like an enormous cray-fish, and is at the head of the rest of the islands. Spreading far out into the sea its two claws, Bombay island stands like a sleepless guardian watching over his younger brothers. Between it and the Continent there is a narrow arm of a river, which gets gradually broader and then again narrower, deeply indenting the sides of both shores, and so forming a haven that has no equal in the world. It was not without reason that the Portuguese, expelled in the course of time by the English, used to call it "Buona Bahia."

In a fit of tourist exaltation some travellers have compared it to the Bay of Naples; but, as a matter of fact, the one is as much like the other as a lazzaroni is like a Kuli. The whole resemblance between the two consists in the fact that there is water in both. In Bombay, as well as in its harbour, everything is original and does not in the least remind one of Southern Europe. Look at those coasting vessels and native boats; both are built in the likeness of the sea bird "sat", a kind of kingfisher. When in motion these boats are the personification of grace, with their long prows and rounded poops. They look as if they were gliding backwards, and one might mistake for wings the strangely shaped, long lateen sails, their narrow angles fastened upwards to a yard. Filling these two wings with the wind, and careening, so as almost to touch the surface of the water, these boats will fly along with astonishing swiftness. Unlike our European boats they do not cut the waves, but glide over them like a sea-gull.

The surroundings of the bay transported us to some fairy land of the Arabian Nights. The ridge of the Western Ghauts, cut through here and there by some separate hills almost as high as themselves, stretched all along the Eastern shore. From the base to their fantastic rocky tops, they are all overgrown with impenetrable forests and jungles inhabited by wild animals. Every rock has been enriched by the popular imagination with an independent legend. All over the slope of the mountain are scattered pagodas, mosques, and temples of numberless sects. Here and their the hot rays of the sun strike upon an old fortress, once dreadful and inaccessible, now half ruined and covered with prickly cactus. At every step some memorial of sancitity. Here a deep vihara, a cave cell of a Buddhist bhikshu saint, there a rock protected by the symbol of Shiva, further on a Jaina temple, or a holy tank, all covered with sedge and filled with water, once blessed by a Brahman and able to purify every sin, an indispensable attribute of all pagodas. All the surroundings are covered with symbols of gods and goddesses. Each of the three hundred and thirty millions of deities of the Hindu Pantheon has its representative in something consecrated to it, a stone, a flower, a tree, or a bird. On the West side of Malabar

Hill peeps through the trees Valukeshvar, the temple of the "Lord of Sand." A long stream of Hindus moves towards this celebrated temple; men and women, shining with rings on their fingers and toes, with bracelets from their wrists up to their elbows, clad in bright turbans and snow white muslins, with foreheads freshly painted with red, yellow, and white, holy sectarian signs.

India is the land of legends and of mysterious nooks and corners. There is not a ruin, not a monument, not a thicket, but has a story attached to it. Yet, however they may be entangled in the cobweb of popular imagination, which becomes thicker with every generation, it is difficult to point out a single one that is not founded on fact. With patience and, still more, with the help of the learned Brahmans you can always get at the truth, when once you have secured their trust and friendship.

The same road leads to the temple of the Parsee fire-worshippers. At its altar burns an unquenchable fire, which daily consumes hundred weights of sandal wood and aromatic herbs. Lit three hundred years ago, the sacred fire has never been extinguished, notwithstanding many disorders, sectarian discords, and even wars. The Parsees are very proud of this temple of Zaratushtra, as they call Zoroaster. Compared with it the Hindu pagodas look like brightly painted Easter eggs. Generally they are consecrated to Hanuman, the monkey-god and the faithful ally of Rama, or to the elephant-headed Ganesha, the god of the occult wisdom, or to one of the Devis. You meet with these temples in every street. Before each there is a row of pipals (Ficus religiosa) centuries old, which no temple can dispense with, because these trees are the abode of the elementals and the sinful souls.

All this is entangled, mixed, and scattered, appearing to one's eyes like a picture in a dream. Thirty centuries have left their traces here. The innate laziness and the strong conservative tendencies of the Hindus, even before the European invasion, preserved all kinds of monuments from the ruinous vengeance of the fanatics, whether those memorials were Buddhist, or belonged to some other unpopular sect. The Hindus are not naturally given to senseless vandalism, and a phrenologist would vainly look for a bump of destructiveness on their skulls. If you meet with antiquities that, having been spared by time, are, nowadays, either destroyed or disfigured, it is not they who are to blame, but either Mussulmans, or the Portuguese under the guidance of the Jesuits.

As last we were anchored and, in a moment, were besieged, ourselves as well as our luggage, by numbers of naked skeleton-like Hindus, Parsees, Moguls, and various other tribes. All this crowd emerged, as if from the bottom of the sea, and began to shout, to chatter, and to yell, as only the tribes of Asia can. To get rid of this

Babel confusion of tongues as soon as possible, we took refuge in the first bunder boat and made for the shore.

From the Caves and Jungles of Hindostan, 1892, pp. 3-11.

An American's First Impressions.

BAYARD TAYLOR.

We came to a stone pier, with a long flight of steps leading down to the water. The top of it was thronged with natives in white dresses and red turbans. Among them were the runners of the hotels, and I soon found the one I wanted. At a small customs office on the pier, my baggage was passed unexamined, on my declaring that I had but two pounds of Turkish tobacco. A line of cabs, buggies and palanquins with their bearers was drawn up on the pier, and in order to be as Indian as possible, I took one of the latter.

It was not a pleasant sensation to lie at full length in a cushioned box, and impose one's whole weight (and I am by no means a feather) upon the shoulders of four men. It is a conveyance invented by Despotism, when men's necks were foot-stools, and men's heads playthings. I have never yet been able to get into it without a feeling of reluctance, as if I were inflicting an injury on my bearers. Why should they groan and stagger under my weight, when I have legs of my own?—and yet, I warrant you, nothing would please them less than for me to use those legs. These wear pads on the shoulders on which rests the pole to which the palanquin is suspended, and go forward at a slow, sliding trot, scarcely bending their knees or lifting their feet from the ground. The motion is agreeable, yet as you are obliged to lie on your back, you have a very imperfect view of the objects you pass. You can travel from one end of India to another in this style, but it is an expensive and unsatisfactory conveyance, and I made as little use of it as possible, in my subsequent journeys.

As I was borne along, I saw, through the corners of my eyes, that we passed over a moat and through a heavy stone gateway. I then saw the bottoms of a row of fluted Grecian pillars—a church, as I afterwards found—then shops, very much in the European style, except that turbaned Hindoos and mitred Parsees stood in the doors, and finally my bearers came to a halt in a wooden verandah, were I was received by Mr. Pallanjee, the host of the British Hotel. I was ushered up lofty flights of wooden steps to the third story, and installed in a small room, overlooking a wide prospect of tiled roofs, graced here and there with a cocoa-nut or brab palm. The partitions to the rooms did not reach the ceiling; there were no glass windows, but merely blinds, and every breeze that came, swept through the whole house. The servants were mostly Portuguese, from Goa, but as India is especially the country of servant and master, every person is expected to have one for his own use. I chose a tall Hindoo, with one red streak and two white ones (the signs of caste) on his forehead, who for half a rupee daily, performed the duties of guide, interpreter, messenger and *valet de chambre*. Nothing can exceed the respect shown to Europeans by the native servants. They go far beyond the Arab and Turkish domestics of the East, or even the slaves in Egypt. No Russian serf could have a greater reverence for his lord. As a natural consequence of this, they are noted for their fidelity; the ayahs, or nurses, are said to be the best in the world.

Bombay, as a city, presents few points of interest to a traveller. It is wholly of modern growth, and more than half European in its appearance. It is divided into two parts—the Fort, as it is called, being enclosed within the old Portuguese fortifications and surrounded by a moat. It is about a mile in length, extending along the shore of the bay. Outside of the moat is a broad esplanade, beyond which, on the northern side, a new city has grown up. The fortifications are useless as a means of defence, the water of the moat breeds mosquitos and fevers, and I do not understand why the walls should not have been levelled long since. The city within the Fort is crowded to excess. Many of the streets are narrow, dark and dirty, and as the houses are frequently of wood, the place is exposed to danger from fire. The population and trade of Bombay have increased so much within the last few years, that this keeping up of old defences is a great inconvenience. So far are the old practices preserved, that at one particular gate, where there was a powder magazine twenty years ago, no person is permitted to smoke. Southward of the Fort is a tongue of land—formerly the island of Colaba, but now connected by a causeway—on which stands the light-house. To the north-west, beyond the city, rises Malabar Hill, a long, low height, looking upon the open ocean, and completly covered with the gardens and country-houses of the native and European merchants.

Visit to India and China, 1856, pp. 35-38.

An Under-Secretary's Impressions.

SIR M. E. GRANT DUFF.

A little before three this morning (28 Nov. 1874) I was awoke by the vessel stopping; and as I looked out of my window, a bright flash met my eyes. It came from the lighthouse on the Prongs, and we were at length in Indian waters. Before dawn, most people were on deck, and were rewarded by a sunrise of great beauty—long lines of violet lying above the flat-topped hills of the Maharatta country, and the numerous islands formed like these of trap, which stud the great inlet of the sea known as Bombay harbour.

Some hours passed in the usual preparations, and about eight o'clock five of us got into a steam-launch, which the Governor had sent out, and proceeded to the landing-place of Mazagon, whence we drove to his country house at Parell. The *trajet* would, I have no doubt, have looked common-place enough to many eyes accustomed to India ; but to mine it was full of novelty and interest. First came the boats, with their graceful sails, formed, most of them, out of many pieces of cloth sewn together ; then the strange sandals of the men on the landing-stairs. Next A. pointed out to me the Cocoa-nut and the Toddy palm, the Mango, the Casuarina and the gold Mohur tree. Then I heard "the inevitable Indian crows," while every group had something to arrest the eye, either from strangeness of attitude or brilliancy of colour.

After the heat of the day was over, Sir Philip Wodehouse took us for a long drive. Passing some of the cotton Mills, which are already beginning to attract the attention of Manchester, we turned to the right, across a hideous flat, on which rice is grown in the rains, and reached the sea-shore just as the sun was setting. A. called my attention to the curious way in which, in this land of sudden darkness, the foreground becomes quite pale and dead, where, in England, it would still be blazing with colour; to the exquisitely graceful growth of the Cocoa-nut palms, in a grove through which we passed; to the Elephant Creeper (Argyreia speciosa); to the pretty lamps suspended in the shops of the native town, and to much else. It was indeed no small privilege to have my first peep of India under the guidance of an eye and mind to which everything was at once familiar and fresh.

Skirting Back Bay, a name rather too famous in the modern history of the Western Presidency, we arrived at the great range of public buildings which has recently arisen under the initiative of Sir Bartle Frere, and which would do honour to any capital. Then we turned and passed homewards, through the crowded streets of Bombay proper, said to be about the best native city in India, but which, even with all the advantage of darkness, and of its many twinkling lights, did not strike me nearly so much as Cairo.

Notes of an Indian Journey, 1876 pp. 21-23.

2.

We went this morning with the Secretary to Government over part of the Secretariat, which commands, I suppose, one of the finest sea views to be had from any Government office in the world, and in which the arrangements of the council-room, &c., had of course a certain interest.

Later, we drove round a large part of the town with Dr. Wilson—a great pleasure—to be put in the same class, as going over Canterbury

Cathedral with the author of the *Memorials*, the Greyfriars churchyard with Robert Chambers, or Holyrood with poor Joseph Robertson. Dr. Wilson has been here nearly fifty years, and has seen generation after generation of officials rise, culminate, and disappear.

It would take too long to enumerate all the things we saw, but I note especially a Shiah mosque, the first I ever looked upon; the street which supplies all Asia with Mahometan books, more being reproduced here (by lithography chiefly) than in Constantinople or any other city; a small mosque, which forms the centre of whatever is fanatical and dangerous in the Mussulman population of Bombay; a tiny temple of the monkey god Hanuman; and opposite it a much larger one, dedicated to Siva. We walked through the second of these, amidst a ghastly but amicable crowd of worshippers, chiefly men from Guzerat. You remember thinking El Azhar one of the most extraordinary places you ever entered. Well, this temple is as much more unfamiliar than El. Azhar, as that is than St. Sophia. The centre is formed by a tank, in which people were bathing, and round which there were, I think, four different shrines. Sacred cattle encumbered the pathway, while hideous and filthy devotees squatted about everywhere—one, who was smeared with ashes from head to foot, being pre-eminently unpleasant.

Notes of an Indian Journey, pages 41-42.

3.

The train from Poona came in sight, and, picking us up by the courteous arrangement of the authorities, carried us down through the magnificent pass known as the Bhore Ghaut, to the lowlands near Bombay. The line is a noble piece of engineering, and the scenery is even more striking than that along the Nervion, between Miranda and Bilbao, which it frequently recalls.

The breeze blew fresh from the sea as we crossed Salsette, and ere long we were once more at the starting-place of our three month's wanderings, under the hospitable roof of Sir Philip Wodehouse.

Parell, March 7th 1875.—It is very hot—the thermometer about 90° in the shade, but there is a delicious breeze. The only really bad time here is the month of May, when the breeze fails.

The garden is looking lovely—two huge white triumphal arches of the imperial Beaumontia being its chief feature.

The Parell mangoes, the best in India, are in full flower.

In the evening I went to the cathedral, and saw the admirable recumbent statue of J-'s excellent friend, Bishop Carr, which I had missed last December, though I sat close to it. On the way back I observed, for the first time, the zodiacal light, which I have looked for in vain so often.

March 8th.—I rose early, and wandered down to the sea across the Mahim palm groves. The cocoa-nut is the prevailing tree, though I saw some of the Borassus, and a few of the Areca. The coast of Ceylon, they tell me, is bordered by just such woods as these for hundreds of miles. The whole scene was thoroughly tropical, a single leaf sometimes stretching over a road where two carriages could pass each other, and the little huts looking like vignettes to *Paul et Virginie.* At length I reached the shore. The tide was far out, but there were few shells, and none at all attractive—a great contrast this to the last beaches we explored together near Suez, and at Ramleh.

Notes of an Indian Journey. pp. 237-9.

Jumble of Nations

SIR JAMES MACKINTOSH.

I am carried in my palanquin by bearers from Hyderabad. I have seen monkeys and their tricks exhibited by a man from Ougein. I condemn a native of Ahmedabad to the pillory. I have given judgment on a bill for brandy supplied by a man who kept a dram-shop at Poonah. I have decided the controversies of parties who live in Cutch; and granted commission to examine witnesses at Cambay, I have, in the same morning, received a visit from a Roman Catholic Bishop, of the name of Ramazzini, from Modena, a descendant of the celebrated physician, Ramazzini, a relation of Muratori, who wondered that an Englishman should be learned enough to quote Virgil; of an Armenian Archbishop from Mount Ararat; of a Shroff (money dealer) from Benares, who came hither by the way of Jyenagur, and who can draw bills on his correspondents at Cabul; and of the Dustoor, or Chief-Priest, of the Parsees at Surat, who is copying out for me the genuine works of Zoroaster. All this jumble of nations, and usages, and opinions, looks, at a distance, as if it would be very amusing, and for a moment it does entertain.

The island of Bombay is beautiful and picturesque; it is of very various surface, well wooded, with bold rocks and fine bays, studded with smaller islands. There is scarcely any part of the coast of England where the sea has better neighbours of every kind. But what avails all this, in a cursed country where you cannot ramble amidst these scenes; where, for the far greater part of the day, you are confined to the house, and where, during your short evening walk you must be constantly on your guard against *cobra capells* and *cobra manills*. The pleasure of scenery is here but little; and so seems to have thought a young artist, whom a strange succession of accidents threw upon our shores, W..., a brother of the Academician, and a young man who seems not destitute of talents.

Memoirs. 1836. Vol I. Pages 212 to 214.

A Picturesque City

SIR HENRY CRAIK

Of the general appearence of Bombay I am conscious that it requires some temerity for a new-comer to speak. One thing adds infinitely to its picturesqueness, as compared with a South African town: there is no banning from the streets of native costume, or even lack of costume, and this, as it seems to me, is all to the good. The ugliest sight one can see in Durban or Johannesburg is the native clad in European dress; the most attractive sight in the thoroughfares of Bombay is the native in his many coloured garb, and with that lissomeness of limb which its freedom gives. All along the Queen's

Road, the promenade which runs along the sea to Malabar Hill, crowded as it is with carriages, motors, and bullock-carts, we come across natives peacefully sleeping on the side paths, or quietly cooking their meals in the airiest of garments. We pass the fishing village, and then climb the road to Malabar Hill, and on between picturesque gardens and the many-coloured villas of the wealthier natives, with their bright tiles glittering in the sun. It is a picture which we could see nowhere else, and even the stifling heat is relieved by the breeze which comes from the wide expanse of sea on each side of us.

Of Bombay as a city, what can one say? Its sea-front looks bright and magnificent from the harbour—what large piles of sumptuous buildings could look otherwise in such a sunlight? The great mass of the Taj Hotel dominates them all. It shows itself frankly for what it is—a large advertisement, brave in its rather exaggerated caricature of an Indian palace. The great ranges of flats and mansions have a sumptuousness of their own, and would find themselves quite at home along the sea-front of Brighton, which they would fitly embellish. The Yacht Club is more quiet and dignified, and tells of comfort without gaudiness in its trim lawns and white balustrade. The principal commercial street would be a splendid thoroughfare in any European capital, and its warehouses, its banks, its insurance offices, need not fear comparison with the best of their kind at home. It is a thoroughfare of generous width bordered with rows of trees, and broken here and there by public gardens rich with flowers. Bombay there displays its wealth, but for real interest we must go to the narrow and crowded streets of the native town, down the passage of the Bazaar where natives of every tribe are chattering and gesticulating, while at every second or third stall the vendor is peacefully sleeping after his morning's work, and crowds of infants grin at us merrily from the corners and the recesses at the back. Occasionally a specially active stall-holder offers us his wares; for the most part they only turn on us a vacant and preccupied glance, and sink back into their own inscrutable indifference.

It is brilliant city, brimful of interest in its native quarter, lavish in its display of wealth in the business streets, picturesque in its residential suburbs, with their wealth of colour and of foliage. It may be a heresy, but to my mind there is one, and only one, British building of real architectural beauty in Bombay. It is the old Town Hall, built, I suppose, in the eighteenth century, when the Adam influence was strong, and when our great-grandfathers struck what one is tempted to think was the true note—that of making their buildings distinctive of our national character, and attempting no flimsy imitations in the Indo-Saracenic style. Those who, no doubt, know better will condemn my bad taste; but, frankly, I must confess that this fashion of aping the beauties of alien style does not attract me. The University does not carry this too far, and has an architectural beauty of its own. The Secretariat might have been even more imposing with advantage, as the outward embodiment of our rule. But the railway stations, with their inharmonious imitation of the Eastern style, strike one only as inept and misplaced.

In some respects Calcutta is in sharp contrast with Bombay. At Bombay one is chiefly struck by the variety of the motley throng, by the picturesque and brilliant colouring, by the entirely Oriental aspect of the place and by the rare occurrence of a white face amidst all the passing crowd. Here in Calcutta it is quite different. A Calcutta crowd does not show the same brightness of colour and the same teeming variety as Bombay. Nor can Calcutta boast the splendid sea front which gives to Bombay its claim to rank amongst the fairest cities of the world. But besides its busy, energetic, vigorous life, and its aspect of solid prosperity, Calcutta has one invaluable possession—the finest expanse of open ground in its great *Maidan* of which any city can boast. But although it cannot rival the beauty of the sea view of Bombay, and does not equal it in brilliancy of colour, Calcutta has a massiveness and an impression of energy which are all its own.

Impressions of India, 1908 pp. 13-16, 209-212.

Czar Nicholas II's Impressions

PRINCE OOKHTOMSKY.

Having driven in state through the streets of Bombay, it is now time to form a clearer idea of what surrounds us, and of the interest attaching to that part of India whither the journey of their Highness has led us. From the roomy verandah of Government House on Malabar Hill, we have a really magnificent view of the ocean we have just crossed, of the chaos of European and native buildings, with stately towers, long open galleries and soft outlines which seem to melt into the radiant distance. Between the city and the Government House, at present the abode of the Cesarewitch, lie the waters of the broad and shallow Back Bay running up into that part of the land which is chiefly occupied by the newer quarters of Bombay. The calm surface of these waters forms a marked contrast to the harbour by the absence of any large vessels, and of the forest of masts, funnels, and sails which lines the dark-blue, foam-flecked sea lying beyond the chief European quarter. We are indeed in India, but in an India widely different from that dreamt of on the way hither when the fancy, oblivious of the sameness and want of beauty which is to some extent peculiar to all seaport towns with a wide commercial development, painted the Malabar coast; without due warrant, as an all but virgin forest, inhabited by a strange people and full of mysterious temples overpowering in their majesty and unequalled beauty. Instead of this, the first impressions received in the interval between our entrance into the harbour and the drive through the streets of the European quarter to the residence of Lord Harris were in reality somewhat calculated to rouse disappointment. What met the eye on the way here did not, either in colours or in form, surpass or efface our recollections of Egypt still fresh and clear in the memory. On the contrary excepting the typical faces of the natives, who from afar off greeted, or rather gazed with curiosity and wonder at the brilliant procession on its way from the landing-place to Malabar Hill, nothing seemed specially individual, particularly picturesque or distinguished by that charm which met us at every step in the yet unforgotten land of thePharaohs.

Now having collected oneself after receiving a mass of new impressions, all that has been seen gradually becomes clearer, the spiritual eye penetrates, as it were, into the reality of the things around us, and gradually leads the feeling that the imagination already reflects a whole new world, distinguished by this remarkable peculiarity that it does not at first produce too deep an impression yet gradually draws the European deeper and more irresistibly into itself. He who has once set foot on the shores of India, who has even for a short time experienced its charms will never forget this beautiful land, with its peoples at first sight, unattractive and with its beautiful scenery.

The house in which we now are guests is undoubtedly one of the most important centres of Government on the face of the earth. From this spot the Governor of Bombay rules over an immense region, with a population of twenty-five millions: his sway extends over the native Principalities adjoining the Presidency or forming part of its territory; Beloochistan in the north is the boundary of the power of the administration to whom the English nation Entrusts on the western coast of India politically the most necessary districts of the Indian Empire.

The greater part of the trade of Europe with the former empire of the Great Moguls is carried on through Bombay. The coast which some two or three centuries ago was regarded as comparatively insignificant from a commercial point of view, desolate, unhealthy, and dangerous, on account of the neighbourhood of pirates, is at present very densely populated, has good sanitary arrangements, is covered with habitations, and may in a sense, be said to be fortified. In any case the time lies far behind us, when not only Europeans, but even the half-savage natives were here the rivals and foes of the English by sea. Strictly speaking it is but a little while ago that the latter gained a firm footing on the Bombay coast. About a hundred years ago they did not even hold the islands that lay nearest the town. Had not fortune shown such extraordinary favour to the countrymen of Clive and Warren Hastings in India during the last century, it is a very doubtful question who would now be ruling over that vast country which the Cesarewitch is about to survey.

Travels in the East of Nicholas II, Emperor of Russia, English Ed. 1900. Vol I pp. 178–9.

IMPORTANCE.

IMPORTANCE.

H. M. King George V on Bombay.

You have rightly said that I am no stranger among you, and I can heartily respond that I feel myself no stranger in your beautiful city. Six years ago I arrived indeed as a new comer; but the recollection of your cordial and sympathetic greeting is still fresh in my memory. The wondrous aspect disclosed by the approach to your shores, the first glimpse of the palms, rising as it were from the bosom of the sea, have not been forgotten, and have lost none of their fascination for me. From Bombay I set forth in 1905, encouraged by your affectionate welcome, to traverse at any rate a part of this vast country, and to strive to gain some knowledge of its people. Such knowledge as I acquired could not but deepen my sympathy with all races and creeds, and when through the lamented death of my beloved father I was called to the Throne of my ancestors, one of my first and most earnest desires was to revisit my good subjects in India.

It is with feelings of no common emotion that I find myself here again to-day with the Queen-Empress at my side and that desire fulfilled.

And I come with a heart full of gratitude that the anxiety due to a threatened scarcity in certain areas of the Presidency has, thanks to favourable and opportune rains, been happily dispelled, and that there is every prospect of your land being blessed with a good spring harvest.

Your eloquent Address has recalled to me that Bombay was once the dowry of a British Queen. As such Humphrey Cook took it over two hundred and fifty years ago, a mere fishing village. You, gentlemen, and your forerunners, have made it a jewel of the British Crown. I see again with joy the rich setting of its beautiful and stately buildings; I note also the less conspicuous but also more profitable improvements lately effected; but, above all, I recognise with pride your efforts to heighten what must always be the supreme lustre of such a jewel as this, the peace, happiness, and prosperity of all classes of the citizens. From my heart I thank you for the generous reception accorded to the Queen Empress and myself to-day.

We earnestly pray that God's blessing may rest upon our Indian Empire and that peace and prosperity may be ever vouchsafed to its people.

Answer to the Bombay Address in Dr. Reed's "King and Queen in India," 1912 pages 41-42.

The Address of Bombay Citizens To Their Majesties.

"The dower of a Royal Alliance, Bombay represents no chance settlement acquired by purchase from petty chiefs, or selected by merchants fugitive from other centres. Its importance and future greatness were foreseen by the sogacity of statesmen, and its acquisition by a Treaty of State constitutes the first intervention by the Royal Government of England in the administration of the land of India. We proudly claim that the high hopes entertained by the statesmen who acquired the Island and by the Governors who faunded and administered the City have met with rich fulfilment, and that this city constitutes the strongest link between the civilization of the East and of the West, which it has ever been the aim of the British Government to weld into one harmonious system.

"We rejoice to think that Bombay is broad based upon the firmest of foundations in being united within itself and that the diverse races and classes whom we represent are actuated by a strong sense of common citizenship.

"In the gracious presence of Your Imperial Majesty the Queen Empress, the people of India, regarding Your Imperial Majesty as the lofty embodiment of the highest ideals of womanhood, will recognise with renewed feelings of gratitude and affection Your interest in them, as evinced by this second visit to their shores."

Dr. S. Reed's 'King and Queen in India,' pp. 38-41.

Edward VII as Prince of Wales on Bombay.

"It is a great pleasure to me to begin my travels in India at a place so long associated with the Royal Family of England, and to find that during so many generations of British rule this great port has steadily prospered. Your natural advantages would have insured a large amount of commerce under any strong Government, but in your various and industrious population I gladly recognise the traces of a rule which gives shelter to all who obey the laws, which recognises no invidious distinctions of race, which affords to all perfect liberty in matters of religious opinion and belief, and freedom in the permit of trade and of all lawful callings. I note with satisfaction the assuranes I derive from your address, that under British rule men of varied creeds and nations live in harmony among themselves, and develop to the utmost those energies which they inherit from widely separate families of mankind, whilst all join in loyal attachment to the British Crown, and take their share, as in my native country, in the management of their own local affairs. I shall gladly communicate to Her Majesty what you so loyally and kindly say regarding the pleasure which the people of India derive from Her Majesty's gracious permission to me to visit this part of Her Majesty's Empire. I assure you that the Princess of Wales has never ceased to share my regret that she was unable to accompany me. She has from her very earliest years taken the most lively interest in this great country, and the cordiality of your greeting this day will make her yet more regret the impossibility of her sharing in person the pleasure your welcome afforded me."

The Prince of Wales' Tour, 1875-6, by Sir W. Howard Russell, pp. 119-120.

Wellington on Bombay

DUKE OF WELLINGTON.

Reply to the address from the British Inhabitants of Bombay. Bombay, 13th March 1804.

'The approbation of this Settlement is a distinction which will afford a permanent source of gratification to my mind; and I receive, with a high sense of respect, the honor conveyed me by your Address.

The events which preceded the war are of a nature to demonstrate the justice of our cause;

while the forbearance with which the British Government refrained from the contest is calculated to manifest that the efficient state of our military equipment was directed to the preservation of peace, and consistant with the principles of our defensive policy. The comprehensive plan of operations for the conduct of the war was equalled by the extent of our resources, and supported by the concentrated power of the empire. The conflict in which the British armies were in consequence engaged presented a theatre capable of displaying at once the most splendid objects of military glory, and substantial proofs of the pervading wisdom of the British councils. To be engaged in such a scene was an object worthy of the highest ambition; and the contingencies which placed a division of the army under my command enabled me to appreciate the permanent causes of our success and power, in the established discipline of our troops, in the general union of zeal for the public interests, in the uniform effects of our consolidated strength, and in the commanding influence of our national reputation in India.

In reviewing the consequences of our success, it is with unfeigned satisfaction that I perceive the increasing channels of wealth which have been opened to this opulent settlement; and it is peculiarly gratifying to my feelings, that I should have been instrumental in renewing the benefits of peace to a settlement, from the resources and public spirit of which, the detachments under my command have derived the most essential aids during the prosecuton of the war.

The occasion which it has pleased you to choose of uniting my name with that of the Governor General has excited the warmest affections of my heart, together with the highest sentiments of public respect; at the same time therefore, that I receive with peculiar gratitude, this mark of your kindness, I cannot, discharge the obligations you have imposed on me, in a manner more conformable to my sense of the honour and welfare of this settlement, or of the reputation and interests of the empire, than by expressing my confidence of your cherishing those principles of loyalty, subordination, and government, which have raised and finally established the British empire in India on the extensive foundations of its present security, prcsperity, dignity and renown."

Duke of Wellington's Despatches—selected by Gurwood, pages 156–157.

Marquess of Wellesley's Praise of Bombay.

Reply to the address from the British Inhabitants of Bombay presented on 22nd March 1804.

The congratulations which you are pleased to offer to me on the happy termination of the late war, manifest the most honourable, zealous, and just spirit of attachment to the public welfare, and to the national fame and glory.

I accept the animated expressions of your confidence and favourable opinion with a due estimation of the liberal sentiments which dictated your address, and with a high sense of the honour conveyed to me by this public testimony of your approbation.

Your vicinity to the theatre of the war in the Deccan has enabled you to appreciate with accuracy and justice, the magnitude of the dangers which have been surmounted, and the extent of the substantial advantages which have been obtained by this signal triumph of the British arms. In the commencement and progress of the war in the western quarter of India, the efficiency of various important branches of our military operations was secured by the active aid of the government, of the civil and military service, and of the British inhabitants of Bombay, and the useful and cordial assistance which you contributed in your several capacities to promote the common cause in the hour of peril, entitles you to participate in the honour which has attended our glorious success.

The exertions of Bombay during the late contest have recalled to my recollection the distinguished services of that settlement in a crisis of equal importance; and I have viewed with confidence and satisfaction the revival of the same energy and zeal which facilitated the success of our arms in Mysore.

It is grateful to my mind, that the conclusion of peace should have established national advantages, from which, peculiar benefit will be derived to the settlement of Bombay, by the security and extension of its commerce, military resources, territorial revenues, and political influence and power. The magnitude and importance of these advantages afford a due reward to the loyalty, public zeal and courage uniformly displayed by the settlement of Bombay during my administration. Having borne a considerable share in the burthen and hazard of war, you have received a just proportion of the benefits of peace.

You may rely on the continuance of my earnest endeavours to promote the improvement of those benefits, in your opulent and public spirited settlement; and to maintain the interests honour, and welfare of Bombay, by a just application of the same principles of public policy which have contributed to secure the general prosperity of the British Empire in Asia.

Marquis of Wellesley's Despatches, Vol. III, pages 595-596.

Queen Among Cities

G. W. STEEVENS.

Bombay is indeed a queen among cities. Drive down from the Ridge by the white flooding moonlight, beneath fleshy green leaves as huge, and flowers as languorously gorgeous, as in any fairy tale,—beneath hundred-fingered fronds of palm and wax-foliaged banyans that feel for earth with roots hanging from their branches; past tall broad-shouldered architecture rising above these, Western in its design, Eastern in the profusion of its embellishment; looking always out to the blue-veiled bay with the golden lights on its horns. Then think of the factory smoke, the numberless bales of cotton, the hives of coolies, the panting steamers in the harbour, the grim-eyed batteries, and the white warships. Bombay is a beautiful queen in silver armour and a girdle of gold.

In India, 1899, page 23.

First to Receive the King

DR. STANLEY REED.

In all India none made preparation to greet the King and Queen more joyously than Bombay. Delhi could rightly claim to be the scene of the Imperial Durbar. Calcutta, as the seat of the Government of India, absorbed a large share of the Emperor's limited time. But none could challenge the title of Bombay to be the first to receive the Emperor of United India. Standing in the midst of a western seaboard which possesses no other great natural harbour and in close touch with the most productive districts of the country, the fortunes of the city are broad based on unshakeable geographical advantages. They are buttressed by a population composed of the most acute trading races of the East. Parsis, Banias, Khojas and Bhattias, inspired by the example of Englishmen, have here united to make this one of the great cities of the world, justifying in remarkable degree the prescience of the Viceroy of Goa who declared that India will be lost on the day when the English nation is settled in Bombay—then a collection of mean islets separated by swamps. Here too the significance of the Royal visit was recognised from the day when it was announced; it was seen that the event was one of profound Imperial significance a demonstration to the peoples of the land, and to the wider Empire of which it forms a great and splendid part, made in the most conspicuous manner possible, that not only is India indissolubly one with the far flung Dominions of the Crown, but has a great and special place in the responsibilities of the Royal House. The citizens of Bombay can also claim, with better right than any other part of India, to be a united people. Not that there are no differences, racial, communal, religious, and sectarian amongst its million inhabitants, but because when occasion arises they are brushed aside like an impalpable cobweb and all act as one enterprising homogeneous body. Commerce has proved a wonderful solvent, and the influence of the Parsis, free from caste restrictions and religious bigotry, standing between Englishman and Indian, has welded all far more closely than has been practicable elsewhere in Asia.

King and Queen in India, 1912, pages 28–29.

The Gateway Between the East and the West

SIR RAYMOND WEST.

There was a city in ancient days founded by a great conqueror,–I am speaking of Alexandria,– and when that great conqueror founded that city he established it as a gateway of communication and as a means of connection between the East and the West. That great city of commerce was the seat of a long line of kings. It had wealth beyond most cities of the ancient world, and it was the favoured resort of many of the great ones of the earth. It has occupied a great place in history, but the greatest place it has taken has been on account of its library, on account of its learned men, and on account of the philosophy and learning which grew up there, and which have left its name, whatever its future fate may be, imperishable in the intellectual history of mankind. Now in our day and our age Bombay occupies quite an analogous position to that of Alexandria in the ancient world. Bombay is for us the gateway between the East and the West. There meet the men of various nations, and there they exchange their merchandise.

There also then, I say, should be that interchange of thoughts and ideas by which Bombay, like Alexandria, may rise to a fame quite independent of the wealth of its citizens, and of any fate which may befall it. Here in Bombay, where converging races from the East and West meet, should rise a school of scholarship and philosophy, which should make this city a worthy successor to the great city founded by Alexander the Great. Surely to forward such a work as this is an ambition worthy of the greatest and most distinguished of our citizens. I hope they will now and in all future time rise to the occasion, and it will be a part of their ambition—certainly it will be the noblest and purest part of their ambition—to endow the learned institutions, and especially the University in this city, with such gifts, make them so rich, and furnish such encouragements to learning, research, and study, as shall make Bombay intellectually the first city in Asia and second to none in the world. Let me remind these citizens that at the period of the Renaissance in Europe, which corresponds in many ways to the awakening of thought and intellectual light which is now making its way in India, the citizens of the great cities were lavish in their gifts and in their expenditure for the encouragement of learning. The great merchants of Florence, as some of their day-books, their "*mels*," preserved down to our own time show, not only had their correspondents in all parts of the world for gathering up rich merchandise, but also to seek out learned men and to send home valuable manuscripts. There is an example for our citizens to follow. Again, I find at the same stage in the world's progress that a city like Bologna spent half of its municipal funds in the support of its University. Padua, another great city, supported at one time thirty Professors in its University—Professors of Law and Medicine and General Literature.

But at the same time that the municipalities of Italy at the period of the Renaissance were so liberal in their gifts in aid of learning, there was still a field left for the princes and nobles and chiefs of that country, and there is still a field left for the princes and nobles and chiefs of India to do a great deal for the University of Bombay. It will be familiar to those of you who have read the history of that great period of the re-awakening of European life and knowledge that the new learning was but somewhat coldly received by the Universities themselves, which by that time after a period of three or four centuries of activity had already sunk pretty deep into the ruts of routine. It was in the courts of Popes and of the princes and nobles of Italy that the great scholars found means for carrying on their studies and the Universities, which were somewhat chary of receiving them, found to their cost afterwards that the wave of learning had in the long run passed them by and left them standing. Here is an example for the chiefs in India, especially chiefs who have any relation to the Presidency of Bombay. Here is an institution which would be in no wise jealous of anything they can do for learning. It invites them to come into its arms and to go hand in hand along with them in the work of assisting and promoting learning, literature, and science. I suppose there are few chiefs of higher rank who would not give a lakh or even two or five lakhs for an addition of one gun to their salutes. I do not ask these gentlemen in any way to despise the salute, which shows the respect felt for them by the Paramount Power in India. Far from it; but I ask them to win a still greater and nobler salute by giving a lakh or two or five to an institution of this kind, and then on every occasion of their entering this building, and showing their face among the community to which they belong, they will receive the noblest salute of a people's applause. I would fain see on every one of the panels of this hall, in which we are assembled, a tablet containing the names of chief after chief, hereditary donors of bounties to this University, hereditary benefactors who would within its sacred walls find a nobler Walhallah than anything that northern mythical imagination can conceive, where instead of drinking mead out of the skulls of their slain foes, they would move about in ideal society, one with the other, an idolized body of benefactors worthy of the recollection and almost of the worship of those who in future generations will flock into this hall, as they have done to-day, to take their degrees and to receive the recognition of those who come to witness the proceedings.

University Convocation Address, 1887, pages 184-186.

2

In this very city we have seen the mill industry grow up, which makes Bombay one of the great manufacturing cities of the world, and here, especially, the want: of technological instruction has been a growing want, which has made itself keenly felt and has been loudly expressed. Now comes an institution which, I trust, will supply that great want: nor let it be supposed for a moment that an institution of that kind need be deficient in the higher elements of intellectual cultivation. It is certainly true that technical instruction, when it is pursued on a scientific basis, affords exercise to the very highest powers of the intellect. If we follow out the development of any one of the great branches of physics or chemistry or any of the great inventions by which the world has been enriched in its material sphere, from the early gropings of its first devotees down to its development in our days, we find in that task a noble and worthy exercise of the highest capacity. If we attempt to appreciate the influence of such an invention or discovery on the world as it exists now, we are involved in a very comprehensive view of the existing conditions of human existence. If we attempt to anticipate what these inventions are to produce in the future, we are engaged on a problem which is worthy of the very highest speculative ability. It should never be said then that technological instruction, when properly pursued on a scientific basis, is in any way opposed to the high cultivation of the mind or to the objects of a University. It takes its part beside, and in no way under, it.

Convocation Address, 1888, pages 199–200.

3

We live at the time of a momentous confluence and conflict of ideas, principles, and interests. You will probably have to take your part in a profound moral strife; but if that part is a noble one, you may rest assured of abundant sympathy. The establishment of the Victoria Jubilee Technical Institute, which will make a new departure in the educational system of Bombay and of India, will stand also, like this University, as a striking and permanent sign of our readiness to admit and welcome every duly accredited addition to the means of advancing the moral and material welfare of the community. It is a wedding by which we bring a new sister into the family, without abating one jot of our love and reverence for the members who were there before. The literature in which we delighted aforetime is still dear to us; the rigorous laws of mathematical science still command our reverence and admiration. But we think that while we keep room for our possible Newtons, Wordsworths, and Macaulays, we may find a place also for our Faradays and Darwins. We may hold out hands of fellowship to an Indian Watt or Arkwright, a Stephenson or Bessemer, and strive by mastering the principles which their genius anticipated to make the path smoother for new conquests of nature. When I see my beloved country seated majestically in her centre of empire, yet thus diffusing the highest blessings she herself enjoys to all who will accept them in this great dependency, I feel myself filled, I confess, with a patriotic pride, which no tales of mere victory could inspire. To her, and her alone, I feel those fine lines of Claudian are applicable:—

Haec est in gremio victos quae sola recepit
Humanumque genus communi nomine fovit
Matris non dominae ritu; civesque vocavit
Quos domuit.

All of you are invited to come in and realize these blessings of a peaceful and beneficent dominion, and share the pride of a common citizenship with the great men whose writings have formed the nurture of your adolescence. But more, you are called on to go forth from this institution as apostles and interpreters to your countrymen in this generation and the next, of the vivifying influence by which in our own day Europe has been renovated. The historical glory of a great civilization glows behind you; the rising splendour of an enlarged nationality, and of a new intellectual world is before you. You may well be stirred with noble emotion at the sight of where you are and what you have to do. Accept this as a command from Heaven, as a divine impulse to work and wait for the complete regeneration of your people, and resolve to act worthily of so high and sacred a behest.

Convocation Address, 1888, pp. 205-206.

Bombay Essential to the Empire

PHILIP ANDERSON.

Amongst the foreign dependencies of the British Crown none is of greater and more increasing importance than Bombay. The growth of the Australian Colonies has been indeed far more rapid, and their sudden acquisition of wealth more astonishing, than any progress which has been made in India. But the possession of Australia and other colonies is not essential to the maintenance of England's power and glory; if their independence was to be at once proclaimed, no serious consequences need be apprehended on her account. It is, however, essential to her prosperity that she should preserve her Indian Empire, and every year strengthens the conviction of thinking men, that whether that Empire be regarded from a political or commercial point of view, its most important possession is the island of Bombay.

For many years the English had been anxious to lay their hands upon this treasure; yet strange to say, when they had obtained it, its value remained for a while hidden from the penetration of their statesmen, the practised eyes of their naval and military commanders, and the keen avidity of their enterprizing merchants. Its retention was considered scarcely worth a struggle, and the question whether it should be resigned was actually debated. Even the Dutch historian (Baldacus) of the age, a shrewd and accurate man, considered that this possession was worthless.

English in Western India, 1854, pp. 50-1.

Mingling of Peoples

"THE TIMES."

But transcending even these natural advantages is the asset Bombay possesses in the character of its people. In all other parts of India society is divided into water-tight compartments. In Calcutta industry and commerce are entirely in the hands of English and Scotch manufacturers and merchants, whilst the retail trade is monopolised by the keen Marwaris. The Bengali loathes the office and the desk, expending all his energies in the law and journalism, and when he has money to invest he puts it in the safest four per cents. In Madras the division between business and the professions in no less sharp. But Bombay is a cosmopolitan city, its trade and industry are shared by every section of the population to a degree unparalleled in any other part of the Indian Empire. When the St. George's Cross was raised over Bombay Castle, the proselytizing methods of the Jesuits and Franciscans had made European domination a hated thing. The British at once established a reign of complete religious toleration, and the keenest brains and boldest characters from all Western India flocked to an island where a security which the native rulers could not guarantee might be had with complete freedom of conscience and religious observance. The Parsis, driven from Persia by the Mahomedan conquerors, centuries before, who had been allowed to settle as hewers of wood and drawers of water in Gujarat, were amongst the first arrivals. They brought freedom from caste prejudice and restriction, and the quickness and clannishness bred of oppression, which made them the natural channel of communication between the English and the children of the soil, and gave them a large share in the seaborne trade shunned by Hindus because of the pollution involved in voyaging across "The Black Water." The Khojas, forced converts from Hinduism, came from Cutch, the Banias from Gujarat, the Bhattias form Cutch and Gujarat, the Konkani Mahomedans from the south, and a sprinkling of Jews from Baghdad. These are amongst the keenest trading races in the world; their natural vogue is commerce; and if they have a fault, it is that they are too speculative rather than ultra-conservative—the besetting sin of most of India. It is on this secure human foundation that the commercial fortunes of Bombay are firmly based.

A full appreciation of the position of the various Indian communities in the city is essential to an understanding of the place of Bombay in India and the Empire. In most parts of India the line of demarcation between the Englishman and the Indian is sharply drawn ; in some parts it is possible for a man to pass a lifetime in the country and never come into intimate contact with an Indian gentleman. In Bombay the line is so faint that it must soon be extinguished. Englishman and Indian, Parsi and Mahomedan, Jew and Hindu, meet in daily and intimate commercial dealing. They sit side by side in the Hall of the Municipality and the Senate of the University, they foregather nightly at the Orient Club, and interdine frequently. Touch any commercial house and you find that its ramifications are so intertwined with Englishman and Indian that acute racial feeling is impossible ; at any public gathering, every race and creed in the cosmopolitan city will be represented. Whilst communal life in Bombay is strong, it is rarely bigoted ; commerce, and the amenities commerce has brought in its train, has been a mighty solvent of particularism and intolerance. In all these respects Bombay is nearly a generation ahead of any other part of India. It has acquired a unique reputation for common sense and sobriety of opinion. The Bengali is generally more cultured, he is almost always a finer orator and rhetorician ; Madras has carried its educational machinery to a higher pitch and produced more accomplished Brahmin administrators ; but Bombay leads India in the sobriety of thought and breadth of view which comes from travel and commerce and the magic influence of property. If it cannot be said that what Bombay thinks to-day India thinks to-morrow, it may be said without exaggeration that at all times of political excitement India looks to Bombay for an informed opinion, and for the brake which will arrest runaway political thought. It is to Bombay that the Government look for the reflection of the best Indian opinion on the politics of the day, and for a lead in currency and finance.

India and the Durbar 1911, pp. 270-272.

"The Eye of India"

W. S. CAINE.

Bombay has been called "The Eye of India". It is the largest, most populous, and enterprising city in the Empire. More than half the imports and exports of all India pass through its custom house. Nine-tenths of the persons entering or leaving the country do so at Bombay; it is without exception the finest modern city in Asia, and the noblest monument of British enterprise in the world. The traveller, eager for the wonders of Agra, Delhi, or Benares, is too often satisfied with a couple of days spent in driving through its spacious streets, neglectful of the wonderful life of this great city and seaport, seeing nothing of its institutions, its arts and manufactures, or the interesting peoples who make up its population of 800,000 souls. A month may be spent in Bombay, and at the end many things will still be unseen that ought to have been seen.

As the steamer rounds Colaba point, and proceeds slowly to her moorings, the panorama of Bombay city, with the noble buildings towering above the masts in her docks, the low coast line beyond sweeping round the vast bay dotted with palm-clad islands, backed by the lofty blue mountains of Matheran and Mahableshwar, fully justify the name given by the old Portuguese navigators in the 16th century—Bom Bahia, the beautiful bay.

Picturesque India, 1891, pages 1-2.

Cosmopolitan yet Homogenous

"THE TIMES."

It is well-nigh impossible for the untravelled Englishman to realize the giant strides that are being made by the commercial cities of India that have sprung into existence under the influence of the Pax Britannica. He needs to sail into Bombay Harbour, to survey its miles of deep water anchorage, and drive round the wharves and quays that accommodate a seaborne trade of four million tons a year. He must drive through the main streets of the city, where he will find roads and public buildings that would not be unworthy of Munich. Most significant of all, he should stand on some eminence looking north, and mark the scores of tall chimneys belching forth smoke, then descend into the industrial quarter, and listen to the roar of machinery that is bound some day to drive Lancashire textiles out of India. All these industrial potentialities are established in a setting of unsurpassed beauty. Alone amongst the modern cities of India, Bombay can claim to be called beautiful, and the glories of its deep bays and noble harbour, of its wooded slopes and saphire sea command the unstinted admiration of the visitor and cannot pall on the oldest inhabitant. And these conditions are found in a climate which, whilst enervating, is never really hot, and in the worst months of the year is tempered by a sea-sweetened breeze. Broad-based as its fortunes are on geographical position, harbour, and industry, the future of Bombay is yet more securely founded on its people. Cosmopolitan to an almost unparralled degree, yet it owns a homogeneity unknown elsewhere in India, and a civic patriotism based on the consciousness that all are citizens of no mean city. No city could be more conscious of its future as the second city in the British Empire, or more willing to spend prodigally in order to be worthy of that destiny; so that Bombay may truly fulfil the ideal of Gerald Aungier, one of the first and greatest of her Governors, as the city that by God's grace is destined to be built.

India and the Durbar, 1911, pages 281–282.

The Modern Alexandria

SIR M. E. GRANT-DUFF.

I leave Bombay with a much stronger impression than I had of its great Asiatic as distinguished from merely Indian importance. It is, and will be, more and more to all this part of the world what Ephesus or Alexandria were to the eastern basin of the Mediterranean in the days of the Roman Empire.

I wish I could give it a fortnight, and be allowed to pick Dr. Wilson's brains all the time; but the "limitations of existence" say 'no' to that.

Notes of an Indian Journey, 1876, page 44.

Bombay an Asylum for All

FRANCIS WARDEN.

If in addition to these local improvements, we estimate the importance of Bombay in a national point of view, in reference to the resources which it has afforded towards the extension and consolidation of the British Empire in India; to the means of promoting the vend of the manufactures of the mother country for upwards of a century and a half in every quarter of India, throughout Persia and Arabia; to the aid which it has afforded in upholding her military reputation and in contributing to her naval power and resources, we cannot too highly extol the liberal policy, which has acquired and cherished those advantages; and in viewing the commanding situation of this possession, either in a commercial or in a plitical light, on the security of which the permanency of our Eastern Empire mainly depends, we cannot be too cautious in preserving unimpaired the resources of the island, by encouraging and conciliating not only its own subjects, but those of the surrounding country; to convert the floating population into permanent residents; that Bombay, and ultimately the adjacent island of Salsette, may continue what it has hitherto proved, an asylum to those who seek for refuge and protection from the oppression of their own arbitrary governments.

The Court of Directors have, from the earliest period, entertained an opinion that the island of Bombay might be rendered an advantageous settlement, and have, therefore, repeatedly enjoined the exercise of a mild and good Government, to encourage people from all other parts to come and reside under their protection; the impartial administration of justice has been anxiously urged, and that every facility might be afforded to the new inhabitants to build themselves habitations.

Land Tenures, 1814, pages 75-76.

Variety of Races and Religions

:MURRAY MITCHELL.

Even in 1838 the importance of Bombay as the great western gate of India was clearly recognished, and one heard of many new mercantile houses springing up. The arrival of the monthly steamer from Suez was working a vast revolution.

Then, as now, the population of Bombay was remarkably mixed. Equal to the variety of races was the variety of religions. Hinduism (to use the term in all its vast and vague comprehensiveness); Mohammadanism in several forms; Jainism; Zoroastrianism; Judaism; and Christianity—the last, especially in its Roman Catholic form. Even in ancient Alexandria the races and the systems of belief could not have been more diversified.

There could not have been a more stimulating field of labour. All of these systems had to be studied, and, if possible (no easy task), understood. It was not difficult to refute, it was tempting to denounce, them; but that did little good. The question was, what gave these systems their terrible power over human hearts?

The Marathas—the inhabitants of Maharashtra, 'the great country'—had long been the leading race in Western India. They had begun to act a conspicuous part more than two hundred and fifty years before. Their first leader, Shivaji, was a man of remarkable skill and energy; and under him the sturdy Maratha was a match for the trained Moslem warrior. The Maratha horsemen soon swept victoriously over the land from Agra to Tanjore. Maratha dynasties were set up far beyond the limits of Maharashtra. But the Marathas were, at best, what Sir Thomas Munro called them, a horde of Imperial robbers. Their work was plunder and devastation. Doubtless the Mohammadan yoke pressed sore on the vanquished Hindus, It did so especially in the time of Shivaji, under the bigoted Aurangzib. And Shivaji waged what may be called mainly a religious war. He had consecrated his sword to the destroying goddess Bhawani and called it by her name. He unfurled a sacred banner and summoned his countrymen to rally round it 'for the Protection of Brahmans and cows.' Yes; and the wily chieftain knew his men; they flocked enthusiastically round him, at the call. Ere long the Peshwas, who were Brahmans, did with the descendants of Shivaji as the Mayors of the Palace had done with the early kings of France. And now everything was modelled according to the Shastras. The Brahman and his fellow-sufferer the cow were reinstated in divine honour.

So through the eighteenth century the Marathas fought on with varying success, but plunging India into greater and greater misery. Still worse were the Pindharis,-lawless freebooters, who were generally their allies. In their rapid movements they spread desolation on every side.

The strength of the Marathas had been broken at the great battle of Asai (Assaye) in 1803; and in 1818 the Peshwa was overthrown near Poona and stripped of his dominions. The shock was tremendous. But the fierce Maratha spirit was only curbed, not crushed; and it fretted with ill-concealed impatience under the British rein.

God grant, for the sake of India even more than that of Britain, that the Pax Britannica may long endure; Let Britain be just and fear not; yet also, to the justice let her add a large measure of sympathy. She seldoms fails in the former; she often fails in the latter.

In Western India, 1899, pages 23-25.

Bombay and Calcutta.

EMMA ROBERTS.

Comparisons are so frequently both unfair and invidious, that I had determined, upon my arrival at Bombay, to abstain from making them, and to judge of it according to its own merits, without reference to those of the rival presidency. It was impossible, however, to adhere to this resolution, and being called upon continually to give an opinion concerning its claims to superiority over Calcutta, I was reluctantly compelled to consider it in a less favourable point of view than I should have done had the City of Palaces been left out of the question.

That Bombay is the rising presidency there can be no doubt, and there seems to be every probability of its becoming the seat of the Supreme Government; nothing short of a rail-road between the two presidencies can avert this catastrophe; the number of days which elapse before important news reaching Bombay can be known and acted upon by the authorities of Calcutta rendering the measure almost imperative. Bengal, too proudly triumphing in her greatness, has now to bear the mortifications to which she delighted to subject Bombay, a place contemptuously designated as "a fishing village", while its inhabitants, in consequence of their isolated situation, were called "the Benighted."

Steam-communication brought the news to Bombay of the accession of Queen Victoria to the throne of England, and this event was celebrated at the same time that the Bengallees were toasting the health of William the Fourth at a dinner given in honour of his birth-day. "Who are the Benighted now?" was the universal cry; and the story is told with great glee to all new arrivals.

Overland Journey to Bombay, 1841, pp. 244-246.

Bombay and Paris

GERSON DA CUNHA.

The great events that have materially contributed to the making of modern Bombay are the Treaty of Bassein, which, destroyed the Maratha Confederacy, the annexation of the Dekkan, and the opening of the Suez Canal, which helped considerably to raise this city to the proud position of the gateway of India. On the ruins of the Peishwa's dominion was thus rising the edifice of a snug little island on the Konkan coast, destined to rule over a great part of a vast Continent. Since then it has passed through various critical phases of growth and development, through years of joy and of sorrow, periods of unnatural inflation alternating with those of apparently hopeless depression; but, in spite of all this, Bombay, like Paris, *fluctuat nec mergitur* and, like Paris, Bombay has grown, due allowance being made for the boldness of the comparison, slowly at first, but rapidly during the last quarter of this century. From Charlamagne to Napoleon, Paris took nearly ten centuries to become a populous city, and Bombay, from Humphrey Cooke to Jonathan Duncan, has spent about one hundred and fifty years to develop frcm a mere hamlet into a fair town.

Thus Bombay resembles Paris, as some other cities, in the rapidity of its expansion within the last quarter of a century. In 1814 the population of Bombay was about 200,000, and the tenements 20,000. Now the population has quadrupled, and the number of buildings has nearly doubled. There is more concentration and pressure of the populace in Bombay than in Calcutta. Like the Adriatic tribes who took refuge in the city of the Lagoons, all tribes in Western India flock to Bombay, and from traditional beliefs, social instincts and tribal affinities are drawn to certain areas in the town where their tendency is to agglomerate rather than to disperse. Within the memory of many of us fields, which once were open and cultivated, have now been built over with houses of all shapes and sizes.

Another feature common to both Paris and Bombay is prestige and influence, which each of them exercises over all the country, far beyond the limits of their own administrative spheres. Bombay draws, as the metropolis, the best talent from provinces and districts around, and dictates laws and fashions to India as Paris does to France.

It is said that Bombay is the Alexandria of India. Its geographical position and commercial relations bear evidently some resemblance to the great eastern *entrepot* of the Mediterranean. As the swampy Rhakotis, a mere fishing village, which Alexander the Great transformed into the splendid city of Alexandria, the desolate islet of the Bombay Koli fishermen was changed into the present capital of Western India. Like Alexandria, it is, moreover, on the highway to other cities. As the visitor hurries from steamer to rail on the way to the Pyramids and to Luxor, the Indian tourist rushes from the Ballard Pier to the Victoria Station on the way to the Taj Mahal, Delhi, and Benares. But in all other respects Bombay is the Paris of India. It is true it does not possess the beautiful, and, according to Lebrun, the honest smiling river—

La Seine aux bords riants, nymphe tranquille et pure,

Porte son doux cristal, ennemi du parjure,

A l'immense Thetis ;

but it has instead one of the most splendid harbours in the world, about which the old Portuguese Viceroy, Antonio de Mello e Castro, wrote to the King of Portugal, D. Affonso VI in 1662: "Moreover, I see the best port your Majesty possesses in India, with which that of Lisbon is not to be compared, treated as of little value by the Portuguese themselves."

The history of the two cities has hitherto proved that they are both endowed with powers of recuperation to meet the effects of disaster. But while Paris possesses the vitality of a virile constitution, seasoned and braced up by the lapse of some centuries, to guarantee its future, Bombay is yet too young to justify any dogmatic prognostications of continued prosperity.

History, like drama, delights in contrasts and coincidences. But if the historical parallels of the past were logical arguments in relation to the changed conditions of to-day, the tragic fate of nearly all the cities in Western India, whose existence could hardly be counted by the cycle of three centuries, would lead us, indeed, to very gloomy forebodings.

I will not claim to possess the prophetic instinct to foresee what is in store for Bombay. But as it has adopted the happy motto of *Urbs prima in Indis*, it may be hoped that this will prove of good augury, and that among other privileges Bombay will own that of priority among the Indian cities for longevity in undecaying prosperity.

Origins of Bombay, 1900, pp. 3-6.

Another Carthage

JAMES DOUGLAS.

It was in 1675 that Dr. Fryer, a member of the Royal Society, suggested that out of all this scum there might arise another Carthage. He was a far-seeing man, for among the long bead-roll of illustrious names on the page of Bombay history, or books of travels, not one among them all ventures to forecast the greatness of the city or even hazard a conjecture thereon. Xavier, Heber, Wilson ?

I do not ask to see
The distant scene, one step enough for me.

And it was ever thus. Not Aungier, not Wellesley, not Elphinstone, nor the eagle eye of Mackintosh which scans the destiny of nations, vouchsafes a single glance to revive the flagging courage of the plodding servant of Government, or animate the hopes of the merchant or the missionary, who had cast his lot on the dreary shores of old Bombaim. To him Bombay is "the most obscure corner of India."

But from first to last it was all the same; we sowed the seed and awaited patiently the harvest. In spite of the blundering and villainy of Cooke, the rebellion of Keigwin, and a climate that mowed us down before the reaper's sickle, we held our ground by sending out fresh men to repair disaster. In the dullest and most discouraging of times there was always some advance. Sometimes floundering but never despairing, our powers of endurance and administrative ability were tested to the very utmost. The work, however, killed seven Governors in one generation—we mean in thirty years. We may also tack on to this, one ambassador and one admiral. These were the days of darkness, when men's hearts failed them for fear, and when the tumults of the people were like the noise of the sea and the waves roaring. It was then we saw the sun set behind the Dutch fleet, which blocked up the view seawards and hung like a black thundercloud at the mouth of Back Bay. It was then that the Great Moghul, or the Seedee for him, was battering at the gates of Bombay Castle. Though the Dutch and the Moghul are now of little account, they were then about the strongest powers respectively in Europe and in Asia. The Dutch in the generation we speak of were the terror of the seas, had burned Sheerness and entered the Medway and the Thames: and Aurungzebe had insulted the majesty of England by tying the hands of our envoys behind their backs and sending the Governor of Bombay about his business.

But we survived it all. There was a providence that watched over the infancy of Bombay, and well did she stand her baptism of fire. By and bye the great Augean stable was partially cleaned out and the Bombay climate became tolerable. Either good or bad, strong or weak as the party is that useth it; like the sword of Scanderbeg. She chased the pirates from the sea and the Pindaris from the land. By opening up roads Bombay unlocked the granaries of Western India for her starving children, and by clearing the sea of desperadoes the Indian Ocean became the property of all the nations of the world. She did not wait for the trumpet blast of the Anti-Corn Law League, but quietly on her own account inaugurated Free Trade in 1812 during the Baroda Famine.

In terms of her first proclamation she became an asylum for all; many men came from the west with the seeds of religion and civilisation, the blessings of which are now apparent. They were welcome. Not one of them was injured. During the long period we have held this island—and it is a blessed fact to be able to record—no man has suffered death for his religion. So perfect was the security of life and property that many of the settlers slept with open doors and windows. At length walls were found to be no longer necessary. They were a hundred years in building, and were demolished not by the hands of an enemy, for no enemy was ever seen within her gates. The same men (or their descendants) who erected them levelled them to the earth, and let him that rebuildeth them beware of the curse of Hiel the Bethelite. Little by little as from the slime and miasma of some geologic era, an island-city rose slowly from the bosom of the sea, fair to look upon, green with the verdure of an eternal summer, beautiful as Tyre and more populous than either ancient Carthage or Alexandria—crowned not only with the monuments of human industry, but with buildings to teach men the art of being industrious; with a Government India had never known before, that protects the weak from the oppression of the strong, and measures out equal law to every one irrespective of his colour or his creed.

Clear innocence her shield; her breastplate prayers,
Armour of trustier proof than aught the warrior wears.

Book of Bombay, 1883, pp. 15-20.

Bombay and European and American Cities

WILLIAM CURTIS.

There are two cities in Bombay, the native city and the foreign city. The foreign city spreads out over a large area, and, although the population is only a small per cent of that of the native city, it occupies a much larger space, which is devoted to groves, gardens, lawns, and other breathing places and pleasure grounds, while, as is the custom in the Orient, the natives are packed away several hundreds to the acre in tall houses, which, with over-hanging balconies and tile roofs, line the crooked and narrow streets on both sides. Behind some of these tall and narrow fronts, however, are dwellings that cover a good deal of ground, being much larger than the houses we are accustomed to, because the Hindus have larger families and they all live together. When a young man marries he brings his bride home to his father's house, unless his mother-in-law happens to be a widow, when they often take up their abode with her. But it is not common for young couples to have their own homes; hence the dwellings in the native quarters are packed with several generations of the same family, and that makes the occupants easy prey to plague, famine and other agents of human destruction.

The Parsees love air and light, and many rich Hindus have followed the foreign colony out into the suburbs, where you find a succession of handsome villas or bungalows, as they are called, half-hidden by high walls that inclose charming gardens. Some of these bungalows are very attractive, some are even sumptuous in their appointments—veritable places, filled with costly furniture and ornaments—but the climate forbids the use of many of the creature comforts which American and European taste demands. The floors must be of tiles or cement and the curtains of bamboo, because hangings, carpets, rugs and upholstery furnish shelter for destructive and disagreeable insects, and the aim of everybody is to secure as much air as possible without admitting the heat.

Bombay is justly proud of her public buildings. Few cities have such a splendid array. None that I have ever visited except Vienna can show an assemblage so imposing, with such harmony and artistic uniformity combined with convenience of location, taste of arrangement and general architectural effect. There is nothing, of course, in Bombay that will compare with our Capitol or Library at Washington, and its state and Municipal buildings, cannot compete individually with the Parliament House in London, the Hotel de Ville de Paris or the Palace of Justice in Brussels, or many others I might name. But neither Washington nor London nor Paris nor any other European or American city possesses such a broad, shaded boulevard as Bombay, with the Indian Ocean upon one side and on the other, stretching for a mile or more, a succession of stately edifices. Vienna has the boulevard and the buildings, but lacks the water effect. It is as if all the buildings of the University of Chicago were scattered along the lake front in Chicago from the river to Twelfth street.

Modern India, pages, 27 to 28.

A Peerless Harbour

Dr. GEORGE SMITH.

Bombay, with the marvellous progress of which, as city and province, Wilson was to be identified during the next forty-seven years, has a history that finds its true parallels in the Mediterranean emporia of Tyre and Alexandria. Like the Phoenician " Rock " of Baal, which Hiram enlarged and adorned, the island of the goddess Mumbai or Mahima, " the Great Mother," was originally one of a series of rocks which the British Government has connected into a long peninsula, with an area of 18 square miles. Like the greater port which Alexander created to take the place of Tyre, and called by his own name, Bombay carries in its ships the commerce of the Mediterranean, opened to it by the Suez Canal, but it bears that also of the vaster Indian Ocean and Persian Gulf. Although it can boast of no river like the Nile, by which alone Alexandria now exists, Bombay possesses a natural harbour peerless alike in West and East, such as all the capital and the engineering of modern science can never create for the land of Egypt. Instead of the "low" sands which gave Canaan its name, and the muddy flats of the Nile delta, Bombay presents ridge after ridge intersecting noble bays, and hill upon hill, rising up into the guardian range of the Western Ghauts. From their giant defiles and green terraces fed by the periodic rains, the whole tableland of the Indian Peninsula gently slopes eastward to the Bay of Bengal, seamed by mighty rivers, and covered by countless forts and villages, the homes of a toiling population of millions. On one-fourth, and that the most fertile fourth, of the two centuries of Bombay's history, John Wilson, more than any other single influence, has left his mark for ever.

Life of Dr. Wilson of Bombay, 1878, pp. 37-38.

Advantage Over Every Port in India

MARIA GRAHAM.

Bombay possesses more natural advantages than any other European settlement in India, but it is, unaccountably, that which has been most neglected; however, it is only a few years since the Mahrattas have been so far subdued as to render the surrounding districts safe. It is nine miles in length and three in breadth; full of towns and villages, and every foot of the land in cultivation. It is connected by a causeway, with the large and fruitful, though neglected, island of Salsette, and forms with it, Caranja, and Elephanta, a most commodious harbour. It has the advantage over every port in India in the rise of the tides, which is seventeen feet, whereas the highest springs in Prince of Wales's Island, and the wonderful harbour of Trincomale only rise to ten feet. It is consequently well adapted for building and docking large ships, the timber for which is furnished by the Malabar coast; and its situation opposite to the Persian and Arabian shores makes it peculiarly fit for commerce. I know no place so well situated. Its excellent well-defended harbour, the fertility of the adjointing districts the agreeableness of the climate, and the extreme beauty of the scenery, all contribute to make it one of the most charming spots in the world, as far as the gifts of nature are concerned, and with the state of its society I have at present nothing to do, although I feel it difficult to restrain myself from talking of a place which is rendered interesting to me by a thousand agreeable recollections.

Letters on India, 1814, pp. 165 to 166.

"The Brightest Jewel of our Dependencies"

MRS. POSTANS.

The "brightest jewel" of our British dependencies is now brought within the observation of the intelligent and "thinking people of England;" and policy seems at last to urge the necessity of attention to the best interests of India.

A full development of its sources of natural wealth must increase the value of that magnificent country, the richest and most productive of all our colonies. To effect this, the commerce of the Presidencies must be encouraged; and to the Provinces must be held out a sufficient stimulus, to arouse the industry of their agricultural and manufacturing classes. The great marts of the ancient world, Tyre, Sidon, and Ophir, with the fair cities of the plain, exist but in the history of the past; the btusite of their desolate grandeur will teach Britain the instability of possessions, which have already cost a heavy price in blood and treasure. The progress of opinion, no less than the force of present circumstances, renders it more than ever desirable, that the natives of Western India most particularly, should, as an intelligent and commercial people, value our allegiance as friends, rather than regard us as the grinding oppressors of their fatherland, whom they require only union and opportunity, to expel from their shores.

That the material exists for restoring freedom and wealth to the people of India, there can remain no doubt. We see the bazaars of the native town of the most interesting Presidency, rich and populous, teeming with an enterprising and mercantile people, and abounding with productions of natural wealth, rich gems, and precious metals. The neighbouring bay is animated with rude and foreign crafts, laden with curious manufactures, or the exuberant produce of the most fertile soils. The dock-yards, justly considered the finest in the world, send forth their teak-built vessels, to enrich with their cargo the isles of the far distant West; and the raw and unpolished material is exported from a land, which possessed a knowledge of those arts calculated to improve the conditon of a people, and whose fine linens, brilliant dyes, costly wools, and glittering jewels, awakened the admiration of the civilized nations of the West, while yet the inhabitants of our remote and sea-girt isle roamed wild and unclad, among the fastnesses of their mountain homes. We look on the East, and her desert lands seem to whisper a reproach that they are not now teeming and fruitful as of old; we see that in the crowded and busy ways of the Burrah bazaars, is accumulated the rich produce of such localities as are calculated to afford increased revenue to our several civil and financial departments, but the art of the weaver and the lapidary is forgotten. We, the consummately civilized, have brought ignorance in the wake of our conquests; and this to a people, "old in arts and literature, before the primeval forests of Britain had started from their ancient silence at the voice of man."

The sinews of war are again strained for territorial protection and acquirement; but the influence of public opinion will, it is to be trusted, change the object of the struggle. The splendid scheme of navigating the noble Indus, will probably become the means of introducing industry and manufacture among isolated thousands; and of bringing justice and wisdom to the courts of their barbarian princes.

In exchange for these benefits, monuments more durable than the altars of the triumphant Greek, will record the dominion of British power; and where the great invader of eastern freedom first felt the strength of an arm determined to support its rights, the rude descendants of the princely Porus may again esteem the arts and elegancies of civilized existence.

The commercial interests of the world would gain much by a liberal line of policy; the stimulus of interest might awaken the slumbering knowledge of olden times; hungry barbarism give place to commercial opulence, and fabrics of costly and inimitable manufacture again attract the wealthy trader; while thus the shores of Western India, with the stores of her great bazaars, might be as eagerly sought in the maritime enterprise of foreign lands, as were the crowning cities of the East, when the princely merchants of Venice displayed their red, gold, and costly stuffs, upon the busy pass] of the Rialto.

Western India, 1839. Vol. I, pages 98-102.

Commercial Importance

GENERAL JOHN TAYLOR.

It may not be improper to offer a few observations on the political and military advantages derived from the settlement of Bombay. It will be allowed that the expenses attending distant colonies or dependencies should be proportionate to their revenues or income. In some cases, either great political reasons, or the prospect of future advantage, counter-balance any extraordinary expense that may be incurred in retaining a distant garrison, or particular colony beyond its internal resources. When this happens, the advantages to be derived, whether present or future, should much more than preponderate in the scale of the expenditure, and this too, should be very clearly ascertained.

That the Island of Bombay is favourably situated for trade, its docks necessary for the repairs of shipping and the construction of durable vessels, that it is an ancient settlement of the Company's, I will readily admit; but when put in competition with these benefits, the immense sum of nearly half a million, which is the annual sacrifice for retaining this settlement, independent of its own resources, we may well wonder that its political value has not been more strictly enquired into. It is far from my intention to depreciate the advantages of Bombay; on the contrary, that island is essential to our interest.

Ist. As the centre of our trade from the northward, from the Mahratta country, and the Gulf of Persia.

2ndly. As a dock-yard for our ships of war and Indiamen.

3rdly. As a harbour for water and refreshment for the use of the ships that protect our trade in the Indian Seas.

4thly. As a place of respectability and strength on the coast of Malabar.

Bombay, in a political point of view, is certainly of very little consequence to our affairs in India; as a place of commercial resort it is no doubt deserving of attention.

Travels from England to India in 1789.
1799, pages 167-168.

Finest Site for Commerce in the World

LORD MAYO.

Saturday, 26th December, 1868—Drove in the morning to see the works of the Elphinstone Land Company, which astonished me by their magnitude. Nearly the whole frontage to the harbour of the commercial port of Bombay is now occupied by the property belonging to the P. and O. Company, the Elphinstone Land Company, and the Government. It is, perhaps, the finest site for commerce in the world. Steamed round the harbour, and saw a portion of the various defences which are proposed. The construction of the batteries has been stopped, pending the decision with regard to the Moncrieff gun-carriage. We then steamed over to the island of Elephanta, saw the caves, and walked round the island. A beautiful view. Mr. W. was very much disgusted on finding the cave occupied by some drunken British soldiers and an American party, one of whom was playing on a banjo. This day enabled me to form an estimate of the works, military and naval, in the harbour of Bombay.

Sir W. W. Hunter's Life of Mayo, 1875, Vol. I, page 168.

An Extensive Emporium

HOBART CAUNTER.

This island owes its original importance to the Portuguese, to whom it was ceded in 1530. They retained possession for upwards of a century, when Charles the Second got it as a part of his queen's portion, During the Portuguese government it was a comparative desert; but almost from the moment it fell under British domination it became a flourishing settlement. It was finally transferred from the crown to the East India Company, the 27th of March 1668, upon payment of an annual rent of ten pounds in gold on the 30th of September of every successive year. In 1691 this island was visited by plague, which, when its ravages ceased, left only three civil servants alive. In 1702 it was again devastated by this dreadful scourge, and the garrison reduced to seventy-six men.

From its position, Bombay commands an extensive traffic with those countries which lie upon the shores of the Persian and Arabian gulfs with both the western and eastern coasts of India as well as with China, where it exports vast quantities of cotton-wool. The other chief exports are sandal-wood, pearls, gums, and drugs, from Arabia, Abyssinia, and Persia; pepper from the Malabar coast; birds' nests and other produce from the Maldives, Lackadives and eastern islands, and elephants' teeth from

Cambay. The China ships generally arrive at Canton towards the end of June or beginning of July, and lie there idle, except delivering and receiving their return cargoes, until the month of December or January.

In 1808 the quantity of cotton brought to Bombay for exportation was eighty-five thousand bales of seven hundred and thirty-five pounds, making a total of sixty-two million four hundred and seventy-five thousand pounds' weight.

This settlement likewise carries on a considerable commerce with Europe and with different parts of America, though their most extensive trade is to China. The imports from Europe are principally articles of the finer manufacture, such as cottons and other piece-goods, wine, beer, and articles for domestic consumption.

Here are excellent rope-walks, equal to any in Great Britain, except in the King's yard at Portsmouth. The dockyard is very capacious, and admirably contrived, being well supplied with naval stores of all kinds, and fitted up with every convenience for shipbuilding and repairs of vessels; for which purposes a large stock of timber is kept up. The new dock constructed by Major Cooper is a noble work, scarcely inferior to the finest docks in Europe.

Oriental Annual, 1836, pages 217 to 219.

Great Cotton Mart

SIR W. W. HUNTER.

After the downfall of the Peshwa in 1818, Bombay became the capital of a large territory, and from that year may be dated her pre-eminence in Western India. She was especially fortunate in her early governors. From 1819 to 1830, she was ruled successively by the Hon. Mountstuart Elphinstone and Sir John Malcolm. The first founded the present system of administration; the second, by opening the road through the Bhor-Ghat, broke down the natural barrier that separated the sea-coast from the table-land of the Deccan. The next stage in the course of onward prosperity was reached when Bombay was brought into direct communication with Europe through the energy and exertion of Lieutenant Waghorn, the pioneer of the Overland Route. In the early years of the present century, express couriers or adventurous travellers used sometimes to make their way to or from India across the isthmus of Suez, or occasionally even through Persia. A monthly mail service was commenced by way of Egypt in 1838 and the contract was first taken up by the Peninsular and Oriental Company in 1855. Bombay is now recognised as the one port of arrival and departure for all the English mails, and also for the troopships of the Indian army. But the city could not have attained this position, if the means of communication on the landward side had not received a corresponding development. In 1850, the first sod was turned of the Great Indian Peninsula Railway, and three years afterwards the line was opened as far as Thana, the first railway in the country. By 1863, the railway had been led up the formidable Bhor-Ghat to Poona, by a triumph of engineering skill. In 1870, through communication was established with Calcutta, in 1871 with Madras. The city has a successful tramway system. There is now a prospect of more direct railway communication being established, *via* Nagpur in the Central Provinces, with Calcutta.

But it is not only as the capital of a Presidency, or as the central point of arrival and departure for Indian travellers, that Bombay has achieved its highest reputation. It is best known as the great cotton market of Western and Central India, to which the manufacturers of Lancashire turned when the American war cut off their supplies. Even in the last century the East India Company was accustomed to export raw cotton as part of its investment, both to the United Kingdom and to China. This trade continued during the early years of the present century, but it was marked by extreme vicissitudes in quantity and price, the demand being entirely determined by the out-turn of the American crop. The war between the Northern and Southern States was declared in 1861, and the merchants and shippers of Bombay promptly took advantage of their opportunity. The exports of cotton rapidly augmented under the stimulus of high prices, until in 1864-65, the last year of the war, they reached a total value of 30 millions sterling, or nearly ten-fold the average of ten years before. Large fortunes were acquired by successful ventures, and the wild spirit of speculation thus engendered spread through all classes of the community. The scenes of the South Sea Bubble were revived. No joint-stock project seemed too absurd to find subscribers. Banks, financial associations, and land companies each with millions of nominal capital, were started every month, and their shares were immediately run up to fabulous premiums. The crash came in the spring of 1865, when the news was received of the termination of the American war. A panic ensued which baffles description, and the entire edifice of stock exchange speculation came toppling down like a house of cards. Merchants and private individuals were ruined by hundreds, and the quasi-official Bank of Bombay collapsed along with the rest. But despite this sudden flood of disaster, honest trade soon revived on a stable basis; and the city of Bombay at the present day, in its buildings, its docks, and its land reclamations, stands as a monument of the grand schemes of public usefulness which were started during these four years of unhealthy excitement.

Imperial Gazetteer. 2nd Ed. 1887, Vol. III., pp. 75-77.

Cotton Green

W. S. CAINE.

Bombay, after New Orleans, is the greatest cotton port in the world, and a visit should be paid to the Cotton Green about noon, at which time "high change" sets in at a yard opposite to the Colaba terminus of the tramway. Any open market in India is sure to be a striking picture of native life, brightened with an endless variety of costume and kaleidoscopic colour. The cotton market of Bombay is no exception. Four million cwts. are exported from Bombay in the year, and over two millions more are consumed in the 82 mills in the Bombay Presidency, the bulk of which are in the city; the value of all this cotton is about twelve million sterling.

Picturesque India, 1891, pages 11-12.

Centre of Gravity of The Empire in the Future

SIR GEORGE BIRDWOOD.

But the past of Bombay is of the deepest and universal interest, not only with reference to its prophetic significance, but in itself; for as the modern representative of mediaeval Tannah, and ancient Kalyan, it has an immemorial history of commercial command, political authority, and religious supremacy. The whole Deccan, with all Hindustan, exclusive of the valley of the

Indus, may be regarded as physically and commercially, and, in the last result, politically, as but the "hinterland" of the Town and Island of Bombay. They are still half mythical regions, "the world's green end," "the abodes of the blameless Æthiops," and "the dancing places of Aurora, the mother of the Dawn, and of the risings of the sun;" very picturesque indeed, and very poetical, but they nowhere provide the offensive and defensive strongholds of a widely extended and mighty transmarine commercial Empire. Bombay can never be silted up as Tannah and Kalyan higher up the same river, successively were; and as Karachi is continually being silted up in spite of every effort to keep the port way clear; and, therefore, Bombay will always remain the accessible, commodious, and safe harbour it has ever been, and predominant over all others throughout the Indian Ocean. If only the opportunity of so vast and impregnable a harbour, and so attractive an emporium of the commerce of East Africa, and Southern Asia, had occurred at, or nearer to the site of Karachi, India, under a powerful Government, would be as absolutely sealed against any menace of invasion from Central Asia, as it is, under our rule, from the sea.

But its actual position detracts very little from the immense strategic value of Bombay; and great as its history has been in the past, it must be greater still in the future. With the concentration of the United Kingdom, the Dominion of Canada, the Commonwealth of Australia, and the coming Confederation of South Africa, into a homogeneous British Empire, with which, moreover, the United States of America are becoming, for all commercial and moral and religious purposes, more and more indissolubly one, the inevitable tendency must be to shift the mercantile and naval and military centre of gravity of the Empire eastward, to Alexandria or Bombay. Alexander founded Alexandria before its time, for he did not anticipate the invasion of Europe by the Goths and Huns and Vandals, or of Anterior Asia and Africa by the Saracens and Turks. But Alexandria will find its fulness of time within the 20th century. Bombay will, however, press it closely; and being absolutely defensible, and commanding all the exhaustless resources of its whole Indian "hinterland," it may yet snatch the crown of mercantile and maritime supremacy from Alexandria. In a word, it is the boundless and incalculable destiny of the sea-throned city of Bombay under British rule, which gives absorbing interest to the story of its auspicious beginnings under the Portuguese and the English which Mr. Forrest will now unfold to you.

Remarks introductory to Mr. L. R. W. Forrest's Paperon Bombay before the Society of Arts—Journal of Society of Arts, 1901, p. 570.

Development of Bombay.

LORD SYDENHAM.

The rise of Bombay from an unknown village to a great commercial and industrial city occupies a very short space in the long vista of the history of India, but it is the most remarkable development, which is exercising a powerful influence extending over a large portion of the Presidency. Only two hundred years ago, Kunaji Angria had just occupied the Keneri Island. and for many years no ship could enter or leave this great harbour without the risk of being captured. Less than a hundred years ago a lady wrote of the country within twenty miles of Bombay that "in the shops every artisan has his sword and spear beside and the cultivators plough with arms in their hands." Peace and security are essential conditions of the prosperity of commerce and industry which have raised Bombay to its present proud position among the great cities of the East. Nature has been bountiful in providing a magnificent area of shelter water. The same has brought the markets of the world within easy and certain reach of these waters, and perhaps the most important of all, the great railway systems of India have enabled the produce to be brought to the sea for export and to be distributed far inland rapidly at small cost. All the circumstances were, therefore, favourable to the development of Bombay as the great western gate of India with the populace contained in its hinter-land. But more was needed. The rapid growth of sea-borne oommerce created many pressing requirements which can be met only by the science of the engineer applied through the agency of a wise and businesslike administration.

Speeches of Lord Sydenham, 1913, ed. Dongre Sec. IV pp. 7-8.

Gateway to a Land of Enchantment

LORD CURZON.

This is the fifth time that I have gazed from the sea upon the majestic panorama of your city of palaces and palms; and if my previous visits have been those of a private traveller only, they have yet given me an interest, which official experience can but enhance, in your city—itself so worthy a gateway to a land of enchantment and in its occupations, so typical of the busy industry to which the peoples of India have turned under the security assured to them by British rule.

In your address you call my attention to the fact that, during the past few years, India has been subject to the triple scourge of war, pestilence and famine, and that your own Presidency has suffered sorely from the ravages of the two latter in particular. In England our hearts have gone out to you in your trouble—our pursestrings have, as you know, been unloosened on your behalf. The unceasing and devoted efforts of your rulers—of the present illustrious Viceroy (The Earl of Elgin) and in this place, of your Governor (Lord Sandhurst) whose application to the onerous work imposed upon him by the plague has excited widespread gratitude and admiration—have, I believe, enabled India to cope with these trials in a manner more successful than on any previous occasions. In this great city the patience of your people, the voluntary co-operation of your leading citizens, and the natural vitality of your resources have greatly assisted in the work of recuperation; and I would fain believe that the corner has now been turned and that an era of reviving prosperity is already beginning to dawn. To that movement it will be my agreeable duty to lend whatever impulse I can; and it is with feelings of sympathy that I regard, and shall take an early apportunity of inquiring into, the great undertaking (City Improvement) to which, with so marked a combination of courage and wisdom, you are about to address yourselves in Bombay.

Reply to the Bombay Municipal Address, Dec. 1898,
Speeches, Ed. Raleigh, Vol. I., p. 32.

Patriotism of Citizens

LORD CURZON.

I have seen it in prosperity and I have seen it in suffering; and I have always been greatly struck by the spirit and patriotism of its citizens. There seems to me to be here an excellent feeling between the very different races and creeds. Bombay possesses an exceptional number of public-spirited citizens, and the sense of civic duty is as highly developed as in any great city that I know. If there is a big movement afoot, you lend yourselves so it with a powerful and concentrated will, and a united Bombay is not a force to be gainsaid. Let me give as an illustration the magnificent success of your reception and entertainment of Their Royal Highnesses the Prince and Princess of Wales. Moreover, you have the advantage of one of the best conducted and ablest newspapers in Asia (The Times of India).

Lord Curzon's Farewell to India, ed. R. P. Karkaria, 1907, p. 1.

Commercial Capital of the East

JAMES ROUTLEDGE.

The first impression received of Bombay after the voyage from England is not easy to represent on paper. The splendid bay, covered with shipping, may perhaps be entered a second time without emotion, but hardly so the first time by an Englishman. After travelling over 6000 miles through the lands and along the shores of strangers, here is English life, strong, intellectual, and self-reliant; a Government-house, a fort, military lines, law courts, a custom house, colleges, markets of uncommon excellence, European residences skirting carriage-drives open to the sea, jetties and wharves, churches and chapels, reading rooms and libraries, clubs, cotton and other mills—everything, in fact, of all that Englishmen have accustomed themselves to term necessaries of civilised (meaning English) life. With an inland trade ever increasing as the Railway system is extended, and a direct communication with England by the Canal, Bombay has put forward substantial claims to become the capital of India, Calcutta being dismissed as too far away from England and as unfit for European residence all the year through, and the old capitals of the Moguls as only suited to a purely military people, possessing no basis on the sea. Nothing of all this, it is true, shakes the imperial position of the great city on the Hoogly, while Allahabad is fast becoming, if it has not already become, the military capital of India. Yet there is something in Bombay that is all its own, and which at least gives it an indisputable right to be called the commercial capital of the East.

English Rule and Native Opinion in India, 1878, p. 21.

Great Work of the Municipality

SIR BARTLE FRERE.

We have been lately reminded that Her Majesty the Queen, in all her vast dominions, has but one city which is more populous than Bombay, and few which are the seats of such important commercial interests. It numbers twice the population of Glasgow, and there are hardly two of your great English cities which in this respect would, if united, out-number the population with which you have to deal. Then consider the magnitude of the task which the Bench has undertaken to discharge—to make good the omissions and neglect of former ages, and to provide all the vast multitude of people with good air, good water, good roads and everything else which should distinguish the second city of of the British Empire. I think, Sir, that to take a part in the great work the Municipality has in hand, is an object in no way unworthy of any Englishman who desires to serve his country in this distant land. But though the task is great and difficult, I have every confidence it will be well performed. Much has been already effected in a very short time, and I look forward with the utmost confidence to the time when we shall hear that Bombay has taken her place among cities, owing as much to art as she does to nature and position.

Reply to Address of the Bench of Justices, 1867, Speeches of Bartle Frere. ed. Pitale, 1870, p. 433.

Importance and Growth of Bombay

LORD SYDENHAM.

Bombay was not one of the many rich gifts of the sea to England, although it must have passed from her hands if naval supremacy had not been asserted at the periods of great national crises. The finest harbour in the East became a possession of the Crown on the marriage of Charles II. to Catherine of Braganza, and was leased to the East India Company in 1669 for the modest rental of £ 10 per annum. Why this important possession was selected by the Portuguese as part of the dowry of their Princess is not clear; but in 1662 the Viceroy of Goa wrote to his King: "I see the best port your Majesty possesses in India, with which that of Lisbon is not to be compared, treated as of little value by the Portuguese themselves." If the great importance of Bombay was not realised by its first European owners, no clearer perception was vouchsafed to their British successors for many years. As ships increased in tonnage and as the trade of India developed, Bombay inevitably grew into a great maritime port, and the opening of the Suez Canal made it at once the main gate of communication between India and the Western world. Bombay now has about one million inhabitants, and is the centre of a great volume of valuable trade and of a most important mill industry. It is one of the best governed and certainly the healthiest city in the East.

A noble city has arisen on the barren island ceded by the Portuguese, and while there is still ample scope for progress the British people may well feel proud of what has been accomplished. The maintenance of peace and order throughout India has led to the creation of a vast trade of infinite value to the people. The enrichment of Indians through the operation of that trade is nowhere so conspicuous as in Bombay, where the Parsis were the pioneers of Indian enterprises which are now rivalled by those of Hindus and Mahomedans successfully following in their footsteps. While the wealth of Bombay tenαs more and more to flow tc Indians of many classes, British administration has left an indelible impress upon the great city, although the guiding hand is now lightly felt.

Man had laid a heavy hand upon the natural beauties which many visitors have recorded. A thick pall of smoke, the wasteful outpouring of numberless chimneys overhangs the island and obscures the splendid background of the Western Ghats. Yet when the sunset paints the waters of the harbour and tinges the sails of the old world craft that still ply their trade unchanged since the time of the Angrias, or when at night the necklace of lights embraces the noble sweep of Back Bay under the stars, none can deny the fascinations of the great

Eastern gate of India, of the city which, in Gerald Aungier's words, was to be built "by. God's assistance."

Introduction to *Bombay in the Making, 1910, pp. 10-14.*

The Most Impressive City in the Orient

"THE TIMES."

The continuous growth of Bombay is one of the brightest and most hopeful episodes in the modern history of India. Seventeen years ago the city was sorely stricken. The appearance of plague in the midst of its teeming population seemed like a disaster of the first magnitude. The inhabitants fled by the hundred thousand. The deaths reached an appalling total. Successive epidemics produced temporary despair. There were moments when the possibility was seriously discussed that Bombay might share the fate of those great cities of Asia which have been deserted and forgotten. But the public spirit of its citizens remained undefeated. Lord Sandhurst set on foot a scheme for the reconstruction of the slums which has since had far-reaching results. Trade revived, the city took heart of grace, and to-day it enjoys a prosperity such as it has never before known.

The story of Bombay in recent years is almost a romance. Its own inhabitants are hardly conscious of all they have achieved. Though the world has heard little about it, their indomitable confidence and preseverance have wrought a change greater than that effected in the stricken city of San Francisco. So many new and palatial buildings have been erected in the business and the new European residential quarters that to those who quitted it twenty years ago, Bombay would now be almost unrecognizable. Long ago Lord Curzon christened it "the city of palaces and palms," and ever since it has striven to deserve the description more worthily. If Lord Sydenham's scheme for great reclamations on the shores of Back Bay is ever carried out, as we trust it may be, Bombay will become the most impressive city in the Orient. We are not sure that in some respects it is not so to-day. No city in Asia, not even Canton seen from its Pagoda, nor Hong-Kong from its Peak, impresses the stranger as does the wide-spread and beautiful panorama of Bombay seen towards sunset from the crest of Malabar Hill. It impresses not only by its hugeness and its beauty, its glorious bay and golden sands and innumerable palms, and its frame of dim blue mountains.

Far more moving is the thought it brings that, to a degree which cannot be said of any other city in India, Bombay though founded by the British, has been the joint creation of Englishmen and Indians working together in friendly unison for a common object. It contains and typifies, could both races see it, the secret upon which the future welfare of the Indian Empire must depend. Bombay was seven islands once. Now it has been made one by the infinite toil of man, and within its narrow confines there has grown a noble city which owes much to both the East and to the West. So, out of divided provinces and myriads of people divided by race and by religion, must an enduring Empire be wrought if India is to find salvation.

The Times (London). 21 March 1914 p. 9

SCENES IN BOBAY.

SCENES IN BOMBAY.

The Yacht Club at Evening

J. A. SPENDER.

At the Yacht Club towards sunset you will find the English colony assembled on a green lawn fronting the sea, with the club-house behind. The view seawards embraces the great circle of the bay, and the distant promontories are deep purple against a flaming orange sunset which is topped by masses of crimson and warm grey clouds. Tone it all down and in the dim light the view might be that from Plymouth Hoe. The twilight passes quickly, festoons of electric light make a dazzle on a hundred tea-tables, and an excellent military band strikes up a selection from "Samson and Delilah." While you are here, you forget the great, seething, miasmic city behind you, and wonder at the cheerfulness, smartness, good looks, and good manners of the Bombay English and their womenkind. Civilians or Soldiers, they are clearly a strong, self-reliant, well-favoured race, with an indefinable air of being in authority. It is an authority, however, which is not flaunted. You see the native policeman everywhere, but the soldier hardly at all. All the military men are in mufti, and there is no outward sign to distinguish the civilian administrator from an Englishman on business. You hear no big talk; it is indeed, the most difficult thing in the world to induce any of them to talk at all about themselves or their duties. They seem to take for granted that they should be there and doing what they are doing. The first dominant impression you bear away is that they have a great interest in governing and none at all in possessing. Hence, in spite of the alien rule, Bombay strikes you as eminently belonging to itself, as being in fact a real Indian town, and as remote as possible from a British colony. This, perhaps, is the greatest tribute that can be paid to the English who made it, or at least made it possible.

The Indian Scene, 1912, pages 26 to 28.

Sunset

"SLEEPY SKETCHES."

When night comes on, and Providence sends a few clouds to make the sunset glorious, then the scene of Bombay harbour is wonderful. Out at sea, at the harbour's mouth, great streaks and blotches and broken points of gold crowd the western sky, bright and dazzling on the background of crimson that runs far along the horizon and rises upwards till it pales and is lost in the pure blue above; the broken water of the harbour burns gold and red and yellow in reflection; the masts and yards, sails and hulls, of the anchored vessels are gold; the ugliest collier has become meet to carry Cleopatra; the houses of Bombay are translated, and the town is a town of gorgeous palaces; the mountains in the distance catch the bright lights and, mindful that true greatness is humble, deck themeselves in soft, faint colours; and over all is the blue sky pure and clear. Then, slowly, the light fades, and darkness approaches and settles down. But sometimes there is a change, and darkness is driven back. Then, all through the air and light, there is a strange, tremulous motion. The ships, the sea and the land, the mountains in the distance, quiver fantastically and seem no longer substantial. It is a battle between the full moon, the sun, and darkness. Darkness is beaten, the sun sets, and the moon begins to rule. The gold, the red and yellow, have all gone; only a steady white light marks the shadows of the ships and the ripples of the water, and charily touches an edge here and there with a brighter emphasis of silver.

The sudden change—a change in a few minutes—from sunset-light to moonlight, is astounding! It is the creation of a new world, of new thoughts. The brightest of bright moonlight nights in England gives no idea of an Indian moonlight night. Ghosts, pixies, trolls, gnomes are not in India; there is no sentiment for them to feed on; and Jinns, Afreets, and Shaitan make but a poor substitute. The moonlight here suggests nothing of the spiritual, nothing of the sentimental. All scenery in daylight is wanting in shadow and depth of colour; each landscape under the sun looks like a faintly-tinted photograph, sharp in outline, but faded till almost invisible in parts. But by moonlight this is changed; deep, heavy shadows sit on the mountains and hills where before were only their neutral tints; and though all bright colour be gone, nature has a sturdy, earnest appearance that is invigorating, after its wan, transparent look of the day. It is this robust look that the landscape gains which is so striking. Life under the moon seems more vigorous. It gives no desire for sentiment, but rather for physical exercise. To sail out in the harbour on a moonlight night is delightful. But it is delightful because it makes one feel brighter and more active, and gives a good appetite for dinner; not because the scene and light set one dreaming of home or love.

Sleepy Sketches, 1877, pp. 28-31.

A Street by Moonlight

SIR FRED. TREVES.

It is at night and under the moon that the streets of an Indian town become filled with the most unearthly spirit of romance. I recall one such night in Bombay when the moon was high in the heavens.

The street was narrow, for the houses on either side of it leaned towards one another. They were lofty and fantastic in shape, so that the gap of light that marked the road made it look like a narrow way through a gorge of rocks. The white glory of the moon, falling from broken housetops, turned into marble the wood-carved mullions of an overhanging window, poured slanting-wise, into a verandah and made beautiful its poor roof, its arches, and its bulging rail, and then dripping through rents and holes in ragged awnings, filled little pools of cool light in the hot, untidy road.

The shops were closed and were lost in the blackest shadows, although, here and there, a splash of moonlight would strike the stone platform which stood in front of them, and reveal a bench, a barred door, or a heavy chest. A few steps of a rambling stair would climb up through the glamour and then vanish in the dusk. The pillars of a stone balcony would stand out like alabaster in the moon, appearing poised in the air, as if the corner of a palace projected into the street. A denser mass of shadow would mask an arched entry whose flagstones led through utter darkness to a courtyard flooded with light.

On the pale stones of one such courtyard was the recumbent figure of a man wrapped from head to foot in a purple cloak, like a corpse laid out for burial. Under the verandahs and in caverns of darkness many other figures were stretched out on mats, on low tables, or on bare stones, all wrapped up so that no face could be seen, all motionless, all lean like the dead. These mummy-like bundles (that were sleeping men) might all have been lifeless bodies put out of doors to wait for some tumbril to come by.

On certain lintels was the mark in red paint which showed that the plague had visited the house, and so quiet was the place and so still the wrapped up men that one could fancy that the lane was in a city of death. The figures looked so thin and lay so flat as to show, under the meagre covering, the feet, the points of the knees, and the outline of the head. One figure drew up a bony leg as I passed, and it seemed as if a man left for dead was still alive.

Some were wrapped in red garments, some in yellow, and a few in white. In every one the wrapping entirely enveloped the head, for the native of India when he sleeps—whether in a room or in the open—will always cover up his face.

Possibly a few of those who slept were servants lying outside their masters' houses, but the greater number of them were the homeless men of the city. Some were asleep in the very roadway, so that the passer-by would need to step over them.

The quiet in the place was terrible. The only sound came from the shuffling feet of two prowling dogs who rooted among the garbage in the gutter. It was just such a street as Doré was wont to paint and such an one as figures in many a rapier-and-cloaked-figure romance. It was a street that breathed murder, and to which would be fitting the stab in the back, the sudden shriek, the struggling body dragged into a dark doorway by knuckles clutching at the livid neck. It was the street of the Arabian Nights, and there was in it the hush that comes before a tragedy.

In one place in the street a bar of red light from an open door fell across the road and across a muffled figure asleep upon the stones. In another place a motionless woman bent over the rail of a verandah, her head outlined against the glare of a lamp in the room behind her. For what she watched, Heaven knows!

Beyond these two streaks of light, which burnt into the arctic pallor of the moon, there was nothing to suggest that the dwellers in the street did more than mimic death.

The Other Side of the Lantern, 1905 pp. 55-56.

The City at Dawn

LORD LAMINGTON.

No one who has filled the post of Governor of Bombay could have anything but a natural pride in having had the privilege of being associated with that province, possessed of so many and varied interests, and having for its capital one of the most magnificent cities of the world. It will ever be a memory to gladden my spirit to recall the view from Malabar Hill. More particularly on one occasion, just before dawn, do I remember the effect produced by the rays of sunlight behind the Ghats, throwing the latter into relief, lighting up the harbour and reddening the roofs and pinnacles of the stately buildings in the Fort, whilst nearer at hand below slumbered Back Bay and its palm-covered shores; and to the North-East streaks of smoke from the tall chimneys showed that the industrial world was awakening, and for once this evidence of human activity really lent a picturesque touch to the scene. At times the disfigurement due to the grimy out-pourings of the factories is deplorable. In private and in public I have discoursed on this theme. Prosecutions did take place but it was very difficult to secure a conviction against individual offenders. I gather from the latest reports that smoke consumption appliances are being adopted. Let us hope that the use of these, combined with the introduction of electricity produced by water power, and with regulations more stringently enforced in the future, will ensure that one of the most glorious of landscapes will cease to be besmirched by a careless and wasteful expenditure of coal.

Paper on Bombay before the Society of Arts, 30 Ap. 1908. Journal of the Society, 1908.

After the Rains

ROBERT BROWN.

The rains are now nearly over, having lasted about three months, though not without intermission, for a deluge continues about a fortnight, then there is fine weather for a week. There are snatches of sunshine too during the deluges, and it is interesting to see people watching a shower coming over the sea, and calculating the time they can stay out with impunity. It is good fun to see some unfortunate wight, who has made rather too fine a calculation, caught in the shower; in about three seconds he is wet to the skin, and a drookit rat is a dry animal and a nice-looking beast compared with him. I speak feelingly on this point, having been lately caught once or twice myself, and I was certainly conscious that I looked a fool ! The grins depictcd on the faces of the natives I passed left no doubt on the subject. Fortunately one never catches cold after a ducking, if you keep the blood in circulation by a smart gallop, and change whenever you get home. We have had some beautiful evenings lately, which reminded me of summer in England, for the air was pure, and very little warmer than you have it, at least I fancied so, and the moonlight nights that followed were lovely in the extreme. It gets dark just now about seven, but people scarcely ever go out here after dinner; a siesta is generally preferred. The other night I dined alone, the first time sincc I arrived here, and I felt very curious, do you know ?—something in the old lodging style at Liverpool; but I suppose I must consider myself a more important man now. After reading some reminiscences of Thomas Campbell, I betook myself to the sleeping bungalow, and seated in the verandah there, while solitude and silence reigned around, interrupted occasionally by the squeak of the lizard, or that hum of innumerable insects which are called into being, as it were, by the night air, while the moon shed its silver light on the Temple of Maha Luxumee, and the billows rolled in on the rocks, their crests beautifully white,—while this was going on, I seated myself in an arm-chair, and breathed out in the most exquisite tones, 'Ye banks and braes.' You may recollect that Orpheus had the power of charming beasts, and even trees, by his music; at the last note of my Scotch air, two goats that were standing on the edge of the verandah fell on their backs, and kicked convulsively for seven minutes ! writhing in the most intense agony, which their medical man opines has caused a constitutional nervousness for life. This is a curious contrast to mesmerism.

Memorials, 1867, pp. 34-36.

In a Bombay Garden

LADY FALKLAND.

I had not been long in Bombay, before it became my habit to sit at early morning, in a verandah, overlooking the beautiful garden attached to our house, wondering at everything.

There was nothing in the scene to remind me of Europe, except perhaps, at very rare intervals, an English servant, determined to wear a black beaver hat, and doing all he could to have a sun stroke. Despite the early hour, it was always overpoweringly hot. There were no clouds rising in the deep blue sky, and the sun would pour down its heat on the burnt-up grass, and trees, and drooping shrubs, Nature herself as well as human beings, apparently sighing for the rains.

The flower garden, though not large, was tastefully laid out; and a terrace at the end of it, having mango trees on one side, and a large piece of water on the other, rendered it a pleasant walk in the evening.

Along the sides of all the walks of this garden are stone channels, into which, the water runs from the wells, and thence into the beds of plants and flowers, which for a time stand in a refreshing pool.

The trees were all new to me, especially a teak, (Tectona Grandis,) with its last year's foliage, the large leaves being very much 'the worse for wear.'

At the end of the garden were superb mango trees so famous for their delicious fruit, that comes into season in April, but unfortunately only last till June. I have met with some persons who do not like the mango, but they are 'few and far between.' It is perfection—you do not wish it larger, nor smaller, nor is it too sweet or too sour. When you have eaten one, it is enough, but a second is by no means too much. The flavour combines that of the melon, apricot, and strawberry. The blossom is beautiful, the rind has tints of green, red, and orange. It must have been the fruit which tempted Eve, and that weak man Adam, who afterwards threw all the blame on his poor wife.

Near me was the Asoka, which in spring bears beautiful red blossoms, many casuarinas with their light and graceful foliage being intermixed and contrasted with the broad leaves of various kinds of palms, among them the lofty *Caryota Urens,* and the traveller's palm, from which a watery juice is extracted, and the broad leaves of which grow in a complete fan-like form; the beauty of the whole scene being enhanced and enlivened by the brilliant-coloured turbans worn by the native servants belonging to the establishment of the 'burra sahib,' of which there are so many that it is not easy at first to know their different offices.

First, a very tall, portly Parsee, who is the *maitre d'hotel,* would walk forth to begin his day's occupations, and then appeared sundry Parsee and Mussulman-servants carrying tea or coffee to their different masters' rooms. These would be followed by the durjeys or tailors going to their work. Everybody has a private tailor in India; the governor has a tailor; captains, councilors, and cadets, ladies, lords, and secretaries, all have one a piece. A separate tailor seems to be considered essential to Anglo-Indian happiness. Then the dobie (washerman) passed by with a red turban, and a long white dress, carrying a basket full of linen, which he meant to wash by beating and slapping it on a stone in the tank, at the back of the garden. Then at a quick pace came the gardeners (mali), having on their heads red cloth skullcaps, and very little other apparel, carrying on their shoulders a long bamboo-stick, at each end of which hangs a large copper chattie, full of water, with which they were going to refresh the drooping plants. Such was the scene from my verandah, looking outwards.

If I turned round, in a room immediately adjacent was an individual (wearing moustaches, like all the natives) clothed in white drapery (twisted round his body and descending to the knees), a white jacket, and a blue and white turban–his black shining legs and feet being uncovered; over his shoulder hung his badge of office–a duster–with which he occasionally rubbed a chair or table; he represents the housemaid;

and, as I have before said, is called a hamal. Near him was another Hindoo in a similar dress, except that he wore a blue turban, and held a tray of small glasses full of cocoa-nut oil to place in the lamps suspended round the room; he is called a mussal; and the lamps and lights are his especial department.

Chow-Chow, Vol. I, pages 31-35.

Nature in Bombay

MADAME BLAVATSKY.

We occupied three small bungalows, lost, like nests, in the garden, their roofs literally smothered in roses blossoming on bushes twenty feet high, and their windows covered only with muslin, instead of the usual panes of glass. The bungalows were situated in the native part of the town, so that we were transported, all at once into the real India. We were living in India, unlike English people, who are only surrounded by India at a certain distance. We were enabled to study her character and customs, her religion, superstitions and rites, to learn her legends in fact, to live among Hindus.

Everything in India, this land of the elephant and the poisonous cobra, of the tiger and the unsuccessful English missionary, is original and strange. Everything seems unusual, unexpected, and striking, even to one who has travelled in

Turkey, Egypt, Damascus, and Palestine. In these tropical regions the conditions of nature are so various that all the forms of the animal and vegetable kingdoms must radically differ from what we are used to in Europe. Look, for instance, at those women on their way to a well through a garden, which is private and at the same time open to anyone, because somebody's cows are grazing in it. To whom does it not happen to meet with women, to see cows, and admire a garden ? Doubtless these are among the commonest of all things. But a single attentive glance will suffice to show you the difference that exists between the same objects in Europe and in India. Nowhere more than in India does a human being feel his weakness and insignificance. The majesty of the tropical growth is such that our highest trees would look dwarfed compared with banyans and especially with palms. A European cow, mistaking, at first sight, her Indian sister for a calf, would deny the existence of any kinship between them, as neither the mouse-coloured wool, nor the straight goat-like horns, nor the humped back of the latter would permit her to make such an error As to the women, each of them whould make any artist feel enthusiastic about the gracefulness of the movements and drapery, but still, no pink and white, stout Anna Ivanovna would condescend to greet her.

From the Caves and Jungles of Hindostan, 1892, pp. 13-14.

The Plague

LOVAT FRASER.

Outwardly "a city of palaces and palms," with a magnificent harbour and life-giving sea-breezes which never fail, it was nevertheless the home of an immense population living under the most unwholesome conditions. At the northern end of the island the native city had been crammed within restricted limits, notby official mandate, but by the greed of property-owners. Huge insanitary tenement houses had been erected, which almost rivalled the "sky-scrapers" of New York in her less aspiring days. Eighty per cent of the million inhabitants were living in tenements of a single room; and the average number of occupants of each room was four. Many of these rooms had neither light nor ventilation; into them the sunlight could never penetrate; large numbers of the houses were deliberately built back to back; and in these noisome dens, with damp mud floors, rats and humanity swarmed. Bombay owed its plight to a rapid influx of populations, to a great rise in land-values, and to defective building regulations inadequately administered by a Corporation which had inherited a situation with which it was unable to cope. When plague came there was a panic. I witnessed the scenes of that first mad exodus at the end of 1896, when the railway stations were crammed with people who fought for places in the trains, and when the roads of Salsette were thronged with fugitives fleeing from the pestilence they knew not whither.

India under Curzon, 1911, pp. 270 to 271.

2

Experienced officers have sometimes told me that in their opinion plague leaves surprisingly little impression upon India. Their argument is that in such a teeming population pestilence has no very abiding result. I am bound to say that my own experience leads to very much the same conclusion. I lived for a considerable number of years in a city from which plague was never absent. I have seen the clerk seized at his desk, the servant stretched dead at my gate, the disappearance of one familiar face after another. I have even, when playing golf, seen a woman stagger and fall upon the green as I approached it, and die of plague before she could be moved. Yet after the first mad terror was over the city waxed busy, and grew, and all the thronging funerals never seemed to give more than a momentary check to its feverish prosperity. I sometimes wonder whether we Englishmen judge the situation correctly, and whether plague has not had a deeper effect upon some parts of India than we are able to discern. If you live long in the presence of a great infliction, it becomes commonplace, and ceases to impress. I know now why men who have endured a protracted siege dislike to talk about it, why the historians of past centuries say so little about plague, although they dwelt in its midst. There came a time when we were wearied of the very name of plague, and looked with dull indifference on the flames of death aglow.

India under Curzon, 1911, page 278.

The Mango Trick

NORMAN MACLEOD.

Through one of my friends, I asked for the wellknown Mango trick. I am told that many intelligent young men profess to know how it is done. When inquiry is made on this point, however, I have hitherto found to my regret, that at the moment of expectancy they always forget it.

While the tom-tom was beating and the pipe playing, the juggler, singing all the time in low accents, smoothed a place in the gravel three or four yards before us. Having thus prepared a bed for the plant to grow in, he took a basket and placed it over the prepared place, covering it with a thin blanket. The man himself did not wear a thread of clothing, except a strip round the loins. The time seemed now to have come for the detective's eye! So, just as he was becoming more earnest in his song, and while the tom-tom beat and the pipe shrilled more loudly, I stepped forward with becoming dignity, and begged him to brin g the basket and its cover to me. He cheerfully complied and I examined the basket, which was made of open wicker-work. I then examined the cloth covering, which was thin, almost transparent, and certainly concealed nothing. I then examined the cloth covering, which was thin, almost trans-parent, and certainly concealed nothing. I then fixed my eyes on his strip of clothing with such intentness that it was not possible it could have been touched without discovery, and badehim go on, feeling sure that the trick could not succeed. Sitting down, he stretched his naked arms under the basket, singing and smiling as he did so; then he lifted the basket off the ground-and behold a green plant, about a foot high! Satisfied with our applause, he went on with his incantations. After having sat a little longer, to give his plant time to grow, he again lifted the basket, and the plant was now two feet high. He asked us to wait, that we might taste the fruit! But on being assured, by those who had seen the trick performed before, that this result would be obtained, I confessed myself 'done' without the slightest notion of the how. I examined the ground, and found it was smooth and unturned. Apparently delighted with my surprise, the juggler stood up laughing, when one of his companions chucked a pebble to him, which he put tnto his mouth. Immediately the same companion, walking backwards, drew forth a cord of silk, twenty yards or so in length; after which the juggler, with his hands behind his back; threw forth from his mouth two decanter stoppers, two shells, a spinning-top, a stone, and several other things, followed by a long jet of fire! If the wise reader regrets so much space being occupied by such a story, let him pass it on to the children, as foolish as myself, who will be glad to read it.

Far East, ed. 1893, pages 17 to 18.

Palm-Tree

NORMAN MACLEOD.

Turning away from man and looking at nature, there is a feature of Bombay which never ceases to please: this is the glorious palm trees! Palms are so associated with the East in our thoughts that we have heard of an artist introducing them into a picture of a scene up-country, where no palm tree ever grows, on the ground that "the British public would expect them in an Indian landscape." I never felt weary looking at them. Their tall stems and picturesque heads cluster in the still air of the sunny sky, and they are always beautiful, whatever their species may be. They are characteristic of Bombay as of no other city visited by me on the continent of India; and they so hide portions of the scattered town as to appear almost an unbroken forest.

Observing wild-looking huts, with out-of-the-way people among the trees, I was told that they are inhabited by a class who extract "toddy" from palms, and thus make their living.

Far East, page 13.

Fish at Bombay

JAMES FORBES

The surrounding ocean supplies Bombay with a variety of excellent fish; some of them are similar to those in Europe, others are peculiar to India. The pomfret is not unlike a small turbot, but of a more delicate flavour; and epicures esteem the black pomfret a great dainty: the sable, or salmon-fish, a little resembles the European fish from whence it is named: the robal, the seir-fish, the grey mullet, and some others, are very good; but the bumbalo, a small fish, extremely nutritive, and caught in immense numbers, is the favourite with those natives who are allowed by their religion to eat fish: they are dried for home consumption, and furnish a principal article of food for the Lascars, or Indian sailors, on board their vessels; they are also a considerable article of commerce in their dried state. Turtle are sometimes caught at Bombay and the adjacent islands; as are sea cray-fish, oysters, limpets, and other shell fish.

Oriental Memoirs, Vol. pages 36 to 37.

The Banian Tree

E. H. A.

(E. H. AITKEN.)

The leaves of the Banian come before the heat, and its shade is a shade indeed. And to sit in contemplation under the majesty of a noble Banian would make a man a Rishi if he were not so before.

What a world it is in itself, populous with beasts and birds and myriads of little things, which though we call them insignificant, are sharers with us in the mystery of life and happiness. And how bountifully the tree feeds them all. It is literally a land flowing with milk and honey.

If you wish to form a just idea of the place which the Banian tree fills in the world you must visit it when every twig is fringed with scarlet figs. If this should be, as it generally is, in the cold season, when food is scarce, then there is indeed a bazaar. Early in the morning the birds begin to gather, the riotous Rosy Pastor and the self-possessed Myna, the graceful Brahminy Myna, with its silky black crest and buffy-red waistcoat, and the yet more elegant Hoary Headed Myna, and the cheery Bulbuls and the Coppersmiths, quiet and silent just now, except when they quarrel and rail hoarsely at each other, and the Golden Orioles, and here and there a great blackguard Crow, devoid alike of shame and fear. They are all in high spirits, and plenty makes fastidious. Watch that Myna as he hops about, judging the fruit with one eye, till he finds a fine, mellow fig, not too raw and not too ripe, but just right. Then he digs a hole in it with his sharp beak. Of parrots there are not many, for the parrot is a sybarite and the fig is plain, wholesome fare. Another fruit-eater also is absent–the Green Pigeon: its mellow whistle is seldom heard in the Banian tree. The reason is that the Green Pigeon cannot dig holes in fruits: it swallows them whole. Now the Banian fig is tough and so firmly joint to the twig that the Green Pigeon has not strength to pull if off.

A Naturalist on the Prowl 1892, p. 50-53.

Native Schools

MRS. POSTANS.

The Native Education Society's Schools are situated near the great bazaars, at the extreme end of the Esplanade. Committees and examinations are held in the library, a splendid apartment fitted with a good collection of useful works with globes, maps, and papers, and adorned at either end with full length portraits of the great benefactors of the institution, Sir John Malcolm, and the Hon. Mountstuart Elphinstone. The last is the work of Sir Thomas Lawrence, and one of those startling and wonderful likenesses, which gained for the magic pencil of the elegant, yet truthtelling artist, its immortality of fame. There is, moreover, an exquisite touch of oriental landscape in the background, to which the eye is agreeably referred, after a full contemplation of the principal subject of the painting; beautifully coloured, the tall minarets seem brightly reflected in the placid waters stealing round the sacred fanes which the artist has chosen for his subject; while the figure of Mr. Elphinstone, seated in a library chair, is animated by a countenance beaming with intelligent benevolence. To a fanciful spectator, this fine portrait might suggest numerous reflections on the history of the great and nobleminded man, who, amidst the pomp and circumstance of eastern greatness, devoted his best energies to the promotion of the happiness of those he governed ; valuing power as it afforded means for the exercise of his enlightened philanthropy.

Western India, 1839, Vol. I, pp. 48-50.

The Mohurrum in Bombay

S. M. EDWARDES.

Although the regular Mohurrum ceremonies do not commence until the fifth day of the Mohurrum moon, the Mahomedan quarters of the city are astir on the first of the month. From morn till eve the streets are filled with bands of boys, and sometimes girls, blowing raucous blasts on hollow bamboos, which are adorned with a tin 'panja '—the sacred open hand emblematical of the Prophet, his daughter Fatima, her husband Ali and their two martyred sons. The sacred five, in the form of the outstretched hand, adorn nearly all Mohurrum symbols, from the toy trumpet and the top of the banner-pole to the horse-shoe rod of the devotee and the 'tazia' or domed bier. Youths, preceded by drummers and clarionet-players, wander through the streets laying all the shop-keepers under contribution for subscriptions; the well-to-do householder sets to building a ' sabil ' or charity-fountain in one corner of his verandah or on a site somewhat removed from the fairway of traffic; while a continuous stream of people afflicted by the evil-eye flows into the courtyard of the Bara Imam Chilla near the Nal Bazaar to receive absolution from the peacock-feather brush and sword there preserved. Meanwhile in almost every street where a ' tabut ' is being prepared, elegiac discourses ('waaz') are nightly delivered up to the tenth of the month by a maulvi, who draws from

Rs. 30 to Rs. 100 for his five nights' description of the martyrdom of Husain; while but a little distance away boys painted to resemble tigers leap to the rhythm of a drum, and the Arab mummer with the split bamboo shatters the nerves of the passer-by by suddenly cracking it behind his back. The fact that this Arab usually takes up a strong position near a 'tazia' suggests the idea that he must originally have represented a guardian or scapegoat, designed to break by means of his abuse, buffoonery and laughter the spell of the spirits who long for quarters within the rich mimic tomb; and the fact that the crowds who come to gaze in admiration on the 'tazia' never retort or round upon him, for the sudden fright or anger that he evokes gives one the impression that the crack of the bamboo is in their belief a potent scarer of unhoused and malignant spirits.

By-ways of Bombay, 1912, 2nd ed. pp. 46-47.

Mohurrum

M. T. HAINSSELIN.

On the final day the streets were crowded beyond imagination all along the route. Sitting in a balcony at any point you could have watched for hour after hour while the thousands of natives thronged past at a run, till you wondered where they could possibly come from in such incalculable numbers. Now a tall tomb of gilded wicker-work, elaborately ornamented with flags and paper streamers, would be borne along on a wagon drawn by two patient oxen; around it a crowd of excited natives, brandishing ten-foot bamboo poles, kept up a perpetual shouting in which the names of Hassan and Hussein were continually repeated. Some half-a-dozen of the crowd would ever and anon separate themselves from the seething human mass and act like chorus-leaders to the rest, turning round to face them and dancing backwards with wild gesticulations, and conducting the shouting till it became, from a mere confused noise, a regularly-timed concert of staccato cries, like the splash of oars in a racing boat. So the tomb and its attendant mob would pass along, and then perhaps for a few minutes a quiet interval when the people dribbled past scantily; then another crowd, thicker than ever, and taking longer to go by, all running and shouting, though they had neither tomb nor anything else to shout at; and every man's white clothes were thickly bespattered with great splashes of coloured dyes, red and purple, to represent the blood of the martyred saints. Here for a moment or two the crowd would thicken at a corner, swaying and surging till it looked as if there was going to be a very ugly crush; but at the critical moment a mounted white policeman, who had all the time been viewing the proceedings with blasé contempt, would quietly back his horse into the thickest part of the crowd, and the natives would scatter and fly. Next, perhaps would come a little band of three or four men, naked, except for the dhooti around their loins, and painted from head to foot in stripes, yellow and white, to represent tigers; these kept up a weird sort of animal dance, with some symbolism attached to it relating to the events in celebration. After them, another tomb, taller still and more elaborate than the former, and then another and still another. And so on, for hours, all wending their way along a winding route all through the city, till they finally reached the bridge, where the tombs were cast over to float away with the tide.

Markham of Mohistan. Pages 180 to 181.

Collins the Armenian Loafer

ARTHUR CRAWFORD.

No acount of Bombay loafers would be complete without a reference to the harmless old fellow whose death, I think, I read of two or three years ago. For a quarter of a century or more, Collins, I believe he was named, was to be found somewhere or other squatted in some favourite nook in the Fort, his preference being for some lane opposite Watson's Grand Hotel. Many of us thought that he was an Armenian, and his features favoured this supposition. He never solicited alms—in fact, he never spoke, but there was a mute appeal in his sad, worn-looking eyes, a dignity in his grand face, with its long gray beard flowing to his waist, which attracted the passer-by, and made him forget the squalid appearance of this curious old fellow. Many a coin was silently passed into his hands by European and Native, and as silently received, to be immediately put away in some place of concealment in the bundle of indescribable rags which made up his clothes. He was popularly supposed to have lost his wits in his youth, after some great domestic affliction, but there was nothing in his eye that betokened a weak intellect—at any rate, he was quite harmless, and was officially tolerated by the Police. To what lair he retreated at night is best known to them. When he died, if I remember aright, a respectable sum of money was found about his person.

Reminiscences of an Anglo-Indian Police Officer, 1894, pp. 247—249.

An Afternoon Scene in the Town

PRINCE KARAGEORGEVITCH.

Afternoon in the bazaar, in the warm glow of the sinking sun, wonderfully quiet. No sound but that of some workmen's tools ; no passers-by, no shouting of voices, no bargaining. A few poor people stand by the stalls and examine the goods, but the seller does not seem to care. Invisible *guzals* vibrate in the air, and the piping invitation of a moollah falls from the top of a minaret.

Then suddenly there was a clatter of tom-toms, and rattling of castanets, a Hindu funeral passing by. The dead lay stretched on a bier, his face painted and horrible, a livid grin between the dreadful scarlet cheeks, covered with wreaths of jasmine and roses. A man walking before the corpse carried a jar of burning charcoal to light the funeral pile. Friends followed the bier, each bringing a log of wood, to add to the pyre as a last homage to the dead.

A Mohomedan funeral now. The body was in a coffin, covered with red stuff, sparkling with gold thread. The bearers and mourners chanted an almost cheerful measure, as they marched very slowly to the burial-ground by the seaside, where the dead rest under spreading banyans and flowering jasmine.

Enchanted India, 1898, p. 23.

LIFE AND SOCIETY

LIFE AND SOCIETY

Society in Bombay

"SLEEPY SKETCHES."

There are features, however, in Bombay society which, I think, distinguish it most favourably from society at home. In the first place, it is far more natural; there is far less of assumption or pretence than in England. I have said there is little musical or scientific society in Bombay. Now, in England, it is true there is not this want ; but in England, while even real lovers of music or science are few, there are immense numbers of people who, without any refined love of or interest in art or science, assume refined love and interest, to gain credit in the fashionable world, to increase the apparent difference between their own being and that of the lower classes. But this is not so in Bombay. There, in truth, we may have no refined taste in music, but we make no pretence that our taste is refined. We do not, hating classical music, suffer long performances of Beethoven or Bach, because to like their music shows refined taste ; we don't care for Beethoven or Bach or classical writers, and we do care for light music; and, without pretending that our liking is other than what it is, we play and sing and listen to, light music only. And so in literature. Darwin, Spencer, Lyell may write books, and we may have no interest in them, preferring instead the romances of Dumas. But we do not pretend to have any such interest. I think I am justified in saying that there is an almost entire absence of humbug amongst us, which makes up almost for our absence of refined interest in art and science. And as a result of this absence of humbug, every one in society is bound to act without assumption; side or swagger cannot be long maintained by any one. The young civilian, army man, merchant, or barrister who, from association with his inferiors, the flattery of relatives, or inordinate vanity, comes out with an arrogant manner, must soon get rid of it or be cut. And all men who come out to India come out to work, and so any position they may gain is owing, in some measure at least, to their new efforts, and, I fancy, no man who is conscious that his place in the world is the result of his own endeavours is guilty of side. Again, we show in Bombay far more general hospitality and kindness one to another, and this from disinterested motives, than is the case in England.

Of course, as all the world over, there are some who form their friendships solely with a view to self-advantage, who consistently cut poor and shabby men, and consistently invite to dinner those who have influence. But it is at the same time a fact, and a very strange fact, that many, very many—I believe myself, the great majority of those who have the means—ask others not in so happy a position, to dine with them, to stay at their houses or go away with them for vacation; *not* because there is any return advantage to be gained, or because there is any obligation from friendships in England, but out of pure kindness and sympathy with the men asked for in their less free position. I believe there are many people in Bombay who, when going away for vacation, look round among their friends, and ask themselves, who is ill and would be better for a change? or who wants to get away and cannot, unless some chance turn up that he may do so at little expense? I myself can say I have benefitted from this; and not once, but often, have I heard other men say the same.

Sleepy Sketches, 1877, pp. 10–13.

Life in Bombay

LADY BURTON.

Turning now to society at Bombay, and indeed Indian society generally, I must say that it is not to be outdone for hospitality. There is a certain amount of formality about precedence in all English stations, and if one could only dispense with it, society would be twice as charming and attractive. I do not mean of course the formality of etiquette and good-breeding, but of all those silly little conventions and rules which arise for the most part from unimportant people trying to make themselves of importance. Of course they make a great point about what is called "official rank" in India, and the women squabble terribly over their warrants of precedence: the gradations thereof would puzzle even the chamberlain of some petty German court. The Anglo-Indian ladies of Bombay struck me for the most part as spiritless. They had a faded, washed-out look; and I do not wonder at it, considering the life they lead. They get up about nine, breakfast and pay or receive visits, then tiffen, siesta, a drive to the Apollo Bunder, to hear the band, or to meet their husbands at the Fort, dine and bed—that is the programme of the day. The men are better because they have cricket and polo. I found nobody stiff individually, but society very much so in the mass. The order of precedence seemed to be uppermost in every mind, and as an outsider I thought how tedious "ye manners and customs of ye Anglo-Indians" would be all the year round.

I found the native populace much more interesting. The great mass consists of Konkani Moslems, with dark features and scraggy beards. They were clad in chintz turbans, resembling the Parsee headgear, and in long cotton coats, with shoes turned up at the toes, and short drawers or pyjamas. There were also Persians, with a totally different type of face, and clothed in quite a different way, mainly in white with white turbans. There were Arabs from the Persian Gulf, sitting and lolling in the coffee-houses. There were athlelic Afghans, and many other strange tribes. There were conjurers and snake-charmers, vendors of pipes and mangoes, and Hindu women in colours that pale those of Egypt and Syria. There were two sorts of Parsees, one white-turbaned, and the other whose headgear was black, spotted with red. I was much struck with the immense variety of turban on the men, and the *choli* and headgear on the women. Some of the turbans were of the size of a moderate round tea-table. Others fit the head tight. Some are worn straight, and some are cocked sideways. Some are red and horned. The *choli* is a bodice which is put on the female child, who never knows what stays are. It always supports the bosom, and she is never without it day or night, unless after marriage, and whilst she is growing, it is of course changed to her size from time to time. They are of all colours and shapes, according to the race. No English-woman could wear one, unless it were made on purpose for her; but I cannot explain why.

The Romance of Isabel Lady Burton,
by W. H. Wilkins, 1897, pp. 589-591.

Byculla Club

SIR BARTLE FRERE.

It has always struck me that in England we are in the habit of doing very scant justice to institutions like this. We have got into the habit of regarding them as mere excrescences in our social organisation, but I have often thought that they take a very important place in the political organization of England, and are a valuable means of preparing Englishmen for that political life which is more or less the part of every one of us. In the first place we acquire in those clubs a complete deference to the verdict of the majority—which is of itself a great thing. We are trained also to a habitual deference to the government of the best and wisest among us, whom we have selected to rule over us. But above all, gentlemen, we are trained to a tolerant regard for the minority; and I cannot help thinking that it is to a great extent to this feeling—which plays so important a part in our club organisation and club habits—that we owe that toleration to which your chairman (Sir A. Scoble) has alluded in speaking of the way in which we treat the Natives of this country. In all party contests, political or otherwise, there is a great disposition on the part of the majority or those who get the victory, to treat with scant consideration those over whom they have triumphed; but it is very different, as you know, in clubs, for when a question is once settled, there is great toleration always shown to the minority, and the object of the committee of a good club is always to make up differences which have been caused by a club quarrel.

Now, Gentlemen, I do not think this is an unimportant matter when so many of our countrymen come out to rule over a nation, or as I may say an assemblage of nations, in India. But, Gentlemen, whatever may be the claims of a Club in England on the gratitude of the community, I think there are very few who will not recognise far greater claims here in Bombay, where this institution has been to so many of our younger brethren a home and a very happy home. We know that in England there is often a choice between a home and a Club; but here, where many of us have no home of our own, we owe a double debt of gratitude to the Club. And, Gentlemen, I have always thought that this institution afforded to us so many of the advantages of club life at home, in establishing a standard of judgment upon all social questions, and passing a free and unbiassed verdict upon all those questions, and in affording a home to our younger brethren and keeping them generally in very good order—that it deserved the gratitude of all who look to the character of Englishmen in this country as of paramount importance to the character of English Government. And I have viewed with satisfaction the growth of such institutions —especially of the infant one at Poona where I had lately the pleasure of being entertained—as a good sign of the advancement of society in Bombay.

Speech at the Byculla Club, 1867. Speeches, ed. Pitale, pp. 472–473.

A Judge's House Establishment, 1828

ELIZABETH GRANT.

Our establishment consisted of a head servant, a Parsee, who managed all, hired the rest, marketed, ordered, took charge of everything, doing it all admirably, and yet a rogue; an under-steward or butler, a Mohammedan, who waited on me; four chobdars, officers of the Supreme Court who attended my father there, waited at meals on him and my mother, and always went behind the carriage; they were dressed in long scarlet gowns edged with gold lace, white turbans, gold belts, and they bore long gilt staves in their hands. The Parsee wore a short cotton tunic with a shawl round the waist, very wide silk trousers, and the high brown silk cap peculiar to the Parsees. My Mohammedan had a white turban, white tunic, red shawl, and red trousers tight to the leg. My father's valet was a Portuguese Christian in a white jacket and trousers, European style. Besides these there were four sepoys for going messages, who wore green and red and gold fancifully about their turbans and tunics—the family livery; two *hammauls* to clean the house, two *bheesties* to fetch the water, two men to light the lamps, one water-cooler and butter-maker (this last piece of business being done in a bottle on his knee), a gardener, a cook with an assistant, two dhobies or washermen, and a slop-emptier, all these being Hindus of various castes, except the cook, who was a Portuguese.

The stable establishment was on a similar scale: two pairs of carriage horses, my father's riding-horse and mine, a coachman, a groom to each horse who always ran beside him whether we drove or rode, and a grass-cutter for every pair. Wages had need to be small in a country where such a retinue was requisite for three people; no one doing more than one particular kind of work rendered this mob of idlers necessary. My mother had her maid and I had mine, whose daughter also lived with us and was very useful. We hired a tailor when we wanted one, a mender, or a mantua-maker or a milliner as required.

Our life was monotonous. My father and I rose before the sun, an hour or more, groped our way downstairs, mounted our horses, and rode till heat and light, coming together, warned us to return. I then bathed and breakfasted and lay upon the sofa reading till Fatima came to dress me. I always appeared at the family breakfast, though but for form. My father, who had been hard at work fasting, made a good meal, and my mother, just up, did the same. We had frequently visitors at this hour; after they went my mother walked about with the *hammauls* after her, dusting her china—of which she soon collected a good stock—

calling out to them *subbr* when she wanted them to go on, and *ahste* when they had omitted a cup or vase, for she never could manage their easy language. I wrote or worked or played or sang while the weather remained tolerably cool; in the hot months I was not able to do anything. My mother and I were cften amused by receiving presents from the natives, and by the arrival of *boras* to tempt us with the newest fashions just procured from "a ship come in last night," shown first to us as "such great ladies." My father took no presents himself, and permitted us to accept none but fruits and flowers ; very valuable ones were at first offered, but being invariably only touched and returned, they soon ceased. The flowers generally came tied up with silver thread in the hands of the gardener, but the fruits, fresh or dried, were always in silver bowls, covered with silver gauze, and brought in on the head of the messenger. Some ladies, it was said, used to keep the bowls, but we better instructed, returned the dull-looking precious part of the offering with its dirty bit of covering, quite content with our simpler share.

The *bora* entered more ostentatiously with a long string of native porters, each bearing on his head a box. All were set down and opened, and the goods displayed upon the floor, very pretty and very good, and only about double as dear as at home, a rupee for a shilling, about. The native manufactures were cheap enough, except the shawls; and, by the bye, Mr. Gardiner gave me one, which cost a hundred pounds. It is a good thing to be the last married of a sisterhood, when one meets such generous brothers-in-law! At two o'clock or rather sooner we had our tiffin, after which we were never disturbed, every one retiring during those hot hours, undressing and sleeping.

The drives were beautiful whichever way we went, on the beach, on the Breach Candy road, or the Esplanade, and twice a week across the rice-fields to Matoonga to listen to the artillery band, all the Presidency collecting there. We drove up and down, stopped alongside another carriage, sometimes on a cool evening got out and walked to speak to our friends. We were all very sociable, and the band was delightful. The equipages were extraordinary, all the horses fine but the carriages very shabby. The smartest soon fades in such a climate; what with the heat of one season, the wet of another, the red dust, the insects, the constant use and not much care, the London-built carriage makes but a poor figure the second year, and as the renewal of them is not always convenient, and a daily carriage drive is essential, they are used in bad enough condition sometimes.

On the sun going down, which he does like a shot—there is no twilight—the crowd separates, the ladies glad enough of a warm shawl on their back return home, for it was often very cold driving back. Then, if we were to pass a quiet evening, a very few minutes prepared us for dinner; but if, as was often the case, we were to be in company at home or abroad, there was great commotion among the ayahs to have their preparations made in time. My Arab, Fatima, was always ready; she was so quick and so quiet. There are many drawbacks to an Indian life, but the servants in Bombay at that time were a luxury.

Lady Strachey's " Memoirs of a Highland Lady, " 1898, pp. 421-423.

A Governor's Life a Century Ago

MOUNTSTUART ELPHINSTONE.

'My dear Adam,—

'Now to answer your questions. How I like Bombay? Very well; and the first month, which you thought would be so disagreeable, better than I expect to like any future month. There were no troublesome forms and ceremonies, and much novelty and variety. The new and unknown details you allude to give me little trouble, as I have always Warden to tell me what is usual; and as to the new business not of detail, I like learning it. Besides, I am not nearly so hard worked as in the Deccan; and much of my work (that is, much of what takes up my time) is half play, such as talking to people who come to me on business instead of puzzling over records or pumping natives, going to Council, going to church. What I dread, detest, and abhor, to a degree which I fancy never was equalled, is making speeehes, and ceremonies of that nature. I avoid them as much as I can by avowing my horror of the practice; but sometimes they occur. All the other people of Bombay harangue to such a degree that if I were Charles Fox I should hold my tongue on purpose to put down the fashion. No party of thirty meets without thirty regular speeches. This, though sometimes amusing, is the great reproach of Bombay; otherwise the society is pleasant and easy, at least as much so as Calcutta. People either always dance or have a good deal of music and singing when there is a party, and no stiff private circle. The Governor too, by the custom of Bombay, constantly drives out, and is quite a private gentleman, which suits well with my habits and tastes (3, Dec. 1819).

Life by Sir E. Colebrooke, 1884, Vol. II, page 108.

Life in Bombay in the Sixties

J. M. MACLEAN.

Many a pleasant evening we spent in those days at the Byculla Club in symposia which were not unworthy to be classed with the "Noctes Ambrosianæ" of Christopher North; and here let me pay a passing tribute to the delightful society which flourished in India forty or fifty years ago. The Anglo-Indians of Bombay then formed a community of a democratic kind such as could not be found elsewhere. It comprised no old men or children, and ccmparatively few women. There were no millionaires or paupers. All menial offices where discharged by the native population. Every Englishman was comfortably off, had been well educated, and belonged either to the civil or military service of the crown, or to the mercantile or professional classes.

Everybody, therefore, lived on a footing of perfect equality; intercourse was easy and pleasant, and there was none of the appalling snobbishness towards good society and people in high places which is the curse of London life, and which has been stimulated to a height never dreamt of even by Thackeray by the eager competition of American and Colonial capitalists anxious to make their way to the front. I suppose that for a parallel to such a community as then existed in Bombay, it wouldbe necessary to go back to the old Greek Republics. Conversation was very frank and outspoken, and criticism very prolific and enlightenend, for the Gevernment had not then thought it necessary, as they now have, to close the safety valve by formally prohibiting public servants, on pain of dismissal, from making any observations on the conduct of their superiors in office.

There were great merchants in those days who lived for many years in Bombay, kept great houses on Malabar Hill, and entertained in good style. Their place has now been taken by clerks who are mere agents for firms at home or for the German or Greek houses which everywhere do so much business under the British flag. Nothing surprised me so much, I went back to India on a visit three years ago, (1899), than to find that the Europeans in Bombay had taken a back seat. All the best houses in the island were occupied by wealthy natives, and Englishmen seemed to possess nothing except the fringe of ground adjoining the harbour on which the Yacht Club is built. In my time the Englishman walked about Bombay as if he realised Goldsmith's description:—

> " Pride in their port, defiance in their eye,
> I see the lords of humankind pass by "

The natives then occupied a distinctly inferior position, and they did not seem to resent it. Most of them had made money through English agency, and they looked up to the heads of the great firms, like Michael Scott, John Fleming, and Donald Graham, with pride and affection. They loved to give great entertainments in honour of their English friends, and never forgot them when the Englishmen came home. The feelings of good will between Englishmen and natives were much stronger and more lasting then than they are now, when there is much less of the feeling of fellowship between the two races.

My personal relations with leading natives were always of a pleasant character, and I made many friends among them, who, when I went to India in 1899, after nearly twenty years' absence, crowded round me, and gave me a cordial welcome. But I always opposed the political views of the ambitious young natives who dreamed of self-government for India, and so aroused the lasting resentment of the Maratha Brahmins of Poona. The Parsees of Bombay, however, have cherished a warm feeling of gratitude towards me since I took up their cause against a mob that had wrecked their fire temples in 1874.

A good many of the Europeans lived in houses of their own, but many of them stayed at the Clubs, which were always a main source of attraction in the evening in a city which, as a rule, was destitute of theatrical performances. When we became more wealthy, we tried the experiment of importing on opera company from Italy, but it did not succeed. When I first went out, soon after the Mutiny, the military element was much stronger than it afterwards became. There were twenty or more commissioned officers to every regiment, and their mess tents were the scene of much hospitality. They had the pleasant custom of inviting residents in Bombay to become honorary members of the mess, and on guest nights it was not unusual for forty or fifty men to sit down to dinner. I thus extended my acquaintance very largely, and became known to many of the men who afterwards made their mark.

Recollections of Westminister & India, 1903, pp. 23-27.

Indian Life

BASIL HALL.

I have no language competent to give expression to the feelings produced by the first contemplation of so strange a spectacle. I was startled, amused, deeply interested, and sometimes not a little shocked. The novelty of the scene was scarcely diminished by a further inspection; which may appear a contradiction in terms, but is not so in reality. The multitude of ideas caused by the first view of such an astonishing crowd of new and curious objects, obscures and confuses the observation, in a certain sense, and prevents us from distinguishing one part from another. In like manner, I remember being almost stupefied with astonishment, when Sir John Herschel first showed me one of the great nebulae or clusters of stars in his telescope at Slough. When, however, the philosopher unfolded the results of his own observations, and ventured to separate and distinguish the different orders of nebulae and double stars, or pointed the instrument to the planet which his illustrious father discovered, and made me understand, or tried to make me understand, the revolutions of its satellites, I felt the confusion by which at first I was distracted gradually subsiding, while the fresh interest of the spectacle, strictly speaking, was greatly increased. And so I found it in India, especially at the most curious of places, Bombay, where the more I saw of the natives, the more there seemed still to discover that was new. It would be absurd to pretend that all this pedantic kind of reasoning process took place at the moment, for, in truth, I was too much enchanted to speculate deeply on the causes of the enjoyment. I shall never forget, however, the pleasure with which I heard a native, with a bowl in his hand, apply to a dealer in corn for some of the grain called Sesame. The word, in strictness, is not the Indian name for this seed, though it is used generally in Hindustan. Til is the native term for the plant from which the oil of sesamum is expressed; Semsem being the original Arabic word. I need not say how immediate the sound recalled the 'Open Sesame!' of the Arabian Nights; and the whole of the surrounding scene, being in strict character with that of the tale, I felt as if I had been touched with some magic wand, and transported into the highest heaven of Eastern invention. As I gazed at all things round me in wonder and delight, I could fix my eye on nothing I had ever seen before. The dresses, in endless variety of flowing robes and twisted turbans, flitted like a vision before me. The Hindoos, of innumerable castes, were there each distinguished from the other by marks drawn with brilliant colours on his brow. There stood Persian merchants with shawls and other goods from Cashmere, mingled with numerous Arab horse-dealers careering about; Malays from the Straits of Malacca, chatting familiarly with those good-natured, merry fellows, the long-tailed Chinese, whose most ungraceful Tartar dress and tuft contrast curiously in such a crowd with the tastefully arranged drapery and gorgeous turbans of the Mahometans and Hindoos.

Some of these groups were fully as much distinguished by their sandals and slippers as by their head-gear; others arrested the attention by the sound of their voices, and many by the peculiarity of their features and complexion. It really signified little which way the eye was turned, for it could rest on nothing, animate or inanimate, which was not strange and full of interest. Most of the trees which shaded us, and especially a tall variety of the palm tribe, commonly called the Brab, I had never seen before. It is named by botanists Barassus flabelliformis, or Tara Palm; Tara or Tari being the native word for the toddy which is yielded by these trees. It grows, in respect to its stem, like the coca-nut, with a glorious set of projecting arms at the top. But these branches, different from those of the cocoa-nut, do not send forth along their whole length lateral leaves resembling the ostrich feather, to which the cocoa-nut leaf is very similar in form. They are smooth and naked to the end, on which is opened out, rather fantastically, a huge circular leaf, marked with divisions like those of a fan, radiating from a centre, each ray or division being sharp-pointed.

But the chief object of attraction, and I may well say of admiration, in this gay scene, was the appearance of the women, who are not only not concealed, but go about freely, and, generally speaking, occupy themselves out of doors in works not requiring any considerable strength, but a good deal of dexterity. Of course, this does not include the highest classes, who are kept quite secluded. The females appear to be the great water-carriers; and the pots or chatties, as they are called, which are invariably borne on the head, are of the most elegant forms imaginable. Indeed, when standing by the side of a Hindoo tank, or reservoir, as I have often done for hours together, I have been reminded of those beautiful Etruscan vases, the discovery of which has given so new a character to modern forms. This practice of carrying all loads on the head is necessarily accompanied by an erect carriage of body, and accordingly the most graceful of dancers, even the matchless Bigottini hereself, might have "snatched a grace beyond the reach of art," from observing the most ordinary Hindoo girl on her return from the tank, with her hand sometimes just touching the vessel poised on her head, and sometimes not, so true is the balance, and so certain the bearer's step. The dress of these women consists chiefly of one strip of cloth, many yards in length. This narrow web is wound round the body and limbs with so much propriety, that while the most scrupulous delicacy could find nothing to censure on the score of deficiency in covering, it is arranged with such innate and judicious taste, that even the eye of a sculptor could hardly wish many of its folds removed. The figure of the Hindoos, both male and female, is small and delicate; and, although their features are not always handsome, there is something about their expression which strikes every stranger as singularly pleasing, perhaps from its being indicative of that patience, docility, and contentment, which are certainly their chief characteristics. We see at least, in every part of our Eastern empire, that, with a little care, coupled with a full understanding of their habits and wishes, and backed by a thorough disinterestedness, and genuine public spirit on the part of their rulers, the above-mentioned qualities of the Hindoos may be turned to the highest account in all the arts of war, and many of the arts of peace.

Perhaps not the least curious sight in the bazaar of Bombay are the ornaments worn by the women and children, by which, with the most lavish profusion, and the most ill-directed taste, they succeed in disfiguring themselves as much as possible. And this might lead us almost to suspect that their taste in the other parts of their dress, like the gracefulness of their carriage, is the result, not of choice and study, but of happy accident. The custom of carrying their water-vessels on the head requires an erectness of gait during the performance of that duty, which may become the easiest and most natural at other times. And probably some circumstances incident to the climate may, in like manner, direct the fashion in adjusting their drapery.

Most of the women wear nose-rings, of great dimensions. I have seen many which hung below the chin; and certainly to us this seems a strange ornament. I forget whether or not the Hindoo women cover their fingers with rings, as our ladies do, but their principal fashion seems to consist in loading the wrists and ankles with armlets and bangles, as they are called, of gold and silver. The virgin gold generally used for this purpose is almost always rich, and grateful to the eye. But, I imagine no art can make a silver ornament look any thing but vulgar. Just as we sometimes see persons in Europe crowd ring upon ring on their fingers, till all beauty is lost in the heap, and all taste sacrificed for the mere sake of ostentatious display, so, in India, I have observed women, whose legs were covered with huge circles of gold and silver from the instep nearly to the knee, and their arms similarly hooped round almost to the elbow. The jingle made by these ornaments striking against one another gives ample warning of a woman's approach; a circumstance which has probably led to the notion that this custom of attaching, as it were, a set of bells to the heels of the ladies, may have been an institution of jealousy devised by the husbands of those warm latitudes, to aid their search after their gadding spouses. I cannot say how this theory squares with history; but I have never heard any hypothesis equally good to account for the still more ridiculous, not to say cruel custom, of covering the legs and arms of their poor little children with these rings. I have seen a girl three years old so loaded with them, that she could not walk or hold out her arms; and I once counted no fewer than twenty heavy gold chains on a child's neck, besides such numbers of rings on its arms and legs, that the little thing looked more like an armadillo of the picture-books than a human being. Such is the passion of some Hindoo parents for this practice, that I have been assured they often convert their whole worldly substance into this most useless form of the precious metals, and thus transform their progeny into a sort of money-chest. Small happiness is it for these innocent wretches, however, who, as the head police-magistrate informed me, are not infrequently murdered for the sake of the property they carry about with them!

I have before remarked, that when a traveller is first thrown into such a scene as I have here alluded to, although his enjoyment certainly is very great, there often comes across him a feeling of hopelessness, when he admits to himself his total inability to record one hundredth, one millionth part, I may say, of the splendid original. Everything is totally new to him; even the commonest implements of husbandry, the pots and pans, the baskets and barrels, the carts and carriages, all are strange to his eyes, and far beyond the reach of his pen; while things which stand higher in the scale come still less within its range. Then what is he to do with the sounds he hears, or the motion he perceives? And strange it is to admit, but true, that the interest is at times actually increased by circumstances which are in themselves very annoying. I well remember submitting even to the intense heat and glare with great patience, and almost relish, in consideration of their being strictly in character with a scene I had so long ardently desired to witness. The formidable smell of assafœtida, which reigns in every Indian market, I nearly learned to bear without a qualm, for the same reason. Other annoyances I cared very little about; and had it not been for the well-cursed mosquitoes, I should not hesitate to declare, that, as far as travelling human nature is capable of happiness, I was perfectly happy when cruising about the bazaars of Bombay.

Full well am I aware, that much of all this will appear to many excellent persons who have been in the East, or who may visit it after me, as sufficiently fanciful and exaggerated; and there are many who will pass through the very scenes which excited in me so much rapture, and will have no more anxious wish than to get safely out of it before they are splashed with mud from the feet of the wild-looking, blue-skinned buffaloes, or have their toes trodden upon by bullocks with great humps between their shoulders. It is impossible to expect general sympathy for such things; and accordingly, my English friends at Bombay used often to laugh heartily when I returned from these Arabian Night sort of excursions, with my head brimful of turbaned Turks, Hindoo pagodas, and all kinds of Oriental associations about the Indus and the Ganges, or Brahma and Vishnu, or with speculations on the customs, languages, and manners, of the extraordinary collection of people I had been rambling amongst.

Fragments of Voyages, 2nd series, 1832, pp. 108-111.

Native Life.

J. A. SPENDER.

I never imagined such variety as Bombay displays in its circuit of twenty miles. I have driven in a taxi-cab for two hours through the native town and out into the villages beyond and am trying in vain to sort my impressions. Every street swarms with people, and no half-dozen seem alike. There are white men, brown men, yellow men, chocolate men, and very nearly black men. Their costume varies from the frock coat to the loin-cloth, through a brilliant scale of orange, vermilion, green, blue, and brown. There are troops of children, apparently free of school, and some of these, again, are stark naked, while others are elaborately decked out, as for some fantastic childrens' carnival. The women are as various as the men and children, and the darker skins affect the brightest colours. Scores of opulent native gentlemen thread their way in and out among the crowds in the newest motor-cars; and other handsome carriages shuttered or curtained, suggest the presence of the *purdah* women. There is an incessant hubbub; the slightest transaction appears to require the unloosing simultaneously of all tongues in a wide circle of disinterested spectators, as well as among those immediately concerned.

The houses are as various as the people. The European part of Bombay might be Vienna slightly orientalized. The native is a grand jumble of all styles, but it gives you the queer impression of an immense hive, very intricate and deeply recessed, with layer of people living in a condition of vertical overcrowding which must give the plague its richest opportunities. The absence of glass enables you to look right into the heart of the houses, and the back rooms are little dark caverns. The main impression is that they swarm with people. Every veranda is crowded; there is a head or two heads at every window. I have some acquaintance with the East End of London and its crowded tenements, but nowhere in London or in any European city that I know, except possibly in one quarter of Naples, have I ever seen anything like this swarming, vivid, various humanity. You might suppose them to be an amiable, tolerant people, jostling each other with a good-natured friendliness which took no account of the differences of creed or race. And so in a superficial way they must be. No multitude could live thus close-packed without establishing some rough rule of mutual forbearance. Yet those who know them tell you that this immense jumble of humanity sorts itself into hundreds of intensely separate little heaps., each of which is guarded from the others by an unimaginable code of pride or prejudice.

The Indian Scene, 1912, pp. 17 to 20.

Bombay Beats the Whole World As a Place to Go Away From

"SLEEPY SKETCHES."

The buoyancy of the life felt in England is never experienced here. Brain-work is irksome, and muscles are unstrung. But we live in big houses and big rooms; there are no windows to shut out the air; the sky is blue, and every morning a cool breeze blows over us from the land, and every evening a cool, soft breeze fans us from the sea. And, if the air, steaming and bubbling with heat, grow unbearable, are there not pegs and icebergs of cold, glistening ice.

And the sun dries up our livers till they are infinitesimal, or swells them till they are monstrous; and the wise have no beer and women no complexions, and we go home.

But Bombay is not a bad place to live in, and beats the whole world as a place to go away from. No one can appreciate the delights of a temperate climate who has not been here. After steaming in Bombay for month after month, the pleasure of getting away to a hill station is indescribable. To sleep under one or even two blankets, to be forced by cold to huddle over a fire, to shiver in the morning bath, and absolutely be obliged to walk about in the sun to get warm, give an indescribable feeling of self-satisfaction that is the result entirely of previous life in a vapour bath.

If we poor devils out here are to be pitied for the discomforts we have to put up with in tropical residence, we are, too, to be envied for the exceptional pleasures we at times enjoy.

Sleepy Sketches, 1877, pp. 22-23.

BAZAARS AND STREETS

BAZAARS AND STREETS

Pen Pictures of Native Town

KARAGEORGEVITCH.

Outside Bombay, at the end of an avenue of tamarind trees between hedges starred with lilac and pink, we came to Pinjerapol, the hospital for animals. Here, in a sanded garden dotted with shrubs and flowers, stand sheds in which sick cows, horses and buffaloes are treated and cared for. In another part, in a little building divided into compartments by wire bars, poor crippled dogs whined to me as I passed to take them away. Hens wandered about on wooden legs; and an ancient parrot, in the greatest excitement, yelled with all his might; he was undergoing treatment to make his lost feathers grow again, his hidéous little black body being quite naked, with its large head and beak. In an open box, overhung with flowering jasmine, an Arab horse was suspended to the beams of the roof; two keepers by his side waved long white horsehair fans to keep away the flies. A perfect crowd of servants is employed in the care of the animals, and the litter is sweet and clean.

Enchanted India, 1898, pp. 25-26.

2

In the evening, as I again went past the Towers of Silence the palm trees were once more crowded with sleeping birds gorged with all the food sent them by the plague. On the other side of Back Bay, above the field of Burning, a thick column of smoke rose up, red in the last beams of the crimson sun.

In the silence of a moonless night nine o'clock struck from the great tower of the University —a pretty set of chimes reminding me of Bruges or Antwerp; and when the peal had died away a bugle in the sepoys' quarters took up the strain of the chimes, only infinitely softer, saddened to a minor key and to a slower measure; while in the distance an English trumpet, loud and clear, sounded the recall in counterpart.

Enchanted India, pp. 31-32.

3.

Here, one by one, in came the nautch-girls, dancers. Robed in stiff sarees, their legs encumbered with very full trousers, they stood extravagantly upright, their arms away from their sides and their hands hanging loosely. At the first sound of the tambourines, beaten by men who squatted close to the wall, they began to dance; jumping forward on both feet, then backward, striking their ankles together to make their *nanparas* ring, very heavy anklets weighing on their feet, bare with silver toe-rings. One of them spun on and on for a long time, while the others held a high, shrill note—higher, shriller still; then suddenly everything stopped, the music first, then the dancing—in the air, as it were—and the nautch-girls huddled together like sheep in a corner of the room, tried to move us with the only three English words they knew, the old woman repeating them; and as finally we positively would not understand, the jumping and idiotic spinning and shouts began again in the heated air of the room.

"Nautch-girls for tourists, like Europeans," said my Indian servant Abibulla. "Can-can dancing-girls," he added, with an air of triumph at having shown me a wonder!

Enchanted India, pp. 28–29.

A Night Scene

COUNT VON KOENIGSMARCK.

At eleven o'clock the party breaks up. But it is still too hot to sleep. I whistle for a cab and shout "Grant Road" to the driver. We pass Munlader's Tank, drive down Abdul Rahman Street, through the Bhendi Bazaar, and at length reach Grant Road, the pleasure-haunt *par excellence* for the native town.

Here the typical life of the Arabian Nights obtains. The narrow, dimly lighted, dirty, unsavoury, dusty street swarms with folk. Howling, shouting, groaning, the gaily coloured tangle of humanity rolls past me unchecked. Wave upon wave flows past, a hurrying flood-tide of human passions. The coachman has to drive at walking pace, and at length pulls up. You alight and mingle with the throng—the rustling, living mass which ebbs and flows, incessantly, without aim or object, all through the livelong night. A strange sight, like a masquerade or a carnival.

But, in spite of this seeming inextricable confusion, law and order prevails. Guardians of the peace rarely show themselves; only a single white policeman stands at the corner of Bhendī Bazaar, a slim young Englishman in khaki kit and helmet. In silent sympathetic interest he watches the flood of humanity speeding past. Bobby is conscious of his white superiority, but he does not rub it in. His presence is enough!

All the houses open on to the street; their inhabitants squat in the doorways, gossiping, eating, drinking, laughing and making merry. It is only late at night that the Indians seem to wake up. You only rarely see women, and yet they are playing the principal part here.

So these are the enchantments of the Arabian Nights! "Once, and never again," the stranger says to himself, and is glad to find his cab once more, to be borne away with all despatch out of the chaotic symposium of voices of this human ant-hill.

A German Staff Officer in India, 1910, pp. 58-59.

A Mart of Nations

MRS. POSTANS.

The early riser, desiring to pursue his ride into the lovely scenes which skirt the town, will find the roads clear, clean, and void of all offence. The porters and artisans then lie shrouded in their *cumlies*; the market people have a wide path, as they bring in the fresh fruits of the neighbouring country ; the toddy-drawer appears, crowned with an earthen vessel, overflowing with the delicious juice of the graceful palm tree ; and Hindoo girls seated behind baskets of bright blossoms, string fragrant wreaths, to adorn the altars of their gods. Thus fresh and tranquil remain the elements of the scene, until the hurry and the toil of life fill it with that suffocating heat and deafening clamour, attendant upon the interests of eager traffic.

Offensive to every sense, as the dust and noise of these crowded ways must be, steaming under the noontide influence of a tropic sun, 'tis worth the cost, to stop a moment at the entrance of a great bazaar, and looking along the wide and busy way, watch the full tide of human beings, jostling and vociferating against each other, as the throng presses onwards, each individual animated with the object of labour or of profit. More strange and interesting is it still, to move among the groups, and passing, mark the varied characters which form the living mass.

To a stranger's eye, the chintz bazaar will afford the most curious scene; the road skirts that particular portion of the bay occupied by native shipping, and is wholly devoted to the purposes of commerce. Here indeed is a "mart of nations," where the genius of traffic reigns triumphant, and the merchandize and produce of all the nations of the east seem garnered in one common store, awaiting an escort to the lands where the arts and manufactures of civilized life will increase the value of nature's gifts. Piles of rich gums and aromatic spices, carboys of oil and rose water, pure ivory from the forests of Ceylon, rhinoceros hides from the burning coast of Zanzibar, the richest produce of Africa India, Persia, and Arabia, is here cast in large heaps, mingling with coir cables, huge blocks, and ponderous anchors, the requisite material of island exportation.

On the highway, porters bending beneath square bales of tightly compressed cotton, stagger to and fro, as if overpowered with their loads; Arabs with ponderous turbans of finely checked cloth, and kabas loosely flowing, lounge lazily along; Persians in silken vests, with black lamb-skin caps, the softest produce of Bokhara, tower above the crowd; Banians, dirty and bustling, wearing red turbans bristling with pens and memoranda, jostle roughly to the right and left; Bangies with suspended bales, or well-filled water vessels; Fakirs from every part of India; Jains in their snowy vests, with staff and brush, like palmers of the olden time; Padres with round black hats and sable cloaks; Jews of the tribe of Beni Israel, all mingle in the throng; while ever and again, a bullock hackery struggles against the mass, or a Parsee, dashing onwards in his gaily painted buggy, forces an avenue for an instant, when the eager crowd, rapidly closing in its rear, sweeps on a resistless torrent as before.

The Arab stables, which occupy a considerable space in the great bazaar, form a powerful attraction to the gentlemen of the Presidency. Military men, of whatever rank, in India, consider it necessary to possess at least a couple of horses. Colts being usually preferred for a new purchase, the stables are eagerly resorted to whenever a fresh importation arrives from the Gulf. The appearance of the poor steeds, on their debarkation, is wretched indeed; the want of pure air and exercise, the filth and close stowage of the Arab boats, "forcing their bones to stick out like the corners of a real," reduce them to the proportions of that horse so good, which appertained to the chivalrous state of La Mancha's knight. In this sad plight good judges secure the best for the turf; and the rest remain in the stables, where they fetch prices, either commensurate with the merits they may possess, or the lack of knowledge in the purchaser.

The horse merchants of the Presidency are not more conscientious than the Tattersalls of the west; and the "griffin logue" are consequently victimised by most grievous impositions. Tempted beyond the power of resistance, the representations of the dealer meet with easy credence from the uninitiated, and his offers of credit are readily accepted.

A good hack, or roadster, may be purchased for about fifty pounds; but a hundred and fifty is considered a fair price for an Arab colt of promise, calculated either for the duties of a charger, or, if possessing "the speed of thought" in all his limbs, for the exciting interests of the turf.

On a visitor to the stables desiring to see the action of a valuable colt, one

> "Wild as the wild deer, and untaught,
> With spur and bridle undefiled,"

an Arab rider grasps its flowing mane, flings himself suddenly on its back, strikes his bare heels into its glossy sides, and with hair and garments wildly flying, urges the noble creature to a furious gallop; then, with a skilful check in mid career, he brings it, with expanded eye and reeking flank, back to the appointed stall.

With the exception of horses intended for the cavalry, it is not customary to subject Arabs to the exercise of the manège; the natural disposition of the "desert born" being itself so noble, so full of nervous energy, yet so tractable and gentle withal, that good treatment is alone required to ensure his ready obedience to the rider's will.

Western India, 1839, Vol. I, pp. 76—81.

Mixture of Types in the Bazaar

LOUIS ROUSSELET.

On entering its huge bazaars for the first time, one is immediately deafened by the din that prevails, and half suffocated by the smells that impregnate the atmosphere. A heavy perfume of "ghee" and grease, which is exhaled from numerous shops belonging to the poorer class of confectioners, turns the stomachs of all who, for the first time, experience it. In spite of this source of discomfort, the visitor cannot help admiring these famous bazaars. A world of peoples and races, of perfectly distinct types and costumes, are crowded together in the streets of this capital, which distributes the products of Europe to two-thirds of India. It is the port of arrival for all who come from Persia, from

Arabia; from Afghanistan, and the coast of Africa; and from it the pilgrims from Hindostan bound to Mecca, Karbala, or Nujiff, take their departure. Beside the indigenous races which still present such varieties, we see the Persian, with his high cap of Astrakan; the Arab, in his Biblical costume; the Somali negro, with fine intelligent features; the Chinese, the Burmese, and the Malay. This diversity gives to the crowd a peculiar stamp, which no other town in the world can present. The corpulent Buniahs of Cutch or Gujerat, with their pyramids of muslin on their heads, raise their voices in rivalry with the natives of Cabul or Scinde; the Hindoo fakir, naked and hideously painted, elbows the Portuguese priest in his sable robe. The Tower of Babel could not have assembled at its foundation a more complete collection of the human race. Palanquins, native carriages, surmounted by domes of red cloth, beneath which dusky beauties conceal themselves, pass by, drawn by beautiful oxen from Surat, as well as handsome open carriages from Paris or London. The street is bordered by small booths, the flooring of which, raised several feet above the roadway, serves for counter and stall; the most diverse branches of industry are there displayed side by side: but those which call for particular notice are the stores of manufactures in sandal-wood, ebony, furniture, and works of art in copper.

The houses which skirt the bazaars are generally laid out in several storeys, and constructed of wood and bricks. Their fronts, adorned with verandahs, the pillars of which are delicately carved and painted in lively colours, afford a peculiarity of appearance altogether unknown in exclusively Mussulman countries. All the streets that traverse this immense town are very large ; the Bhendi Bazaar, amongst others, is one of the finest. Here are the famous Arab stables, from which come all the magnificent and costly horses used in the island, and which, for the sportsman, form one of the most interesting places of resort. Here are to be found the finest kinds of horses in the East. Most of them come from the provinces bordering on the Persian Gulf, from Kattywar and from Cabul ; but the most excellent are those of Djowfet and Nedjed, of the purest Arab race. Unfortunately their value is considerable, the prices ranging from £ 120 to £240 or £250 for those of the best class, and from £40 downwards for the inferior sort.

These stables attract the attention of all the horse-riding people of this part of the world, and the coffee-houses facing them present, therefore, a very singular appearance. All day long we may see there Arabs, Negroes, Bedouins, squatting on couches of rope drawn up alongside the shops, and quaffing aromatic drinks, or smoking the long hubble-tubble; the Persians, in their long caps, assemble in the shops devoted to *meethæee*, where they consume enormous balls, composed of flour, sugar, and milk ; and at the corners of streets the natives of Cabul, in their long and disgustingly dirty linen smocks and blue turbans, regale themselves frugally on dried dates. Continuing our excursion across the Black Town, we reach the China Bazaar, which is always encumbered by a dense crowd. It extends along that part of the port reserved for native vessels. The quays are covered with all the rich products of Asia—buffalo-horns, tortoise-shells, elephant-tusks, bags of spices, coffee, pepper, &c. Coolies of great strength pass through the crowd, bearing on each end of long bamboos bales of merchandise; and Parsees take note of the arrivals, or discuss prices. Everything, in fact, presents this mixture of types, which is universal at Bombay, and always surprising to strangers.

India and its Native Princes. 1882, pp. 7-9.

The Bombay Bazaar, Unique

J. H. STOCQUELER.

Few things can afford more interesting or picturesque effects than the great bazaar, beginning with the gay, open Esplanade, its pretty bungalows and animated groups, with the Fort and Bay in advance, and ending with the dark cocoa-nut woods in Girgaum and Mazagon, speckled with the handsome villas of the European gentry.

The beautiful Parsee women, with their gay green and orange-coloured sarees, chatting at the wells to the graceful, handsome sepoys, whose high caste compels them to draw water for themselves; the crowded ways, peopled with professors of almost every known creed, and natives of almost every land; the open shops, filled with goods to suit all tastes, "corn, and wine, and oil," in their literal sense, with women's bracelets (a trade in itself), culinary utensils, and fair ivory work; the quaint, though barbarous, paintings that deck many of the exteriors of the houses; the streets devoted to the cunning work of gold and silver; the richly-carved decorations; the variety of costumes that meet the eye, and the languages that fall upon the ear; the native procession that stops the way; the devotee, performing his unnatural penance; the harmonies of light and colour; the rich dresses; the contrasts of life and character—such as the stately yet half-nude Brahmin, the English sailor, the dancing-girl, and the devotee, with the intermediate shades—each and all, to the reflecting mind, are full of interest; and although, towards twilight, the bazaar is deeply shadowed, and the fresh breeze reaches it not,—although the dust rises in clouds, the air is stagnant, and the native drivers care nothing for the right of road, pressing to either side as suits them best, causing irritation, suspense, and danger to all whom they encounter; still, the Bombay bazaar outbalances, in interest, all its worst annoyances and is, in its peculiarities, *unique*.

Hand-book of India, 1844, pp. 323-325.

Animated Life of the Bazaars

LADY FALKLAND.

The same evening we drove through the native town and bazaar of Bombay. Here I was quite bewildered with the novelty of the scene around me—too much so, indeed—as we passed rather quickly though the streets, to note separately the endless variety of groups and pictures that presented themselves, in all directions; still I saw a great deal. A bridal-party first drew my attention. The young bride rode *á califourchon* on a miserable pony; and behind her, on the same animal, sat the bridegroom. They both wore gilt-paper crowns; and down their faces hung many strips of tinsel, and coloured beads, completely concealing their features; relations and friends on foot, and men beating the 'tom-tom' (native drum) and playing on musical instruments, both followed and preceded the happy couple.

The street from that part of the bazaar which is called the 'Bhendy Bazaar,' to the Esplanade, is crowded from sunrise to nine o'clock at night; and, as the people walk generally in the middle of the streets, the coachmen and gorah-wallahs (running footmen), who attend the carriages of Europeans and wealthy natives, are constantly calling out to the pedestrians to get out of the way.

The most interesting part of the native town begins at the horse-bazaar; where, in the cool of the evening, the picturesquely-clothed Persian and Arab horse-dealers sit in the open air, sipping coffee and smoking with their friends. All is much 'Europeanized' in Bombay, to use an Anglo-Indian expression; and these men, instead of squatting on the ground, sit on old chairs and stools.

Proceeding onwards, the scene becomes more animated; and one is constantly looking to the right and left, fearing to miss some new and curious sight. Many of the houses are lofty, and the ornaments outside carved in wood. Presently, we pass what I am told is a Jain temple, and I strain my eyes to look inside, but only see the pillars and external ornaments, painted red and green, and I wonder who the Jains *can be.* Some are pointed out, wearing very high turbans, passing in and out of the building. I learn they are a sect of Buddhists, and long to know all about them; but there is no time for hearing more just now. A Brahmin priest passes, he is turbanless, his hair floating in the breeze, his white robes falling in ample folds around him; in one hand he holds a copper drinking vessel; in the other, a few sacred flowers—an offering to some god in a temple close by. To the right is a Musjid, or Mussulman temple, into which the followers of the prophet are crowding for their evening devotions. Near us is a Fakir, or religious (Mussulman) fanatic, with a long beard, calling out to passers-by for alms; close to him stands a Hindoo saint who has devoted himself by a vow to a life of begging, meditation, and idleness;

his face and matted hair are besmeared with ashes, as also is his body, on which he has as little covering as may be. I have scarcely time to look at this unpleasant specimen of humanity, when I see a group of women, with their heavy anklets, 'making a tinkling with their feet,' their sarees folded over their heads and persons, and carrying little chubby children on their shoulders, or astride on their hips; and now these are lost to sight, a fresh group appears, consisting of Hindoo women of various castes, clothed in jackets and sarees of divers colours, and wearing 'the chains and the bracelets,' 'the ear-ring,' 'the rings and the nose-rings.' (Isaiah III, 16). I must not forget the toe-rings, which are thick and heavy, and must cause, I should think, some pain and inconvenience to the wearers. On their heads they bear large copper water-pots, and they walk with a stately and measured step, though the crowd presses on them, some not even holding the vessels with one hand. Next comes a hackery, or peasant's cart, drawn by two pretty little Indian bullocks, with rings through their noses, through which a cord is drawn, which serves the purpose of a bridle. In the vehicle are several native women, returning from a féte, with flowers in their black hair; then a European carriage, painted light blue, and elaborately mounted in silver, in which a fat native gentleman is sitting, rushes furiously past driven by a Parsee coachman.

On all sides, jostling and passing each other, are seen Persian dyers; Bannian shop-keepers;

Chinese with long tails; Arab horse-dealers; Abyssinian youths, servants of the latter; Bohras (pedlars); toddy-drawers, carrying large vessels on their heads; Armenian priests, with flowing robes and beards; Jews in long tunics and mantles, their dress, half Persian, half Moorish; Portuguese, small under-sized men, clad in scanty short trousers, white jackets and frequently wearing white linen caps. Then we meet the Parsee priest, all in white from top to toe, except his dark face and black beard; Hindoo, Mussulman, and Portuguese nurses or attendants on European children and ladies, mingle in the crowd, and everywhere I see something new to look at every moment. What bits to sketch! what effects here! what colouring there!

At times the crowd is broken into by the gorah-wallahs belonging to the carriage of a 'burrah bibi' (great lady), wife of a European sahib, 'high up' in the military or civil service of the Honourable Company.

I have as yet said nothing of the shops, where the sellers sit squatting and waiting for purchasers. In the East, it is usual for all the members of a trade to live in the same vicinity, and thus we find a row of many shops here, all tenanted by coppersmiths, there, by cutters of stones, by vendors of gold and silver ornaments, of wearing apparel for the natives, each having their proper *locale*—a custom we read of among the ancient Jews; for 'Zedekiah the king commanded that they should commit Jeremiah into the court of the prison,' and that 'they should give him daily a piece of bread out of the *bakers' street.*' (Jeremiah, XXXVII, 21.) Amidst such a variety of novel sights it is impossible to note all. There are sellers of flowers for weddings—of flowers for offerings at temples; shops where rice, split peas, salt, oil, vinegar, ghee or clarified butter, made from the milk of the buffalo, betel-nuts, pawn-leaves, and fruits are retailed; beside confectioners, dealers in snuff and tobacco, or copper vessels for household use among the natives, and lamps, some of which are very curious, and indeed classical in form. Here and there the foliage of palms, and other trees, particularly that of the pipul, mingles with the houses. From the branches of the last-named tree hang clusters of flying foxes, head downwards, apparently by one leg: these animals are in a dormant state from sunrise to sunset, at which time they show signs of life, and commence their nocturnal wanderings. They have the wings, body, and legs of the bat, and the head of a fox most exquisitely and delicately formed, resembling that of the quadruped alike in colour, shape, and fur. The body is generally about a foot long, and the wings, when extended, from three to four feet between the extremities. By day, when seen suspended from the pipul, they look like very large *cotelettes á la maintenon* attached to the frailest boughs; but while flying, in the dusk of the evening, they have the appearance of crows of a large size. Their flight is heavy, and apparently slow, as if they were never quite awake.

The variety of colour exhibited in the turbans and costumes of the natives, astonishes a European. The dresses of the men (at least of those who do wear clothes) are frequently white, but the turbans are of all colours, and the forms various,—the reds are particularly fine; indeed, all the dyes are beautiful.

Such were my impressions on my first drive through the native town of Bombay, and, after all, I saw very little compared with what there was to see.

Chow-Chow, 1857, Vol. I, pp. 4—11.

The Horse Bazaar

BALCARRES RAMSAY.

As you roam through the bazaars you will often come upon an Arab horse-dealer's stable; most of them are commission stables—that is to say, an Arab merchant will bring a batch of some twenty or thirty to sell, and will sit all day smoking with oriental indifference, not even rising to receive you. In the hottest weather these Arabs were wrapped in thick woollen garments. The Persian dealers wear an open tunic over a light vest and wide sleeves, with a high conical fur cap. The horses of high caste were kept apart from the others, and only brought out when likely purchasers appeared. Amongst the rest, all that average fourteen hands were bought for the cavalry and artillery; so that at the dealer's you can only buy horses of great value or mere ponies. These dealers were apparently very indifferent as to selling their horses. The probability was, if a stranger went in, he would with difficulty induce them to bring out their valuable horses; and then they asked ten times their value, and if remonstrated with, coolly ordered the horses to be taken back, taking no further notice of the intending purchaser. This was not flattering to the vanity of the stranger, accustomed to the civility and blandishments of an English horse-dealer; but the fact is, these men were aware that every horse of value that is landed was known to all the gentlemen whose patronage they were anxious to secure, and to some of whom they would be sure to sell the horse. And they would rather sell a likely horse for the turf to a well-known man, who would bring him out on the race-course, at a lower figure, than to a stranger at a high price; for they have a very laudable ambition, and crowds of them may be seen every morning at the race-course. They generally gave a cup to be run for, and were therefore glad to see their best horses pass into the hands of such men as Elliot, Blood, Howard, Coghlan, &c.

A person newly arrived in the country should be very careful as to trusting to his own judgment in buying a horse, as however good a judge he may be at home, it is impossible that he can at once understand all the points of the Arab, especially in the miserable condition they are landed from the Gulf, apparently only fitted for the knacker's yard—frequently cruelly mangled by the ropes which confined them, and hardly able to stand. I was recommended by Captain Thornhill, the remount agent, to give 1200 rupees for a miserable-looking animal, to my idea only fit for the knacker's yard. He could not stand, had a frightful gash on his flank, and two hind legs the size of mill-posts. However, acting on the best advice, I bought him, and he turned out one of the handsomest horses in the Presidency. My advice to the new-comer is, distrust your own judgment. There are always men long resident who know every Arab by heart, and will help you to choose.

I was never tired of rambling in the bazaars when I had a chance. Captain Basil Hall, the celebrated traveller, experienced the same delight, and was often laughed at by his Bombay friends for his love of wandering about them.

Rough Recollections, 1882, Vol. I, pp. 79–81.

A Gay Street

LOUIS ROUSSELET.

Girgaum, the Bréda Street of Bombay, is a vast wood of cocoa-nut trees, which extends from the bazaars to Chowpatti, at the head of Back Bay. In the midst of this picturesque forest are innumerable huts, half concealed by a rich tropical vegetation, in which reside bayadères of every nation, and of all colours,—the demi-monde of this immense capital. As the night draws on, the depths of the wood become lighted up ; on all sides resound the tom-tom, the guitar, and the voice of song ; and the illumined windows are filled with women in dazzling costumes. One would say that a great fête was in preparation. The uninitiated stranger stops, hesitates, asks himself whether it is for him that these garlands of flowers have been suspended, these coloured lamps hung out. But soon it would seem as if all the nations in the world had arranged a meeting in this wood of Cythera. The refreshment-rooms in the taverns are thronged by Europeans, Malays, Arabs, and Chinese. Far into the night will the songs resound, and the lamps shed their light; then, when the morning is come, all will return to gloom, and the worthy English merchant, driving past in his shigram, or office carriage, may wonder who can be the inhabitants of this sombre grove.

India and its Native Princes, 1882, pp 11-12.

Scenes in the Bazaars

BALCARRES RAMSAY.

It was a constant source of pleasure to me to pass through the bazaars. A year's residence did not wear off the novelty. The only feeling that generally possesses the resident with regard to them is how to reach his destination without passing through them, but to me they were replete with interest: Hindoo temples, Mussulman mosques, Portuguese Christian churches, with quaint and curiously carved doors, and every sort of architectural curiosity, present themselves to you at every turn. People of every nation are sauntering about in rich and varied costume. The stately Parsee or fire-worshipper, the grave Mussulman, Hindoos of every caste—the distinguishing mark of which is a daub of paint (white, red or yellow) on his forehead—the Persian horse-dealer, the Sindee, the Greek, the Chinaman, the Bokhara and Cabul merchants; the Africans—conspicuous for their want of costume—most of them employed on board our steamers as firemen. Now you come upon a grand Mohammedan festival, then a Catholic procession of the Host; while at a corner of the street you see the Hindoo prostrate before a stone daubed with red paint and covered with flowers, his god.

Rcugh Recollections, 1882, Vol. I, pp. 77-78.

The Crawford Market

WALTER CRANE.

The Crawford Market is one of the sights of Bombay. Outside, with its steep roofs, belfry, and projecting eaves, it has a rather English Gothic look, but inside the scene is entirely oriental, crowded with natives in all sorts of colours, moving among fish, fruit, grain, and provisions of all kinds, buying and selling amid a clamour of tongues—a busy scene of colour and variety, in a symphony of smells, dominated by that of the smoke of joss-sticks kept burning at some of the stalls as well as a suspicion of opium, which pervades all the native quarters in Indian cities. There is a sort of court or garden enclosed by the buildings, and here the live stock is kept, all sorts of birds and animals.

India Impressions, 1907, p. 26.

Flower and Fruit Market

MRS. GUTHRIE.

G. kindly took me to see the markets before the heat had tarnished the early beauty of the flowers and fruit. We found the [Crawford] Markets exquisitely clean and admirably arranged. The flower, fruit, and vegetable market is a circular building, lighted from above, which encloses a beautiful public garden.

Never had I seen such a luxurious profusion of beautiful flowers and fruits as was set forth upon the white marble slabs, which sloped up on each side of the broad promenade, which was thronged, not crowded, by endless streams of people, in strange costumes and gay apparel, ever passing into strange combinations, like the bits of coloured glass in a kaleidoscope. There were pyramids of flowers, not set forth in the European fashion, but picked with little stem and no leaves, and heaped up carelessly. There were lovely pale pink roses, and an endless variety of double jessamine flowers, pink and white, probably destined to be threaded together for the adornment of temples. The tuberoses were almost too sweet. There were gorgeous hillocks of the double yellow marigold, to be woven into coronets for women, their intense colour being well calculated to set off the dark skins and shiny black hair which they were meant to adorn. Some of the smaller flowers and fragrant leaves, made into tiny sprigs, were intended to be thrown into the finger-glasses which figure at every Anglo-Indian's meal, the lemon-scented verbena being often employed for this purpose.

Glowing fruits peeped forth from beds of cool green leaves. The more delicate sorts were placed in wicker baskets, artistically lined with pieces of the plantain leaf cut into shape. We bought one of these little boats, with its cargo of dull-hued lilac figs, luscious and small, with just one tear of liquid sugar upon each—the true *goutte d'or*. Among the fruits with which I was familiar, were many species which I had never seen before; but to enumerate them would be tedious. The vegetables were of infinite variety, including gourds of the most grotesque forms, which nature must have imagined in a mirthful hour. Some of them were intended for eating, but others would be carefully cleaned out, and the hard rinds converted into vessels for water, and other liquids. The capsicums and chillies were curious and pretty, some being large, shiny, and intensely green, while others were small and red and pointed, and made one hot to look at them. There were many varieties of the egg-plant, some of them white and smooth like ivory, others resembling balls of gold; and the long purple aubergines were very handsome. I could have spent hours with satisfaction in these markets, which were the finest I had ever seen; but time pressed and we passed into the interior garden, a charming, cool, and verdant spot, in which there were numerous varieties of the palm tribe, all sorts of velvety, long-leaved plants and trembling ferns of exquisite beauty. It was strange to see caneless clumps of the caladium of tender green, spotted with white and red, along with other plants, only at home to be seen in a hot-house, where one lingers for a moment, in mortal dread of catching one's death of cold on again breathing the raw air outside. I should have liked to have explored the fish market, which no doubt contained many curious and strange varieties; but the sun was up, and as we hesitated at the door of the market, we perceived that its atmosphere was not as odoriferous as that of the floral Paradise which we had quitted.

My Year in an Indian Fort, 1877, Vol, I, pp. 54-57.

The Bazaars during the Feast of Lamps

SIDNEY LOW.

Get into your gharry and tell the driver to take you by the Grant Road past the Mumbadevi Tank, along Abdul Rahman Street, by the Bhendi Bazaar, and about the native quarter generally. You will not lack entertainment: especially if you strike Bombay, as I did, on the eve of a Royal visit, and at the new moon of the month Kartik, which is the Hindu Feast of Lanterns.

The night, indeed, like Prospero's isle, is 'full of noises': the Indian night always is, even in the quieter suburbs of the towns, for there are the noises of beast and bird, as well as the sounds made by human hands and throats. The field crickets and grasshoppers are chirping with a loud metallic clank; the grey-backed crows, which you have noticed all day feeding on dead rats and other carrion, retire to their nests with raucous cawings; weird squeals and chatterings are heard from a thicket, and you know—that is, you know when your driver tells you—that they are emitted by the monkeys who are swinging in the boughs.

When you reach the native bazaar, your coachman must drive at a foot's-pace, with many stoppages. The narrow twisting streets are swarming with people, spreading all over the roadway in close groups and solid columns. You will make better progress by leaving your carriage and walking; besides, this will give you an opportunity of observing the people in their various types and tribes.

The bazaar is always crowded from early morning until late night; it is always full of people walking, sitting, lying on the ground, jostling against one another like ants. But perhaps the throng is a little more than normal on this Feast of Lamps, the Diwali, which is one of the great festivals of the Hindu year. The Diwali is held in honour of Lakhshmi, the Venus of the Indian Pantheon, the wife of Vishnu the Preserver. Lakhshmi, like her Hellenic antitype, arose out of the foam of the sea waves, and she is the Goddess of Beauty; but she is also the Goddess of Wealth and Prosperity, and is therefore held in special honour by shopkeepers and tradesmen.

On the Feast of Lamps the gains of the year are dedicated to the goddess, and every house is lighted for her. The larger Europeanised stores in the bazaar, the 'cheap jacks,' where they sell all sorts of things, from bicycles to safety-pins, the motor garage where the wealthy native buys his up-to-date car, are hung with tiers of electric lights and glow-lamps; but each little square booth has its own small illumination. All the shops are open, and the owners are seen sitting beside the implements and objects of their trade. The goldsmith has rows of candles to set off his golden bowls, his cups and chains and jewellery work; the *shroff*, the small money-lender or usurer, piles up his account-books in a heap, with a kerosene lamp on top. A white Hindu temple is all festooned with ropes and wreaths of flowers; a yellow Jain chapel sparkles with colouredo lights, and looks rather like a Paris café, with its open rooms and balconies and lounging groups. Only the Mohammedan mosque stands grimly shut and dark and silent; for Diwali is a Hindu festival, and the children of the Faith have no part in it. There were times when the celebration was a fruitful source of faction-fighting and serious riot. But the vigilant Bombay constables, little sturdy men in blue, are scattered freely among the crowds, and in the very centre of the whole turmoil, where the chief Mohammedan street crosses the Hindu bazaar, there is a small square brick building, which is the police post. Here a couple of sepoys are talking to a khaki-clad sowar of the mounted force standing beside his horse, ready to ride to the barracks for assistance, if need be; and against the door-post leans a tall young Englishman, in white uniform and helmet, surveying the passing stream of humanity with good-humoured, but not inattentive, indifference—a symbol of that impartial tolerance, combined with the vigorous assertion of public authority in the maintenance of order, which is the attitude of the British *raj* towards the creeds and sects of India.

A Vision of India, 1906, pp. 12–16.

Streets During The Diwali

MRS. JOHN WILSON.

On returning from chapel at 9 o'clock this evening, the whole native town was illuminated in honour of the Diwali. A torrent of light seemed to issue from every house; lamps were suspended in gardens, and in the streets; and the air reverberated with incessant and deafening clamour of the countless throngs who walked to and fro in the bazaars. The heat was oppressive, and the atmosphere heavily charged with electricity. Above our heads, the sky was clear and beautiful; an innumerable multitude of stars walked their midnight rounds; and you can scarcely imagine the relief gained in looking upwards to their pure light, for it was impossible to shut our eyes upon the rude but splendid exhibitions in the streets. The lightning issuing from a distant cloud had a magnificent and awful appearance, and reminded me of the accounts given in Scripture of the advent of the Son of Man, and of His terrible majesty, when He shall come in the clouds of heaven with power and great glory.

Dr. Wilson's Memoir of Mrs. John wilson, 1838, page 429.

The Streets During The King's Visit, 1911

TEH HON. JOHN FORTESCUE.

The crowd was immense, and the variety of shades indescribable–here a group of men in rich dark-red turbans, with perhaps one of vivid grass green flaming among them ; there a group of children, wide-eyed and open-mouthed, with one or two little maids in blazing crimson silk huddled into their midst ; there again a body of Parsi ladies in simple gowns of the palest pink, blue or dove-colour, draped on one side with light transparent muslin in graceful folds, which made the delicate hues more dainty still. There was no rest for the eye in the ever-changing feast of colour.

The most striking of all was the scene in the quaint irregular buildings and narrow streets of the native town. There is no appearance of wealth in the houses, the stucco being often decay ed and fortunately rarely repainted; but there are quaint wooden stairways, balconies and loggias, which the wealthy owners had beautified with the best and simplest of all street-decorations by simply throwing over them rugs and carpets, or occasionally a great sheet of rich dark silk shot with gold. The houses were crammed with spectators. The housetops and the highest stories were occupied chiefly by peeping women, nearly all of whom displayed at least a scrap of costly red material; the lower windows were simply packed with tier upon tier of heads—I counted over thirty in one of no extraordinary size—and even the steep narrow scraps of verandah over the native shops were swarming with men and boys.

Royal Visit to India, 1912, pp. 110-111.

Legions of Dark-hued Faces

SIR HENRY CRAIK.

As we pass through the streets, what are our impressions? The countless legions of dark-hued faces, the strange rarity of the white complexion. It is not that we are outnumbered. To all intents and purposes, so far as numbers go, we simply do not count. And next, amongst these countless dark visages, the endless variety of physiognomy, with only one common attribute, that of absolute inscrutability. They are solemn and self-important, or careless and self-forgetful; they are dreamy and ferocious, melancholy and merry; but all alike are to us simply masks. They look at us as if they were divided from us by centuries, and as if they were gazing at sticks and stones. Their lives lie hidden away from us by an impenetrable veil. In London we hear glib talk of the need of greater sympathy with the native. What easy words to utter!

Next the quietness, the coolness, the patience, the reserve of authority, of the few white faces that we meet. No wonder that with men like these, who know their work, its hard conditions and its dangers, and have learned to face it, the recklessness of loose tongues is met by a momentary anger, perhaps, but, after the first moment, with the apathy of contempt. There is something of strain, and no great measure of light-heartedness, in the faces of that ruling class; but no fretfulness and nervousness, and no assumption of bullying or domineering. They are there to do their duty; and almost the only comment, if we refer to the wild mouthings of self-advertising frivolity, is, "why heed him?"

Impressions of India, 1908, pp. 11-13.

Modern Town and Native Town

MRS. GUTHRIE.

We passed through the modern town, which is full of fine buildings, public offices, and private houses. Handsome equipages rolled along, but the tall dark men, with peculiar liveries and naked feet, who stood behind each well-appointed carriage, had a strange appearance. The reclining ladies were such as may be seen any fine afternoon in Hyde Park or the Bois. Far more interesting were the numbers of Parsi women who were walking about in short satin skirts of the most brilliant hues—an exquisite pale cherry and an emerald green appeared to be the favourite colours—flowers were in their glossy black hair, and they wore quantities of gold lace and handsome ornaments.

When we reached the native town how changed was the scene. Europe was left behind, and the East was realized—the narrow, winding streets, the open shops, small, but highly characteristic, where the owner, Hindoo, Mahomedan, or Jew, squatted amidst his wares. Those of the same trade congregated together, the workers in brass and copper, with bright vessels of curious shape, such as the *lota* with its narrow neck and bulging sides, the lamp of many beaks, the little bells with images at the top, used in the temples. Then there are the leather workers, from whom one may select embroidered slippers, turned up at the point, saddle bags, and trappings for horses, covered with gold and silver, and cowrie shells. There were rows of wood-carvers, who work upon the blackwood furniture peculiar to the Bombay Presidency, and fine specimens of their art were placed about to attract attention. The general merchant had his small store, heaped from floor to ceiling with bales of cloth, gaudy shawls, and cottons, with various patterns printed upon them, vases, and griffins, and pagodas, for furniture, and dark but deep-hued checks and stripes for garments. There were little niches where betel-leaves and pungent seeds were sold, and, most picturesque of all, were the shops of the Indian druggists, where one was sure to see a venerable old man with a flowing white beard; probably a learned man, and one who possibly dabbled in magic, his drugs ranged about in jars of china, which would have made the fortune of a European bric-a-brac shop. By a Christian these jars were not, alas! to be bought for love or money.

No two houses were alike, some were tall and pink, others were squat and yellow, and both perhaps were neighboured by dwellings of a superior order, which stood back, not hidden, but sheltered by plantain-trees, and tall cocoa-nut palms, spreading their elegant fan-shaped leaves against a crimson background, for the fervid sun was setting. These houses had in general two tiers of wooden verandahs, with shutters. The ground-floor was partly open; and supported by pillars of wood, richly carved, and on the projecting beams and latticed frames there was many a quaint device. I was charmed with these irregular old dwellings. A dead wall, with the pyramidal summit of a Jain temple appearing above it, would vary the scene, or a mosque, with broad dome and airy pinnacles, and sometimes we came upon a Hindoo temple, adorned with highly-coloured mythological subjects, with lights in its interior, which cast a glow upon some hideous copper idol, or figure of stone, daubed with red paint, and greasy with libations of melted butter. Every step was a surprise.

My Year in an Indian Fort, 1877, Vol. 1. pp. 44-48.

The Bazaar to the Artistic Eye

VAL. PRINSEP.

What a sight the bazaars of Bombay present to the artistic eye! All sorts of Indian forms, from black to white; all sorts of dresses, from nothing at all to tinsel and *kincaub*; colours of the most entrancing criginality, and forms of the wildest beauty. Every day since my arrival have I been wandering through these streets, and yet I feel quite dazed and have done absolutely nothing. The infinite variety and "rummyness" of the whole thing quite unhinges one.

Imperial India, 1879, pp. 13-14.

The Native Town

EMMA ROBERTS.

The native town extends considerably on either side of the principal avenue, one road leading through the cocoa-nut gardens, presenting a great variety of very interesting features; that to the left is more densely crowded, there being a large and well-frequented cloth bazaar, besides a vast number of shops and native houses, apparently of considerable importance. Here the indications shown of wealth and industry are exceedingly gratifying to an eye delighting in the sight of a happy and flourishing population. There are considerable spaces of ground between these leading thoroughfares, which by occasional peeps down intersecting lanes, seem to be covered with a huddled confusion of buildings, and, until the improvements which have recently taken place, the whole of the town seems to have been nearly in the same state.

The processes of widening, draining, pulling down, and rebuilding, appear to have been carried on very extensively; and though much, perhaps, remains to be done in the back settlement, where buffaloes may be seen wading through the stagnant pools, the eye is seldom offended, or the other senses disagreeably assailed, in passing through this populous district. The season is, however, so favourable, the heat being tempered by cool airs, which render the sunshine endurable, that Bombay, under its present aspect, may be very different from the Bombay of the rains or of the very hot weather. The continual palm-trees, which, shooting up in all directions, add grace and beauty to every scene, must form terrible receptacles for malaria; the fog and mist are said to cling to their branches and hang round them like a cloud, when dispersed by sun or wind elsewhere; the very idea suggesting fever and ague.

Though, as I have before remarked, the contrast between the muslined millions of Bengal and the less tastefully clad populace of Bombay is unfavourable, still the crowds that fill the streets here are animated and picturesque. There is a great display of the liveliest colours, the turbans being frequently of the brightest of yellows, crimsons, or greens.

The number of vehicles employed is quite extraordinary, those of the merely respectable classes being chiefly bullock-carts; these are of various descriptions, the greater number being of an oblong square, and furnished with seats across (after the fashion of our taxed carts), in which twelve persons, including women and children, are frequently accommodated. It is most amusing to see the quantity of heads squeezed close together in a vehicle of this kind, and the various contrivances resorted to in order to accommodate a more than sufficient number of personages in other conveyances, not so well calculated to hold them. Four in a buggy is a common complement, and six or nine persons will cram themselves into so small a space, that you wonder how the vehicle can possibly contain the bodies of all the heads seen looking out of it. The carts are chiefly open, but there are a few covered *rhuts*, the conveyances probably of rich Hindu or Mohamedan ladies, who do not content themselves, like the Parsees, with merely covering their heads with the veil.

Young Parsee women of the better class are frequently to be seen in carriages with their male relations, nor do they object to appear publicly in the streets following wedding processions. They are the only well-dressed or nice-looking women who drive or walk about the streets or roads. The lower classes of females in Bombay are the most unprepossessing people I ever saw. In Bengal, the saree, though rather too scanty, is a graceful costume, and at a little distance appears to be a modest covering. Here it is worn very differently, and without the slighest attempt at delicacy or grace. the drapery being in itself insufficient, and rendered more offensive by the method of its arrangement.

Overland Journey to Bombay, 1841, pp. 225-228.

A City of Strange Contrasts

S. M. EDWARDES.

Hark, through the hum of the crowd, above the rumble of wheels and the jangle of bullock-bells, rises the plaintive chant of the Arab hymn-singers, leading the corpse of a brother to the last "mukam" or resting-place; while but a short distance away,—only a narrow street's length,—the drum and flageolets escort the stalwart young Memon bridegroom unto the house of the bride. Thus it is ever in this city of strange contrasts,—Life and Death in closest juxtaposition, the hymn in honour of the Prophet's birth blending with the elegy to the dead. Bagpipes are not unknown in the Mussalman quarters of Bombay; and not infrequently you may watch a crescent of ten or twelve wild Arab sailors in flowing brown gowns and parti-coloured head-scarves, treading a measure to the rhythm of the bagpipes blown by a younger member of their crew. The words of the tune are the old words "La illaha illahlah," set to an air endeared from centuries past to the desert-roving Bedawin, and long after distance has dulled the tread of the dancing feet, the plaintive notes of the refrain reach you upon the night breeze. About midnight the silent streets are filled with the long-drawn cry of the shampooer or barber, who, by kneading and patting the muscles, induces sleep for the modest sum of four annas; and barely has his voice died away than the Muezzin's call to prayer falls on the ear of the sleeper, arouses in his heart thoughts of the past glory of his Faith, and forces him from his couch to wash and bend in prayer before Him "Who fainteth not, Whom neither-sleep nor fatigue overtaketh."

By-Ways of Bombay, 1913 2nd. ed. pp. 17-18.

Drive Through the Town

MRS: ELWOOD.

It being Sunday, which is with the natives as much a holiday, perhaps I should rather say, *idle* day, as with the English, they were likewise taking their evening drives and promenades. It has been said, that Bombay is more populous, and contains a greater variety of inhabitants than is to be found so small a space in any other part of the world; and certainly the scene which presented itself, and which I subsequently found was of no unfrequent occurrence, was one of the most amusing and singular I ever beheld. The difference of costumes, and equipages, reminded me of the two or three last days of the Carnival at Florence. There was the grave and respectable looking Parsee, who is the decendant of the ancient Persians, looking as consequential and as happy as possible, in his clean white vest, and ugly, stiff, purple cotton turban, with a shawl thrown over his shoulders like a lady, driving an English buggy in the English fashion. Then followed a hackery, or common cart of the country, creaking slowly along, drawn by oxen, and appearing as if about to tumble down, with a Hindoo family; the men half naked, but invariably with turbans on their head; the women, clothed in the saree or long piece of cloth or silk, which is twisted round their persons so as to fall gracefully in folds to the feet, like the drapery of an antique statue, and, after forming a petticoat, is brought over the right shoulder, across the bosom, and falls over the head like a veil. This, with a small bodice fastening before or behind, according to fancy, constitutes the whole of their attire, and it is infinitely prettier, and far more elegant than the Frank female costume.

The saree so completely covers the whole of the person, and so effectually conceals the figure of the wearer, that it is likewise infinitely more modest and delicate than our style of dress, and it also possesses the advantage of being more quickly put on; one minute will suffice a Hindoo belle to arrange her attire, but they make up for the simplicity of this part of their toilet by a profusion of ear and nose rings, and ornaments of every sort and description, which are frequently composed of precious stones and valuable pearls. Necklaces of gold mohurs, or Venetian sequins, bangles of gold and silver on their arms and ankles, and costly rings on their toes, frequently decorate the persons of the females of the humblest and meanest classes, for, as there are no such things as savings-banks in India, they convert their money into these trinkets, as the most portable method of carrying their riches about with them though sometimes, in times of war this has given rise to most dreadful personal cruelties.

After the hackery, would dash by an English Officer in full regimentals, or a civilian in the light Anglo-Indian costume, on spirited Arabs, followed perhaps by native grooms in turbans and white cotton vests. Then would appear a couple of Persians, carefully guiding a pair of horses in an English curricle, attired in long flowing robes, and graceful and becoming turbans, with peculiarly fine features, handsome and intelligent countenances, and dark beards sweeping their breasts. In heavy coaches, lighter landaulet, or singular looking shigrampoes, might be seen, bevies of British fair, in Leghorn hats, silk bonnets, blond caps, and Brussels lace veils. Feathers waving, flowers blooming, and ribands streaming, in all the freaks and fancies of every French and English fashion, which may have prevailed in Europe, during the last half dozen years. In India the veriest *adorateur des modes* must be content always to be *one* year behind the belles of London and of Paris and, in the out stations, at least two or three—but, however, there is no deficiency of finery, whatever there may be of *ton,* in the appearance and attire of the ladies of Bombay. These would be driven by a coachman, and attended by footmen in Parsee, Mahometan, or Hindoo attire, whilst a *Ghorawalla* or horse keeper, would run by the side of the carriage on foot, and keep up with it, though driven at a tremendous rate, carrying a painted chowree in his hand, with which he would keep the flies from annoying the horses.

In addition to these, might be seen numerous Portuguese, whose very dark complexions and short, curly, coal-black hair, looked more singular and more foreign in their white cotton Frank costume than even the Asiatics in their loosely flowing robes. There were also Roman Catholic priests in their robes, respectable-looking Armenians with their families, numerous half-castes in neat English dresses, and a few Chinese, looking exactly as if some of the figures on a China jar had stepped forth to take an evening walk. These were most effeminate in appearance, with a long silky plaid of dark hair, twisted neatly round their heads; yet their sleepy countenances, and flat and singular features, had an air of stupid benevolence, such as may be seen in the figures of Bhood, or Bhudda. The wild looking Arab, and the majestic Turk in his magnificent and superb attire, were of rare occurrence. The Cutchee "Burra Sahib" in a fine gilt palanquin, with a turban a yard high, richly adorned with gold, was also to be seen, and there was an endless variety of Mussulmans, and Hindoos of different castes; the Holy

Brahmin, with the sacred Zennar [janoi] or cord, suspended from his shoulder; the Purbhoo or writer-caste, with their very neat turbans; the Bunyans in their deep-red, and the Bengalese with their flat ones; the Maharattas, the Malabarese, the Malays, and the Boras, who are said to be Mahometanized Jews, and who are the pedlars of the country. In short, every religion, every caste, and every profession, of almost every nation, from the shores of China to the banks of the Thames. Even in a fancy ball in London, or during the Carnival in Italy where every one strives to be in a particular and original costume, it would be impossible to meet with a greater variety, than presented itself in this short drive, which indeed was only what may be seen every day in the Island of Bombay.

Narrative of a Journey Overland, 1830,
Vol II. pp. 374-378.

Bhendy Bazaar

WILLIAM SHEPHERD.

We enter the Bhendi Bazaar, very different from our English idea formed upon the model of that in Oxford street, or Soho Square. This is one of the principal thoroughfares of the native town, quite separate from the English portion, where stand the British Hotel, Town-hall, pay offices, Cathedral, banking-houses, post-offices, and shops of Parsees and English. This is a long, tolerably wide, irregular street, with high irregular houses on either side, containing many windows, built principally of wood, some of the projecting parts rudely, yet rather richly carved, some painted, all full of dirt and darkness, and crowded with inhabitants. The lower story is usually devoted to the goods to be sold, where the vendor sits, cross-legged, on the same shelf as his bread, cakes, flour, grains, oil, stuffs, calicos, earthenware, wine, or whatever other article he has for sale, lazily smoking his "hubble-bubble;" or, half dozing. If he be a Persian or Mahomedan, leaning upon dirty cushions, and sublimely indifferent to purchasers.

Slowly we drove through the crowded bazaar, crowded with vehicles of all kinds, rough carts, buggies conveying drunken sailors to and from places, where they are easily deprived of their money and their senses, carriages of rich Hindoos and Parsees, miserable shake-down shandrydans of all sorts; men, women, children, dogs, horses and bullocks in gharries and otherwise, all straggling about, with no concern for their own safety, or the convenience of others.

We drive on towards the large Tank, situated in an open space, where four cross roads meet in this bazaar; frequented at certain hours by picturesque groups of natives, in gay garments, and almost no garments, with water vessels on their heads or pendant, (held by ropes from a bending bamboo yoke,) red, yellow, black rudely formed of clay. "Bhistees," with their humped bullocks, bearing water-skins, "Paniwallas," stooping under theirs; women, with long flowing robes, silver bracelets and anklets, a brass water "chatti," filled, and carried gracefully on the head, reminding one of the fair Rebecca; bullocks (drawing carts) brought there for refreshment, and also for washing the beasts, and perchance, their drivers, who habituated to an extremely minute portion of clothing, have little of that article to remove, and not any scruples, in performing their ablutions in public;—these various groups, approaching, retiring, and surrounding the well, present a most Eastern and interesting appearance.

From Bombay to Bushire, 1857, pp. 15-21.

Stroll Through the Streets

SIDNEY LOW.

The thing to see in Bombay is Bombay itself. It has no sight to show, no spectacle to offer, at all equal to that presented by its own streets, seething with miscellaneous humanity, especially if one can examine them at leisure and on foot, mingling with the populace and peering into the open houses. In the East people do not live in sealed compartments, and the front door, the shield of our own cherished domesticity, can hardly be said to exist. The climate and the local habits are opposed to it. Before the sun has risen, or after his setting, everybody seeks space and air and coolness out of doors; nor is there any jealous shrinking from observation, even in the day time. People do all sorts of things in public which to our thinking should be transacted in privacy, such as dressing, shaving, washing, and sleeping, and, in spite of the caste rules and religious restrictions, even a good deal of eating.

Going into one of the large sheds in the quarter of Bombay where the hand-loom weavers carry on their work, I saw two men crouching in the dust by the outside wall. They proved to be a barber and his client. The latter was naked to the waist; the barber, a respectable old gentleman in robe and turban, was sitting on the ground beside his victim, on whom he was operating in a very complete fashion, passing his razor not merely over the chin, but over the head, arms, and shoulders, and performing the whole toilet in full view of passers-by and of various other persons engaged in minor manufacturing or domestic avocations at intervals of a few yards along the wall of the shed. So it is everywhere. As you pass along the streets of the bazaar you can look right into half the houses. The shops are simply boxes, set on end, with the lids off. You can, if you please, stand and watch the baker rolling his flat loaves, the tailor stitching and cutting, the coppersmith hammering at his bowls and dishes, the jeweller drawing out gold and silver wire over his little brazier. The Indian townsman does not mind being looked at. He is accustomed to it. He passes his life in the midst of a crowd.

A Vision of India, 1906, pp. 23-24.

A Drive Through the Native Bazaar

WALTER CRANE.

A drive through the native bazaar of Bombay is a revelation. The carriage works its way with difficulty through the narrow, irregular street, crowded with natives in every variety of costume forming a wonderful moving pattern of brilliant colour, punctuated by swarthy faces, gleaming eyes, and white teeth. Shops of every kind line each side of the way, and these are rather dark and cavernous openings, shaded by awnings and divided by posts or carved pillars, on the lowest story, raised from the level of the streets by low platforms, which serve the purposes of counter and working bench to the native merchant or craftsman, who squats upon it, and often unites the two functions in his own person. He generally carries on his work in the presence of his whole family, apparently. All ages and sexes crowd in and about the shops, carrying on a perpetual *conversazione*, and the bazaar literally swarms with dusky, turbaned faces, varied by the deep red sari of the Hindu women, with their glittering armlets and anklets, or the veiled Mohammedan in her—well, pyjamas!

The older house fronts above the shops were often rich with carving and colour, the upper storeys being generally supported over the open shop by four columns. It reminded one of the arrangement of a mediaeval street, as also in its general aspect, the shops being mostly work-shops; and, as in the old days in Europe, could be seen different crafts in full operation, while the finished products of each were displayed for sale. There were tailors stitching away at garments, coppersmiths hammering their metal into shape, leather workers, jewellers, cook-shops, and many more, the little dark shops in most cases being crowded with other figures besides those of the workers—each like a miniature stage of life with an abundance of drama going on in all. The whole bazaar, too, was gay with colour—white, green, red, orange, yellow, and purple, of all sorts of shades and tones, in turban or robe—a perfect feast for the eye.

In the course of our drive through the bazaar we met no less than three wedding processions, though rather broken and interrupted by the traffic. In one, the bridegroom (who, with the Hindus and Mohammedans, is considered the most important personage in the ceremony as well as the spectacle) was in a carriage, on his way to fetch the bride, in gorgeous raiment and with a crown upon his head. He was followed by people bearing floral trophies, perhaps intended for decoration afterwards. These consisted of gilt vases with artificial flowers in them, arranged in rows close together, and carried in convenient lengths on a plank or shelf by young men bearers.

Another of the bridegrooms was mounted on a horse, crowned and robed like a Byzantine emperor with glittering caparisons and housings, a tiny little dusky girl sitting behind him and holding on, who was said to be his little sister.

The third bridegroom we saw was veiled, in addition to the bravery of his glittering attire. Flowers were strewn by boys accompanying him, and a little bunch fell into our carriage as we waited for the procession to go by, in which, of course, the musicians went before. We afterwards passed the house where the wedding was being celebrated, the guests assembling in great numbers to the feast, a tremendous noise going on, drums beating and trumpets blowing. In one of the processions very antique-looking trumpets or horns were carried of a large size, much resembling the military horns of ancient Roman times. These were all Hindu weddings.

We had also a glimpse of a Parsee wedding. This was in the open court of a large house arcaded from the street, brilliantly illuminated where sat a great crowd of guests all attired in white.

India Impressions, 1907, pp. 26-28.

Variety in the Native Town

BARON VON HÜBNER.

One of the most attractive features of Bombay is its variety—variety in the sites, in the appearance of the streets, and in that of the population. Starting from Colaba lighthouse, we proceed northward between two sheets of water, inlets of the ocean, and reach the Apollo Bander. Thence, after an excellent and well-served luncheon at the Yacht Club, we penetrate into the town proper. First comes the Esplanade with its imposing buildings, the Secretariat, containing the various public offices, the University, and the Sailors' Home; farther on, the Anglican Cathedral built in 1718, the Town Hall, and a host of other buildings suggestive of modern English taste.

We next turn our steps towards the quarters of the Parsees and Hindoos, where we are constantly stopped, either by passers-by or by something curious, pretty, or hideous, but at any rate novel, which rivets our attention. A few paces more and we might imagine ourselves in Europe, judging by the broad thoroughfares leading towards Byculla, the northern suburb which gives its name to a club far famed in the Anglo-Indian world. Here the town ends, and noise and bustle cease abruptly. To return to Parell I had to cross an immense and somewhat lonely flat, and that at night. But no matter; in India, from Cape Comorin to the banks of the Indus and the foot of the Himalayas the European—I do not say the native–can travel by day or night in perfect safety, under the talismanic protection of his white skin.

But let us go back to the native town. With the exception of the Parsees' quarter, which, like its inhabitants, has a character of its own, this part of Bombay differs little from any other town of India. But the people are different. In the first place there are numbers of women, whereas elsewhere they are extremely scarce. Here you meet them everywhere. Look at that group; they are Parsee women. You know them by their brilliant-coloured robes and the artistic drapery of their shawls, their slim, lissom, and graceful figures; their clear complexions, their eyes fringed with long eyelashes, and the oval outline of their cheeks which, like their bare necks and arms, recall the masterpieces of Greek statuary. Great animation prevails amongst them. They are talking, gesticulating, and laughing. To see an Indian smile is a rarity, but laughter is a thing unheard of. I have indeed seen Hindoo servants draw their lips together, out of deference to their master; but it was always a grimace, and not a frank smile. Here, in good society, no one thinks of laughing, any more than we do of yawning.

In the background, beyond this bright and sunny group, under the shade of the houses, appear some Hindoo girls, each clothed in white and carrying on her head a vase of classic shape—

real goddesses descended from Olympus, disguised as simple mortals. The dervish, that scourge of native society, with his ill-favoured countenance, spiteful look, and shaggy hair and, clad with nothing but a few rags to hide his nakedness, is gliding among the busy crowd of men of every race and every creed. This multitude, now blocked by bullock-carts, now hustled back by the smart carriages of European merchants, surges to and fro between two rows of houses built of painted or carved wood-work, and in front of temples great and small, with their grotesque idols displayed on their facades. These sanctuaries are not shut in by walls, but stand with their doors opening on to the street, and devotees can go freely in and out. Verily, the old gods still reign supreme! The spirit of Christianity has not yet prevailed over this form of civilisation, which, though less perfect, is more ancient than our own. They are like two streams that meet, cross and dash against each other, but never mingle.

Through the British Empire, 1886, Vol. II. pp. 9-12.

The Jubilee Illuminations, 1887

THE LATE LADY BRASSEY.

In a pleasant, informal way, we were told off to carriages from which to see the illuminations, an escort of cavalry and of the bodyguard being provided to prevent, as far as possible, our small procession being broken up by the crowd. In the suburbs the illuminations were general but simple in design. There was a more pretentious display in front of the Veterinary Hospital, consisting of transparent pictures of horses and cows. This hospital was established by Sir Dinshaw Manockjee Petit, one of the largest mill-owners of Bombay, who has received the honour of knighthood as a Jubilee gift.

Presently the crowd became more numerous, and began to run alongside the carriages, shouting, and carrying blue lights, a compliment with which we could well have dispensed; for the smoke, the clouds of powder which they occasionally threw into the air, the dust raised as they rushed along, and the general heat and want of air in the narrow streets, had a stifling effect. The illuminations were not only artistically beautiful, but afforded a proof that members of every religion and class had united to do honour to their Sovereign. Among the most striking buildings were a Mahomedan Mosque, the lines of which were clearly defined against the starlit sky by rows of pure white lanterns; a Hindoo temple, where court within court was lighted in a simple and effective manner by butties filled with cocoa-nut oil; and several Jain temples brightly illuminated with coloured lights. In the native quarter the houses were lighted up in the peculiar Indian fashion by chandeliers suspended from the windows or across the streets—perhaps the most wonderful part of the scene.

After driving through the crowded streets we proceeded to the Apollo Bunder—now officially called the Wellington Pier—to witness the illumination of the harbour and the grand display of fireworks. The harbour, with its thousands and thousands of twinkling lights, was a sight to be remembered. Even the little 'Sunbeam,' though somewhat over-shadowed by the huge 'Bacchante', displayed with good effect a row of coloured lights from stem to stern.

As we drove home we much admired the illumination of the public gardens on Malabar Hill. The name 'Victoria' was written in lines of fire on its steep slopes, and was reflected with beautiful effect in the still waters of the bay below.

Last Voyage of the Sunbeam, 1889, pp. 62-64.

A Gay Street of a Century Ago

"ADVENTURES OF QUI HI?"

After a little drink and talk,
They ask our youth to have a walk;
"They're only going for a spree,
"An hour or two to Dungaree"

They told Qui Hi that they were sure,
He could not solitude endure;
Begg'd him to go along with them,
And they would shew him famous game.
Then said—" my boy! come let's be off;
" At all events, we'll have a laugh."

The moon majestically rose,
And did all Dungaree disclose
To Qui Hi's view, who thought the change
Of prospect was as new as strange;
For now our youth conceiv'd he'd got
Transported to some magic spot,
Where midst a wood of toddy trees,
Fairies and sprites, and fiends he sees.

Now here and there a female imp—
A police peon—perhaps a—,—
Chasing the dingy queens of beauty,
In execution of their duty:
And now a tar, hard in the wind,
For fighting, or for love inclin'd,
Come in the rear, and, with a blow,
Lays one of Goodwin's Sepoys low;
Then follows up the victory,
And all the vanquish'd sepoys fly.

Now from a darken'd corner ran,
A grave, religious, married man,
Who fancied in the woods to range,
And left his turtle for a change.

Here serious characters resort,
And quit domestic broils, for sport.

Qui Hi determin'd to retreat,
Nor for his new found friends would
wait;
But to his tent he slyly creeps,
Gets into bed, and soundly sleeps.

Adventures of Qui Hi? by Quiz, 1816, pp. 214-216.

A Sea of Turbans

MADAME BLAVATSKY.

The hall was full of natives. We four alone were representatives of Europe. Like a huge flower bed, the women displayed the bright colours of their garments. Here and there, among handsome, bronze-like heads, were the pretty, dull white faces of Parsee women, whose beauty reminded me of the Georgians. The front rows were occupied by women only. In India it is quite easy to learn a person's religion, sect, and caste, and even whether a women is married or single, from the marks painted in bright colours on everyone's forehead.

The Parsee women could only be distinguished from their Hindu sisters by very slight differences. The almost white faces of the former were separated by a strip of smooth black hair from a sort of white cap, and the whole was covered with a bright veil. The latter wore no covering on their rich, shining hair, twisted into a kind of Greek chignon. Their foreheads were brightly painted, and their nostrils adorned with golden rings. Both are fond of bright, but uniform, colours, both cover their arms up to the elbow with bangles, and both wear saris.

Behind the women a whole sea of most wonderful turbans was waving in the pit. There were long-haired Rajputs with regular Grecian features and long beards parted in the middle, their heads covered with "pagris" consisting of, at least twenty yards of finest white muslin, and their persons adorned with earrings and necklaces; there were Mahratha Brahmans, who shave their heads, leaving only one long central lock, and wear turbans of blinding red, decorated in front with a sort of golden horn of plenty; Bangas, wearing three-cornered helmets with a kind of cockscomb on the top; Kachhis, with Roman helmets; Bhills, from the borders of Rajastan, whose chins are wrapped three times in the ends of their pyramidal turbans, so that the innocent tourist never fails to think that they constantly suffer from toothache; Bengalis and Calcutta Babus, bareheaded all the year round, their hair cut after an Athenian fashion, and their bodies, clothed in the proud folds of a white *toga-virilis* in no way different from those once worn by Roman senators; Parsees, in their black, oil-cloth mitres; Sikhs, the followers of Nanak, strictly monotheistic and mystic, whose turbans are very like the Bhills', but who wear long hair down to their waists; and hundreds of other tribes.

From the Caves and Jungles of Hindustan, 1892, pp. 38-40.

Sonapur: The City of the Dead

LOUIS ROUSSELET.

"But behind this screen of palms what a change of scene may be witnessed! It is there, on the damp seashore, that past generations are reposing—the Mussulman, under his stone behind the poor European, who, blighted in his hopes, has never been permitted again to see his native land.

Numerous are the tombs of our countrymen, who sleep beneath the shade of these palm-trees, their names effaced by the parasitic plants, just as is all remembrance of them in the land to which they have been conveyed. Death comes so quickly in India that every one thinks only of himself, and forgets those who are no more. The crosses are thrown down, the stones broken; such is the aspect of these scenes of desolation, over which the rich and charitable nature of the tropics has been kind enough to throw a mantle of flowers. Nothing can be more beautiful than this immense and silent City of the Dead; the foaming waves contest with them their tombs, and every year gives up some of them to be engulfed in the deep.

During the searches I made to discover the tomb of poor Jacquemont, I used to contemplate this sheet of water and its extensive westward horizon—that quarter to which every European in this country turns when he thinks of home. Assuredly, if the dead rise from their graves, as legends aver, they have a spectacle as sublime and as melancholy as they can desire. The spot where our brave fellow-countryman Jacquemont reposes is marked by a simple stone, on which may with some difficulty be read his name. The martyr of science, he has come to the end of his travels on the shores of this ocean, which separated him from the land of his birth.

Not far from the Mussulman cemetery is situated the field where the bodies of the Hindoos are burnt to ashes. From a considerable distance the processions, bearing corpses placed on open litters, and directing their course to this point, sufficiently indicate the route you should follow to reach it. Death has no terrors for the Hindoo, since for him it is only a change of existence. The enclosure in which the funeral piles are erected is situated on the summit of a lofty terrace of granite, of which the base is accessible only at low water. The fires form several ranks in line; on one side are placed the corpses which are waiting their turn; on the other an honest dealer in wood is selling the necessary combustibles. Do not expect, however, to find there the slightest symptoms of meditation. Some are cutting the wood or arranging the pile; others, sitting on the summit of the walls, play on their instruments a dismal strain. The pile being prepared, the relatives place the corpse upon it, and cover it with small pieces of wood till it is entirely concealed. The eldest son, or the nearest relation of the deceased, approaches, beating his breast, and raising lamentable cries. Seizing a torch, he sets fire to the four corners of the pile; the flame rises rapidly, and the attendants augment it by throwing on oil. Soon the body appears a burning mass. When all is reduced to ashes, they water the place, and throw some of the calcined remains into the sea.

But for the presence of the corpse which crowns this mortuary trophy, the ceremony itself presents nothing repulsive, provided always that one keeps out of reach of the noisome smoke.

India and its Native Princes, 1882, pp. 12-13.

Hindu Burning-Ground

LADY BURTON.

I must also describe our visit to the Hindu Samsan or burning ground, in the Sonapur quarter, where we saw a funeral, or rather a cremation. The corpse was covered with flowers, the forehead reddened with sandalwood, and the mouth blackened. The bier was carried by several men, and one bore sacred fire in an earthenware pot. The body was then laid upon the pyre; every one walked up and put a little water in the mouth of the corpse, just as we throw dust on the coffin; they then piled more layers of wood on the body, leaving it in the middle of the pile. Then the relatives, beginning with the nearest, took burning brands to apply to the wood, and the corpse was burned. The ashes and bones are thrown into the sea. It was unpleasant, but not nearly so revolting to me as the vultures in the Parsee burying-ground. All the mourners were Hindus except ourselves, and they stayed and watched the corpse burning. Shortly the clothes caught fire, and then the feet. After that we saw no more except a great blaze, and smelt a smell of roasted flesh, which mingles with the sandalwood perfume of Bombay. The Samsan, or burning-ground, is dotted with these burning-places.

Wilkins' "The Romance of Isabel Lady Burton," 1897, page 588.

Walkeswar Village

LADY FALKLAND.

Near Malabar Point, on the right hand as you drive towards the compound in which the Governor's bungalows are situated, is to be seen a wall and an entrance in it, from which a long flight of steps leads down apparently to the sea. The further you proceed the more is your curiosity excited. Half way down this flight there is a handsome temple to the right, where I stopped to sketch a small curiously carved window, and beyond are more and more temples, with red-flags, waving on their roofs. Continuing to descend, I found myself in the midst of a small village, full of life and animation—it was like a dream. The little town or village, is called Walkeshwur. In the middle of a large square is a tank, round which are built temples, houses, and tall white obelisk-shaped pillars, called *deepmals*, painted in parts red and green, on which lamps are suspended on great festivals, and numbers of little altars containing the Tulsi plant. Temples of all sizes and forms are here: there is the lofty one shaped like a sugar-loaf; here one with a domed roof, on it a pinnacle and turret, with similar ones at each corner, and a third elaborately carved, in which are small images of gods in niches placed in the numerous turrets on the roof. Then there are flat-roofed temples, and little square ones, standing about four feet high, with pointed roofs, and built under trees.

It is a village of temples, full of busy Brahmins, and lazy fakirs, who sit on the ground, under a dirty bit of canvas stretched on four poles, with a hubble-bubble (a pipe, the smoke of which is made to pass through a cocoa-nut filled with water; being an humble imitation of a hooka) with their long hair twisted round their heads, and covered with ashes and dirt.

A wall surrounds this little corner of the island of Bombay on three sides; towards the west it is open to the sea. The narrow passages (for streets they cannot be called) were dark and gloomy; on each side were temples, houses, and dingy walls, with the foliage of tall trees overshadowing the way, and nearly obscuring the day-light; and on all sides there were numbers of mysterious corners, little barred windows in walls: small, dark inlets here, and outlets there, so that I almost expected Hunooman (the monkey-god) would creep out from one of them, and Gunputty (the elephant-god) with his trunk; grin at me, through an open, carved window in a temple. Every now and then a Brahmin, in white drapery, flitted by like a ghost, and religious mendicants slunk along the wall, looking like spirits from the nether world.

After passing through this singular town, I came to a staircase, and when half way up the numerous steps, I was startled by a cow, driven by a man—it came ungracefully bustling down; scared, as all Hindoo cows are, at a European, it endeavoured to turn back and retrace its steps; my servant drove it up, and the owner drove it down, while I stood on the low parapet of a wall, till it was decided which way the animal was to take, and at last I found myself on the top of the staircase, and in the world again.

Chow-Chow, 1857, Vol. I, pp. 87-89.

Malabar Point

EDWARD MOOR.

At the very extremity of a promontory on the island of Bombay, called Malabar Point, is a cleft rock, a fancied resemblance of the Yoni, to which numerous pilgrims and other persons resort for the purpose of regeneration by the efficacy of a passage through this sacred type. This Yoni, or hole, is of considerable elevation, situated among rocks, of no easy access, and, in the stormy season, incessantly buffeted by the surf of the ocean. Near it are the ruins of a temple, that present appearances warrant us to conclude was formerly of rather an elegant description. It is said, with probability, to have been blown up by gunpowder, by the pious zeal of the idol-hating Portuguese, while Bombay was under their flag. Fragments of well-hewn stone are now seen scattered over and around its site, having a variety of images sculptured on their surface: many of those most useful in building have been carried away by the Hindus to help their erections in the neighbouring beautiful Brahman village, its fine tank, and temples. With the view, neither pious nor sacrilegious, of discovering to whom this temple was dedicated. I have particularly examined its remains; and, with the help of my servants, I succeeded in removing the stones and rubbish from the surface of the ground, and discovering what was buried beneath.

Returning to the cleft, or Yoni, at Malabar Point, I repeat, that it is a type much resorted to. When Ragoba (as he is colloquially called, but more properly Ragonaut Rao; classically spelled Rhagu-Natha-Raya), the father of the present Peshwa, Baajy Rao, while exiled from Poona, was living in Bombay, he fixed his residence on Malabar hill, where he built a lofty habitable tower, since removed. He was in the habit occasionally of passing through the cleft in question; and being a Brahman of considerable piety, was doubtless much benefited by such regeneration. It is related of Sivaji, the daring founder of the Mahratha state, that he has been known to venture secretly on the island of Bombay, at a time when discovery was ruin, to avail himself of the benefit of this efficacious transit: this relation is, I believe, in Orme's *Fragments,* and other works, but I have them not at hand. Sivaji was a Mahratha, proving that high and low sects have faith in this sin-expelling process. Women also, as well as men, go through this operation; and I have witnessed some ridiculous, and indeed, some embarrassing and distressing scenes in the unsuccessful efforts of individuals, loaded either with sin or flesh, or both.

It is necessary to descend some steps on rugged rocks, and then, by first protruding the hands, you ascend head first up the hole. After the feet be lifted from their last support, the ascent is very difficult, and sometimes impracticable: in which case the essayist remains with his head and hands exposed to the laughing or commiserating spectators above; and it is necessary that some one should go below to aid the disappointed aspirant in his or her descent. I have several times attempted this regeneration, but could never effect it; although I have often seen my superiors in bulk, and, I conclude, in skill, as well as faith and good works, perform it with apparent ease.

Hindu Pantheon, 1810, pp. 307-309.

Tombs Near Love Grove, Mahaluxmi

MARIA GRAHAM.

The Mussulmans have contributed greatly to adorn the cities of India with tombs, whose magnificence has never been surpassed, and though all superstitious reverence for the dead be strictly forbidden by the Koran, they have borrowed from their Hindu subjects much of that kind of devotion; and a Pir's *kubber*, or tomb of a Mussulman saint, might pass for the shrine of St. Frideswide or St. Agnes. These buildings, in the parts of India I saw, are of very various sizes and degrees of beauty; they have all domes, under which is the tomb. generally unadorned, however rich the superstructure may be. Two of them at Bombay, one on the point of Love-grove, and the other on the rocks close to the sea-shore, have an interesting story attached to them. Two lovers were together in a pleasure-boat, enjoying the cool breezes of the ocean, when their little bark struck on a concealed rock and sank; the youth easily got on shore, but finding that his beloved was still struggling in the waves, he returned to save her, but in vain: the bodies of both were afterwards drifted to the land, where they were buried on the different spots on which they were found. Peculiar reverence is paid to these *kubbers* both by Mussulmans and Hindus; and I believe that the priest in whose guardianship they are, makes no small profit of the offerings made to the *manes* of the unfortunate lovers.

Letters on India, 1814, pp. 321 to 322.

Bombay Buildings

SIR RICHARD TEMPLE.

The objects of beauty in Indian art, and especially of architecture, are equal to those in nature, like gems set in gold, where the jewels are worthy of their setting.

For a long time the British Government contributed little or nothing to the category of national architecture. Indeed, the style of many British structures was so erroneous or defective as to exercise a debasing influence on the minds of those Natives, who might be induced to admire or imitate it as being the production of a dominant, and presumably a more civilized race. Most of the early buildings erected under British rule were, and many of the recent buildings still are, of a plain and uncouth fashion architecturally, however useful or commodious they may be practically. Of late years the Government has moved in an æsthetic direction, and at Calcutta, Madras and Bombay, fine edifices have sprung up in which the Gothic, Italian and Saracenic styles have been adapted with much taste and skill to the necessities of the East. A department of architecture has been established, from which the Native princes are beginning to obtain artistic designs for their palaces, colleges and civil structures.

At Bombay, along the shore of the bay, there is a long line of stately piles befitting a capital city in any country of the world, some of which were designed by Sir Gilbert Scott. The view of them as seen from Malabar Hill, with the blue sea before them, the city on their flank, the harbour behind them, the several ranges of Koncan hills in the distance, and the Western Ghat mountains bounding the horizon, has often been compared with the scenery of the Bay of Naples. It probably would rival the Neapolitan scenery, if only there were the transparent atmosphere and azure sky of the Mediterranean.

Many of the largest public works under British rule, though not designed for artistic effect, do yet incidentally present a very handsome appearance and have surroundings fraught with interest. For example, the Bhor Ghat incline, between Bombay and Poona, where the railway ascends the Ghat range to a height of nearly 2000 feet, has very fine scenery in the rainy season, when the thunderclouds are blown away by the wind and display the precipitous and wooded mountain-sides, streaked in all directions with rain-swollen torrents, which leap in many series of cascades from the crests to the bases of the precipices. This spectacle, when seen to full advantage, is admitted by all railway travellers to be one of the most remarkable in the Empire.

India in 1880, pp. 23-24.

NOTABLE EVENTS

NOTABLE EVENTS

The Royal Visit, 1911: An Interesting Episode

DR. STANLEY REED.

There is a favourite expression of Mr. Pepys that is the only fit description to apply to the great concourse of children that was massed on the Maidan: it was "as pretty a sight as ever I saw." Twenty-six thousand children in their best clothes, and all happy! It was a sight that one would go far to see, and that one will long remember. They began to assemble before the violet grey mists of dawn had disappeared and they continued to arrive in little companies up till about 8-30, and as they came each company was directed to its allotted position—some in the Stadium where the seats formed a semi-circular background to the picture, others on each side of the avenue left clear for the King's carriage to drive from the Gymkhana into the Exhibition. It was a fine piece of organisation. Mr. Cadell and his Committee seem to have acquired the Pied Piper's facility for leading children where they will, but with what patience and labour they acquired that knack they only know: however, their weeks of drudgery were fruitful of a splendid result. As the assembled host waited, there was no lack of entertainment for them. A military band played to them, and four Pipers of the Cameron Highlanders delighted them with their magnificence and their music. Occasionally as the day grew older there was a false report that the King was coming, and the arrival of H. E. the Governor and Lady Clarke was the signal for a cheer which started near the gateway, gradually spread over the whole mass, and finally developed into a paroxysm of cheering that lasted for several minutes.

As the Royal Procession drove on to the ground by the Gymkhana gateway, the cheers of the children again broke out with renewed force and were maintained for so long that the singing of "God Save the King," in English, was almost inaudible until near the close. This unrehearsed effect was probably unavoidable, as the problem of enforcing silence on so large a gathering of excited children was too difficult to face. But during the singing of the Gujarati Anthem, the cheers, except in the Stadium, had subsided though occasionally they were heard again.

While this singing was going on the children in the background in addition to cheering waved the flags with which most of them had been provided. The flags in most cases were blue ensigns, on which were portraits of the King and Queen, and the appearance of these thousands of uplifted flags was very remarkable. The children in their dense masses and groups of colour were like what gardeners call "carpet bedding," but when their flags appeared the floral nature of the scene was more clearly defined than ever. It was like a sheet of bluebells as one sees them on a late spring morning in an English copse ruffled with the wind. Here and there a white ensign gleamed a speck of white, like a wood anemone half strangled in its growth by the stouter wild hyacinth. And all this mass of gorgeous colour was constantly in motion swaying backwards and forwards, rippling and flowing before the eyes of the dazzled onlooker.

After the National Anthem had thus been sung in many tongues came the singing and dancing of the Garbi. The form of the dance defies description. It is first of all a song to which the dancing and gestures are subsidiary. And the song is a song of triumph, of welcome, and of blessing. For the singing an immense amount of energy is required. The circles wheel and turn, hands are uplifted and gracefully waved in benediction, one gesticulation succeeds another. Now the dance seems modelled on the Lancers or on Plaiting the Maypole, as the girls go in and out of the chain; and now it seems to be derived from what one supposes to have been the evolutions of a Greek chorus circling with stately tread round the altar of Dionysus. It is a swirling mass of colour as the girls turn and bend clapping their hands in rhythmic beat.

Some of them carry bright, shining lotas which glitter in the sun. The dance ended, the damsels withdrew, and the symbols round which they had danced were removed. In the Stadium a display of daylight fire-works, more noisy than spectacular, was begun and Their Majesties and suite drove through the crowds of children into the Exhibition.

The King and Queen in India, 1912, pp. 51-56.

Reception of The Prince and Princess of Wales, 1905

DR. STANLEY REED.

The drive from the Apollo Bunder to Government House carried the Prince and Princess through the most characteristic scenes in the civic life of Bombay. First through the modern town that has grown up beyond the line of the old ramparts and upon land filched from the sea—a quarter distinguished by its broad boulevards and splendid architecture; then through the densely populated native town; and finally, touching the hem of the mill district, to the shady slopes of Malabar Hill, where the wealthy of all communities love to dwell. As the Royal cortege moved off at a walk from the Bunder, as far as the eye could range stretched a splendid array of nodding plumes and flashing swords and dancing pennons, helmet and turban, horse and artillery. Each balcony and window was bright with keen eyes and animated faces, with gay frocks, and brilliant *saris*. Behind the stolid ranks of the Infantry was wedged a mass of humanity, clad in the variegated, yet always graceful colours of the East. As the shrill notes of the bugle gave the signal to advance, every verandah and vantage-point broke into a fluttering kaleidoscope of handkerchiefs and flags, and from ten thousand throats rose a joyous cry of welcome an earnest outpouring of the deep spring of loyalty which exists in every true heart, and welled over at the advent of the heir to the British throne.

Through scenes such as these Their Royal Highnesses passed the handsome Home which Khande Rao of Baroda built to shelter the seamen of the port, in commemoration of the visit of the Duke of Edinburgh, the fountain which preserves Bombay's connection with the Duke of Wellington, to the floral trophy erected to the name of the greatest of her Governors, Sir Bartle Frere. Here, in the heart of the modern city, the Koli fishermen had bridged the road with a scroll, fringed with emblems of the Sacred Fish, and bearing this inscription: "The Koli early settlers greet the Prince and Princess of Wales under the Sacred Fish Banner"--a reminder of the day when the Island of Bombaim was peopled only by hardy fisher folk whose rude huts clustered under the palm trees. Nor could the trading instincts of the enterprising peoples permit them to miss the opening for a little cheap advertisement. One small shopkeeper improved the occasion by allowing his loyal message "God bless the Prince and Princess of Wales, Long live our Noble King" artfully to lead to this announcement, "Further reductions at the popular sale expressly for the Royal visit." Another individual wished his "Royal patrons" long life at an expenditure of much red paint and white calico, and delicately reminded them that his wares were "of English make, as supplied to Queen Alexandra." But though the expression was occasionally quaint, the sentiment was unmistakeable. A continuous roar of welcome greeted the Royal carriage as soon as it was discerned, the school-children, massed on giant stands, joining their shrill trebles—a reception the more remarkable because the Oriental is not commonly given to vocal expression and expresses his greeting by reverential salaams.

Alone among the modern cities of India Bombay reproduces the character and charm of the older centres of population. The native town is no mere desert of dull, unattractive, squalid barracks. The houses ascend four, five and six storeys, their facades are broken with airy balconies enriched with graceful carving and painted all colours of the rainbow. Indeed, the most populous streets bear a far closer resemblance to those of Amritsar and Lahore than to anything in the other towns that have grown up under British rule, and they are always crowded with representatives of every race in Asia. Here, in the decorations, the oriental love of colour ran riot. Emerald and orange, crimson and azure, everywhere met the eye, and were flashed back from the crowds who thronged the streets and studded even the house-tops in their gayest attire. At every stage one was reminded of the wide variety of races who coalesce into the population of this many-tongued city. The Parsis welcomed Their Royal Highnesses as they passed the fire-temple with these words: "Parsis pray that the consecrated fire of the heart of the British Empire may burn bright and flourish for ever." The emancipated women-folk of this community broke the garishness of the street decorations with a vision of silks of the most delicate hues. The Jains exhibited the temple insignia usually exposed only on festival days. The Marwaris offered prayers at the Mumbadevi temple for the safe-keeping of the Prince and Princess, and here the temple girls were massed, robed in accordion-pleated skirts like those of an Empire ballerina and loaded with jewels.

In the Bhendy Bazaar, which ranks with the Chandni Chowk of Delhi and the Burra Bazaar of Calcutta as one of the famous highways of the Orient, the clash of races was indescribable. The giant Afridi, who sniped the Sirkar's troops in '97 and has just settled an old blood feud, jostled the mild Hindu. The Arab in his brown *burnous* elbowed the fair Parsi. Mahomedan and Chinaman, Sindis in their inverted "toppers," and jet black negroes rubbed shoulders in their desire to greet the Emperor's son, whilst the storeyed houses rippled with the chatter and the gay saris of the women of a dozen nationalities. Passing from the Bhendy Bazaar, the Moslems welcomed the Royal visitors with this graceful reference to Queen Alexandra:—

> "Son of a Sea King's daughter over the sea
> We Moslems welcome thee!"

On the fringe of the mill district the operatives were massed in tens of thousands. A sharp turn brought the procession from this, the least attractive part of Bombay, to the snores of the bay which is the natural glory of the city. Here school-children cheered in piping treble and waved their little flags. Breasting the slope of Malabar Hill the horses soon passed into the leafy shade of the avenue to Government House, where Lord Lamington and Lady Ampthill—who acted as hostess in the absence from India of Lady Lamington—received the Prince and Princess.

Royal Tour in India, 1906, pages 19–21.

Golden Jubilee Celebrations in Bombay, 1887

THE LATE LADY BRASSEY.

Four o'clock of the morning of February 16th found me in the verandah outside our bungalow listening to the roaring of the cannon, which ushered in the day on which was to be celebrated in India the Jubilee of Victoria, its Queen and Empress. The hours are early here, and at a quarter to eight Lady Reay, Captain Gordon, Tom [Lord Brassey] and I started to 'assist' at the grand ceremony at the Town Hall, followed later by the Governor and his aides-de-camp. As we neared the city the crowd became greater, everyone being dressed in holiday attire, and all apparently in a great state of enthusiasm and excitement. It looked like a many-tinted bed of flowers; for the Parsee ladies, unlike their Mahomedan and Hindoo sisters, have no dislike to display their toilettes in public, and are always clad in the gayest colours, arranged with perfect taste. The only specially distinctive mark in their costume is a rather unbecoming white band drawn tightly over the brow. In many cases, however, this had been judiciously pushed back so far as nearly to disappear under the bright-coloured silk sari which only partly concealed their jet-black and glossy tresses.

Near the Town Hall the scene became still more animated, and the applause of the multitude, though much more subdued in tone than the roar of an English crowd, was quite as enthusiastic. The men from H. M. S. Bacchante lined the approaches to the building, and the Bombay Volunteers acted as a guard-of-honour. We were ushered into the gallery, where chairs were placed for Lady Reay and myself close to the Governor's throne. The sight from this 'coign of vantage' was indeed imposing. Immediately in front stretched a fine flight of steps, covered with red cloth, and crowded with European and native officials in every variety of costume. The approach to the steps was through a pretty garden, where the wealth of tropical vegetation was set off by flags and gaily coloured banners. A dense crowd of natives ringed this enclosure round, whilst lofty houses, their gaily draped balconies and windows filled with bright and happy faces, made a brilliant background. Presently the Governor was seen approaching, escorted by his own body-guard and a company of mounted Volunteers (now called the Bombay Light Horse), who looked very picturesque and soldierlike as they dashed through the crowd. All dismounted at the west entrance to the garden, where a procession was formed, at the head of which the Governor advanced and, amid a flourish of trumpets, took his stand in front of the throne to receive the addresses and telegrams presented by, or on behalf of, various classes of the community in the Bombay Presidency.

The Governor's replies to the addresses were most happy, and evidently touched the feelings of his hearers. As he uttered his final words two young middies, perched on a dangerous-looking corner of the parapet, scrambled on to the roof, and, at a given signal, smartly unfurled an immense Royal Standard, amid the thunder of an imperial salute of 101 guns. The effect of the whole scene was deeply impressive, as well as suggestive. I have seen many ceremonies both at home and abroad, but never one more picturesque or of more thrilling interest.

From the Town Hall we went, still in procession, to the Cathedral, which stands close to the Elphinstone Garden, where a musical service was held. 'God save the Queen' was magnificently rendered, and the two specially written verses which were added to the National Anthem were most effective.

Last Voyage of the Sunbeam, 1889, pp. 58-61.

Landing of King Edward VII as Prince of Wales, in Bombay, 1875

SIR WILLIAM HOWARD RUSSELL.

The cannon spoke, the crews aloft cheered, bands played, marines and guards of honour on deck presented arms, officers saluted as the Royal Standard passed each man of war, and from all the shipping uprose a mighty shout.

The Prince's barge was preceded by boats bearing the members of the suite, who had to land before him. Looking back from one of these, a noble pageant, lighted up by the declining sun, met the eye—the hulls of the fleet, bright streamers and banners, long rows of flags from yard to yard and mast to mast, white boats, a flotilla of steam-launches, gigs, pinnaces, and a crowd of onlookers hastening fast as oar could send them in wake of the Royal barge to the Dockyard.

The flotilla sped on shorewards. A vast triumphal arch, spanning the waterway between two piers, but gay with banners, branches and leaves, and with decorations of palm and cocoanut, appeared in front of us. It could not be imagined that this dockyard stair in its normal state was one of the most commonplace and ugly of landings. But it had now not only been decked out with all the resources of art, which in this land are various and fantastic, but there was assembled beneath its great span perhaps the most strange and picturesque assemblage ever seen of late days in any part of the world. On each side of the way, under the vaulted roof, were long lines of benches rising in tiers, draped with scarlet cloth. This material was also laid down on the avenue to the gate, a hundred yards away, where the carriages were waiting. In the front rows sat or stood, in eager expectance, Chiefs, Sirdars, and native gentlemen of the Presidency, multitudes of Parsees, rows of Hindoos, Mahrattas, and Mahomedans dressed in their best—

which was oftenest their simplest,—a crowd glittering with gems and presenting, as they swayed to and fro to catch sight of the Prince, the appearance of bright enamel, or of a bed of gay flowers agitated by a gentle breeze—the officers of the Government, the Corporation with its address, the Municipal body of Bombay, and the naval and military officers who could be spared, representatives of the faculties, corporate bodies, dignitaries, and all the ladies who could be found within the radius of some hundreds of miles, and who had hastened to greet the Prince with their best smiles and bonnets. An abundance of sweet-smelling flowers, many of rarity, was displayed in pots along the avenue, and others commingled with shrubs of new forms were arranged in masses near the entrance,—banners hung from the roof,—words of "Welcome," in various characters were inscribed in gold over the entrance.

The Prince of Wales' Tour 1875-6,
pp. 115-116. (1877).

Bombay's Reception of King Edward VII

SIR W. HOWARD RUSSELL.

The impression produced by the aspect of the streets can scarcely be conveyed in any form of words; certainly if one were to try to set the sights down on paper, he might well be puzzled.

He would have to give an account of every yard of the many miles through which the Prince passed, each presenting extraordinary types of dress and effects of colour. There was something almost supernatural in those long vistas winding down banks of variegated light, crowded with gigantic creatures tossing their arms aloft, and indulging in extravagant gesture, which the eye—baffled by rivers of fire, blinded with the glare of lamps, blazing magnesium wire, and pots of burning matter—sought in vain to penetrate. For the most part the streets indulge in gentle curves, and as the carriages proceeded slowly, new effects continually opened up, and fresh surprises came upon one, from point to point, till it was a relief to close the eyes out of sheer satiety, and to refuse to be surprised any more. After several miles of these melodramatic effects, no wonder there was an inclination to look for one welcome little patch of darkness to receive us in its grateful recesses ere the night was over. Certainly it was a spectacle worth going far to see—the like of it will never probably be seen again. This is generally said of any spectacle of any unusual magnificence, or of extraordinary grandeur; but taking it all in all, I believe that very few who witnessed the sight would care to miss it, or to go through it all once more. To the spectators, no doubt, the passage of the cortege of the Prince, who was the central point on which all eyes turned, presented an absorbing attraction. But it was a pleasure which lasted but for a moment, for the carriage was soon out of sight; and then silence gave way to the noisy interchange of ideas as to what had been seen, for there was no certainty among the mass of natives respecting the Prince's place in the procession. To those who were passing between these animated banks of human beings, there came at last an ennui, and a sense of sameness, although, as I have said, every single yard of the way was marked by many distinctive types. Who could take them all in? Windows filled with Parsee women—matrons, girls, and children—the bright hues of whose dresses, and the brilliancy of whose jewels, emulated the coloured fires burning along the pavement—scarcely attracted one's notice before it was challenged by the next house filled with a crowd of devout Mahommedans, or by a Hindoo temple opposite, with its Brahmins and its votaries on steps and roof; flanked appropriately by a Jew Bazaar, or by an Armenian store, or by the incongruity of a European warehouse; or was solicited by the grotesque monitors on a Jain Temple. For if the changes in the chess-board are so numerous as to furnish matter for profoundest calculations, the extraordinary varieties of race and population in Bombay present endless subjects for study, to which only one thing was now wanting—adequate time. Night had long fallen; at last the whisper came from the front and ran down the line—"We are nearly at home," and Parell received the Prince with all due honour, the most illustrious of the many guests who have been sheltered under the roof of the old Jesuit convent.

The Prince of Wales' Tour 1875-6, pages 122-124.

Welcome to The Duke of Edinburgh, 1870

DR. JOHN WILSON.

We all deeply sympathise with the object of his [The Governor's] absence, that of welcoming, along with our distinguished Viceroy, the Earl of Mayo, and the other magnates of this great country, the second son of our most Gracious and Illustrious Queen Victoria to the shores of India. We ourselves (I venture to speak not only for this large assembly, but for the whole of the West of India) most cordially join in that welcome. We, the dwellers on "Cambay's strand," unite our most cordial felicitations with those of our fellow-subjects sojourning near "Ganges' golden wave" on the arrival, in this distant land, of our Sailor Prince, who is gracefully carrying the expression of the imperial and personal interest of her Majesty in all her subjects to the remotest places of the globe. We go further than this, and humbly beg His Royal Highness to spare as much time as he conveniently can for this most populous and rapidly growing city, with its numerous and diversified tribes and tongues congregated together, with its capacious and beautiful harbour, with a commerce the most valuable of the "Greater Britain," needing the protection of the Royal Navy, with most curious and instructive antiquities within easy reach, some of which extend back beyond the Christian era, and with the most picturesque and sublime scenery in its neighbouring isles, hills, and mountains.

Convocation Address, 1870, page 47.

The Bombay Riots of 1874: A Remarkable Episode

JAMES MACLEAN.

On Monday, the 16th February, the sun again rose upon an excited city. As some of the Seedees and Mahomedans who died on Sunday were expected to be taken from the Jamsetjee Hospital and buried by their friends, the Parsees looked forward to another riot, and indeed the most exciting circumstance that occurred on this day was the burial of an old Mussulman named Hajee Ahmed. We take the following account of this remarkable affair from the *Bombay Gazette.* While it is interesting in the details given of what actually took place, it is also highly expressive of the state into which Bombay had been plunged:—

Shortly after our visit to the Jamsetjee Jejeebhoy Hospital on Sunday, Hajee Ahmed and two of the mangled unknown Seedees died. Hajee Ahmed is the old man who was found lying insensible on the road near Sonapore with his fractured jaw hanging down upon his chest. We thought when we saw him gasping, that the world would hear no more of Hajee Ahmed than that he was one of the victims of the Sonapore Riot, but he has been fated to have a wider fame after death than during life. The "unknown" Seedees died unknown, and having no friends in Bombay were quietly bestowed in the usual way of unknown corpses that make their exit from the Jejeebhoy Hospital; but to Hajee Ahmed was reserved the notoriety of having the most extraordinary funeral ever seen in Bombay. The poor little old Mussulman, whose age and feebleness make it probable that he met his death-wound not when he was an active rioter but when he was a real mourner who had been hustled into the midst of the melee, has had a greater procession at his funeral than the most famous that ever died in this city. Hajee Ahmed when alive was nobody; dead, his name will become a household word in the Mussalman community. He was followed to his grave by hundreds of his community; by a Commissioner of Police and many Superintendents and Inspectors belonging to that body; by police on foot and on horseback; by a regiment of native soldiery. And after he was laid in the earth, the fact was marked by the presence in the principal streets of a Brigadier-General, several companies of European infantry, and a diminutive detachment of native cavalry. "Like Hajee Ahmed's funeral" may well become a synonym with Bombay Mussulmans for something very grand.

The men, whom Mr. Souter employs to feel the native pulse, reported to him on Monday morning that the Mussulman community—at least the Soonee portion of it—were very excited about Hajee's death, and proposed to follow his body to Sonapore grave-yard in large numbers. They also said it was their belief that the excitement at the funeral would be so great that an attack upon the Parsees in revenge for the old man's murder was as likely an event as not. Mr. Souter at once asked the Brigadier-General for the assistance of the military and before two o'clock the precautionary measures were taken.

The relatives of Hajee Ahmed had gathered in the vicinity of the Jamsetjee Hospital at an early hour and began to clamour for his body. But permission to remove it was denied until the result of Mr. Souter's negotiations for a military force were known. The multitude swayed about impatiently and at half past one the nearest relative of the Hajee went to Mazagon Police Office and asked Mr. Edginton to grant his permission to remove the body. The Soonee, however, had just to wait until the news arrived that the military precautions were complete, which it did, as we have said, about two o'clock. The body was soon taken out of the ward, and mounted on a bier borne by a number of willing shoulders. At sight of this the assemblage raised a mournful sound, and the bier with its simple covering of a white spotted red piece of cotton became an object of the most reverend attention. At a signal the funeral procession fell in, but very quietly there moved along with it a number of persons who were not exactly mourners. In front marched a number of sepoys and one or two Police Superintendents while closing in the rear came a small body of police and then a small body of the 21st Regiment; and at a short distance further off came a couple of companies of the 21st Regiment, under Lieutenant-Colonel Macleod and Captain Becke. The mourners round the bier leaped and cried and beat their heads; the police marched quietly on; the military's fixed bayonets glittered as they moved; a Police Superintendent on horseback darted suddenly to this side or to that, at each rush making a crowd of loungers fly; and so the procession moved up Bhendy Bazar. It turned down towards Null Bazar, where the number of mourners, or pretended mourners became considerably larger, and as this place is the notorious haunt of Bombay ruffiandom, the character of the procession as to respectability was increased by the addition. The Police Superintendents galloped here and there, but their enthusiasm could not alter the fact of thousands of people clustering on the foot-path or craning their necks over the windows of the houses. A short halt was made near the Null Bazar, during which the military split into lines and guarded the road.

When the procession moved on again, it turned down a narrow lane called Ali Oomer Street, the quaint architecture of the wooden and green, blue, yellow, and even red houses in which shared attention with the motley character of its residents. In this street Hajee Ahmed's house was situated and collected near it there must have been five hundred people. The cries of the mourners echoed through the street and continued till the bier disappeared beneath the deceased's doorway, in front of which a rough mat was hung. The bier reappeared covered with the same old piece of cotton and everybody who had been squatting on the road rose to his feet, and soon the procession was formed again. It would be difficult to describe the appearance of the funeral party and their military accompaniments as they moved down between the narrow defiles of streets, gazed upon by thousands of people from roofs, verandahs, and windows. The combined murmur of the huge surging crowd, the shouts of the mourners, the yells of the sowars as they wheeled about and drove back with their batons too curious half-dressed people who were crowding in upon the bier; the steady tramp of the military, all made up on effect beyond description. At Bapu Khote Street a crowd was waiting which must have numbered many thousands, but it was prevented from joining the mourners by the European Superintendents, riding in among the people and driving them back. In Bhoiwada street, where the narrowness of the road extenuated the procession considerably, the windows in the high houses were filled with Hindoo men and women spectators. Frequent halts had to be made, during which the Commissioner of Police rode among the mourners and warned them against breaking the peace.

At the end of this road, where Bhuleshwar Temple, half hidden by cocoanut trees rises on an eminence, which was on this occasion crowded by Hindoos even down to the verge of the shimmering tank, the procession became slightly unsteady, and a halt had to be made for a short time; but in a few minutes the mourners had again room to leap about and scream and beat their heads and breasts, and the procession moved onwards past the Roman Catholic chapel and then into the Agiary Lane—the abode of Parsees, and therefore looked upon with some anxiety by the authorities. The procession moved on through the dreaded Agiary Lane. In front of the Dady Sett Fire Temple, round which a good deal of Sunday's rioting raged, a small company of soldiers and police was stationed, but the Mussulmans showed no disposition whatever to offer violence to the edifice and went on with their noisy chant of grief round Hajee's body. At the entrance to the Sonapore gully, which was the scene of another of Sunday's free fights, a number of police and military were drawn up. A temporary halt was made, during which the Commissioner of Police and Superintendent Mills rode down the narrow stinking place to see whether the Parsee residents had closed their houses. Not a single window was found open, and the usually teeming lane was as quiet as the grave. The procession turned down the lane, some of the mourners showing their excitement by extra furious dancing and singing.

The graveyard has a small gateway, situated in a dilapidated alley, and for five minutes the members of the procession streamed through it. Near the gate a little mosque stands and strikes the stranger as being more useful than ornamental, its masonry being alternated with indifferent specimens of thatching. Here some priests received the body, and a glimpse of the red bier could be caught sight of as it appeared across some archways on its way to the inner recesses of the edifice. The graveyard round the mosque surged with excited people, but speedily the murmur of the crowd was silenced, giving place to a prayer chanted over the body by the Mahomedan priests. While further ceremonies were being performed inside the mosque, the majority of the crowd dispersed across the graveyard, and formed parts of groups which stared through the gateway at the military, whose red coats and bayonets ornamented the sides of the lane as far as the eye reached: or squatted on the earth, and lit their *bidees,* and joked and laughed as though the occasion was rather a jolly one than otherwise. This latter fact indicated, in our opinion, that a huge proportion of the so-called mourners had honoured the procession with their presence simply because some fun was to be expected.

The burying ground had been reached about four o'clock, and the body had been within the mosque for half an hour or so, when it reappeared in the archways, and a signal from a priest set the people down upon their knees, where they genuflected for a short time in the direction of the declining sun after which the bier was picked up and taken to the place of burial, followed by a lamenting crowd. While the members of the procession were absent, a commotion occurred in one of the lanes adjoining the graveyard, but this was from no more alarming cause than the arrival of two companies of the 2nd Queen's, who had been conveyed to Churney Road Station by train from Colaba. The men were "as fresh as larks" and their appearance must have had a considerable moral effect upon the Mussulmans within the churchyard, who came to stare at them. They were accompanied by Brigadier-General Gell and Major Sexton, while Major Gibbs was the officer in charge of the detachment. These European troops were marched through the Parsee quarters and down to the Bhendy Bazar Road. They had scarcely disappeared round the Sonapore Lane, when the trampling of horses was heard, and twenty-five men of the 1st Cavalry (His Excellency the Commander-in-Chief's escort) rode on to the ground, Captain Karslake following. They proceeded at once through the parts of the town where the peace was menaced, and their moral effect must have been almost as great as that of the European troops.

Soon after this the Mussulmans issued from the graveyard. They were addressed by a little man with a turban and a yellow handkerchief round his waist, after which the procession moved on towards the town again. They were perfectly peaceful. True, not a Parsee was to be seen on their whole line of march; but that they were not very much disposed for rough play was sufficiently shown by their quiet demeanour. They quickly reached the Bhendy Bazar, and thence dispersed, every man to his own way. When the crowd had passed through the Agiary Lane and Sonapore Lane, the hidden Parsees threw open their doors and windows and the whole place soon looked as lively as though Hajee Ahmed's much dreaded funeral had never taken place. The Parsee community are to be complimented for their forbearance on this occasion and the Mussulmans for their discretion in not risking a collision with Her Majesty's troops.

The Bombay Riots, 1874, pp. 23-27.

"Silver Times" in Bombay

ARTHUR CRAWFORD.

It was about the beginning of the great speculation mania that set in in Bombay in 1862-63—a mania beside which, I believe, if facts and figures were compared, the South Sea Scheme would sink into insignificance—that the loafer came to the front. How many are alive still to remember those silver times? When Reclamation schemes turned every body's brain—when "Back Bays" fluctuated between twenty and forty-five thousand rupe es premium—when "Mazagons" and "Colabas" followed suit—when there was a new Bank or a new "Financial" almost every day—when it was a common thing, in strolling from your office to the dear old Indian Navy Club, to stop a moment in the seething Share Market and ask your broker, "well, Mr. B. or Bomanji! what's doing!" "Oh, Sir! So-and-so Financials are rising—they say Premchand is buying." "Ah! well, just buy me fifty or a hundred shares" (as your inclination prompted you). You went to your "tiffin," or luncheon, at that memorable long table; you ordered a pint of champagne—no one ever drank any thing but champagne in those days—you tried to get as near as possible to Doctor D. or poor T., the presiding geniuses of the meal, to obtain an "allotment" of a certain toast, which T. was justly celebrated for. Getting this you were filled with exultation, for it was, and with reason, regarded as the precursor of other and more lucrative "allotments." Four o'clock saw you on your way back to office, and you stopped to ask your broker how your "Financials" stood. "Rising slowly, sir!" would be the answer; with a calm conscience you said, "Then please sell mine," and the morrow brought you a cheque for fifty, a hundred or two hundred rupees, as the case might be.

Why does not some abler pen than mine give an historical account of this great mania? When fortunes were made and lost in a few days; when the fatal telegram came announcing the peace between the North and South American States, and all our houses of cards came tumbling about our ears,—when Back Bays (of which I was the happy possessor of one) rose to half a lakh premium,—when "allotments" were sent to you "willy nilly," mostly worth some money,—when poor Doctor D. and Mr. T. were millionaires on paper! Many a pathetic story could be related of those times, and of the awful crisis afterwards.

Reminiscences of an Anglo-Indian Police Official, 1894, pp. 242-244.

The Share Mania

DR. GEORGE SMITH.

Visiting Bombay, as an outsider, at the height of the mania in 1864-65, and one of the earliest to make the journey by mail-cart across the province and Central India to the railway at

Agra, we witnessed a state of things, economic and social, which no report could gauge. In the five years during which the cotton market of the world was transferred from New Orleans to Bombay, Western India received eighty millions sterling over and above the normal price of her produce before and since. So far as this reached the cultivators it was well. That it largely reached them, in spite of their ancestral usurers backed by the civil court procedure, has of late been unhappily proved by the quantities of silver ornament sent down to the local Mint, in years of enhanced land tax and repeated scarcity and famine. So far as the sudden profit could be utilised for the public good it was also well. Against the fatal mismanagement of the semi-Government Bank of Bombay must be set Sir Bartle Frere's sale of the land on which the walls of the old Fort stood, to form a fund for the creation of New Bombay.

But the bulk of the profit was literally thrown into the sea, and with it the reputation and the happiness of not a few of the leading European, Parsee, and Hindoo merchants and bankers of the province. The catastrophe culminated in 1867, in the fall of the old Bank of Bombay, which led even members of the Government of India to recommend the prosecution of the guilty parties in the criminal courts; in the collapse of the fund for building New Bombay, which necessitated an addition to the ever-increasing debt of India; in the flight of speculators like him who, after buying the Government-House at Dapoorie with paper, left an umbrella as his assets; and in the exposure of countless scandals under the insolvent jurisdiction of the High Court by Mr. Chisholm Anstey, who as an acting Judge was no less pitiless to the gambling traders than he had proved to be to the obscene high priests of Krishna. But England cannot throw a stone at Bombay, for it was in the year before 1867 that Overend, Gurney and Company had led the panic race.

The millions which might have enriched and beautified Bombay and its various communities, were early and almost altogether directed to the mania of reclaiming the foreshore of an Island which already covered eighteen square miles. The harbour, beautiful and spacious by nature, was destitute of wharf and jetty accommodation for the necessary commerce. Before the mania, there had been undertaken the legitimate and praiseworthy enterprise of removing the reproach by establishing the Elphinstone Company. The prospects and success of this really sound project fired the possessors of the surplus capital of the cotton trade with a dream of the profits to be obtained from reclaiming land. The foreshore of the shallow and useless Back Bay, fit only for fisher craft, became the object of the maddest of the Companies. Just above that, forming the eastern side which shelters it from the great Indian Ocean, rises Malabar Hill, and looking down on the generally peaceful water is "The Cliff." One morning when we happened to be breakfasting with Dr. Wilson, he handed to us a letter received by urgent messenger. "That," he said, "will show you to what we have come in Bombay; but I do not give the mania more than a year to collapse." It was an offer from a substantially rich native speculator to purchase the cottage and garden for a sum twenty times their original value. He of course put it from him at once; for, all other reasons apart, he was one of the few sane men of Bombay at that time. Officials, chaplains, bankers—none escaped the infection, it was said, save *three,* of whom he was the chief. His entreaties, his counsels, his warnings, especially to his native friends, were in vain.

Life of Dr. Wilson of Bombay, 1878, pp 573-575.

The Share Mania

BOSWORTH SMITH.

For some years past, a spirit of wild and reckless speculation had, more or less, infected all classes in India, and now it was followed by the inevitable reaction. Colossal fortunes made by gambling are generally followed by colossal failures, which, unfortunately, do not always fall upon the gamblers themselves in exact proportion to their folly or their guilt. Calcutta itself had not been altogether free from the epidemic. But it was in Bombay that the mania reached its height. Owing to the American war, vast quantities of cotton had been exported to England during the last two years from its spacious and expansive harbour; and by their own admission, the Bombay authorities were completely carried away by the torrent. Bubble companies were started by the hundred, the shares in which went up to fabulous amounts. But, like bubbles, one after another, they burst, bringing upon all connected with them, not only ruin but, often, also shame and disgrace. The heir of the famous Parsee baronet, Sir Jamsetjee Jeejeebhoy, the Rothschild of Bombay, failed for half a million of money. The hardly less famous Hindu millionaire, Premchund Roychund, failed for over two millions. And, unfortunately, the Bank of Bombay, which might have done much to check the mischief, and which had, among its Directors, nominees of the Bombay Government, did its best, in spite of earnest and reiterated warnings from Calcutta, by reckless gambling to foster and to spread it. And now, throughout India and England, disaster followed upon disaster. The failures of the "Commercial Bank" of Bombay, of the famous House of Overend and Gurney, and, worst of all perhaps for India, of the Agra Bank—the bank in which the little-all of so many widows and orphans of Anglo-Indians were deposited—followed one another, in melancholy and startling succession. But the worst offender of all, the Bombay Bank, still held its own—though with a loss of half its capital—still plunging itself and others, in spite of all that remonstrances from the Governor-General, and urgent requests both by telegram and letter for information could do, more deeply into the mire; till at last it fell, deep alike in ruin and in guilt, the full dimensions of which were only to be revealed by the Commission of Inquiry which an outraged people demanded and, at length, succeeded in obtaining.

Life of Lord Lawrence, 1883, Vol. II., pp. 354-55.

How the Mutiny Was Nipped In the Bud

CHARLES FORJETT.

The Mohorrum is a festival causing great excitement and religious enthusiasm among Mahomedans: so much so, that the presence in the native town, as stated by General Bates, of strong detachments of troops, both European and native, were always, previous to my time, found necessary for the preservation of the peace; but having a police force equal in my estimation to any emergency on the part of the population, the idea of being dependent on military aid proved distasteful, and with the assistance of the Chief Secretary to Government—now Sir Henry

Anderson—I discontinued the practice, and it was attended with the happiest results.

As the Mohorrum of 1857 was approaching, suspicion seemed to be directed towards the Mahomedans of the town, and the excitement was becoming very great. A similar excitement, just previously, had led to a panic, and it was followed by the wildest hurrying off on board ships in the harbour. I deemed it necessary, therefore, to call a meeting of all the leading members of the Mahomedan community. I was accompanied to it by Colonel, now Lieutenant-General, Birdwood, and his son, Doctor George Birdwood. The gathering was unusually large, and my address to the assembled native gentlemen was delivered in the native language.

After I had finished, Colonel Birdwood addressed some excellent remarks to the large assembly. He dwelt principally on the check which every species of improvement in India would receive in consequence of the revolt in the North-West; and concluded with the words of a well-known Mahomedan ditty, that our just Government was by scoundrels hated and by the good beloved. After Colonel Birdwood had spoken, a leading member of the Mahomedan community assured me that the Mahomedans were most peaceably disposed, and that there was no fear of a disturbance taking place.

The Governor, the Judges of the Supreme Court, and other high functionaries being present at the time in Bombay, I was not quite sure, when on the following morning I saw my address published, that I had committed no breach of official propriety in declaring to the Mahomedan gentlemen that those whose fidelity there was reason to suspect would be speedily dealt with, undeterred by the "trammels" of the law, and that "every guilty man would be strung up before his own door." And this doubt was by no means allayed when a trooper brought me a note from the Private Secretary, telling me that it was the Governor's wish to see me. I was received by his Lordship with his usual kindness, and resting his hand on my shoulder, he said, "You had a meeting yesterday of Mahomedan gentlemen; in addressing them you made use of very strong language; *but I am glad you did so.*" I was of course thankful.

I then touched upon the protest I had placed in the hands of the Private Secretary for his Lordship's information, against the military and police arrangements ordered by Government for the preservation of the peace during the Mohorrum. His Lordship said he was sorry he did not know my views before those suggestions were made; but having made them, and the Brigadier—the chief responsible military authority—having adopted them with the concurrence of the chief magistrate, he did not see his way to countermanding them; but he hoped everything would pass off quietly. I then respectfully intimated that I should be obliged to disobey the orders of Government in respect to the police arrangements, for, I added, "I must keep my Europeans together and have them in hand in case of a sepoy outbreak." His Lordship kindly remarked, "It is a very risky thing to do to disobey orders; but I am sure you will do nothing rash." And I may now add, that it was happy for Bombay, happy for Western India, and happy probably for India itself, that one so noble and clear-headed as Lord Elphinstone was Governor of Bombay during the period of the Mutiny; but for which it is impossible to state what the results would have been.

Our Real Danger in India, 1878, pp. 122-128.

2

Happily this intended mutiny was nipped in the bud by the very opportune assistance rendered by Colonel Barrow. And it will, I think, be admitted that I had exercised a wise discretion in evincing the determination I did at the sepoy lines, when the sepoys, many with arms in their hand that were found loaded, were abusing me, and their officers, keeping them back sword in hand, were crying out to me, for God's sake, to go away, and that my presence was exciting the men. It will be admitted too, I think, that I exercised an equally wise discretion, when, believing sepoy loyalty not to be depended upon, I formed the resolution of disobeying the orders of Government, and keeping my Europeans together, and so posting them as to have led to the postponement of the outbreak that had been arranged to take place on the last night of the Mohorrum.

If the mutiny in Bombay had been successful, Lord Elphinstone was of opinion, and this is indisputable, that nothing could have saved Hydrabad and Poona and the rest of the Presidency, and after that, he said, "Madras was sure to go too."

Our Real Danger in India, pp. 143-144.

A Page from Early Bombay History.

KINLOCH FORBES.

A contest now ensued with the Bahmuny sovereign of the Deccan, in which his usual success attended the arms of Ahmad Shah. An interesting fact is here disclosed—the possession by the sovereigns of Guzerat of Salsette and of the islands of Mahim and Moomba Devee, which, in their united form, constitute the present island of Bombay. Mahim was then held by a tributary Hindoo prince with the title of Rai, who afterwards gave a daughter to the harem of the son of Shah Ahmad. There is no record of the separate conquest of this territory by the Mohamedans, nor does it appear that either the

Viceroys or the Sultans of Guzerat were ever sufficiently unemployed up to this time, or possessed of sufficient resources, to have enabled them to undertake an extension of their dominions into this detached and distant quarter. We have seen, however, that the sovereigns of Anhilwara pushed their armies deep into the Dekkan; that they not only held possession of the northern part of Khandeish, in which Kurun Waghela long maintained himself after Guzerat had been overrun, but that they also occupied the Konkan, and threatened the kingdom of Kolapur. We may therefore conclude that the northern Konkan fell into the possession of the Mohamedans on the extinction of the Waghela dynasty, as part of the recognised territories of the lords of Anhilwara,—a fact which, taken in connection with the glimpses we possess of their naval supremacy, is calculated to add no little interest to the illustrious line of Sidh Raj.

Kootb Khan, the governor of Mahim on the part of Ahmed Shah, dying, the Bahmuny Sultan seizing the favourable opportunity, occupied that island without loss, and also took possession of Thana in Salsette. Ahmad Shah immediately assembled a fleet of seventeen sail at with Diu, Gogo, and Cambay, which, in co-operation an army advancing along the northern Konkan, attacked and recovered Thana. The Bahmuny general retreated to Mahim, and on the face of that island, which was exposed, constructed a very strong wattled breast-work. This stockade was carried, not without considerable loss, by the troops of Ahmed Shah, who now found themselves opposed to the whole of the Dekkan line. A bloody and indecisive action ensued, which was terminated at nightfall; but while darkness lasted, the Dekkan general abandoned his position, and retreated to the contiguous island of Moomba Devee. The Guzerat fleet blockaded the island, and effected a landing upon it for the troops, and the general of the Bahmuny Shah was compelled to fly to the continent. After another action, fought under the walls of Thana the Dekkany troops were ultimately defeated and dispersed, and the fleet of Guzerat returned home, carrying with it "some beautiful gold and silver embroidered muslins," taken on the island of Mahim.

Ras Mala, 1856, *pp.* 269-270.

The Cylone of 1854

CHARLES LOW.

Bombay will not soon forget the memorable cyclone which burst over it at midnight of the first of November, 1854, desolating the city and strewing the harbour with wrecks. The wind veered round the compass, and at three a.m. of the 2nd November, the pressure of the wind actually registered 35 lbs., to the square foot. On the following morning Bombay harbour presented a scene of desolation: five square-rigged ships and three steamers were on shore, most of them dismasted, and one hundred and forty-two smaller crafts, mostly native, were wrecked. The 'Assaye' drifted towards the Castle walls and carried away her bowsprit, but was fortunately saved from total shipwreck by the exertions of her officers and men. The 'Hastings' receiving ship, drove from her moorings, sprung a leak, and, while being towed by the 'Queen' fouled the ship 'Mystery'; and, ultimately, after battering against the fort walls, which she damaged to a considerable extent, was brought to Mazagon in the last stage of decrepitude; and, though she was patched up sufficiently to do duty a little longer as receiving ship, the old frigate was soon consigned to the limbo of the ship-breaker's yard. The surveying brig, 'Palinurus,' was dismasted, and got aground off the dock-yard break-water, where her situation was one of extreme peril, until she floated off with the tide. The Governor's and Sir Henry Leake's barges, and nearly all the pleasure yachts and bunder-boats usually moored off the Apollo Bunder, were lost, and the cutters 'Margaret,' 'Nurbudda' and 'Maldiva' were seriously damaged. The 'Elphinstone' had a narrow escape, as she grounded off the Custom House basin, and was only got afloat by the discipline and smartness of the crew and skill of the officers; backing astern, she set a stay-sail and threaded her way through the crowded harbour to the anchorage outside the shipping.

History of the Indian Navy, 1877, Vol. I pp. 296–297.

The Great Fire of 1803

On the 17th February a most alarming fire broke out in the very extensive and populous Bazar situated within this garrison. It is not exactly known whence the fire originated. Notwithstanding surmises and suggestions to the contrary, in our opinion there is no sufficient reason to consider it arose from any other cause than accident. The fire broke out early in the day and the wind continuing unusually high the flame increased with astonishing rapidity. So great and violent was the conflagration, that at sunset the destruction of every house in the Fort was apprehended. The flames directed their course in a south-easterly direction from that part of the Bazar opposite to the Cumberland Ravelin quite down to the King's barracks. During the whole of the day every effort was used to oppose its progress, but the fierceness of the fire driven rapidly on by the wind baffled all attempts; nor did it visibly abate till nearly a third part of the town within the walls had been consumed.

The apprehensions excited by this calamitous event were considerably increased by the direction of the wind impelling the flames towards the arsenal. For whatever security the magazines might be supposed to afford against access to the fire, still the smallest crevice was sufficient to admit a spark to the great mass of gunpowder within the Castle. It was impossible to view otherwise than in a state of awful suspense the destruction to the whole garrison which was thus within the bounds of possibility. Before midnight the wind changed more to the northward whence it veered round gradually to the eastward, abating at the same time in its force. From this rather than from any human effort, the conflagration visibly decreased and the danger which threatened gradually diminished. While using every practical exertion to check the progress of the flames, we derived particular and most useful assistance from the presence of Vice Admiral Rainier, who repaired to the spot with all the officers and a due proportion of the men of His Majesty's squadron. From their active interference and uncommon exertions was derived the greater part of any opposition that could be made to the extention of the conflagration. This help proved more eminently advantageous in the two or three days that followed the first extensive destruction by pulling down the crumbling ruins and thereby smothering the remaining fire and smouldering embers. Otherwise we might have had to lament far greater devastation than has occurred.

The loss of lives has been small though there has not yet been time to take any exact account.

But the fire having raged chiefly throughout the day, afforded opportunity to the inhabitants to save not only their lives, but many of them a considerable share of their portable property. The damage sustained on this occasion by the Honourable Company has been proportionably inconsiderable. At the same time the occurrence of the calamity has rendered manifest to all who witnessed it, the danger to which the garrison would have been exposed in the event of the appearance of an enemy before Bombay. The number of houses in the Bazar, the very exceptionable mode of their construction, and the combustible materials of which the greater part of them are composed and with which many of them were also filled in the commercial pursuits of their owners, would have exposed us to nearly equal hazard from the enemy's throwing in only a few shells. Whilst from the confined situation joined to the distress that must at all times have been incident to such a conflagration, the means of effectual defence must soon have been rendered impossible without any consideration to the number of the garrison or to the strength of the works.

Bombay Government to the Court of Directors, 22 Feb. 1803. apud *Bombay Gazetteer, Vol. XXVI, Part, 1. pp. 431—435.*

Royal Visit, 1911.

Bombay, the port selected for the honour of Their Majesties' arrival, has in more senses than one earned the title of the Gateway of India. It was the first possession of the British Crown in India two hundred and fifty years ago, and it has seen the landing of two successive heirs to the Crown within the last half-century. It is now also the terminus for the great steamship lines that link up East and West, and as a modern city, with manufactures of its own, it has a special character of eastern West and western East that makes it obviously the portal of transition. Nowhere in the East has contact with the West produced more remarkable results. For a long period, notwithstanding its extraordinarily favourable position as regards the rest of India and the fact that in the first decade of the eighteenth century it became the head-quarters of the East India Company, it remained a settlement of very ordinary dimensions, with trade in dried fish and cocoanuts. But in the middle of the nineteenth century, with the development of communications, it commenced the rapid and wonderful growth which has now made it, with nearly a million inhabitants, second only to Calcutta in population, and in some ways, perhaps the most splendid city in India, with its world-wide trading interests, its magnificent public buildings, and its unrivalled scenery and harbours. The Bombay of to-day is scarcely recognizable even as the same which King Edward saw not forty years before; but it still preserves the wondrous atmosphere and colour of the East.

Busy and swarming with life as the city always is, it had never displayed such intensity of interest, wonder and deep feeling, as on the morning of the 2nd. December 1911. The arrival of the Sovereign was an event that made an extraordinary appeal to the imagination of all classes of the people. The day before had been Queen Alexandra's birthday, the ceremonies in honour of which added not a little to the expectations and excitement of the multitude. The open spaces round Bombay were occupied by the troops who had come for duty in the pageants, and for many days thousands of people, men, women and children, had been pouring in by rail and road from all parts of the Presidency and beyond. The streets were already packed already long before sunrise with a gay, good-natured throng, which presented almost inexhaustible variety of human types and brilliant costumes, flowing along in a seething tide towards the harbour. The life and movement in the streets were indescribable. Whole families could be seen hastening to secure places which would ensure a view of the procession, fathers carrying sons on their shoulders, and mothers with the last born on the hip and a bundle of food on the head, all dressed in their best and excitedly hailing their friends.

Historical Record of the Imperial Visit to India, 1911-1912. (published by the Government of India, 1914). pp. 35-36.

Royal Progress through the City, 1911.

The formal decorations were a mere framework, but it was the teeming mass of humanity, with colours and contrasts unimaginable in the West, that gave the scene its character. Bombay had never made public holiday in the quite the same wholehearted way before, or given so real a welcome. Every balcony, roof, and window was bright with joyous faces brilliant-coloured clothing. Stands had been erected on the open spaces and all along the route where the road was not too narrow, and these were crowded with men of every Indian race, while in the first part of the route there was a fair sprinkling of Europeans. At every side street a densely packed throng pressed forward to the line of march, and the populace of many cities seemed to have poured out into the streets. The people had come for the event of a life-time, and in spite of excessive heat and the weary hours of waiting, a better-tempered and a more easily managed crowd could scarcely have been possible. A wonderful effect of overwhelming numbers that rendered the setting barely visible was the result, and it was by this more than anything else that the welcome was distinguished. It was the kind of greeting that Their Majesties most desired, and it was particularly noticeable where, as at many parts of the route, the school children of all castes and creed were assembled in their thousands and, as the Imperial carriage passed, started to their feet, waving small flags and filling the air with treble cheers and shouts. Even where, as at many points in the native city, the crowd remained passive, there was something unmistakable about the attitude maintained. The interest, though constantly changing throughout the course, never for one instant flagged, and Their Majesties were evidently much moved by the demonstrations and manifestations of loyalty which had marked their whole progress.

Historical Record of the Imperial Visit, p. 45

Raynal's Panegyric on Sterne's Eliza

ABBE RAYNAL.

Territory of Anjengo! thou art nothing; but thou hast given birth to *Eliza*. A day will come when these staples of commerce founded by the

Europeans on the coasts of Asia, will exist no more. Before a few centuries are elapsed, the grass will cover them, or the Indians avenged will have built upon their ruins. But if my works be destined to have any duration, the name of Anjengo will not be obliterated from the memory of man. Those who shall read my works, or those whom the winds shall drive towards these shores will say: there it is that Eliza Draper was born;—and if there be a Briton among them he will immediately add with the spirit of conscious pride,—and there it was that she was born of English parents.

Let me be permitted to indulge my grief and to give a free course to my tears. Eliza was my friend. Reader, whoso'er thou art, forgive me this voluntary emotion. Let my mind dwell upon Eliza. If I have sometimes moved thee to compassionate the calamities of the human race, let me now prevail upon thee to commiserate my own misfortune. I was thy friend without knowing thee; be for a moment mine. Thy gentle pity shall be my reward.

Eliza ended her days in the land of her forefathers, at the age of three and thirty. A celestial soul was separated from a heavenly body. Ye who visit the spot on which her sacred ashes rest write upon the marble that covers them: in such a month, in such a year, on such a day, at such an hour, God withdrew his spirit and Eliza died.

And thou, original writer, her admirer and her friend, it was Eliza who inspired thy works, dictated to thee the most affecting pages of them. Fortunate Sterne, thou art no more and I am left behind. I wept over thee with Eliza; thou would'st weep over her with me; had it been the will of Heaven, that you had both survived me, your tears would have fallen together upon my grave.

The men were used to say that no woman had so many graces as Eliza: the women said so too. They all praised her candour; they all extolled her sensibility; they were all ambitious of the honour of her acquaintance. The stings of envy were never poured against unconscious merit.

Anjengo, it is to the influence of thy happy climate that she certainly was indebted for that almost incompatible harmony of voluptuousness and clemency which diffused itself over all her person and accompanied all her motions. A statuary who would have wished to represent voluptuousness, would have taken her for his model; and she would equally have served him who might have had a figure of modesty to display. ·Even the gloomy and clouded sky of England had not been able to obscure the brightness of that aerial kind of soul, unknown in our climate. In everything that Eliza did, an irresistible charm was diffused around her. Desire, but of a timid and bashful cast, followed her steps in silence. Any man of courteousness alone must have loved her, but would not have dared to own his passion.

I search for Eliza everywhere: I discover, I discern some of her features, some of her charms, scattered among those women whose figure is most interesting. But what is become of her who united them all? Nature who hast exhausted thy gifts to form an Eliza, didst thou create her only for one moment? Didst thou make her to be admired for one instant and then to be forever regretted?

All who have seen Eliza regret her. As for myself my tears will never cease to flow for her all the time I have to live. But is this sufficient? Those who have known her tenderness for me, the confidence she had bestowed upon me, will they not say to me, she is no more, and yet thou livest.

Philosophical and Political History of the Indies (1770) Vol. II pp. 86-88.

ROUND ABOUT BOMBAY.

ROUND ABOUT BOMBAY.

Bobbery Hunt in the Suburbs

"QUIZ."

Next morning's sun had just arisen,
And drove the dusky clouds from heaven,
Ere Qui Hi, on his Arab horse,
Sets off to find Byculla course;
Where 'twas determin'd, ev'ry man
Should meet before the hunt began.
Their breakfast now the sportsmen take,
Merely a "plug of malt," and steak;
The bugle's signal now, of course,
Summon'd the bobbery to horse:
They get the word, and off they move,
In all directions to Love-Grove.
A jackass, buff'lo, or tattoo,
The sportsmen anxiously pursue.
Old women join the beasts in running:
"The junglewallas now are coming!"
So off they travel, helter-skelter,
In holes or corners to take shelter.
A loud "view—hollo" now is given:
"A dog! a Paria, by heaven!
"Surround him—there he goes—a head:
"Put all your horses to their speed."
He's lost—the knave has taken cover!
Old L——n now perceives another.

" Hark! forward, sportsmen—'tis the same:
" The rascal he shews famous game.
" See now the fellow scours along,
" In a direction to Girgaon:
" Dash after him; he turns again;
" We'll find him on Byculla plain.
" Oh luckless! we have lost all hope—
" He's taken cover in a tope."
Thus, spoke the huntsman, and he swore
He'd find him, or he'd hunt no more.
The horsemen fearlessly push in,
Contending who *the ear* should win;
For, gentle reader! know, that here
A *brush* is nothing to *an ear.*
But Qui Hi, disregarding care,
Fell headlong on a prickly pear:
Making, incautiously, a bound,
Both horse and rider bit the ground;
But luckily, except some dirt,
They both escap'd without a hurt.
The Paria in the tope they caught;
His ear extravagantly bought.
The cur had run them such a heat,
As put the hunters in a sweat;
They vow'd that on a future day,
They'd take his other ear away;
Now jumping-powder, wine and beer,
The riders and the horses cheer.
The huntsman now informed them all,
They were to tiff at Bobb'ry Hall.
Mounted again, the party starts,
Upsets the hackeries and carts;

Hammalls, and *palanquins,* and *doolies,*
Dobies and *burrawa's,* and *coolies.*
Malabar hill at last they gain'd;
Our hero at its foot remain'd;
His horse he could not think to ride,
Like others, up its rugged side,
So wisely took another path,
That led directly to *the bath,*
Where soon he found the party met
Were all for tiffin sharply set.

The Adventures of Qui Hi? by Quiz.
1816, pp. 228–230.

Environs of Bombay.

SIR EDWIN ARNOLD.

That section of the Great Indian Peninsula Railway which runs from Bombay to the capital of the Mahratta country may compare in interest with any hundred miles of iron road in the world. Leaving Byculla Station the traveller threads the thoroughly "Hindu" suburbs of Parel, Dadur, and Chinchpoogly, his train flying through groves of date and cocoa palms, amid temples, mosques, synagogues, and churches; dyeing-grounds spread with acres of new-dipped brilliant silks and calicoes; by burning-ghauts and burying-places; by mills, stone-yards, and fish-drying sheds, through herds of wandering brown sheep and grey goats, droves of buffaloes and kine and great throngs of busy people; all these combining into a continuous picture. Crossing an inlet of the sea at Sion Causeway, the line next coasts the island of Salsette amidst the most characteristic Oriental scenery, and arrives, by many a low-roofed village and tangled patch of jungle, at Thana. Here the outlying spurs of the Syhadri Mountains—steep eminences, coloured red and black, and capped with extraordinary square rocks, like walled fortresses, or domes and pinnacles constantly resembling temples—shut in the sea-flat upon which the town stands; and we are advanced to a spot where, with natural beauty on all sides, the thickets on the hills shelter tigers and panthers, and the water swarms with alligators. Of late years these wild creatures have been largely evicted by sea and land, and even the pretty striped palm squirrel–whose back is marked with Parvati's fingers–and the green parroquets with rosy neckrings, are becoming rare in places which once abounded with them.

India Revisited, 1886, pp. 69–70.

Picturesque Hills in the Neighbourhood.

CAPT. ROBERT GRINDLAY.

It is generally admitted that the earlier portion of the day is most favourable to the contemplation of the grandeur of mountain scenery; and this remark applies with peculiar force to the scenery of the Ghauts in India, when the daylight bursts suddenly upon a wondrous scene of gigantic pinnacles, apparently floating in an ocean of white mist, which rising in successive rolling masses and dissipating under the increasing influence of the sun, gradually developes the connecting range of mountains and the widespread plain below, studded with forests and cocoa-nut groves. In the neighbourhood of rivers and marshes the mist is more dense, and often lingers till noonday in picturesque wreaths along the mountain-side, or envelopes its fantastic peaks, investing the scene with a poetical and picturesque effect, which the excessive brightness of the atmosphere might otherwise destroy.

In the annexed plate it is attempted to convey an idea of the appearance of two mountains, called Bava Malang and Parbul, from Kallian, about thirty miles N. E. of Bombay.

The singular form of these mountains and their almost insulated position give them the appearance, when first discovered at daybreak, of gigantic Gothic cathedrals; and some of their pinnacles are surmounted with those forts, in the impregnability of which the natives of India had, through so many ages, placed reliance, until British intrepidity has shewn them their error.

The river represented (the Ulhas) falls into the northern part of Bombay harbour, and is navigable for the small craft which convey agricultural produce, cocoa-nuts, &c. to that port.

Scenery in Western India, 1830 pp. 41-42

In the Harbour.

JOHN SEELY.

Nothing in the shape of an aquatic excursion in India can be more delightful than a sail on a secure and large bay, with a fine refreshing sea breeze wafting you to your destination, with the scenery, as far as the eye can reach, grand, beautiful, and picturesque in the extreme. An excursion of this kind, with agreeable companions, after a few months grilling in the interior, makes the mind joyful, and the soul glad. On one side, as you proceed up the harbour, you have the mighty range of mountains stretching away their cloud-capt tops in every fantastic and romantic shape; peaks, cliffs, and hollows indented here, and thickly wooded there; the busy and noisy suburbs of Bombay lying on your left, where handsome English mansions, rural-looking native huts, monastic buildings of the Portuguese, with large Mahratta houses, inhabited by wealthy natives, denote opulence and splendour; while the whole scene is embellished with that variety of cultivation and foliage peculiar to tropical climates. As you pass on is an extensive and handsome range of barracks for the king's troops; a little further on brings you to the town of Mazagaum, chiefly inhabited by Portuguese and natives. Many pretty views present themselves on the shore in passing up the harbour, while the city and the shipping are gradually receding to the sight. In front is a large old-fashioned house built by Governor Hornby; beyond that is a large, handsome, white tomb, conspicuously placed on a promontory, containing the mortal remains of a distinguished Mussulman. The curious-looking hill called the Funnel, from its similarity of shape, rises abruptly in front, while on the right a Mahratta fort, called Shoon Ghur (probably Arzoon Ghur), raises its romantic turrets in solitary grandeur in the heart of the mountains. Surrounded by jungle, in all the wildness of nature, on the left the view is bounded by the hills of Salsette, which afford an agreeable back-ground to the whole of this magnificent scenery. Various inlets and salt-water streams may be seen running in different directions inland, which diversify the prospect, whilst a variety of boats are seen swiftly cutting the briny flood, hurrying on to their pursuits and destinations.

Considerably to our right, and almost in mid-bay, is Butcher's Island, where is a large range of buildings used as hospital barracks for the seamen of his majesty's navy in time of war.

After sailing three or four miles further, the bay begins to contract: it is still a noble expanse of water; and, from the great variety of luxuriant scenery and its size, would bear a comparison with the celebrated bay of Naples. I am transcribing my original book from the neighbourhood of Weymouth. This is said to be one of the finest bays in England, but it is not a twentieth part of the size of Bombay.

Wonders of Elora, 1824, *pp.* 16-22.

Sail in the Harbour.

LOUIS ROUSSELET.

On a fine morning in September I arrived at the Apollo Pier, where the bunder-boats congregate, amongst which I found my own, which was soon stored with the provisions, guns, hammocks, &c., which I took with me on this my first expedition. The sun had not yet risen, and the spectacle presented by the harbour was most beautiful. Close by, a fleet of vessels, black and silent, lay beneath the sea walls of the fort, and seemed to occupy only an insignificant space in this majestic bay, whose unbroken surface is lost in the distance of ten miles in the mists of the islands. The horizon was bounded by the Ghats, whose imposing line of terraces and fantastic peaks were beginning to glow in the early brightness of the dawn. I hurried the boatman, and we were soon sailing over this superb lake. The bunder-boats, which are employed in the harbour, are graceful barques of about thirty tons, carrying broad latteen sails, and having large and comfortable cabins astern, surrounded with blinds and furnished with benches. The crew consists of six or seven sturdy lascars. As we proceed, the beauty of the panoramic view increases. The tops of the mountains blaze; and the tallest peak, and the one mos remarkable for its bizarre form,—Funnel Hill,-assumes the shape of an obelisk, dark below and of purple hue above. The islands and the wooded shores, lately hidden from us by the mist, suddenly appear; a light and cool breeze sweeps over the water, and the dull noise of awakened Bombay reaches us. How charming is this hour in the tropics! All around is gay and beautiful. The foliage of the trees, refreshed by the dews of night, the songs of birds, the soft light of day-break, and the splendour of the rising sun, combine to form a whole that speaks to the heart and fills it with the most agreeable emotions. But the sun mounts above the roseate peaks of the Ghats; the scene rapidly changes, and the vivid light peculiar to these regions spreads everywhere. Karanjah, the island towards which we are directing our course, is still far distant. The faint outline of its mountains, in the form of a camel's back, rises in the midst of a dense mass of vegetation, which covers all the level portions of the island to the very centre, and extends down to the coast. The straits which separate it from the neighbouring continent are sprinkled over with innumerable fishing-boats; and these myriads of white points set off the deep blue of the sea.

India and Its Native Princes, 1882, pp. 38–39.

Ruskin's Salsette and Elephanta.

JOHN RUSKIN.

How awful now, when night and silence brood
O'er Earth's repose, and Ocean's solitude,
To trace the dim and devious paths, that guide.
Along Canarah's steep and craggy side,
Where—girt with gloom—inhabited by fear,
The mountain homes of India's gods appear.
Range above range they rise, each hollow cave
Darkling as death, and voiceless as the grave,
Save that the waving weeds in each recess
With rustling music mock its loneliness,
And beasts of blood disturb with stealthy tread
The chambers of the breathless and the dead.
All else of life, of worship, past away,
The ghastly idols fall not, nor decay,

Retain the lip of scorn, the rugged frown,
And grasp the blunted sword and useless crown,
Their altars desecrate, their names untold,
The hands that formed, the hearts that feared—
how cold!
Thou too—dark Isle, whose shadow on the sea
Lie like the gloom that mocks our memory
When one bright instant of our former lot
Were grief, remembered, but were guilt, forgot.
Rock of the lonely crest, how oft renewed
Have beamed the summers of thy solitude,
Since first the myriad steps that shook thy shore
Grew frail and few—then paused for evermore.
Answer—ye long-lulled echoes! Where are they
Who clove your mountains with the shafts of day,
Bade the swift life along their marble fly,
And struck their darkness into Deity,
Nor claimed from thee—pale temple of the wave—
Record or rest, a glory or a grave?
Now all are cold—the Votary as his God,
And by the shrine he feared, the courts he trod,
The livid snake extends his glancing trail
And lifeless murmurs mingle on the gale.
Yet glorious still, though void, though desolate,
Proud Gharapori, gleams thy mountain gate,
What time, emergent from the eastern wave,
The keen moon's crescent lights thy sacred cave
And moving beams confuse with shadowy
change,
Thy column's massive might and endless range.
Far, far, beneath where sable waters sleep,
Those radiant pillars pierce the crystal deep,

And mocking waves reflect with quivering smile
Their long recession of refulgent aisle:
Yet knew not here the chisel's touch to trace
The finer lineaments of form and face,
No studious art of delicate design
Conceived the shape, or lingered on the line.
The sculptor learned, on Indus' plains afar,
The various pomp of worship and of war,
Impetuous ardour in his bosom woke,
And smòte the animation from the rock.
In close battalions kingly forms advance,
Wave the broad shield, and shake the soundless lance,
With dreadful crest adorned, and orient gem,
Lightens the helm, and gleams the diadem;
Loose o'er their shoulders falls their flowing hair,
With wanton wave, and mocks th' unmoving air,
Broad o'er their breasts extend the guardian zones
Broidered with flowers, and bright with mystic stones,
Poised in aetherial march they seem to swim,
Majestic motion marked in every limb;
In changeful guise they pass—a lordly train,
Mighty in passion, unsubdued in pain,
Revered as monarchs, or as gods adored,
Alternately they rear the sceptre and the sword.
And mightier ones are there—apart—divine,
Presiding genii of the mountain shrine,
Behold, the giant group, the united three,
Faint symbol of an unknown Deity!
Here, frozen into everlasting trance

Stern Siva's quivering lip and hooded glance;
There, in eternal majesty serene
ProudBrahma's painless brow,and constant mine;
There glows the light ofVeeshnu 's guardian smile,
But on the crags that shade yon inmost aisle
Shine not, ye stars. Annihilation's Lord
There waves,with many an arm, th' unsated sword,
Relentless holds the cup of mortal pain,
And shakes the spectral links that wreathe his
ghastly chain.

Oxford Prize Poems, 1839, *pp.* 359-364.

Thana Creek.

JOHN SEELY.

Nothing can be more delightful than a sail by the salt-water channel that divides Salsette from the continent, passing by the town of Thana. Inland, the views on either shore are beautifully wooded, the lands picturesque and romantic, with many rude and venerable relics of Mahratha forts and Portuguese churches. You may proceed as far as Bassein, circumnavigating the interesting island of Salsette and part of Bombay for upwards of 60 miles, and enter the ocean again a little beyond Bassein; and all this agreeable journey may be performed in the greatest safety, and with perfect ease, sailing or rowing amid mountains, hills, and dales, with the shore close at hand on either side, and that shore richly ornamented with the most luxuriant and varied foliage; while an idle hour may be whiled away in fishing or shooting, or in viewing many old ruins that occasionally show their hoary points in the deepest solitudes of the forest.

Wonders of Elora, p. 23.

An Excursion to Salsette.

MRS. HEBER.

An excursion to Salsette to see the cave temple of Kanhari, together with some interesting places on the island, had for some time been in contemplation, and we set out to join Mr. Elphinstone and a large party at Toolsey. On leaving Matoonga, an artillery cantonment about the centre of the island, the country became interesting as well from its novelty as from its increased beauty. The road lay principally through a valley formed by hills of a moderate height, covered, wherever the rocks allowed of its growth, with underwood to their summits, while the valleys were planted with groves of mangoes and palms, with some fine timber trees. A very shallow arm of the sea divides Bombay from Salsette, and on an eminence commanding it, is a fort, apparently of some strength, built originally as a defence against the Mahrathas, and still inhabited by an European officer with a small guard; the islands are now connected by a causeway. The mountains in Salsette are considerably higher than those of Bombay, but covered with thicker jungle, while the valleys are more shut in, and consequently less healthy. We saw but few traces of inhabitants during a drive of eight miles, passing but one small village consisting of a most miserable collection of huts.

At Vehar we left our carriages, and proceeded on horseback and in palanquins through the jungle to Toolsey, the place of our encampment. This lovely spot is surrounded by mountains of considerable height, forming a small wooded amphitheatre, in the centre of which grows a fine banyan-tree. Here our tents were pitched, and I never saw a more beautiful scene than it afforded. The brilliant colours and varieties of dress on innumerable servants, the horses bivouacked under the trees with each its attendant sayces, the bullocks, carts, hackeries, and natives of all descriptions in crowds, the fires prepared for cooking, the white tents pitched in the jungle, together with the groups formed by the different parties on their arrival, altogether formed a *coup d'œil* which I can never forget, and which can be only seen in a tropical climate.

Our tent was pitched close to a tiger-trap then unset; there are a good many tigers in the sland, and one was killed a short time previous to our arrival. This was the first night I had ever slept under canvass, and but for the heat, which was intense, I could not have wished for more comfortable quarters; but Toolsey, from its peculiar situation, is reckoned one of the hottest places in India.

Early the next morning the Bishop and I mounted our horses, and took an exploring ride among the rocks and woods; some rain had fallen in the night, which had cooled and refreshed the air. The morning was delightful, a number of singing-birds, among whose notes I could distinguish those of the nightingale and thrush, were performing a beautiful concert, while the jungle-fowl were crowing merrily all around, and monkeys, the first which I had seen in their natural state, were sporting with their young ones among the trees; I enjoyed the ride exceedingly, and left the rocks with regret, though, from the sun being clouded over, we had been already enabled to stay out till eight o'clock.

At four o'clock in the evening we set out, some on horse-back, and some in palanquins, to the caves, with which the hill is literally perforated . . . . . It was late before we returned. Our path wound along the sides of the rocks, and was hardly wide enough in places for a palanquin to pass. The effect of so large a party proceeding in single file, with torches, occasionally appearing and disappearing among the rocks and woods, with a bright Indian moon shining over-head, was picturesque and beautiful in the highest degree. I happened to be the last, and had a full view of the procession, which extended for nearly half a mile. In northern latitudes one can form no idea of the brilliancy of the moon, nor of the beauty of a night such as this rendered more enjoyable from the respite which it affords from the heat of the day.

We left our tents early the next morning, Mrs. Macdonald and I, with most of the gentlemen of the party, on horseback to proceed to Thana, a town with a fort, on the eastern coast of the island. From thence to Salsette we went in a bunder boat, and there embarked on board the Governor's Yacht, where we found breakfast prepared, and sailed for about seven miles through scenery of a very remarkable character. The islands between which we passed lie so close to each other, that I could scarcely believe myself on the sea. On one side the prospect is bounded by the magnificent Ghats, with their fantastic basaltic summits, and the islands are occasionally adorned with ruins of Portuguese Churches and convents. In one of these, Ghodbunder, situated on sateep eminence, and guarded by a fort, we dined and slept.

Mrs. Heber's Journal, 1825, in Bishop Heber's *Journey, Vol. III pp: 84-86.*

View from the Kanhari Caves.

HOBART CAUNTER.

From the portico of one of the caverns the prospect is singularly striking. A long ledge, of several feet in width, supported at either end by the solid rock from which it is cut, protects the spectator from the influence of the sun, and allows him to enjoy without inconvenience the beauties of a scene remarkable for its peculiarity and grandeur. The portico is terminated towards the body of the building by a row of tall massive columns, gracefully proportioned and with no ornament, except on the bases and capitals. With the superincumbent ledge, which they support, they form a vestibule of great elegance. Under its grateful shade I stood for some minutes, contemplating the splendour of the view around me, beholding everywhere a mighty record of God's omnipotence. It is hardly possible to imagine how frequently this conviction is forced upon the mind while travelling in this magnificent country—for here the prodigies of Art bear a sort of collateral testimony to the wonders of Nature; but yet, how does the vast and stately grandeur of the mountain, crowned with everlasting snow, rising in solemn dignity from the plain, with all its accompaniments of animal, vegetable, and mineral production, and projecting, its lofty crest into the clouds, as if to hold communion with beings of a higher world,—how does it bring down to the lowest extreme of comparative insignificance the mightiest productions of human labour! It is clear that Nature has everywhere furnished the elements of Art; the one is an accessory to the other; and consequently, wherever Art prevails in its greater dignity and success, the glories of Nature are heightened to the contemplations of the philosopher, and even to the commonest admirer of the Creator's works.

In no country upon earth. not even excepting Upper Egypt, have the prodigious powers of the human mind been displayed to a greater extent than in India; and I confess I never entertained so exalted an idea of human capability as it deserves until I had witnessed those stupendous productions of man's ingenuity, so frequently presented to the traveller's eye on the peninsula of Hindustan.

Struck by the scene before me, I sat myself down upon a stone under the rocky perch of the cavern. Before me gushed a narrow but deep stream, which tumbled down the mountain in a broken line, appearing at the distance like a narrow strip of silver lace upon a green velvet mantle, but, upon a nearer approach, bounding and hissing over opposing rocks with the force and energy of " a thing of life." Just before it reached the place where I had seated myself, its waters gurgled and fried over a bed of rocks, which formed a considerable slope in the hill, and produced a cascade that sung one of Nature's lullabies with a far more sublime, if with a less harmonious cadence than babbling brooks.

Oriental Annual, 1836, pp. 284-286.

Cave Temples near Bombay.

GARCIA DA ORTA.

Bacaim [Bassein] is a very great city, and under its jurisdiction there are many lands and cities. It gives a rent to the king of more than 160,000 cruzados with its land and fortresses, afterwards granted to Francisco Barreto. The said lands are called Manora. They include, in one part, an island called Salsette where there are two pagodas or houses of idolatry under ground. One is under a very lofty hill built of stones in greater quantity than in the fortress of Diu, and which may be compared, in Portugal, with a town of four hundied houses. This hill has a grand ascent, and on arriving at the hill it is found to be a great pagoda worked and cut within the rock, where the Friars of San Francisco afterwards built a church called San Miguel. There are many pagodas of stone on the ascent, and near the summit there are other stone houses with their chambers, and still higher are houses cut in the rock, and in them there is a tank or cistern of water, with pipes to lead down the train water. Altogether there must be three hundred houses, and all contain idols sculptured in stone. But they are very heavy and dark, as things made for worshipping the devil.

They have another pagoda in a part of the island called Maljaz, [Mandapeshwar, or Monpensir] which is a very grand thing, also cut out of the rock. Within there are many other pagodas very dark and dismal. All who enter these houses say that it makes their flesh creep, it is so dreadful. Another pagoda, the best of all, is on an island called Pori, which we call the Isle of the Elephant [Elephanta]. On it there is a hill and in the upper part of it is a subterranean house worked out of the living rock, and the house is as large as a monastery. Within there are courts and cisterns of good water. On the walls, all round, there are sculptured images of elephants, lions, and many human images, some like Amazons, and in many other shapes well sculptured. Certainly it is a sight well worth seeing, and it would appear that the devil had used all his powers and knowledge to deceive the gentiles into his worship. Some say that it is the work of the Chinese when they navigated to this land. It might well be true, seeing that it is so well worked and that the Chinese are artists. It is true that, at the present day, this pagoda is much defiled by cattle getting inside, but in the year 1534, when I came from Portugal it was a very fine sight. I saw it at the time when Bacaim was at war with us. Soon afterwards the King of Combaya [Cambay] ceded it to Nuno da Cunha.

Colloquies (1563), tr. C. Markham 1913, page 443 to 445.

Kanhari and Bassein.

LADY WEST.

To-day we left Bombay in a hired barouche with our own horses to Parell, where Hormasjee Bomanjee lent us a pair of horses which took us to Coorla six miles. We had to pass over a very narrow road, two miles long, which joins the island of Salsette to Bombay. I am grown so tired, I had a Palankeen waiting to take me over. Mrs. Heber and I travelled in company, and the Bishop and Edward rode to Toolsey, where we found Mr. Elphinstone waiting to receive us and all our tents pitched in the most picturesque spot in a valley, with fine mountains nearly all round, and fine banyan trees which hung over us to shade us.

Edward got up early and took a ride. At three we started in our Palankeens to see the Kanhari Caves,—picturesque scenery, but the path sadly steep, rugged, and bad for horses. The caves are certainly very curious, one very much in the same style as the Karlee Caves, but not so large or in so perfect a state.

We were up this morning at a quarter to four. At five Edward got on his horse and Batt and I in our Palankeens to go six miles to Thana. But at the top of the Vehar Hill I found the Governor's carriage, which he had sent for me. I could not do otherwise than use it, and was much delighted with the driver to Thana. The descent of the hill is exceedingly steep, and the scenery very wild and beautiful. Thana seems a pretty place and they are now finishing a fine church there.

At two we had again to get into Bundar Boats to row to Ghodbunder, as the yacht got aground. The views all day were very beautiful, and employed the Bishop and Sir Charles Chambers in taking some pretty sketches.

We arrived at Ghodbunder at three—a Portuguese church, beautifully situated at the top of a high mountain, to which you ascend by an immensely long flight of stone steps. The encampment was at the foot of the hill, and was voted too hot, and all the ladies were lodged in the church, where we had a fine large room for eating, which was not forgotten anywhere. It would make an excellent dwelling house, and the views from it quite magnificent, on one side overhanging the water, which had the appearance of a fine lake.

In the evening Col. Rienzi harmonised us by singing to an ill-strung fiddle. He has a good voice, and some execution.

We breakfasted early this morning to go and see the old ruined city of Bassein eight miles off, and were to go in the yacht and sent our Palankeens on to await our arrival. But we had so little wind and had to tack about so much, it was thought advisable to get into the Bundar

Boats and row to Bassein. When we arrived there the Palankeens were not arrived. We all got out to walk under the umbrellas, and I believe I may say that no one ever felt greater heat or more scorching sun at 12 o'clock under a high wall, with the black sand half over one's shoes, which literally blistered our feet :—it was so hot. After half an hour's walk apparently three sides round a large castle, we saw a bullock cart with a little tilt; we (Mrs. Heber, Lady Chambers, and myself) were gladly lifted into and squeezed into this machine, and really no chaise and four would have been more welcome to us at that moment. We were driven very dexterously through ruined gateways and walls to a church, a fine and complete ruin, and saw some tombstones, of 1606, of Portuguese families. Soon after this the Palankeens arrived and we went to see a Hindu building not at all decayed, and a most perfect fine carved stone cow which they worshipped. We went to another church where there were remains of fine stone carving, and the entrance very fine. The arches and Corinthian pillars and some of the iron of the gate very finely embossed with iron nails. There are the remains of innumerable fine houses and streets.

It really fills one with melancholy when one reflects that this once magnificent place is now a perfect desert with not one single inhabitant, and it is not accounted for except that it is thought that the Mahrathas drove the Portuguese out of it. We were much pleased with it, and only regretted that we could not stay longer, but we were too tired and hot to prolong our researches, and as we had two Palankeens I took Lady Chambers into mine, and Sir Charles, took Mrs. Heber, and in half an hour we got back to the yacht, where we found an excellent dinner waiting for us, and to that, and claret and water, we did ample justice. We sailed back so soon that we found ourselves at Ghodbunder by the time dinner was over, and by the time our adventures had been related the carriages and horses were ready, and at 5 o'clock our agreeable and cheerful party dispersed. I think I may say that every one enjoyed it extremely; nothing could exceed Mr. Elphinstone's attention, civility, and wish of obliging; he was my devoted Cavaliere Servente the whole time. He certainly shines in these parties, and I am sure we all regretted that it was Saturday and that we must return home. Hormasjee's horses took us the first twelve miles to Ambolee; the hired horses took us to Bandora where we had to ferry over to Mahim, and by driving very fast we were soon home, as we found our horses the other side of the water, and drove the ten miles in an hour and twenty minutes.

The ferrying over is a curious process; there is a large cage put upon two boats, the horses are taken off, and one is pushed up the inclined plane into this cage in one's carriage. The horses stand by the side, and in a quarter of an hour one is rowed over. We saw the chief part of the island of Salsette. The whole of the drive to-day was very rich, almost like a gentleman's park with large mango trees where I suppose there have been houses, and now and then ruins of them and also churches with a Cross in front; it is indeed sad to think that all this fine country seems nearly depopulated; the Governor has tried to do what he can, but it does not seem to answer, in fact I suppose it is hot and unhealthy. In some degree Bassein reminded one of Goa, though there the Churches were kept in repair, and inhabited by the monks. The view of Bassein was very pretty from the water, walled all round. I regretted then, as I always do, that I cannot sketch.

Lady West's Journal. 1825, in Drewitt's
Bombay in the days of George IV. 1907,
pp. 178-181.

Elephanta.

BAYARD TAYLOR.

I visited to the Cave-temples of Elephanta. These celebrated remains are upon the Island of Elephanta, in the bay, and about seven miles distant from Bombay. I was accompanied by the captain of an American bark. We engaged a bunder-boat, a craft with a small cabin, something like the kangia of the Nile, embarked at the Apollo pier, and went up the bay with the flood tide. We passed the fort and floated along the shore as far as Mazagaum, where the wind favoured us for a run out to the island. The scenery of the bay is beautiful, the different islands rising from the water in bold hills covered with vegetation, while the peaks of the Malabar Ghauts cut their sharp outlines against the sky, on the opposite side. Butcher's Island, which lies between Bombay and Elephanta, is comparatively low and flat, and has a barren appearance, but it contains a number of European bungalows, and seems to be a favourite place of residence. Elephanta, on the contrary, which is about a mile in length, is lofty and covered with palm and tamarind trees. Its form is very beautiful, the summit being divided into two peaks of unequal height.

The water is shallow on the western side, and as we approached several natives appeared on the beach, who waded out two by two, and carried us ashore on their shoulders. A well-worn foot-path pointed out the way up the hill, and in a few minutes we stood on the little terrace between the two peaks and in front of the temple. The house of the sergeant, who keeps guard over it, still intervened between us and the entrance and before passing it, I stood for some time looking across to Bombay and Salsette, enchanted with the beauty of the prospect before me. More than half the charm, I found, lay in the rich, tropical foliage of the foreground.

Turning, I passed around the screen of some banana trees and under the boughs of a large tamarind. The original entrance to the temple is destroyed, so that it is impossible to tell whether there was a solid front and doorway, as in the Egyptian rock-temples, or whether the whole interior stood open as now. The front view of Elephanta is very picturesque. The rock is draped with luxuriant foliage and wild vines, brilliant with many-coloured blossoms, heightening the mysterious gloom of the pillared hall below, at the farthest extremity of which the eye dimly discerns the colossal outlines of the tri-formed god of the temple. The chambers on each side of the grand hall are open to the day, so that all its sculptures can be examined without the aid of torches. The rows of rock-hewn pillars which support the roof, are surmounted by heavy architraves, from which hang the capitals and shattered fragments of some whose bases have been entirely broken away.

Visit to India and China, 1856, pp. 46-48.

Elephanta.

BASIL HALL.

It must be owned, that, of all the lions of India, there are few to compare with the cave temples of Elephanta, which, from lying within less than one hour's sail of the town of Bombay, form the scene of many a pleasure party; a circumstance which ought to add considerably to the recommendation I have already given, that any person wishing to behold at a glance all the wonders of the East should select Bombay, rather than any other place. The island of Elephanta lies only a few miles further up the harbour than the spot where the ships anchor off the fort; and as large and commodious boats, covered with awnings, are to be had at a minute's warning, nothing is so easy as to transport one's self from the midst of the European society of the presidency, or from the bustle of the crowded native bazaar into the most complete solitude. As the island is not inhabited, the traveller finds himself at once undisturbed amidst some of the oldest and most curious, or, at all events, most striking, remains of the ancient grandeur of the Hindoos, which are anywhere to be met with. The effect, I have no doubt, is considerably augmented by the unusual abruptness of the change from a scene of such particular bustle to another of entire stillness. There are many points of intrinsic local interest about Elephanta which rank it very high in the scale of curiosity; yet it is one of those wonders which, although it may far exceed in interest what we expect, necessarily baffles anticipation. No drawing can represent it. Even a panorama, which, in the case of Niagara, has already conveyed to European senses most of the wonders of the great American cataract, could make nothing of Elephanta. The only device that could give a just conception of the form, size, colour, and so on, of these caves, would be a model of the full dimensions, similar to what Belzoni exhibited of an Egyptian mummy pit.

Fragments of Voyages, 2nd series, 1832, page 129.

2

The caves of Elephanta are not, by any means, of the same stamp; but they possess their own share of deep interest, which will not let them slip off the recollection. I was not more anxious to get sight of Niagara than to have a look at Elephanta: nor can I pretend to say which of the two gratified me most at first. Comparisons, after all, between such incongruous things are not only useless, but absurd. It is like comparing the pleasure of viewing the Elgin marbles with the surprise caused by hearing a concert played on one string. The former is pure, sublime, and enduring; the latter is strange, inexplicable, and transient. One we recollect merely for its singularity, the other for its instruction in genuine taste and refined fancy. Elephanta, therefore, considered as a work of art, may be compared to one of Paganini's extravaganzas in music. Niagara, on the other hand, in grandeur and severe simplicity, is about as difficult to match amongst the natural wonders of the earth as the Parthenon of Athens amongst the works of man. Rivals, no doubt, may be found; but I suspect they will both remain for ever at the top of their respective classes.

Fragments of Voyages, 2nd series, 1832, pp. 129, 131.

Elephanta.

SEELY.

On quitting Butcher's Island, called by the natives Deva Devi, or Island of the Gods, not far up the bay stands the celebrated Elephanta Island. It is of considerable elevation, and famous for its caves hewn out of the solid rock from the face of the mountain; they are considerably injured by time,—

"Whom stone and brass obey,
Who giv'st to every flying hour
To work some new decay."

These caves are very much injured by the action of the sea-breeze, and from not having drains cut on the top of the mountain to carry off the rain water; nor has any care been taken to have trenches made at the foundation; so that in the periodical rains they are often inundated, and abound with reptiles particularly snakes. From their vicinity to Bombay they are frequently visited by parties of pleasure; and to preserve them from wilful injury by casual visitors, a wall with a gate has been lately erected in front, and left in charge of an invalid sergeant, with a few invalid sepoys, to protect them. The old man has a good house adjoining, and has a comfortable sinecure of it, as most visitors do not forget his long stories and the accommodation for refreshment which his house affords. The view from the caves is very fine, as they are situated about 350 feet above the level of the sea. Here is the famous colossal figure of the Trimurti,—Brahma, Vishnu, and Shiva, the creating, preserving, and destroying powers of the Hindoo mythology. The cave is large, but by no means equal to the large temples of Karli, or the far-famed ones at Elora.

Wonders of Ellora, 1824, pp. 20-21.

On the way to Mahableshwar.

MRS. GUTHRIE.

In the soft twilight we picked our way over the rocks by the water, and when the moon shone out we crossed a stretch of ground where innumerable specks of crystal shone like diamond dust. On the viaduct we paused and looked down upon the temples grouped up and down the river. The broad deserted ghats were silent now. The sacred Krishna, bound on her long career, flowed by them a stream of silver. So lovely, so tranquil was the scene that it seemed all unreal—a vision in a dream. We moved away at last, and, bending our steps towards the distant lights, we found ourselves in the central square of the town. Alone as we were, we had no fear; even of an uncivil word. As the population of the place was Hindoo, musicians were beating their drums and twanging the 'vina' in front of an old palace, ornamented with colour and carving—a relic of other days. Afzul Khan probably lived in it when he was governor of the Wai district. His gallant train would have found ample accommodation in its vast courts and galleries.

In the one long street of the bazaar, throngs of men were walking up and down; while women and children, grouped under the verandahs, made the air resound with their shrill cries. People were making purchases at the open stalls. A knot of girls, gaudily attired, were buying strings of jessamine, and crowns of yellow flowers, destined to set off the great knot of glossy black hair raised upon their shapely heads. Handsome creatures they looked as they stood in the red glare of a cresset, flaming with cotton-seed steeped in oil. Numbers of white-robed votaries were wending their way to prayer. We peeped into no less than five temples, catching sight of long aisles of pillars, lit at the top by small lamps. At the end of these vistas were brilliantly-illuminated shrines, before which men in the attitude of prayer were performing 'puja.' Most of these halls had been mosques, but it was now the turn of the Hindoo.

Life in Western India. 1881. Vol. I, pp. 25-26.

Charm of Mahableshwar.

ROBERT BROWN.

I thought it better to defer writing until I could tell you of my arrival and proceedings at this far-famed and universally admired sanatorium. I have stood on the pyramids of Egypt, I have gazed with rapture on the mountain scenery of Ceylon, I have contemplated the beauties of my own heather hills, but not yet have I seen a landscape so extensive, so diversified, as that by which I am now surrounded; and whilst in the full enjoyment of such scenery, you will easily imagine that I am somewhat averse to the use of the pen.

The chief attraction of the place is its magnificent scenery and fine bracing English climate, the temperature ranging from 65 to 70 degrees, while in Bombay it is at least twenty degrees above that just now. It is a sort of sanatorium, founded by Sir John Malcolm, from whom the village takes its name of Malcompeth. It has a fine dry atmosphere, with a cooling breeze that braces every nerve and sinew of one's body, and enables one to undergo fatigue with quite a feeling of pleasure. We are here elevated some 4,000 or 5,000 feet; and at such an altitude you will easily imagine that we command a most extensive view of the surrounding country. On every side, far as the eye can reach, mountain upon mountain raises its lofty summit, contrasting beautifully with the rich luxuriance of the fertile valleys; and while the mind loses itself in the silent contemplation of such a scene, and naturally recurs to the recollection of other scenes in other climes, the ear is suddenly awakened by the roar of the mountain torrent, which, swollen by the last night's thunder-plump, now rolls down the precipitous raving with an impetuosity which no object in nature can check, plunging into the abyss beneath, and dashing the spray like smoke along the mountain-side; until, as if tired of exulting in its mad career, it gradually subsides into a peaceful stream, meandering through the rich green fields of plain beneath, and forming altogether a beautiful and striking object in the surrounding landscape. Gaze on it while you may; for see, the mist is rolling in dense clouds along the mountains, and the curtain of night will soon obscure the landscape from your vision. Look again! and that mountain-peak is shrouded in darkness, when—hark! a peal of deafening thunder rends the heavens and the lightning's flash penetrates the awful obscurity of the scene, and blinds the senses with its lurid brilliancy. A death-like silence succeeds, and while with long-drawn breath I await the next peal, a shriek from my favourite spaniel pierces my ear; I rush to his rescue, but only in time, alas, to see the footprint of the tiger's destroying paw!

Memorials. 1867. pp. 60–62.

Sunsets at Mahableshwar.

MR. GUTHRIE.

My first visit to this spot (Bombay Point) was made just as the sun in crimson glory dropped down into the sea. The hazy tints of golden amethyst that lingered about the mountain depths were indescribably beautiful.

During the dull months when the cold, dry winds blustered, the sunsets were the redeeming charm of the place, a foretaste of "the better land." No spot commanded a finer view of the departing day than our own verandah. Sometimes the orb set in peaceful beauty against a clear background of tender green and violet. Sometimes its beams would suddenly rend the leaden masses of cloud that concealed the sea horizon, and shoot up flaming like some great volcano. Early in the morning the sea that lay more than thirty miles away, was misty and blue; but in the evening it was crimson, like the sky. With the naked eye ships could be distinguished on its bosom. On one occasion, just as the great solar disc touched the water. a black object, no bigger than a man's hand, passed across it—a ship voyaging to gather pearls and spices on far shores. In India there is a bewitching beauty in "the parting hour," but finest of all was it to see a great lone planet all aflame in the deep orange of the after-glow.

Life in Western India, pp. 51-52.

A Journey to Mahableshwar, 1829.

ELIZABETH GRANT.

At last we were off, and as the sun declined and the air cooled, and the ascending path brought the mountain air to us, I was able to look up and out, and enjoy the singular scene presented by our party.

A *burra sahib* needed a large retinue when travelling in the East years ago. First went Nasserwanjee on a *tattoo* (a little pony) leading us all, sword in hand, for the scabbard only hung by his side the naked blade flourished at every turn above his head; next were some sepoys or peons, then my mother's palanquin and her spare bearers, then mine and more peons, then my father's, then the two ayahs'; next, the upper servants on ponies, but without swords then under servants on foot or on bullocks; the luggage, tents, canteens, trunks, all on bullocks, peons and coolies running beside them to the number altogether of fifty or sixty. It was a long train winding round among the hills, always ascending and turning corners, and when night came on, and the torches were lit—one in about every fourth man's hand—the effect was beautiful, the flames waving as the arms moved, leaves, branches, rocks, gleaming in turn among the dusky train that wound along up the steep footway. Daylight might not have been so picturesque, but it would have been far more suitable to the kind of journey, and the distance being considerable, many a weary step was taken before we reached our resting-place.

It was near midnight when we came to three tents sent by General Robertson for our accommodation. All we wanted was soon ready, for a fire was there, burning in a furnace made of stones, the usual travelling fireplace. Our curry was heated, I had nearly a whole bottle of beer, and my bed being ready by the time this supper was over, I was soon fast asleep in a region as wild as Glen Ennich.

My mother became quite reconciled next morning to our journey, for a messenger arrived very early with two notes for my father, one from General—then Colonel Robertson—and one from Colonel Smith; they were notes of welcome with directions, which, warned by the sufferings of the day before, we obeyed; very kind they were—everybody is kind in India—but it was not the kindness that pleased my mother, it was the messenger! He was one of the irregular horse, a native, light made, handsomely dressed, in coloured trousers, flowing robe, and yellow cap (I think). He rode well and caracoled his little spirited horse before us for just as long as we pleased to look at him. She took it into her head that he was one of Colonel Smith's regiment—which regiment was Heaven knows where—in Gujarat, I believe—so she asked Nasserwanjee for a rupee to give him, and did the civil with the air of a princess.

After breakfast we started again, a long ascent, and then, just at dark, a stretch of level road, brought us to the end of our journey, a large double-poled tent of Colonel Smith's, which was to be lent to us during our stay on the hills. We had a very good dinner very well served, and retired to our sleeping-tents in great good-humour. The night was piercing cold, and the chill of the water next morning was really painful; but a canter warmed me and gave me also a good view of the curious place we were settled on, a wide plain on the top of a long ridge of mountains. The Governor's small bungalow, and the Resident's a little way off, were the only houses at the station: everybody else lived in tents, scattered about anywhere in groups of from five to six according to the size of the establishment.

The mountain air was enchanting, the sun hot in the middle of the day, yet quite bearable, the mornings and evenings delightful, the nights rather cold. The society was on the pleasantest footing; the way of life most agreeable as soon as we got into it. The first few days we kept our Bombay hours, late dinners, and so on, therefore an exchange of calls with our neighbours was the extent of our intercourse, but as soon as we showed ourselves well-bred enough to conform to the habits of the place we got on merrily: dined at the Robertsons' often, lunched here and there, gave little dinners and little luncheons, and went with parties to the only two lions that there were, the sources of some river and a hill fort.

Lady Strachey's *Memoirs of a Highland Lady*, *1898, pp. 436–438.*

A French Artist on Matharan.

LOUIS ROUSSELET.

I mounted a pony and commenced my ascent. Night was drawing on, and the mountain-top was purple with the last rays of the setting sun; but as the moon was then at her full, I did not hesitate to enter the gorges that open behind Narel, trusting to the mild light of the satellite to guide me on my way. To the height of nearly 1,500 feet the rock forms a perpendicular wall, which seems inaccessible, and rests on elevated basements, radiating in every direction over the plain. The mountain is entirely isolated from the remainder of the chain of the Ghauts, and looks like a vast island of between nine and ten miles long, by one and a half or two miles broad. Its summit, which forms a long horizontal table-land, is nowhere more than 2,000 feet in height. A very good road rises zigzag up its northern face, but it is too steep to allow of carriages being used in the ascent.

I soon found myself in the midst of a fine forest of teak, which covered the whole outline of the mountain basements. Most of the trees had already lost their foliage, or retained only a few withered leaves. Lofty plane-trees, with their whitish trunks and curved boughs, were massed together at the brink of the precipice; and here and there a silk-tree spread out its arms, dry and spinous, bearing long white flakes.

The forest was intersected with glades, which allowed me to see, from time to time, the tangled array of ravines and hills which I was going to traverse. My rapid course in the midst of this solitude savoured of the fantastic. The wind was blowing among the trees; a thousand rumbling noises resounded on the mountains; and the vivid light of the tropical moon brought out in strong relief all the details of the surrounding landscape. At the foot of the steps which, staircase-like, climb the perpendicular flank of the principal mass, I pulled up my pony;

and, dismounting, I walked on, leading him by the bridle. The road, narrow and cut out of the rock, was continually turning this way or that, bringing me sometimes in view of the plain, which beneath the light of the moon resembled a vast lake, sometimes among the gloomy recesses of the precipices. In some places extensive landslips had formed a steep declivity, covered with a thick growth of forest-trees, rising from the bottom of the ravines to the summit; and here and there rills of spring-water followed the road for a moment and then bounded into space. The higher I climbed, the sharper and more agreeable became the cold. At last I reached the upper tableland, and rested for an instant at a chowkey—a small police-station. Here the transition is abrupt. You feel that you have entered a region entirely different from that you have left; for whilst the vegetation on the sides of the mountain is still purely tropical, that which covers the summit is of a wholly European aspect. One might believe oneself in a well-kept park; the thickets are bushy, and the trees gracefully formed and arranged in groups, while the air is cool and embalmed by thousands of flowers. A beautiful road, spread with gravel like a garden alley, running for several miles through the forest, brought me at last to the bazaar, a long row of native stalls in the midst of a glade. Next morning I went out at an early hour to visit the different points of view, the beauty of which I had so many times heard vaunted. A light mist covering the forest, and the leaves, whitened by an abundant dew, recalled memories of Europe. The houses of the Europeans, substantially built of red stone, crowned every height; alleys ran in every direction, opening out superb vistas. One of the points of the mountain, Louisa Point, terminates abruptly, and forms an immense precipice, at the bottom of which enormous rocks, owing to the fall of a landslip through the infiltrations of the rains, makes a sublime scene of chaos. At my feet stretched the whole Konkan down to the sea, which glittered in the sun. Bombay and its islands looked like dark points surrounded by silvery lines. The plain appeared parched and bare, and the watercourses by which it is furrowed were clearly defined by the green lines of the trees bordering them, while here and there small villages, surrounded by plantations of rice, lent some little animation to the desert tract. Nearly in front of me rose an isolated mountain, which my guide informed me was Mount Parbul, and which is plainly visible from Bombay; an enormous gulf, more than two miles wide, separated me from its level summit, which is at the same elevation as the spot whereon I stood. Pretty roads that go all round the tableland of Matheran extend along by the edge of the precipice, and display a richly varied panorama. The salient points of the mountain are marked off by them like the angles of a fortress, and so furnish magnificent foregrounds of rocks and forests at their several points of view. Far from being completely level, the ground is decidedly undulating, and forms, even on the summit of Matheran, small valleys and peaks.

The finest view to be obtained from Matheran is that which is commanded from the point called that of Panorama. Before the spectator rises the chain of Bava Malang, the crest of which, bare and jagged, appears to be crowned with innumerable strong castles, with towers and belfries; and in the distance, on the other side of a vast plain covered with forests and rivers and sprinkled over with villages, extends the long line of the Thull Ghauts, with their terraces, straight and perfectly horizontal, up to the summit, resembling a gigantic rampart. On another side, the sea and the islands, with the rich vegetation along the coast, complete the magnificence of this panorama.

India and its Native Princes, 1882, pp. 59-61, 63.

View from Panorama Point, Matheran.

"THE TIMES OF INDIA."

This height a ministering angel might select;
For from the summit of this hill, the amplest range
Of unobstructed prospect may be seen
That Konkan ground commands:—low dusky tracts,
Where Ulhas is nursed, far southward! Sahyadri hills
To the south and east, a multitudinous show;
And in a line of eye-sight linked with these,
The hoary peaks of Deccan that gave birth
To Godavari's sacred stream,
Crowding the quarter whence the sun comes forth,
Gigantic mountains rough with crags; beneath,
A little from the imperial station's western base
Main Ocean, breaking visibly, and stretched
Far into silent regions blue and pale,
And visibly engirding Bombay's isle
That now appears a dwindled object
And submits to lie at the spectator's feet.

These graphic lines of Wordsworth, slightly altered and adapted, give an exact description of the splendid view to be obtained from this the highest Point on Matheran. Strictly speaking it does not belong to Matheran proper, which extends from Hart Point north to Chowk Point south. It is the northern end of a small range which abuts on the east of Matheran, and extending to Garbut and Sondai in the south spurs away to the south-west Sahyadris. It is this range that is first seen from the railway and that hides Matheran proper from view. Owing to its great height of nearly 2,700 feet above sea-level, and favourable position, it commands, as its name implies, a panorama unequalled in these parts for its wide sweep of hill and plain, and for its wild grandeur. Those who have seen the famous Matterhorn call this Point its miniature. It boldly juts out like a cape into space and owing to the very small width of its headland, views from both its right and left are easily obtained at the same time.

From its northernmost ledge the eye has a sweep of over sixty miles of the most picturesque country in Western India,—the near hills with their sides clothed with thick forest, the green plain of the Konkan through which meander several rivers and streams, on one side the massive wall of the distant Ghauts with the famous peaks and fortresses of the Deccan rising above their shoulders, and on the other the broad sea as well as its creeks and estuaries wedging into the land. Right in front of us and stretching away from our feet, lie the range of eccentric hills and crags known as the Cathedral Rocks, some of whose peaks are battered and shaped into the most fantastic forms. Nearest to us and looking almost like a continuation of our range, is the pointed hill of Peb or Vikatgad, with its steep and almost inaccessible but nevertheless fortified top. Next to it is the rounded peak of Nakhinda, with its sloping back, standing out from the plain and appearing from certain points like a huge war-elephant on the run. Here the Cathedral range takes a turn to the west with the blade-like peak of Chanderi, the tent-like Mhas-Mara, the finger-like pinnacles of Navara-Navari, and the fortified top of Tavli which appears from here like a camel with its big hump and curved neck.

The range ends with the famous Bava Malang, standing out in stately grandeur like a huge cathedral with its upper outline sharp cut as if by human hands into regular form. Ruskin in a well-known passage calls all mountains the cathedrals of nature set in our midst to proclaim the glory of God. But Malangghad is not only metaphorically a cathedral: it really requires no great stretch of the imagination to see the form of a cathedral in its stately and regular outline. It is seen to its best advantage from here, rising to its full height, and its steep sides with the belts of green forest unobstructed by intervening hills. From Bombay too it appears a marked feature in the view of the Konkan hills to be obtained there; and when the rays of the setting sun resting on its top for a while illuminate its bold outlines with all the colours of the rainbow, the scene as best viewed from Malabar Hill is striking beyond measure and one not easily forgotten.

Beyond the Cathedral range to the north are seen some of the highest peaks of Salsette and south Gujarat. Between Malang and Tavli appear the high cone of Kamandurg and its neighbour, the flat hill-top of the wooded Tungar, ten miles from Bassein, which Sir Theodore Hope had once tried hard to make a rival sanitorium to this of Matheran. To their left rises another high conical peak, that of Dugad, and behind it the steep fortified height of Takmak, while beyond in the dim distance stretches the Surya range, with its chief peak of Asheri, the once famous and important fortress of the Portuguese commanding the rich and fertile plains of Kelve Mahim. The steep sheer rock of Mahalakshmi known to English sailors, who used to take bearings at sea from it, as Valentine's Head, twenty miles east of Dahanu in Gujarat, is visible on the horizon over the point of Peb; and the still more distant and higher fortress of Gambhirghad, eighty miles off, just peeps over the horizon as a small speck. Much nearer than these in the valley of the Tansa is the forked ridge of Mahuli, the highest among these hills, being more than 2,800 feet above sea-level, with its three fortified peaks, Palasgad to the north, Bhandargad to the south and Mahuli proper in the centre. To the east of Mahuli appears the pyramidal peak of Vatwad, with which in the north-east begins the view of the Sahyadri hills.

Raised on these hills is the plateau of the Deccan, and the districts of Nasik, Ahmadnagar and Poona can be made out from here with most of their noted peaks. Of the Nasik hills above the Sahyadri range appear the famous Trimbak, whence rises the sacred Godavari, and Anjaneri, the hot weather hill of the city of Nasik, fourteen miles to the east of it. In the adjoining Ahmadnagar district, on the border appear the two neighbouring forts of Alang and Kulang, and behind and between them the pointed peak of Kalsubai, the loftiest peak on the Sahyadris attaining a height of nearly 5,500 feet. The high fortresses of Ratangad, Harischandragad, and Bahirugad in Ahmadnagar are cut off from our view here by the crest of the Sahyadris, which here turn west to Sidgad, whose sugar-loaf peak stands out detached from the main line. The two other detached hills near are those of Gorakhghad and Machhindraghad.

Exactly opposite to us and right to the east is the sacred hill of Bhimashankar, at the top of one of the old highways from the Konkan to the Deccan and a noted place of pilgrimage. In front of Bhimashankar is the fort of Tungi and a little to its south are Kotaligad and Peth. Furthest to the south-west visible from here is the Kusur Ghaut another of the passes leading from the table-land into the plains of the Konkan below. The remaining Sahyadri peaks not quite visible from this point, but seen from this headland a little further off, are the flat-topped Dhak, six miles east of Karjat, the terraced peak of Rajmachi, the famous Nagphani or Duke's Nose near Khandala, and the historical forts of Lohgad and Visapur beyond Lanowli.

Bounded by the distant Sahyadri hills lies the Konkan plain, studded with numerous villages and hamlets and several forests, and furrowed by many streams, the largest being the river Ulhas, which coming down from the Ghauts into the plains at Karjat, winds into a regular circular course between Narel and Wangni before it meets the Kalyan Creek. The village of Narel is clearly seen from here with its station and the railway line, which is also discerned throughout its length from Karjat to Ambarnath till it winds round Bava Malang to go to Kalyan and Thana. Abutting on our Panorama-Garbut spur is the hill of Gardul, along whose side is cut the road from Narel to Matheran, distinctly visible from here. At our feet on the eastern side slopes the Mhar forest, the well-known picnic place of visitors here, which runs as a belt a few hundred feet below the top and meets the Kala forest on the other or western slope. Looking to the south-east we observe the massive green knolls of Mount Barry and Governor's Hill, between which loom on the horizon the distant peaks of the Sahyadris again; while a little to the left of the latter knoll we get a glimpse of Chowk at the south end of Matheran just peeping over the intervening part of the hill.

Turning from the east to the west, we see the Salsette and Thana hills rising wave-like in three lines one behind the other, and containing the two Bombay reservoirs of Vehar and Tulsi. In one corner appears Persik hill, through two tunnels in which the railway passes soon after leaving Bombay and beyond it glitter in the sun the waters of Kalyan creek. At our feet is the plain of Maldoonga, green with several villages, through which winds the thin streak of the river of that name which, flowing past the Talonje hills, meets the estuary at Panwell visible from here. Looking south-west we get a fine view of the northern points of Matheran and its thickly-wooded beautifully green top, through which peep out one or two house-tops, notably Craigieburn. Hart, Monkey, Maldoonga and the wedge-like Porcupine Points, all slope, gracefully clothed in green, into the Maldoonga valley below, while a thick green line of trees run right from the course of the renowned Malet's Spring. Behind Porcupine Point rises the twin hill of Prabal appearing quite different from what it appears from the nearer western Points of Matheran. From Prabal spur away to the Panwell plain many smaller hills, notably Morpa and Vansa, which alone are wooded.

Beyond the Panwell plain shines the sea of the Bombay harbour, dotted with several big islands,—Trombay to the north, and the two Karanjas, on one of which is Uran, to the south, with Elephanta and Hog Island, in the middle. Behind Trombay are the Coorla and Bhandup marshes, and to their south stretches the long line of Bombay town and island, which appears from here as a gem set in the sea, to use Ruskin's fine expression about Venice. Beyond Bombay which is about thirty miles in a line from here, shines the broad Arabian Sea, with its waters rolling free unbroken by any land for thousands of miles. The south Thana hills, of which the most prominent are the massive pyramidal peak of Manikgad and the tall funnel of Karnala, are the only ones round about Matheran that are not visible from here. But with this slight exception this Point really, as its name implies, commands an unrivalled panoramic view of the country, which we have endeavoured to describe with the aid of the Gazetteer, G. T. Survey maps, and the knowledge obtained by frequent tramping through the picturesque country itself, "meet nurse for a poetic child."

Times of India, 16 April 1897.

The Ghauts.

IMPERIAL GAZETTEER.

The great wall of the Western Ghats probably represents the primaeval water-divide of the bygone Peninsula as it represents that of to-day; but the upheaval to present altitudes must be comparatively recent, inasmuch as the steep-sided valleys of the rivers draining westward, and their tendency to deepen and reach back eastward at their sources, seem to testify to a yet unadjusted gradient. With a general elevation of 3,000 feet, the rugged outlines of the Western Ghats are shaped into steep-sided cliffs and square-crested flat-topped peaks, which present a remarkable appearance. The weathering action of ages has shaped the trap formation into natural citadels and fortresses which dominate the crest of the hills, and were found most useful as military positions in the wild days of Maratha supremacy. South of Bombay the seaward face of the hills is clothed with dense forest, and passes inland from the coast are few. But in the north the interior plateau is approached by several roads, famous in history, from the level coast strip on the western side. Of these the Borghat is the best known, for where the railway now curls and twists around the spurs of a tremendous ravine to a height of 2,027 feet above the sea was once the military road which has ever been regarded as the key to the Deccan. It opened the way from the rising port of Bombay to the plains of India. The Thalghat (1,912 feet) to the north-east of Bombay is another historic pass which likewise now carries a railway; and a third (almost equally celebrated) connects Belgaum with the little port of Vengurla. The precipitous square-cut peaks, which give such a fantastic appearance to the scenery of the Western Ghats, are to be found wherever horizontal strata of varying degrees of resistance are subject to subaerial denudation. They repeat themselves in the Droogs of Deccan scenery.

The seaward face of the Western Ghats is steep, a veritable 'landing stair' (ghat) from the sea, and the intersecting valleys are filled with luxuriant vegetation, nourished by the sea-borne mists and vapours which condense upon the crest of the hills and stream down the steep-sided gullies in endless procession during the monsoon season. The narrow space of lowland bordering the sea below (from twenty to fifty miles wide) is much broken by spurs throughout the northern province of the Konkan, and in North Kanara the hills approach the sea very closely; but farther to the south they recede, leaving the fertile plains of South Kanara and Malabar comparatively open. In the District of Malabar the Western Ghats merge into the irregular uplands of the Nilgiris, rising in altitude to 7,000 and 8,000 feet ere they drop suddenly to a remarkable gap (the Palghat Gap), through which the railway is now carried eastward from the coast port of Beypore.

The low-lying plains bordering the sea throughout the whole length of Western India, from the Kathiawar promontory to Cape Comorin represented in mediaeval ages most of the wealth and strength of India, and are still noted for their great fertility. Ancient ports and factories (Arab, Portuguese, and Dutch) are to be found scattered along the coast line, and amid the palm groves of Malabar are many relics of the days when the commerce of the East centred on this coast. The long, firm, curved outline of the western sea-board south of Bombay is lost in Malabar. Here inlets and backwaters break across the dividing line of sea and shore, rendering the coast scenery impressively beautiful. Cascades plunge down the steep-sided cliffs into depths spanned by rainbows; and the deep stillness of primaeval forest encloses the clear reaches of the sea.

3rd ed. 1908. Vol. I *pp. 38-40.*

Scenery of the Ghauts.

FITZCLARENCE, EARL OF MUNSTER.

As we approached the limits of the great table-land of India South of the Narbuddah, the country became less cultivated and more romantic; and within a mile of this termination the views became every instant more magnificent. The bare points of the rocks and hills appeared above the trees and verdure: and the immense mountain to the south of the pass, which overhangs the plain, is seen threatening all below. The vast chasms, and perpendicular walled valleys, many hundred feet beneath the level of the land on which I stood, were finer than anything I had ever beheld; and the numerous forts on the different pinnacles of the mountains, some near, others more distant, added to the sublimity of the scene. I wished for a glimpse of the sea, and since I have arrived here have been told that from one particular spot this can be obtained, though my longing eyes were disappointed in viewing that which an Englishman feels to be next neighbour to his native country.

The number of beautiful views which continually presented themselves were delightful. I never in any part of Spain or Portugal saw finer scenery. One valley, bounded with mural sides, was so deep, that I could not perceive the bottom, except from the very brink of the precipice; and, being covered with trees and shrubs of the most charming foliage, added much to its other beauties. We found it tolerably easy to descend that part on which our pioneers had been employed, but the remainder was extremely difficult; and it took us till twenty minutes after six (near one hour and a half) before we overtook the escort and my palanquin below in the plains of the Konkan. But magnificent and stupendous as the scenery is around, it does not, I am told, in any degree equal the Ghauts to the southward.

Journal of Route 1819, *pp.* 319-320.

ACCOUNTS OF BOMBAY.

ACCOUNTS OF BOMBAY.

Streynsham Master.

1672.

Having given you a particular account of the Religion and Practice of the Inhabitants of Guzzaratt farr exceeding the leaves of Paper I thought the Relation thereof would have taken up; I shall adventure to trespass a little farther on your Patience and give you a Small account of our Island of Bombay, where I now am, and according to the little time I have had to informe myselfe of this I desire you would measure the imperfect account I am able to render of it.

Bombay is an Island lying upon the Coast of India in about 18 degress North Latitude; 'twas given to the King of England in Dowry with Queen Katherine, the Daughter of Portugal, anno 1662. But not delivered to the English until anno 1668; and in 1668 his Majesty was pleased to give it to the East India Company by reason of some ill government. Since it hath been in the possession of the English both under the King and Company it hath not flourished or Increased in Commerce soe much as it might otherwise have done, and tis hoped will hereafter doe, and by reason there are other Islands lye between the Maine land and this, especially one called Salsett upon which the Portugals have a notable Pass called Tannah, by which noe Vessell can pass into the adjacent River and Maine, but by their Permission, for which they exact intollerable dutys, soe that the Comerce between this Island and the Neighbour Country of Decan is thereby wholy Impeded, therefore the only way to bring Trade to it and to mrke it famous must be by Sea, which is very facill, only a little and but a little Expensive at the first; whereof I shall not insist here. Presuming the President (who is Governor of Bombay) and Councill have represented the matter more effectually to the Company.

Bombay is Inhabited by all the severall Nations or Sects of People I have before mentioned. Here is Mahumetans, and a place where they say one of the Saint of their Religion was buryed, to which many come in Pilgrimage and doe homage at the grave; here is Hindooes of all Sorts and a place to which they goe to pay their Devotions, esteemnig it sacred and antient; here is allsoe some Parsees, but they are lately come since the English had the Island, and are most of them Weavers, and have not yet any place to doe their Devotion in or to Bury their Dead. But the greatest and the ruling part for some years past (that is since the Portugalls have had it) is that of the Christians, the Portuges haveing erected 5: very fair and large Churches, and divided the Island into soe many Parishes, though God knows the major Part of these Christians are very little Different from the Hindooes or naturall Indians, and understand as little of Christian Religion; for they goe by the name of Rice Christians, that is those that profes and owne the Name of Christianity for Sustenance only, being a most miserable poore People, and kept in horrible Slavery, Subjection, and Ignorance. But though since we have had the Island their yoke is much eased, and they seem to be desirous of knowing our Religion, to the Propagation whereof on this Island a fair feild seems to be laid open, and how farr it may spread from hence God knoweth, who may increase into the Courts of all these Eastern Princes and the Bowells of the Neighbour Countrys, if He have such Mercy in Stoere for soe meek, gentiele, and charitable a peopye. And if we were supplyed with able, sober, and orthodox and grave divines for the Ministry, there is great hopes of success. But the Company were (in our Judgment) much mistaken in those two sent out anno 1669 for this worke, one of them to preach and the other to teach a free schoole who were both soe very averse to all things taught and used by the Church of England, that instead of making new Proselits, they had lost many of our owne People, who refused to come to heare them, claiming the same liberty and priviledge which they very roughly and indiscreetly blobbed out to have themselves, that they would not hear the Common Prayer or Soe much as come into the place where it or the Lords Prayer, Apostles Creed, or Ten Commandments were said, directly contrary to the Hon'ble Company's Laws which were sent out the same year they came, wherein they require that in Publique the King's Majestie, the Peace, Happiness and Prosperity of his Kingdomes, and the good and wellfare of the English East India Company be prayed for, and every Sunday the Apostles Creed, or sometimes in place thereof *Athanasius* Creed, and the Ten Commandments, or the Summary thereof out of the 24 Chap. of St. Matthew 37, 38, 39 and 40, ver. be read,—these people, I say, were soe farr from observing this order of the Company that neither of them could be prevailed with at any time to read the Apostles Creed, nay or to say the Lords Prayer, which though the Company's Laws require it not, yet we thought as good and necessary as the other things it doth require. But one of them would some times, tho' a long time first, and that very rarely, would read one of the Chapters where the 10 Commandments was, and some times where the Lords Prayer was, but the other of them never or would did to his Death. And when they marryed any they did it in a strange manner, making the marryed Sweare before God and the Congregation or Company present, which the Soldyers made very ill use of; and because they would not bury the Dead many of them were highly offended, and indeed all their ways were new and soe contrary to the Custome and Education, and humour of the generallity there that it gave great offense and occasion of much debate, that not only the Portugez, to whose Priests, who are generally too well learned for such of our Ministers, these things were very novall and strange but also the Natives would enquire what Class or Sect of Englishmen they were, and to make the busynes worst, there was a Souldyer that came out that yeare allsoe, who pretended the light of the Spiritt, which moved him to Preach, and he had sometimes Delivered his Doctrine in Publicke among them, offering to dispute it with any of the two Ministers, that he was as lawfully sent to Preach the Gospell as they were. But the Deputy Governour did not thinke it convenient to let him have the like liberty, and therefore tooke hold of him and clapt him in Prison, where after a short time he came to a soberer understanding.

"To conclude this paragraph of Bombay, I say we here upon the place doe find that men of this New Straine of opinion and learning are not at all fitt to plant the Gospell here; for it must needs be that they will be disliked of the generallity of the English, which must certainely much divide and distract the opinions of new Proselites. And the honour of these People, may I thinke the air of these Climates, doth much incline to the old orthodox Doctrine and episcopall government, for we find generally those of that persuasion are not soe positive and dogmaticall but more moderate and charitable (a virtue very agreeable to these People), and better learned, espetially in the antient Fathers, and Soe more able to hold a sound argument against the Romish Priests then those of the other Persuasions.

"I shall not trouble you with more at present, having, I doubt, too much trespassed on you allready; if you thinke this discourse may give satisfaction to any of the Company or Committee, who we hear, and by some passages have reason to believe soe, are of opinion we that live here are men of noe conscience or honesty, bringing noe Religion with us on this side the Cape, if you thinke it may be satisfactory to them, or others concerned in the Trade, or for their Relations in these parts, I leave it wholy to your self to shew as your wisdom shall thinke fitt, reserving such part as Treats of particular concerns, &ca.

"Sr: yours, &ca.

"*Bombay, January* 18: 1671" (*i.e. N.S.* 1672).

Diary of W. Hedges, ed. with unpublished records by Yule, 1888, Vol. II.

Fryer.

1675.

I

Bombaim is the first that faces Choul, and ventures farthest out into the Sea, making the Mouth of a spacious Bay, from whence it has its Etymology: Bombaim, quasi Boon Bay.

Beyond it lies Canorein, Trumbay, Munchumbay, with their Creeks, making up the North side of the Bay: Between whom and the Main lies Elephanto, Kerenjau, Putachoes, with the great Rock or barren Islet of Henry Kenry: These, with some part of the Main, constitute the South-East side of the Bay; all which together contribute to the most notable and secure Port on the Coasts of India; Ships of the greatest as well as smaller Burthen having quiet Harbour in it; wither if they can, they chuse to betake themselves, if they happen, as oft they do, to lose their Voyages by the Monsoons.

East India and Persia, 1698 Vol. I, page 160.

(Hakluyt Society's Edition by W. Crookes, 1908).

Fryer.

2

Where at first landing they found a pretty well Seated, but ill Fortified House, four Brass Guns being the whole Defence of the Island; unless a few Chambers housed in small Towers in convenient Places to scowre the Malabars, who heretofore have been more insolent than of late; adventuring not only to seize their Cattle, but depopulate whole Villages by their Outrages; either destroying them by fire and sword, or compelling to a worse Fate, Eternal and intolerable Slavery.

About the House was a delicate Garden, voiced to be the pleasantest in India, intended rather for wanton Dalliance, Love's Artillery, than to make resistance against an invading Foe: For the Portugals generally forgetting their pristine Virtue, Lust, Riot and Rapine, the ensuing Consequences of a long undisturbed Peace where Wealth abounds, are the only Remarkable Relique of their Ancient worth; their Courages being so much effeminated, that it is a wonder to most how they keep any thing; if it were not that they have lived among mean spirited Neighbours. But to return to this Garden of Eden, or Place of Terrestrial Happiness, it would put the Searchers upon as hard an Inquest, as the other has done its Posterity: The Walks which before were covered with Nature's verdent awning, and lightly pressed by soft Delights, are now open to the Sun, and loaded with the hardy Cannon; The Bowers dedicated to Rest and Ease, are turned into bold Rampires for the watchful Centinel to look out on; every Tree that the Airy Choristers made their Charming Choir, trembles, and is extirpated at the rebounding Echo of the alarming Drum; and those slender Fences only designed to oppose the Sylvian Herd, are thrown down to erect others of a more Warlike Force. But all this not in one day.

East India and Persia, Vol. I, *page* 164-5.

Fryer.

3

From whence let us walk the Rounds. At distance enough lies the Town, in which confusedly live the English, Portugueze, Topazes, Gentues, Moors, Cooly Christians, most Fishermen.

It is a full Mile in length, the Houses are low, and Thatched with Oleas of the Cocoe-Trees, all but a few the Portugals left, and some few the Company have built, the Custom-house and Warehouses are Tiled or Plastered, and instead of Glass, use Panes of Oister-shells for their Windows (which as they are cut in Squares, and polished, look gracefully enough). There is also a reasonable handsome Buzzar.

At the end of the Town looking into the field, where Cows and Buffoloes graze, the Portugals have a pretty House and Church, with Orchards of Indian Fruit adjoining. The English have only a Burying Place, called Mendam's-Point, from the first Man's Name there interr'd, where are some few Tombs that make a pretty Shew at entring the Haven; but neither Church or Hospital, both which are mightly to be desired.

There are no Fresh Water Rivers, or falling Streams of living water: The Water drank is usually Rain-water preserved in Tanks, which decaying, they are forced to dig Wells into which it is strained, hardly leaving its braçkish Taste; so that the better sort have it brought from Massegoung, where is only one fresh Spring.

On the backside of the Towns of Bombaim and Maijm, are woods of Cocoes (under which inhabit the Banderines, those that prune and cultivate them), these Hortoes being the greatest Purchase and Estates on the Island, for some Miles together, till the Sea break in between them: Over-against which, up the Bay a Mile, lies Massegoung, a great Fishing Town, peculiarly notable for a Fish called Bumbelo, the Sustenance of the Poorer sort, who live on them and Batty, a course sort of Rice, and the Wine of the Cocoe, called Toddy. The ground between this and the great Breach is well ploughed, and bears good Batty. Here the Portugals have another Church and Religious House belonging to the Franciscans.

Beyond it is Parell, where they have another Church, and Demesnes belonging to the Jesuits; to which appertains Siam, manured by Columbeens, Husbandmen, where live the Frasses, or Porters also; each of which Tribes have a Mandadore, or Superintendent, who give an accôunt of them to the English, and being born under the same degree of Slavery, are generally more Tyrannical than a Stranger would be towards them; so that there needs no other Taskmaster than one of their own Tribe, to keep them in awe by a rigid Subjection.

Under these Uplands the Washes of the Sea produce a Lunary Tribute of Salt, left in Pans or Pits made on purpose at Spring-Tides for the over flowing; and when they are full, are incrustated by the heat of the Sun. In the middle, between Parell, Maijm, Sciam, and Bombaim, is an Hollow, wherein is received a Breach running at three several places, which drowns 40,000 Acres of good Land, yielding nothing else but Samphire; athwart which, from Parell to Maijm, are the Ruins of a stone Cawsey made by Pennances.

At Maijm the Portugals have another compleat Church and House; the English a pretty Custom-house and Guard-house: The Moors also a Tomb in great Veneration for a Peor, or

Prophet, instrumental to the quenching the Flames approaching their Prophet's Tomb at Mecha (though he was here at the same time) by the Fervency of his Prayers.

At Salvesong, the farthest part of this Inlet, the Franciscans enjoy another Church and Convent; this side is all covered with Trees of Cocoes, Jawks, and Mangoes; in the middle lies Verulee, where the English have a Watch.

On the other side of the great Inlet, to the Sea, is a great Point abutting against Old Woman's Island, and is called Malabar-hill, a Rocky, Woody Mountain, yet sends forth long Grass. A-top of all is a Parsy Tomb lately reared; on its Declivity towards the Sea, the Remains of a Stupendious Pagod, near a Tank of Fresh Water. which the Malabars visited it mostly for.

Thus we have completed our Rounds, bringing in the Circumference Twenty Miles, the Length Eight, taking in Old Woman's Island, which is a little low barren Island, of no other Profit, but to keep the Company's Antelopes, and other Beasts of Delight.

The People that live here are a Mixture of most of the Neighbouring Countries, most of them Fugitives and Vagabonds, no account being here taken of them: Others perhaps invited hither (and of them a great number) by the Liberty granted them in their several Religions which here are solemnized with Variety of Fopperies (a Toleration consistent enough with the Rules of Gain), though both Moors and Portugals despise us for it; here licensed out of Policy, as the old Numidians to build up the greatest Empire in the World. Of these, one among another, may be reckoned 60000 Souls; more by 50000 than the Portugals ever could. For which Number this Island is not able to find Provisions, it being most of it a Rock above Water, and of that which is overflowed, little hopes to recover it. However, it is well supplied from abroad both with Corn and Meat at reasonable Rates; and there is more Flesh killed for the English alone here in one Month, than in Surat for a Year for all the Moors in that Populous City.

The Government here now is English; the Soldiers have Martial Law: The Freemen, Common; the chief Arbitrator whereof is the President, with his Council at Surat; under him is a Justiciary and Court of Pleas, with a Committee for Regulation of Affairs, and presenting all Complaints.

The President has a large Commission, and is ViceRegis; he has a Council here also, and a Guard when he walks or rides abroad, accompanied with a Party of Horse, which are constantly kept in the Stables, either for Pleasure or Service. He has his Chaplains, Physician, surgeons, and Domesticks; his Linguist, and

Mint-Master: At Meals he has his Trumpets usher in his Courses, ahd Soft Music at the Table: If he move out of his Chamber, the Silver Staves wait on him; if down Stairs, the Guard receive him; if he go abroad, the Bandarines and Moors under two Standards march before him: he goes sometimes in his Coach, drawn by large Milk-White Oxen, sometimes on Horseback, other times in Palankeens, carried by Cohors, Musslemen Porters: Always having a Sombrero of State carried over him: And those of the English inferior to him, have a suitable Train.

East India and Persia, Vol. I, page 171-178.

Fryer.

4

Happy certainly then are those, and only those, brought hither in their Nonage, before they have a Gust of our Albion; or next to them, such as intoxicate themselves with Laethe, and remember not their former Condition: When it is expostulated, Is this the Reward of an harsh and severe Pupilage? Is this the Elysium after a tedious Wastage? For this, will any thirst, will any contend, will any forsake the Pleasures of his Native Soil, in his Vigorous Age, to bury himself alive here? Were it not more charitable at the first Bubbles of his Infant-Sorrows, to make the next Stream over-swell him? Or else if he must be full grown for Misery, how much more compassionate were it to expose him to an open Combat with the fiercest Duellists in Nature, to spend at once his Spirits, than to wait a piece-meal'd Consumption? Yet this abroad and unknown, is the ready Choice of those to whom Poverty threatens Contempt at home: What else could urge this wretched Remedy? For these are untrodden Paths for knowledge, little Improvement being to be expected from Barbarity. Custom aud Tradition are only Venerable here; and it is Heresy to be wiser than their Forefathers; which Opinion is both bred and hatch'd by an innate Sloth; so that though we seem nearer the Heavens, yet Bodies here are more Earthy, and the Mind wants that active Fire that always mounts, as if it were extinguish'd by its Antiparistasis: Whereby Society and Communication, the Characteristick of Man is wholly lost. What then is to be expected here, where sordid Thrift is the only Science? After which, notwithstanding there is so general an Inquest, few there be acquire it: For in Five hundred, One hundred survive not; of that One hundred, one Quarter get not Estates; of those that do, it has not been recorded above One in Ten Years has seen his Country; And in this difficulty it would hardly be worth a Sober Man's while much less an Ingenuous Man's, who should not defile his purer Thoughts, to be wholly taken up with such mean (not to say indirect) Contemplations; however, a necessary Adjunct, Wealth, may prove to buoy him up on the Surface of Repute, lest the Vulgar serve him as Aesop's Frogs did their first rever'd Deity.

East India and Persia, Vol. I, page 180-181.

II

This passage from Philip Anderson gives Fryer's account in convenient, form.

PHILIP ANDERSON.

We will now endeavour to take a dioramic view of Bombay in its improved condition. The population was composed of English, Portuguese, Hindus, Mussulmans, and native Roman Catholics, called "Cooly Christians," who were chiefly engaged in fishing. The dwellings of these different classes were not fixed in separate quarters of the town, but were placed indiscriminately. The town was a mile in length. The houses were low, and for the most part thatched; a few only, which had been built by Portuguese or English, being of substantial construction. None of the windows were glazed; but in many, oyster shells were used as a substitute for glass. There was a burial ground at a place called Mendairn's Point, from the name of the individual whose corpse was first interred there. Within six hundred yards of the Fort the land was being gradually cleared of trees and cottages. There was one Church, a pretty object, belonging to the Portuguese. On Malabar Hill stood a Parsi tomb recently erected, and the ruins of a large Hindu temple. At Mahim was a Portuguese Church, with a house and other handsome buildings attached. There were also an English Guard-House and Custom-House. The Jesuits possessed a Church and extensive demesnes at Parell, and Sion was also their property. On the low ground to the South-east of Sion were salt pans, the Court having sent out directions that they should be constructed on the model of those at Rochelle in France, and Santavalli in Portugal.

Colaba, or old Woman's Island, as it was called for long, had been taken possession of peaceably in 1674 after an arrangement made between Gerald Aungier and the Portuguese. For many years it was only used "to keep the Company's antelopes, and other beasts of delight." None of its land was appropriated to individuals, as from the first it was reserved to be a military cantonment.

In the Harbour, Butchers' Island—as it was then and still is called—was only used as a run for a few cattle, and a place where small vessels were hauled ashore and cleaned. Elephanta was also used only for cattle, and remained in the hands of the Portuguese. The figure of an elephant carved out of a black stone—from which the island received its name—was standing unmutilated, and so also was the figure of a horse. The tract on the main land extending from the south point of the Harbour to the river Penn was called "The Corlahs," and Bombay was dependent upon it for its supply of provisions, particularly at such times as the Portuguese prohibited all exportations from Salsette.

At the other side of the small Strait which separates Salsette from Bombay were the Aquada Blockhouse, and on the hill a mile beyond Bandora the Portuguese Church, which so gracefully overlooks the sea. The Roman Catholic services were well performed. A new landing-place led to a College of Paulitines, as the Jesuits were then called. Before the College stood a large cross, and before that was a space, which, when the traveller from whose work this account is chiefly taken, visited it, was "thwack'd full of young blacks singing vespers." The collegiate establishment was defended, like a fortress, with seven cannon, besides small arms. Great hospitality prevailed, and distinguished guests were, on their arrival and departure, saluted with a roar of artillery. The Superior possessed such extensive influence that his mandates were respectfully attended to in the surrounding country, and the traveller who had the good fortune to be provided with his letters commendatory, was met by the people, wherever he halted, with presents of fruit and wine. The town of Bandora was large, with tiled houses. A view from midchannel embracing the town, colleg., and Church of St. Andrew, was extremely picturesque. At a distance of four miles was another Church, described as magnificent; and the whole neighbourhood was studded with the villas of Poruguese gentlemen, many of whom lived in considerable state.

To the East of Salsette, the sail by way of Thana to Bassein, which is now so justly admired, must in those days have been of unrivalled beauty. Trombay was adorned with a neat Church and country seat. When Thana had been passed, the traveller's eye rested at every half mile on elegant mansions. Two of these deserve special mention. One, the property of John de Melos, was three miles from Thana. It stood on a sloping eminence, decorated with terraced walks and gardens, and terminating at the water side with a banquetting house, which was approached by a flight of stone steps. A mile further was Grebondel, [Ghodbandar], the property of Martin Alphonso said to be "the richest Don on this side Goa." Above rose his fortified mansion, and a Church of stately architecture. Within Bassein were six Churches, four convents, a College of Jesuits, another of Franciscans, and a library of moral and expository works. The Hidalgos dwellings, with their balconies and lofty windows, presentedan imposing appearance. Christians only were permitted to sleep within the walls of the town, and native tradesmen were compelled to leave at nightfall.

English in Western India, 1854, pages 67–69.

OVINGTON.

1689

This Island has its Denomination from the Harbour, which allows the safest Rideing for Ships of any in these parts, and was originally called Boon Bay, *i.e.*, in the Portuguese Language, a Good Bay or Harbour. By Ptolomy it was described under the Name of Milizigeris. And before it fell into the Hands of the English, was under the Dominion of Portugal, from whence it was translated to the Crown of England, upon the Marriage of the Infanta of Portugal to King Charles the Second, Anno. 1662. And is now put into the Possession of the East-India Company, for the convenience of their Ships and Traffick.

Before we espyed the Main of India, several Snakes of different sizes came swimming round our Ship near the surface of the Water, by which we knew we were not far from Land, because they are never seen at any great distance from the shore; they were washed from it, I presume, by the violence of the Rains in the times of the Mussouns, which I shall afterwards describe. This was seconded by another sign of our approaching the Land, viz. by a multitude of Locusts, which came flying upon our Masts and Yards, when we were distant from it Thirty Leagues, as we found by our Computation afterwards. They were above two Inches in length, and their reaching us at that distance from the Shore, argued their great strength of Wing to flie to us so very far; by which they mounted aloft, after they had rested themselves a while, and took their Flight directly upwards.

A Voyage to Suratt, 1689, pp. 129–130.

OVINGTON.

2.

They have here abundance of Coconuts, which bring some Advantage to the Owners, but very little either of Corn or Cattle, but what is imported from the adjacent Country; and these not in great Plenty, nor of very good Growth. A Sheep or two from Suratt is an acceptable Present to the best Man upon the Island. And the Unhealthfulness of the Water bears a just Proportion to the Scarcity and Meanness of the Diet, and both of them together with a bad Air, make a sudden end of many a poor Sailer and Souldier, who pay their Lives for hopes of a Livelihood. Indeed, whether it be that the Air stagnates, for the land towards the Fort lies very low, or the stinking of the Fish which was used to be applied to the Roots of the Trees, instead of Dung; or whatever other Cause it is which renders it so very unhealthful, 'tis certainly a mortal Enemy to the Lives of the Europeans. And as the Ancients gave the Epithet of *Fortunate* to some Islands in the West, because of their Delightfulness and Health; so the Modern may, in opposition to them, denominate this the *Unfortunate* one in the East, because of the Antipathy it bears to those two Qualities.

We arrived here (as I hinted before) at the beginning of the Rains, and buried of the Twenty Four Passengers which we brought with us, above Twenty, before they were ended; and of our own Ship's Company above Fifteen: And had we stay'd till the end of the next Month, October, the rest would have undergone a very hazardous Fate, which by a kind Providence ordering our Ship for Suratt's Rivermouth, was comfortably avoided. A fortunate Eacape indeed! because neither the Commander, nor myself, were in any Hopes of surviving many Days: neither Temperance, the most Sovereign Medicine, nor the safest Prescription in the Physical Art, could restore the Weakness of our languishing decay'd Natures. And that which thoroughly confirm'd to us the unhealthfulness of the place we had lately loosed from, was the sudden Desertion of our Diseases, and return of Health, before half the Voyage to Suratt was finished. In the middle of which Passage we manifestly perceiv'd in our Bodies as evident an alteration and change of Air for the best, as our Palates could distinguish betwixt the Taste of Wine, and that of Water.

The Deputy-Governor, Mr. George Cook a pleasant and obliging Gentleman, sollicited me upon the account of my Function to reside with him upon Bombay, and invited me with all the Proposals of a frank and generous Civility, to wave my Voyage, and continue with him there, because they were then destitute of a Minister. And indeed the Deference I bore to such kind Expressions, and to the Duty of my Calling, were invincible Arguments for my Stay, had I not been satisfied of the immediate infallible sad Fate I was under, like that of my Predecessors; one of whom was interred a Fortnight before this time, and three or four more had been buried the preceding Years: Which common Fatality has created a Proverb among the English there, that Two Mussouns are the Age of a Man. This is much lamented by the East-India Company, and puts them upon great Expenses for supplying the Island with fresh Men, in the room of those that are taken away, and providing able Surgeons, furnish'd with Drugs and Chests from Europe, to take care of the Infirmaries, and all that are sick.

A Voyage to Suratt, 1689, pp. 140-143.

OVINGTON.

3.

The Island lies in about Nineteen Degrees North, in which is a Fort, which is the Defence of it, flanked and Lined according to the Rules of Art, and secured with many Pieces of Ordinance, which command the Harbour and the parts adjoining. In this one of the Companies Factors always resides, who is appointed Governour to inspect and manage the Affairs of the Island; and who is vested with an Authority in Civil as well as Military Matters, to see that the several Companies of Soldiers which are here, as well as Factors and Merchants, attend their various Stations, and their respective Charge.

The Island is likewise beautified with several elegant Dwellings of the English, and neat Apartments of the Portuguese, to whom is permitted the free Exercise of their Religion, and the Liberty of erecting publick Chappels of Devotion; which as yet the English have not attain'd to, because the War with the Mogul interrupts the finishing of a stately Structure which was going on for their publick

Church. For want of this a particular Room is set apart in the Fort for Publick Service twice a day, at which all are enjoyn'd to be present ; and for performance of which, and other Sacred Offices, a Salary of an 100 l. annually, besides the convenience of Diet and Lodging, is allowed to the Minister by the Company.

The Gentiles too, as well as Christians, are permitted the Freedom of their Religion, and conniv'd at in their Heathen Worship. I accidentally once entred into one of the Gentiles Chappels, but durst not stay for fear of disturbing the Bramin with the Visit. The smallness of it would scarce admit of above Nine or Ten to enter into it. At the remotest part of it was placed the Pagod upon the ground, which was only a Face form'd of Tin, with a broad flat Nose, and Eyes larger than a Crown Piece. On the right side of this Image hung a small Purse for the People Oblations; on the left, very near it, lay some burnt Rice, which the Bramin had sacrificed ; and at the entrance of the Door stood a Trumpet, which sounded all the while he was a sacrificing.

The Island by the War with the Mogul was much Depopulated and Impoverished, both by destroying the English Inhabitants, and wasting the Fruit of the ground, especially of the Coco-Trees, whose Nuts are the staple Income upon it.

A Voyage to Suratt, 1689, pp. 147-149.

Richard Cobbe.

1715.

Bombay Castle, Oct. 5, 1715.

MY LORD,

Having had the honour of paying my respects to your Lordship a little before I left England, I remember the charge you were pleased to lay upon me, the giving your Lordship some account of this island, and the state of religion here; particulars of which I hope, you will excuse, nor having as yet been sufficiently instructed in the manners and customs of the inhabitants of this Place; but, generally speaking, they are a people wholly given up to idolatry and superstition, ignorant and poor; they consist chiefly of Moors, Gentous, Portuguese and Cooley Christians, some converts which the Portuguese have made by marrying into their families, the better to ingratiate themselves with the natives.

The whole island in circumference is about twenty miles, and eight in length, much healthier than heretofore, or than is usually reported; which may be attributed not only to the prohibiting the Bucksho, the smaller sort of Fish, with which they used to dung their ground and trees in these parts; but to the stopping up and repairing several sea-breaches, which formerly overflowed a third part of the island. The soil itself is poor and barren, a sandy rock, producing little else besides Batty, Coco-nuts and a few Greens; however we are plentifully supplied with variety of provisions from the neighbouring Coasts; Syrash [Siraz] Wine, which is our chief liquor, we have from Persia, very strong and wholesome, but not so well tasted; Arrack from Goa or Batavia; and extraordinary good Wheat from Surat, with which we make the best bread in all India. We have three good forts here, and one strong built and well fortified castle.

The number of inhabitants, together with the English, are reckoned about 16,000 souls, of different languages as well as religions; the Moors and Gentous have their Mosques and Pagoda's, the Portuguese several, I think five Churches, supplied with Padres and Clerico's from Goa; but the English have only a private Chapel for their public Devotion. Here are indeed the remains of a spacious Church formerly intended, but never brought to perfection, the ruins of which are to this day a standing monument of reproach to us, among the heathen to a proverb; but this reproach we hope in a little time to wipe off, having already gotten considerable large contributions from the neighbouring factories, as well as this place, in order to rebuild it; which good design I hope your Lordship will not think it amiss to approve of and encourage. Another favour I have to beg, to know what name your Lordship will please to give it when finished; and whether my reading Prayers in it will suffice, for want of a regular Consecration.

Letter to the Bishop of London, Dr. John Robinson.

Bombay Church, 1766 pp. 21 to 23.

Captain Alexander Hamilton.

Circa 1723.

Bombay comes next in course, an island belonging to the crown of England. It was a part of Katharine of Portugal's portion, when she was married to Charles II of Great Britain, in anno 1662. Its ground is sterile, and not to be improved. It has but little good water on it, and the air is somewhat unhealthful, which is chiefly imputed to their dunging their cocoa-nut trees with Buckshoe, a sort of small fishes which their sea abounds in. They being laid to the roots of the trees, putrify, and cause a most unsavoury smell; and in the mornings there is generally seen a thick fog among those trees, that affects both the brains and lungs of Europeans, and breed consumptions, fevers, and fluxes.

Mr. Cook, according to the treaty, took possession of the island, in the King's name, and forthwith began to fortify regularly, and, to save charges of building an house for the governor, built a fort round an old square house, which served the Portuguese for a place of retreat, when they were disturbed by their enemies, till forces could be sent from other places to relieve them.

After the fort was lined out, and the foundations laid, Sir Gervas Lucas arrived from England with two ships, but affairs being settled before he came, did not stay at Bombay longer than January 1666, and left the government of the island in the hands of Mr. Cook and his council, the presidency for the then company, residing at Surat. Their trade flourished, and increased wonderfully; but, after the fort was finished, the King finding, that the charge of keeping Bombay in his own hands would not turn to account, the revenues being so very inconsiderable, he made it over to the East India Company in fee tail, which continues so till this time.

In building the fort where it is, Mr. Cook shewed his want of skill in architecture, where a proper and convenient situation ought to be well considered, for it is built on a point of rocks that jets into the sea, where there are no springs of fresh water, and it stands within 800 paces of an hill, called Dungeree, that overlooks it, and an enemy might much incommode it from that hill, as we found by experience in anno 1689, when the Mogul sent an army on Bombay. As for the magnitude, figure, and materials of the fort, there is no fault to be found in them, for it is a regular tetragon, whose outward polygon is about 500 paces, and it is built of a good hard stone, and it can mount above 100 pieces of cannon; and that is all that is commendable in it: but had it been built about 500 paces more to the southward, on a more acute point of rocks, called Mendam's Point, it had been much better on several accounts. First, it had been much nearer the road for protecting the shipping there, it had been farther off Dungeree Hill, it would have had a spring of pretty good water, which served the hospital that was afterwards built there, and the shipping had been better secured that lay in the little bay between the point where the fort now stands and Mendham's Point.

They went about building several other little forts and sconces in convenient places, to hinder an invasion, if any of their neighbours should have attempted one. At Mazagun there was one, at Souree one, at Sian one, at Mahim one, and Worlee had one, and some great guns mounted on each of them. Notwithstanding the company was at so much charge in building of forts, they had no thoughts of building a church, for many years after Sir George Oxendon began to build one, and charitable collections were gathered for that use; but when Sir George died, piety grew sick, and the building of churches was grown unfashionable. Indeed it was a long while before the island had people enough to fill a chapel that was in the fort, for as fast as recruits came from Britain, they died in Bombay, which got the island a bad name.

There were reckoned above 5,000 £ had been gathered towards building the church, but Sir John Child, when he came to reign in Bombay, converted the money to his own use, and never more was heard of it. The walls were built by his predecessors to five yards high, and so it continued till the year 1715, when Mr. Boone came to the chair, who set about building of it, and, in five years time, finished it by his own benevolence, and other gentlemen, who, by his persuasions, were brought in to contribute. The Company also contributed something towards that pious end.

About the year 1674, President Aungier, a gentleman well qualified for governing came to the chair, and, leaving Surat to the management of deputies, came to Bombay, and rectified many things that were amiss, and brought the face of justice to be unveiled, which before lay hid in a single person's breast, who distributed her favours according to the governor's direction. He erected a formal court, where pleas were brought in and debated; but that method lasted but a few years, when Sir John Child came to the chair the court was done. Mr. Aungier advised the Company to enclose the town from Dungeree to Mendham's Point, for securing the trading people from the insults of their troublesome beggarly neighbours on the continent; but his proposals were rejected, and that necessary piece of work was reserved for Mr. Boone also. And happy it was for the inhabitants that the town was secured by a wall, otherwise Connajee Augarie [Angria] would have harassed them with continual insults since his war with the English began.

The name of Mr. Aungier is much revered by the ancient people of Surat and Bombay to this day. His justice and dexterity in managing affairs, got him such esteem, that the natives of those places made him the common arbitrator of their differences in point of traffick: nor was it ever known that any party receded from his award.

There are no dangers in going into Bombay Road, but one sunk rock that lies about half a league from the castle. It is dry at low water, and has a channel within it deep enough for the greatest ships to pass. I never heard of any damage done by that rock, but to a small ship called the Baden, which by carelessness, run on it at noonday, and was lost.

New account of the East-Indies, 1739;
Vol. I, pp. 183-189.

"Description of the Port and Island of Bombay."

1724.

The haven of Bombay near fifty leagues southward of Surat, in nineteen degrees of north latitude and comprehends all the waters that enter between Colayr on the west point of the island Salsett, and the two small islands of Hunary and Cunary on the South near the main.

It is reputed one of the most famous havens of all the Indies, as never being choked up by the storms, or yearly monsoons, but affords at all seasons reception and security for whole fleets.

Within this haven or bay stands the Island of Bombay which gives title and denomination to the whole sea that enters there, but as for the Island itself, it is barren and incapable of raising sufficient provisions for its inhabitants.

There are as appears by the annex'd chart some small islands scarce worth the notice, but two others are of consideration, namely Caranjah, which is wholly encompass'd by the waters of the Port of Bombay and Salsett, a much larger island, in figure almost square, against two sides whereof the water of this Harbour strikes; the west side of Salsett is wholly exposed to the Ocean, and the north side is wash'd by an inlet of water called the Road of Bassein reaching as far as the east point of Salsett.

On part of the Island of Bombay stands Mahim, the name formerly of the whole Island.

There was in old time, built here by the Moors, a great castle; and in the time of the Kings of Portugal, this was the place where his court and custom-house was kept and here were the duties paid by the vessels of Salsett, Trombay, Gallian [Callian] and Beundy [Bhiwundy] on the main.

Description of the Port and Island of Bombay, 1724, pp. 1-3.

Ives.

1754.

Bombay is a small island, but for its size, perhaps the most flourishing of any this day in the universe. Though the soil is so barren as not to produce any one thing worth mentioning, yet the convenience of its situation will always more than make up for that defect. It may be justly stiled "the grand store-house of all the Arabian and Persian commerce." When this island was first surrendered to us by the Portuguese, we hardly thought it worth notice; but, in a very few years afterwards, we experimentally found the value of it, and it is now become our chief settlement on the Malabar coast.

The natives are shorter and stronger made than those on the Coromandel coast; only four Cooleys carry a Palanquin here, whereas six are generally used at Madras and Fort St. David. The inhabitants of this place are numerous, and are made up of almost every nation in Asia.

Voyage from England to India, 1773, p. 31.

2.

Bombay is the most convenient place among all our settlements in the East Indies, for careening or heaving down large ships; and for small ones they have a very good dock. At the time we were there, they were making great improvements in it, which when finished, will not fail to make it still more commodious. They have also a very good rope-yard. Indeed, this is the only place, in that distant part of the world, for shattered ships to refit at; having always a good quantity of naval stores, and its very name conveying an idea of a safe retreat in foul weather.

On this island are many little forts and batteries, as Dungaree, Massegon, Mahee, Mendham's Point, and Sion hill. Some guns are mounted on each of them; but the principal fort which defends the place, has above an hundred. This building is a regular square, and the materials thereof are very good. The church also is not less substantial than the fort; it is a very handsome, large edifice, and in comparison of those which are to be met with in the other settlements, it looks like one of our cathedrals. It was built by a voluntary subscription among the gentlemen of this factory, and the Rev. Mr. Cobbe, (father to my late worthy friend Mr. Richard Cobbe, Admiral Watson's chaplain) was the chief promoter of this truly pious work: he at that time resided at Bombay as chaplain to the factory. The whole time we spent here, passed very agreebly; for as the island lies in 19° north, the heats must of course be more tolerable than they are at Fort St. David, which is in the latitude of 11° 48′ north.

The admiral's family resided at the Tankhouse (so called from a large tank or pond near to it) and here, as well as at all their other settlements, the Company allowed the admiral and his principal attendants Palanquins, over and above the five Pagodas a day, which were given him to defray part of the expenses of his table. As the Indian horses are of little value, and yet very scarce, oxen are here frequently made use of in their stead; and the admiral had a chaise and pair of these oxen allowed him also by the Company. They are commonly white, have a large pair of perpendicular horns, and black noses. The admiral oftentimes went in this chaise for an afternoon's airing to Malabar hill, and to the end of Old Woman's island, to Marmulla, and many other places. In England, if these creatures are forced out of their usual slow pace, it is too well known that they will faint or lie down under their burthen; but at Bombay they trot and gallop as naturally, as horses, and are equally serviceable in every other respect, except that by their being subject to a loose habit of body, they sometimes incommode by the filth thrown upon you by the continual motion of their tails. Whenever we got to the end of our ride, the driver always alighted, and put the near bullock in the other's place; then he would put his hand into both their mouths, and after pulling out the froth, mount his box again, and drive back. It seems this precaution is absolutely necessary, for as they travel at the rate of seven or eight miles an hour, they would otherwise be in danger of suffocation.

Whilst we were at Bombay, I took particular notice, that at the death of a friend, the Indians collected together and sung, either in the house of the deceased, or under the window; agreeable to that passage in St. Matthew's gospel, "when Jesus came into the ruler's house, and saw the minstrels and the people making a noise, He said unto them, give place, &c." There it was that I also first saw the ceremony of their burning the dead. As the place was very populous, there were seldom less than three or four burned every night near the water's edge, under Malabar-hill.

During my stay at this place, I hired by the month, a chaise drawn by a pair of bullocks. In the several excursions I made in this carriage, I had frequently passed by one of those religious persons, or anchorets, who in India are called Joogees; and who, in consequence of a vow made by their parents, and during their mother's pregnancy with them, are devoted to the service of heaven. One evening, I and a companion had an inclination to pay a short visit to this Joogee; who always sat in one posture on the ground in a shady cocoa-nut plantation, with his body covered over with ashes, and his long black hair clotted, and in the greatest disorder. As we approached him, we made our salutation, which he respectfully returned; and then with the assistance of our Indian driver, who could speak English, we began a conversation with him, that principally turned on the wonderful efficacy of his prayers, and which he pretended had given health to the sick, strength to the lame, sight to the blind, and fecundity to women who for their whole lives had been deemed barren. When we were about to take our leave of him, I offered him a present of two rupees which he bade me to throw on the ground, and then directed his servant, who was standing by, to take them up; which he did with a pair of iron-pincers, throwing the rupees at the same time into a pot of vinegar. After they had lain there a little while, the same servant took them out, wiped them carefully, and at last delivered them to his master; who soon afterwards, by way of return, presented us with a few cakes of his insipid pastry. I then requested of him, that in his next prayers he would petition for an increase of my happiness; to which, with great complacency in his countenance, he replied: "I hardly know what to ask for you: I have seen you often, and you have always appeared to me to enjoy perfect health; you ride in your chaise at your ease; are often accompanied with a very pretty lady; you are ever well cloathed, and are likewise fat; so that you seem to me to be in possession of every thing that can be any way necessary to happiness. I believe therefore, when I pray for you, it must be in this strain: that God would give you grace to deserve, and to be thankful for those many blessings which he has already bestowed upon you." I told him that I was thoroughly satisfied with the mode of his intended supplication for me and with a mutual exchange of smiles and compliments, we parted.

Our hospital at Bombay was without the town-wall; and in order to make my attendance on it the more convenient, Mr. Delaguarde (a factor in the Company's service) was so obliging as to give me the use of a very commodious house, which lay near the hospital, and belonged to him as superintendant of the powder-works. Here I took up my residence, with other gentlemen who assisted me in the execution of my duty. At a little distance from the front of this house is a capacious bason of water, which for the greater part of the year is perfectly dry, but during the continuance of the rainy season, and for some time after, serves as a pond for watering cattle, and swarms with a species of fish about six inches long, and not unlike our mullet. The natives catch them in great plenty soon after the rain sets in, and more than once I had them served up at my own table. This would be looked upon as a very extraordinary circumstance in any other place; but as these fish are found in almost every pool and puddle at Bombay, it ceases to be a matter of wonder among the inhabitants of that island. Various have been the speculations of curious and inquisitive men to account for this phænomenon. Some have supposed, that exhaling power of the sun is so strong in the sultry seasons, as to be able to raise the spawn of the fish into the atmosphere, and there suspend and nourish it, till the rains come on, when it drops down again in the state of living and perfectly-formed fish. Others, perhaps with a greater degree of probability on their side, imagine, that after the ponds become dry, the spawn may possibly fall into deep fissures made in the earth below the apparent bottom, where there may remain through the whole sultry season, a sufficient quantity of moisture to prevent the animalcule from corrupting; and when the rain-waters come on and fill the pond again, the fish is produced and made to appear in such abundance. This, among other hypotheses which I have heard offered on this curious subject, seems best to account for it; but whether even this solution be adequate to the effects produced, I shall not presume to determine.

Voyage from England to India, 1773, *pp.* 33-36.

There is another [Baman] tree of this sort in the Cocoa-nut grove at Bombay, on the road to the arbour near Malabar-hill, which is the third largest and most shady of any I have ever seen; but this last differs from the other two in this remarkable circumstance, that none of its branches have descended into the earth, and formed (as the two others have done) new trunks or trees. It appears indeed to have made some efforts towards it, but the rooty shoots have not yet struck the ground. The single body however, or trunk of the tree at

Bombay, is of much larger dimensions than any one of the many bodies of trunks belonging to those near Fort St. David and Gombroon. Under that on the Coromandel Coast, are the ruins of some houses; and it is commonly related (in order to make the tree appear the more marvellous) that this one tree once shaded a whole town. At a small distance from this tree near Gombroon, there is a Pagoda or temple, in a very ruinous condition, except a small part, which is kept in good repair, and much frequented by the Gentoos in their devotions. The Gentoos likewise worship under the shade of those trees which grow near Fort St. David and Bombay, but with this material difference, that at the two last places they have no Pagodas built with mens hands, any more than the Druids of old had, who under their consecrated oak worshipped one supreme God, immense and infinite, and could not think of confining their adoration to the narrow limits of a temple, which they deemed would be quite inconsistent with those attributes. In like manner, the Banian tree is held sacred by the Gentoos, who are almost as sensibly hurt by your cutting or lopping off one of its superfluous branches, as if you were to mutilate or destroy a cow, between whose sacred horns they often place their hand, when they make their most solemn oaths, and appeals to the Deity.

Voyage from England to India, pp. 199-200.

The island of Bombay has of late been rendered much more healthy than it was formerly, by a wall which is now built to prevent the incroachment of the sea, where is formed a salt marsh, and by an order that none of the natives should manure their cocoa-nut trees with putrid fish.

Voyage from England to India, pp. 448.

Carsten Niebuhr.

1764.

The isle of Bombay is two German miles in length, by rather more than half a mile in breadth. A narrow channel divides it from another small isle of little value, called by the English Old Woman's Island. Bombay produces nothing but cocoas and rice; and on the shore a considerable quantity of salt is collected. The inhabitants are obliged to bring their provisions from the continent, or from Salset, a large and fertile island not far from Bombay, and belonging to the Marattas. Since I left India, the English have made an attempt upon Salset, which is indeed very much in their power, and the public papers say that they have been successful. I know not whether they may be able to maintain themselves in it against the Marattas, whose armies are very numerous.

The sea breezes and the frequest rains, cool the atmosphere, and render the climate of this island temperate. Its air was formerly unhealthy and dangerous, but has become pure since the English drained the marshes in the city and its environs. Still, however, many European die suddenly here; but they are new comers, who shorten their days by mode of life unsuitable to the climate; eating great quantities of beef and pork, which the Indian Legislator has wisely forbidden, and drinking copiously of the strong wines of Portugal in the hottest season. They likewise persist obstinately in wearing the European dress, which by its ligatures impedes the free circulation of blood, and by confining the limbs renders the heat more intolerable. The Orientals again live to a great age, and are little subject to diseases, because they keep the body at ease in wide flowing robes, abstain from animal food and strong liquors, and eat their principal meal in the evening after sunset.

The city of Bombay, situate in the northern part of the island, is a quarter of a German mile in length, but narrow. It is defended by an indifferent citadel towards the sea, and at the middle of the city. On the land side its fortifications are very good. During the war the East India Company expended no less than 900,000 French livres a-year, in the construction of new works for its defence; and, although these works are no longer carried on with the same activity, yet the fortification of Bombay still continues, so that it must be in a short time the most. considerable fortress in India. Besides the town, there are in the island some small forts sufficient to protect it from any irruption of the Indians.

In this City are several handsome buildings; among which are the Director's palace, and a large elegant church near it. The houses are not flat roofed here, as through the rest of the east, but are covered with tiles in the European fashion. The English have glass windows. The other inhabitants of the island have their windows of small pieces of transparent shells framed in wood, which renders the apartments very dark. In the east it is the fashion to live during the dry season in chambers open on one side. The houses of Bombay are in general neither splendid nor commodious in any great degree.

The harbour is spacious and sheltered from all winds. A valuable work, which has been constructed at the Company's expence, is, two basons, hewn out in the rock, in which two ships may be at once careened. A third is now preparing. This work which has been very expensive, likewise brings in a considerable annual return; strangers pay very dear for liberty to careen in these basons. While I was there I saw a ship of war belonging to the Imam of Sana, which he had sent to Bombay, solely on purpose that it might be refitted.

The toleration which the English grant to all religions has rendered this island very populous. During these hundred years, for which it has been in the possession of the Company, the number of its inhabitants has greatly increased; so that they are now reckoned at 140,000 souls, although within these twenty years they did not amount to 70,000.

Of these the Europeans are naturally the least numerous class; and this the rather as they do not marry and their numbers consequently do not multiply. The other inhabitants are Portuguese, or Indian Catholics; Hindus, the original possessors of the country; Persians from Kerman; Mahomedans of different sects; and in the last place some Oriental Christians.

The English, as I have mentioned, have an handsome church at Bombay, but only one English clergyman to perform the service of religion in it; and, if he should die, the congregation would be absolutely deprived of a pastor; for the Company have no chaplains in their ships, and entertain no clergy in their settlements on the coast. Wherefore, when a child is to be baptized, which is not often, as the English rarely marry in India, a Danish missionary is sent for, to administer the sacrament of baptism.

The Catholics, a scanty remainder of the Portuguese, and a great number of Indians, their converts, are much more numerous than the Protestants. They have abundance of priests as well Europeans as Indians, who attend their studies at Goa. To superintend this herd, the

Pope named some years ago a bishop of Bombay, but the Governor of the island sent him away declaring that they needed not Catholic priests of so high a rank. The Catholic churches are decent buildings, and are sumptuously ornamented within. The Jesuits had once a college and a church in the middle of this island. Their college is at present the country house of the English Governor. And the old church has been converted into a suite of assembly rooms.

All religions, as I have already remarked, are here indulged in the free exercise of their public worship, not only in their churches, but openly in festivals and processions, and none takes offence at another. Yet the Government allows not the Catholic priests to give a loose to their zeal for making proselytes. When any person chooses to become Catholic, the reasons must be laid before government and if they are judged valid, he is then allowed to profess his conversion. The priests complain of the difficulty of obtaining this permission. They, however, have considerable success in conversion among the slaves, who, being struck with the pomp of the Romish worship, and proud of wearing the image of a saint upon their breasts, choose rather to frequent the Catholic churches than any others, and persuade their countrymen, as they successively arrive, to follow their example.

Voyage to Arabia, in Pinkerton's Voyages, Vol. X., pp. 201-203.

John Henry Grose

1758

Bombay is an Island, in the latitude of eighteen degrees, forty-one minutes of north latitude, near the coast of Deckan, the high mountains of which are full in view, at a trifling distance; and is so situate, as, together with the winding of other islands along that continent, to form one of the most commodious bays perhaps in the world; from which distinction it received the denomination of Bombay, by corruption from the Portuguese Buon-bahia, though now usually written by them Bombaim. Certain it is, that the harbor is spacious enough to contain any number of ships; has excellent anchoring-ground; and by its circular position, can afford them a land-locked shelter against any winds, to which the mouth of it is exposed. It is also admirably situated for a center of dominion and commerce, with respect to the Malabar coast, the Gulf of Persia, the Red-Sea, and the whole trade of that side of the great Indian Peninsula, and northern parts adjoining to it: to the government of which presidency they are vey properly subordinated.

Considering too that this island is situated within the tropics, the climate of it is far from intolerable on account of its heat, in any time of the year; though never susceptible of any degree of cold beyond what must be rather agreeable to an European constitution. In the very hottest season, which immediately precedes the periodical return of the rains, the refreshment of the alternate land and sea-breezes is hardly ever wanting, the calms being generally of a very short duration; so that perhaps, in the year, there may be a few days of an extraordinary sultry heat, and even those may be made supportable, by avoiding any violent exercise, by keeping especially out of the malignant unmitigated glare and action of the sun, and by a light unoppressive diet. Great care too should be taken of not exposing one self to the dangerous effect of the night-dews, and of the too quick transition from a state of open pores, to their perspiration being shut up; which is so often the case of those, who, from an impatience of heat, venture to sleep from under cover in the raw air of the night, pleasantly indeed, but perniciously cooled by the absence of the sun: a circumstance yet more fatal, to such as have besides been heated by any intemperance in eating and drinking.

Bombay, in fact, had long borne an infamous character for unhealthfulness. It was commonly called the burying-ground of the English; but this was only until an experience, bought at the expence of a number of lives, had rendered the causes of such a mortality more known, and consequently more guarded against. Among others, the principal ones doubtless were:

First, the nature of the climate, and the precautions and management required by it, not being so sufficiently known, as they now are; if that knowledge was but prevalent enough, with many, for them to sacrifice their pleasures of intemperance, or the momentary relief from a present irksomeness of heat, to the preservation of their healths.

Formerly too, there obtained a practice esteemed very pernicious to the health of the inhabitants, employing a manure for the coconut-trees, that grow in abundance on the island, consisting of the small fry of fish, and called by the country-name Buckshaw; which was undoubtedly of great service, both to augment, and meliorate their produce: but through its quantity being superficially laid in trenches round the root, and consequently the easier to be exhaled, diffused, as it putrified, a very unwholsome vapor. There are some, however, who deny this, and insist on the ill consequences of this manure to be purely imaginary, or at least greatly exaggerated; giving for reason, that the inhabitants themselves were never sensible of any noxious quality in that method; and that if the island is now less unhealthy, the change must be sought for in other causes. But all are agreed, that the habitations in the woods, or coconut-groves, are unwholesome, from the air wanting a free current through them; and from the trees themselves, diffusing a kind of vaporous moisture, unfavourable to the lungs, a complaint common to all close-wooded countries.

There has also been another reason assigned, for the island having grown healthier, from the lessening of the waters, by a breach of the sea being banked off; which however does not seem to me a satisfactory one. There is still subsisting a great body of salt water on the inside of the breach, the communication of which with the sea, being less free before the breach was built, must be in proportion more apt to stagnate, and breed noxious vapors; so that this alteration by the breach cannot enter for much, if any thing, into the proposed solution, which may perhaps be better reduced into the before-mentioned one of the different diet, and manner of living of the Europeans: not however without taking into account, the place being provided with more skilful physicians than formerly, when there was less niceness in the choice of them.

Whatever may be the reason, the point is certain, that the climate is no longer so fatal to the English inhabitants as it used to be, and incomparably more healthy than many other of our settlements in India.

Voyage to the East-Indies, pp. 29-33.

John Henry Grose.

This island is however a stong instance of the benefits of a good government, and a numerous population, by not a spot of it remaining uncultivated: so that though it is far from producing sufficient for the consumption of the inhabitants; and notwithstanding its many disadvantages of situation and soil, it yields, in proportion to its bigness, incomparably more than the adjacent island of Salsett; whether under the government of the Portuguese, or, as it now is, under that of the Morattoes.

Voyage to the East-Indies, page 48.

Abraham Parsons.

1775.

The Town of Bombay is near a mile in length from Apollo gate to that of the Bazar and about a quarter of a mile broad in the broadest part from the Bunda (Bandar) across the Green to Church gate, which is nearly in the centre as you walk round the walls between Apollo and Bazar gate. There are likewise two marine gates, with a commodious wharf and cranes built out from each gate, beside a landing place for passengers only. Between the two marine gates is the castle properly called Bombay Castle, a very large and strong fortification which commands the bay. The works round the town are so many and the bastions so very strong and judiciously situated and the whole defended with a broad and deep ditch so as to make a strong fortress, which while it has a sufficient garrison and provisions may bid defiance to any force which may be brought against it. Here is a spacious green, capable of containing several regiments exercising at the same time. The streets are well laid out and the buildings (namely gentlemen's houses) so numerous and handsome as to make it an elegant town. The soil is a sand, mixed with small gravel, which makes it always so clean, even, in the rainy season, that a man may walk all over the town within half an hour after a heavy shower without dirtying his shoes. The esplanade is very extensive and as smooth and even as a bowling-green which makes either walking or riding round the town very pleasant.

Travels in Asia, etc., p. 216.

Philip Stanhope.

"MEMOIRS OF ASIATICUS."

1778.

On the fourteenth we reached Bombay where I have taken up my quarters in a most excellent tavern, till the Indiaman which is to convey me home shall sail.

The island of Bombay is situate in seventy-two degrees of East longitude, and eighteen of latitude, and is about seven leagues in circumference. It originally belonged to the crown of Portugal, but in the year one thousand six hundred and sixty-three it was given to Charles the Second, as part of the portion of the Infanta Catherine, and that Monarch presented it as a mark of royal favour to the East India Company, who fortified it at a vast expence, and it is now in the elegance of its buildings very little inferior to Madras.

The manners as well of the English as of the natives are much the same here as in other parts of India. At present the settlement not being divided by factions, there is more society than at Madras, and the sources of wealth being fewer, there is less of luxury and parade than at Calcutta.

I have dined with the Governor, who is a gentleman of plain good sense, and unaffected politeness, and has sat in the chair with equal honour to himself, and satisfaction to those under him, for five-and-twenty years. I have had pleasure of seeing the beauties of Bombay, at the monthly ball, and I have spent an agreeable evening with Mr. Draper, who is senior member of the Council, and is the husband of the charming Eliza, whose fame will ever live in the celebrated writings of the immortal Sterne.

Memoirs of Asiaticus, pp. 168 to 170.

Samuel Pechel.

1781

The island of Bombay is the antient property of the English East India Company; it hath hitherto been, of all her settlements, the most conducive to the greatness of the nation in Asia; yet, through the splendor of atchievement, great acquisition of territory, and immense harvests of wealth in Bengal and the Coast of Coromandel, it hath been in some measure overlooked, and, as if in a corner of the world, unnoticed.

It receives great importance as well from its situation, so advantageous not only in regard to external trade and the internal in the neighbouring provinces, as from the docks which are the only ones the Company have in India, and without which therefore there can be no maritime power in those regions. Hitherto the expence of maintaining hath not been defrayed by the produce; but the present situation of affairs in the neighbouring provinces, well improved, may place things on a different foot, and that expence not only be cleared, but a considerable revenue yielded, and a great influence in the western part of Indostan obtained.

Historical Account of Bombay, 1781, *pages* 1-2.

James Forbes.

1783.

We found the population of Bombay very much increased, and constantly increasing. The troubles on the continent had compelled many to seek an asylum from the calamities of war; personal security and protection of property, under the British flag, was another great inducement; while a flourishing commerce and many other causes allured a number of merchants to leave their fluctuating situations in other places, for a more permanent settlement on this little rocky island; which to the higher tribes of Hindoos has some peculiar inconveniences, and to the lower classes of every description must be far more expensive than any part of the continent.

The price of most kinds of provisions was nearly doubled since I first knew Bombay; but there appeared no deficiency either of European or Indian commodities. The shops in the bazar were well stored with articles for luxury and comfort from all parts of the world; and every breeze wafted a fresh supply. But if private expenses were thus increased, great indeed was the accumulation of public expenditure since my arrival in India, and still more so since my departure.

The island of Bombay should now no longer be considered as a settlement, or separate colony, but as the metropolis (surrounded indeed by a large moat) of an extensive domain. For this island, only twenty miles in circumference, and almost covered with houses and gardens, will soon become a city, similar to the outer towns of Surat and Ahmedabad; smaller indeed by eight miles in its circumference than the latter in the zenith of her glory, and much less than London at this present day.

Oriental Memoirs, Vol. II, pages 380-381.

Abbe Raynal.

1788.

It is computed that there are at present at Bombay near 100,000 inhabitants, seven or eight thousand of whom are sailors; a few of them are employed in manufactures of silk and cotton. As the larger productions could not prosper upon a rock where the soil has very little depth, the attention of the people has been turned towards the cultivation of an excellent kind of onion, which together with the fish that is dried there, is advantangeously sold in the most distant markets. Those labours are not carried on with that degree of indolence so common under a burning sky. The Indian has showed himself susceptible of emulation; and his character has been in some measure changed by the example of the indefatigable Parsees. The latter are not fishermen and cultivators alone. The construction, fitting out, and dispatching of ships; everything in a word which concerns the road or navigation, is intrusted to their activity and industry.

Philosophical and Political History of the Indies, Vol. II, pp. 109–110

Viscount Valentia.

1804.

The rage for country houses prevails at Bombay as generally as at Madras, and the same inconveniences attend it; for as all business is carried on in the fort, every person is obliged to come in the morning, and return at night. The Governor is almost singular in living constantly in town, having lent his country house at Perelle to Sir James Mackintosh. This place was the property of the Jesuits, and is the handsomest in the island. The apartments and verandahs are extremely handsome, and the former chapel on the ground floor is now a magnificent and lofty dining room. It has, however, the inconvenience of not being open to the sea breeze, and appears to be far from healthy, for Sir James and Lady Mackintosh, with a great proportion of their family, had been attacked by an intermittent fever. The generality of the country houses are comfortable and elegant; and if they have not the splendid

Grecian porticos of Calcutta and Madras, they are probably better adapted to the climate, and have most unquestionably the advantage of charming views; for even the Island of Bombay itself is broken by several beautiful hills either covered with cocoa-nut tree groves, or villas of the inhabitants.

It cannot be expected that the third Presidency in point of rank, should vie with the others in splendor or expence. The society is less numerous, and the salaries are smaller, economy is consequently more attended to by a kind of tacit compact; the style of living is however frequently elegant, and always comfortable and abundant. I confess that having so lately quitted my native country, I preferred it to the splendid profusion of Calcutta. The necessaries of life are here dearer than in the other parts of India; the wages of servants are consequently much higher. Rice, the chief food of the lower orders, is imported from Bengal, even in favourable years: at present the famine has raised it to an alarming price. Grateful, however, must the inhabitants be to Providence, for having, at such an eventful period, placed them under the British protection, and relieved them from those sufferings, which afflict the nations around them. The subscriptions, which were entered into to extend this benefit beyond the limits of their territory, do honour to the gentlemen of the settlement. Hospitals were opened for the gradual administering of relief to such as were too much exhausted to feed themselves, and hircarrahs were placed on the confines to bring in those whose strength had failed them before they could reach the fostering aid, that was held out to them by the hands of British benevolence. The preservation of several hundreds of thousands on the Malabar coast may be attributed to the overflowing supplies which Bengal was able to pour out for their support, in consequence of the fifty years' tranquillity which she has enjoyed under her present masters. India, under our supreme controul, can never expect to feel the effects of famine; for a season which causes a scarcity in one part, generally produces an increase of produce in another; and the devastations of hostile armies will be at an end, which can alone counteract this beneficent arrangement of Providence. For the sake of the population of sixty millions, as well as for our own sake, we may therefore wish that the British influence in India may remain unshaken by external force, or internal dissatisfaction.

Voyages and Travels, 1803-5, Vol. II, pages 169-171.

Bishop Heber.

1825.

The island, as well as most of those in its neighbourhood, is apparently little more than a cluster of small detached rocks, which have been joined together by the gradual progress of coral reefs, aided by sand thrown up by the sea, and covered by the vegetable mould occasioned by the falling leaves of the sea-loving-coco. The interior consists of a long but narrow tract of low ground, which has evidently been, in the first instance, a salt lagoon, gradually filled up by the progress which I have mentioned, and from which the high tides are still excluded only by artificial embankments. This tract is a perfect marsh during the rainy season, and in a state of high rice cultivation. The higher ground is mere rock and sand, but covered with coco and toddy-palms where they can grow. There is scarcely any open or grass land in the island, except the esplanade before the fort, and the exercising ground at Matoonga, which last is the head-quarters of the artillery. The fort, or rather the fortified town, has many large and handsome houses, but few European residents, being hot, close-built, with narrow streets, projecting upper stories and rows, in the style which is common all over this side of India, and of which the old houses in Chester give a sufficiently exact idea.

The Bombay houses are externally less beautiful than those of Calcutta, having no pillared verandahs, and being disfigured by huge and high pitched roofs of red tiles. They are generally speaking, however, larger, and on the whole better adapted to the climate.

Journey in India from Calcutta to Bombay, 1824-25; *Vol. III, pp.* 129-131.

2

The island of Colabah is situated at the entrance of the harbour, and is connected with that of Bombay by a pier, which is, however, overflowed at high-water. Adjoining this pier are the docks which are large, and, I believe, the only considerable ones in India, where the tides do not often rise high enough to admit of their construction. Cotton is the principal article of export, great quantities of which come from the north-west of India, and I have frequently been interested in seeing the immense bales lying on the pier, and the ingenious screw with which an astonishing quantity is pressed into the canvass bags. Bombay is the port from whence almost all the trade of the west and north is shipped for China and England; there are several ships building in the slips, and the whole place has the appearance of being a flourishing commercial sea-port.

Pearls and turquoises are brought from the Persian gulph in great numbers, some of which are very valuable, and fine cornelians and agates also come from Surat.

Journey in India from Calcutta to Bombay, 1824-25, Vol. III, page 129.

3

We could not leave Bombay without regret. There were some persons whom we were sincerly pained to part with there. We had met with much and marked kindness and hospitality, we had enjoyed the society of several men of distinguished talent, and all my views for the regulation and advantage of the clergy, and for the gradual advancement of Christianity had met with a support beyond my hopes, and unequalled in any other part of India.

I had found old acquaintances in Sir Edward West and Sir Charles Chambers, and an old and valuable friend (as well as a sincerely attached and cordial one) in Archeacon Barnes. Above all, however, I had enjoyed in the unremitting kindness, the splendid hospitality, and agreeable conversation of Mr. Elphinstone, the greatest pleasure of the kind which I have ever enjoyed either in India or Europe.

Mr. Elphinstone is, in every respect, an extraordinary man, possessing great activity of body and mind, remarkable talent for, and application to public business, a love of literature, and a degree of almost universal information, such as I have met with in no other person similarly situated, and manners and conversation of the most amiable and interesting character.

Journey in India from Calcutta to Bombay, 1824-45, pages 131-132.

Walter Hamilton.

1820.

Bombay is a small island, formerly comprehended in the Mogul province of Aurungabad, but now the seat of the principal British settlement on the west coast of India. This island is formed by two unequal ranges of whinstone rock, running nearly parallel to, and at the distance of about three miles from each other. The western range of hills is little more than five miles long; the eastern, exclusive of Colaba, may exceed eight in length. At their northern and southern extremities they are united by two belts of sand, now forming a kind of stone, rising but a few feet above the level of the sea. These natural boundaries were formerly breached in several places, where they admitted the sea, and according to Fryer's account of Bombay in 1681, about 40,000 acres of good land were then overflowed. It appears also that the Goper river, which rises among the hills of Salsette and disembogues itself into the channel between that island and Bombay, when swollen by floods, used to enter the breaches at the northern extremity, and after traversing the whole extent of the latter, discharge itself into the ocean. In fact, Bombay was nothing originally but a group of small islands with numerous backwaters, producing rank vegetation, at one time dry, and at another overflowed by the sea. So unwholesome, in consequence, was the situation reckoned, that the older travellers agreed in allotting not more than three years for the average duration of life at this presidency.

The fort of Bombay stands on the south-eastern extremity of the island, on a narrow neck of land formed by Back Bay on the western side, and by the harbour on the eastern. The Worlee sluices are at the north-western end of the island, a distance of nearly six miles from the fort. Formerly a coco-nut wood not only covered the esplanade, but the fort also, down to the channel between Bombay and Colaba. At that remote period of time, Mahim was the principal town on the island, and the few houses of the present town, then in existence, were interspersed among the coco-nut trees, with the exception of those built on the ridge of Dungaree hill, adjoining the harbour, which appears to have been then occupied by fishermen. When the fortifications were erected, but very little more land was cleared of the coco-nut trees, beyond what was absolutely indispensable, leaving the space within the body of the fort, and without its walls up to the very glacis, a coco-nut grove. From time to time, by various means, the esplanade was gradually cleared of trees to 600 yards from the fort, and the esplanade was extended to 800 yards. By this time, the more wealthy inhabitants had built houses in a detached irregular manner, throughout the coco-nut woods contiguous to the esplanade, and Dungaree ridge was also built upon to the extent of two miles and upwards from the fort; the little vacant ground remaining had in consequence risen to an enormous price. In this state of things, the sufferers by the fire and the indigent from the esplanade had no alternative but to resort to the Honourable Company's salt batty ground, scarcely recovered from the sea, neither had government any ground to give in exchange for the valuable land taken when extending the esplanade. All these causes combined, serve to account for what is called the new town of Bombay being built in such a low, muddy, unwholesome tract of land, which during the monsoon has the appearence of a shallow lake, many of the houses being then separated from each other by water, so that the inhabitants suffer from the inundation and its effects, during seven or eight months of the year. At all seasons the ground floor of many of its houses are on a level with high-water mark, some below, and but few actually above it at full spring tides. Much also of the rain water that falls on the old town and the esplanade, passes through the new town and thence across the breach hollow to the sluices at Worlee.

Under these circumstances, the surface of the island is so circumscribed, rocky, and uneven, (except where a considerable part is overflowed by the sea) that it does not produce a sufficiency of grain in the year to supply its population for one week, yet each spot that will admit of tillage is brought under cultivation of some sort or planted with coco-nut trees. The vellard, which communicates between Breach Candy and Lovegrove, has prevented the ocean from making a breach through the centre. This substantial work, with smaller ones of the same construction, have preserved the low lands of the island from being inundated by the spring tides, which but for them would have destroyed all but the barren hills. Although the sea be now excluded, the rain water still collects in the lower parts of the island, where the surface is said to be 12 feet under high-water mark, during the rains forms an unwholesome swamp. In 1805, Mr. Duncan completed a vellard, or causeway, across the narrow arm of the sea, which separated Bombay from the contiguous island of Salsette: an operation of infinite service to the farmers and gardeners who supply the markets, but which is said to have had a prejudicial effect on the harbour.

The fortifications of Bombay have been improved, but are esteemed too extensive and would require a numerous garrison. Towards the sea they are extremely strong, but on the land side do not offer the same resistance, and to an enemy landed and capable of making regular approaches, it must surrender. The town within the walls was begun by the

Portugueze, and even those houses that have since been built are of a similar construction with wooden pillars supporting wooden verandas; the consequence of which is, that Bombay bears no external resemblance to the other two presidencies. The government house is a handsome building, with several good apartments, but it has the great inconvenience of the largest apartment on both floors being a passage room to the others.

The northern portion of the fort is inhabited by Parsee families, who are not remarkably cleanly in their domestic concerns, nor in the streets where they live. The view from the fort is extremely beautiful towards the bay, which is here and there broken by islands, many covered with trees, while the lofty and curious shaped hills of the table-land form a striking background. The sea is on three sides of the fort, and on the fourth is the esplanade; at the back of which is the black town amidst coco-nut trees. Substantial buildings now extend to very nearly three miles from the fort.

Bombay appears for many years to have been left to itself, and individuals were permitted to occupy what land they pleased, nor was there any system or regulation established for the security of the public revenue. In 1707, the greater part of the present limits of the fort had become private property, but by purchases and exchanges, between 1707 and 1759, it became again the property of the Company, and has been subsequently transferred to private persons. It is an extraordinary fact that the principal part, if not the whole, of the landed property which the Company possesses within the walls of Bombay has been acquired by purchase, having, within the memory of many persons now living, bought it of individuals who were always considered to be merely the Company's tenants at will. The property thus acquired to the Company by purchase and exchanges, cost, since 1760, altogether about 737,927 Rupees.

The buildings within the walls of the fort including the barracks, arsenal, and docks, may be valued at one crore five lacks of rupees; the rent of the houses within the fort in 1813 amounted to 527,360 rupees, including the Company's property. The great price given for ground within the fort which is daily increasing, the buildings carried on in every quarter of the European part, the commodious and costly family dwellings constructed by many of the natives, and the immense shops and warehouses belonging both to the natives and Europeans, furnish the strongest evidence of the high price of ground within the fortress of Bombay, and that it might afford to pay a rent of 100 guineas per acre for the support of the police, which upon 259,244 squares yards would yield 22,036 rupees.

Bombay is literally a barren rock, and presents no encouragement to agricultural speculations; but its commercial and maritime advantages are great. It is the only principal settlement in India, where the rise of the tides is sufficient to permit the construction of docks on a large scale; the very highest spring tides reach to 17 feet, but the usual height is 14 feet. The docks are the Company's property, and the king's ships pay a high monthly rent for repairs. They are entirely occupied by Parsees, who possess an absolute monopoly in all the departments; the person who contracts for the timber being a Parsee, and the inspector on delivery of the same caste. On the 23rd of June, 1810, the Minden, of 14 guns, built entirely by Parsees, without the least assistance, was launched from these dock-yards, and since then the Cornwallis and Wellesley, and another of equal strength, have been launched under similar circumstances; besides two of 38, two of 36, two of 18, and two 10 guns. In addition to these, since the dock-yard has been established, there have been built for commercial purposes, nine ships of 1,000 tons; five about 800 tons, six above 700 tons, and five above 600 tons, besides 35 of inferior tonnage; all constructed by the Jumsetjee [Wadia] Parsee family as head builders. The teak forests from whence these yards are supplied lie along the western side of the Ghaut mountains, and other contiguous hills on the north and east of Bassein; the numerous rivers that descend from them affording water carriage for the timber. The ships built at Bombay are reckoned one third more durable than any other Indian built ships.

This little island commands the entire trade of the north-west coast of India together with that of the Persian gulf. The principal cargo of a ship bound from Bombay to China is cotton, in the stowing and screwing of which, the commanders and officers are remarkably dexterous.

Description of Hindostan, 1820, Vol II, pp. 152-156.

SUPPLEMENT.

SUPPLEMENT.

A Noble Introduction to India.

SIR RICHARD TEMPLE.

At Bombay, the western capital, the tourist would have no time to stop and examine the various institutions, unless, indeed, there might be some particular, say, educational institution in which he took an interest, and which could be looked at in two or three hours. But he should make sure of seeing from some point on Malabar Hill, say Malabar Point, the Governor's marine villa, the long and magnificent series of public buildings, one of the finest sights of its kind in the world. The buildings are in themselves grand, but other cities may have structures as grand, though probably separate. Bombay, however, has all her structures in one long line of array, as if on parade before the spectator. And all this is right over the blue bay, with the Western Ghaut Mountains in the distant background. This constitutes a noble introduction for the traveller to picturesque India.

Then we pass through the vast harbour of Bombay, with a comparatively narrow mouth, guarded by fortifications, surrounded by hills, and studded with islands again with a mountain background. This harbour is in the very first rank of the harbours of the world taking an equal place with Sydney, with San Francisco, with Rio de Janeiro.

A Bird's-Eye View of Picturesque India, 1898, pp. 20-21.

A Glowing Sunset.

WALTER CRANE.

We had a glimpse of some of the palaces on Malabar Hill, seeing the latter first against a glowing sunset. Fringed with palms and plantains, with its fantastic buildings silhouetted on the sky, it recalled the banks of storm cloud I had seen on the voyage, with their vaporous trees and aerial hanging gardens.

From the Hill there is certainly a magnificent view of the city of Bombay: especially if seen just before sundown, when a golden glow seems to transfigure the scene; and later, looking down on the vast plain, the white houses partly hid in trees scattered along the shore, the quays, and the ships at anchor in the bay, all seem to sink like a dream into the roseate atmosphere of sunset. But even that lovely light is darkened by a heavy smoke cloud drifting on the city from the forest of gaunt factory chimneys rising in the east like the shadow of poverty which is always cast by the riches of the West.

India—Impressions, 1907, pp. 29-30.

Of no mean city am I!

RUDYARD KIPLING.

So thank I God my birth
　　Fell not in isles aside—
Waste headlands of the earth,
　　Or warring tribes untried—
But that she lent me worth
　　And gave me right to pride.

Surely in toil or fray
　　Under an alien sky,
Comfort it is to say:
　　'Of no mean city am I!'

(Neither by service nor fee
　　Come I to mine estate—
Mother of cities to me,
　　For I was born in her gate,
Between the palms and the sea,
　　Where the world-end steamers wait.)

Now for this debt I owe,
　　And for her far-borne cheer
Must I make haste and go
　　With tribute to her pier.

'*The Seven Seas.*'

City So Full of Fate

MRS. WALTER TIBBITS.

Bombay! How shall we speak of you? City so full of fate for us. Well may the old Portuguese dons have named you "the beautiful," would that my pen could describe you as eloquently as you always speak to me whenever I set foot upon your palm-girt shore. Queen of all Eastern cities, standing at the portal of that wonderful country of Hindustan which has been as a fairy god-mother to so many of the Anglo-Saxon race, often beneficent, sometimes malign, always fateful, with what mixed emotions have we, the children of the West, greeted and paid adieu to your matchless bay!

The Voice of the Orient, 1909, pp. 7-8.

Malabar Hill by Moonlight.

WILLIAM SHEPHERD.

The first time we visited Malabar Hill was by moonlight; slowly ascending the road cut along the rock, the waters of Back Bay glittering under the moon's rays on one side, the tall pines, rooted on huge masses of black rock, on the other, the scene was very Eastern and striking; the broad branching leaves of the palms intensely dark against a sky luminous with incredible moonlight, which served to make their spiny fronds more fine and delicate; and yet to mass the whole, and throw over all that grand quietness, which that time, and perhaps the absence of colour, tend to produce,—impressed us greatly, and we went home with a strong feeling of the grandeur of tropical foliage.

From Bombay to Bushire, 1857, pp. 12.

Harbour Scenery.

EDWARD NOLAN.

The harbour scenery is very fine: Mr. Hamilton, thirty years ago, noticed this in his description. Mrs. Postans, in her lively little volume on western India, many years after, expressed in graceful terms her admiration of it. Many modern writers have followed in their wake, and few have exaggerated the claims of Bombay in this respect, although some have gone so far as to call it "the most lovely in the world," and to describe the island on which the city stands as the fairest of all. "The isles that join Old Ocean's purple diadem." It is certainly very lovely, the azure above, reflected in the wave below, the bright Indian sun shedding its glory over sky and sea, constitute a magnificent prospect from the verandahs of the inhabitants whose houses command the view. The harbour is dotted with palm isles, and the contrast of their green feathery foliage with the bright blue water is strikingly picturesque. In the distance the ghauts tower to the heavens, presenting all imaginable forms, and covered with all imaginable hues; in one direction tinged with the crimson sunset, in another as if clothed in a pale purple robe, elsewhere hung with fleecy drapery; and all these ever changing as day dawns or sets, as its pours its burning noon upon the gleaming rock, or as deep shadows sink upon them with the descending night. Heber, with his soft poetic pencil, has impressed the images of these scenes upon his pages, so as no eye that has rested upon them can ever forget. The island of Elephanta and the island of Salsette, are covered with beautiful trees, which extend their boughs over the rippling waters, presenting every variety of graceful form, and of tint, such as oriental foliage only can exhibit. Yachting being a favourite amusement, pretty pleasure boats may be seen gliding among "the palm tasselled islets:" so that amidst the prospects of soft beauty, and in view of the glorious mountain distance, tokens of human life and pleasure are perpetually indicated, adding that peculiar charm which solitary scenery, however fine, cannot impart. From the harbour the appearance of the city is not attractive; it lies too low, the new town being lower than the old, most of the houses having their foundations on the sea level, and many still lower. The walls of the fort flank the water's edge and first strikes the the eye of the beholder; then the esplanade, with its clusters of tents; and, stretching to the west the island of Colabah, covered with palm-trees and having the light-house at its extreme point.

British Empire in India, 1859. Vol. I., p. 149.

Harbour of Bombay.

ILTUDUS PRICHARD.

The harbour, one of the finest in the world, is formed by a crescent-shaped group of islands, of which Salsette (connected by a causeway), Elephanta, and Colaba are the most familiar to English readers. The rays of a tropical sun are tempered by a delicious breeze; innumerable boats glide here and there on errands of business or pleasure; stately ships ride securely at anchor in the offing; picturesque islets rise abruptly from the ocean, clad from the summit to the very edge with the richest tropical verdure; and the branches of the trees hang so close over the water that they seem to coquet with the rippling waves as they toss themselves in wanton sport upon the pebbly shore. Such a scene, under the clear blue Indian sky and bright sunshine, as it meets the eye of the exile who enters India by its western gate, is well calculated to impress him favourably with the land of his adoption.

Administration of India, 1869, Vol. I, pp. 224.

Sunset in the Harbour.

MRS. GUTHRIE.

In returning, (from Elephanta) the tide was with us, and we stood well out into the middle of the bay, which is very beautiful. The amphitheatre of mountains, the Eastern characteristics of the island we had just quitted, the smiling shore, with here and there a domed and pinnacled mosque, rosy red in the rays of the setting sun, made a delightful scene. Many islets were dotted about—Butcher's Isle, and Old Woman's Isle, and a third, with long rows of empty barracks, built at vast expense, and then deserted.

As we approached the harbour, the scene became most animated. Noble three-masted P. and O. steamers lay at ancher. A little apart from these were others, belonging to different companies, amongst which our own 'Hindoo' cut no mean figure. There were stately sailing vessels and small craft innumerable, which were not huddled together in confusion, but lay at a friendly distance from one another. Every spar, every rope stood out against a back-ground of fiery crimson—such a sunset, such vivid colouring as I had never pictured to myself as possible even in an Indian sunset. As the soft twilight stole on, the hue intensified—the world below the horizon might have been in flames. It was a magnificent conclusion to one of the most delightful days I ever spent.

My Year in an Indian Fort 1877, Vol. I, pp. 70-71.

Scenery of Mahableshwar.

MEADOWS TAYLOR.

Magnificent as is the scenery of the Western Ghauts of India throughout their range, it is nowhere, perhaps, more strikingly beautiful than in the neighbourhood of the great isolated plateau which rising high above the mountain ranges around it, and known under the name of Mahableshwar, from the temple at the source of the sacred river Krishna on its summit is now the favourite summer retreat and sanatorium of the Bombay Presidency. Trim roads, laid out so as to exhibit the beauties of the scenery to the best advantage, pretty English-looking cottages, with brilliant gardens, and a considerable native town, are now the main features of the place; but at the period of our tale it was uninhabited, except by a few Brahmins and devotees, who, attracted by the holiness of the spot, congregated around the ancient temple, and occupied the small village beside it. Otherwise the character of the wild scenery is unchanged. From points near the edges of the plateau, where mighty precipices of basalt descend sheer into forests of everlasting verdure and luxuriance, the eye ranges over a sea of rugged mountain tops, some, scathed and shattered peaks of barren rock—others with extensive flat summits, bounded by naked cliffs which, falling into deep gloomy ravines covered with dense forests, would seem inaccessible to man.

To some readers of our tale, this scenery will be familiar; but to others it is almost impossible to convey by description any adequate idea of its peculiar character, or of the beauty of the ever changing aerial effects, that vary in aspect almost as the spectator turns from one point to another. Often in early morning, as the sun rises over the lower mists, the naked peaks and precipices, standing apart like islands, glisten with rosy tints while the mist itself, as yet dense and undisturbed, lies wrapped around their bases, filling every ravine and valley, and glittering like the sea of molten silver.

. .

Again, as the morning breeze rises in the valleys below, this vapour breaks up slowly; circling round the mountain summits, lingering in wreaths among their glens and precipices, and clinging to the forests, until dissipated entirely by the fierce beams of the sun. Then, quivering under the fervid heat, long ridges of rugged valleys are spread out below, and range beyond range melts tenderly into a dim distance of sea and sky, scarcely separated in colour, yet showing the occasional sparkle of a sail like a faint cloud passing on the horizon. Most glorious of all, perhaps, in the evening, when, in the rich colours of the fast rising vapours the mountains glow like fire and peak and precipice, forest and glen, are bathed in gold and crimson light; or, as the light grows dimmer, shrouded in deep purple shadow till they disappear in the gloom which quickly falls on all.

Tara, *1863*, chap. *69*, *pp. 401-402.*

Great Fire of 1803.

ADMIRAL CARDEN.

On the 18th February 1803 at noon observed the City of Bombay on fire in several places when the signal was made by the Admiral (Rainier) for Captains, Officers and crews from each ship of four of our squadron to proceed on shore and assist in saving the city. The four Captains of the squadron landed with their crews and ships' fire-engines and took different stations in the city, nine being on the north side in the circle of the magazines. The houses being chiefly built of wood the progress of the flames was awful, and the religion of the fire-worshippers being that of the chief of the inhabitants, no effort to arrest its progress could be expected from them. The numerous inhabitants, women, children and aged, who could or would not depart from their houses until the last extremity, or were dragged out by our men, must have been immense, and the numbers who perished in the flames no one could calculate, among whom I had to regret two of my brave crew. Every ladder was in requisition and thus only could the upper stories be reached to help the women and children who were borne down the ladders on the seamen's backs or by ropes. It certainly was heart-rending to hear the shrieks of those in the upper stories of the houses in flames, when no possible help could be afforded.

While the fire was raging violently in the district I had to act in, the Governor, Jonathan Duncan, Esq., came up to me and while I was replying to some questions or remarks he had made, up came several of his staff officers and exclaimed, 'Sir, you had better quit the citadel directly. Such and such street is in flames and in a house in that street there is a deposit of five hundred barrels of gunpowder which the bomb-proof magazine would not contain. It must soon take fire and then no person can sustain the shock nor can one stone be left on another of the walls of this city; therefore do not stay a moment.' The Governor replied 'I will never quit the City on such an occasion.' And he having previously thanked me for my unceasing exertions, now turned round to me and said, 'Captain Carden, see if you can save us all.' I replied in a hurry and ejaculating orders to collect my brave crew told the Governor I should not quit my station or slacken my exertions and would do all that could be expected.

My officers and men were soon around me and water being close at hand in a pond near the Citadel, off we started with as much water in our fire buckets and engine as those vessels would contain. We were led to the street and house, when I found that the Governor's staff officers had stated what was quite correct. The street was in flames on both sides and we found the temporary magazine therein was only more secure than any other house in that street by having a double door, wood porch, and closed windows. This porch had now begun to ignite, which we soon extinguished, and breaking the door open (for no key was to be found in the confusion that prevailed) I beheld the dread combustible matter on the ground floor of a large house. I ordered my men to doff their duck jackets and shoulder each a cask placing the jacket over it to screen it from the falling fire from the house. The distance from the sea wall did not exceed one hundred yards. There seemed to be some hesitation on the part of my men, when I doffed my blue jacket, placed it over the first barrel of gunpowder on my back, and was directly followed by every man of my crew, the officers first, and all unhesitatingly followed. We got safe through the flames of fire falling in all directions and deposited our first burthen in the sea over the sea wall and off again double quick to renew the effort. On placing my jacket on my arm, I found my cambric handkerchief in its pocket in a state of fusion, the fire having fallen into it on our way down the street. And thus we trust providentially successfully and opportunely repeated our efforts, until the contents of this dreaded store were cleared. When this work was completed I felt much exhausted, but, it was visible, much was yet left to do. The City continued in awful flames for three days and two nights, and scarcely a vestige of the City except the citadel and the houses occupied by the European officers civil and military, escaped. They were built of stone, with slated roofs and who generally resided in the south of the City.

Two days after this fire had subsided, I dined with the Governor, all his staff and a large party around him, and on my name being announced the Governor exclaimed with a corresponding motion of his arms, 'I request you all to stand back and allow Captain Carden to come forward, the officer who, under Providence has saved our City of Bombay and all that are in it.' I felt the full effect of this reception and do so to this day. But here except in words exprsssed to Admiral Rainier by public letter from the Governor in Council, was obtained all the advantage derived by me as compensation for my determined and fatiguing exertions. And as a proof of this, I did subsequently enclose letters to the Board of Directors of the East India Company with my request that they would grant a cadet appointment in their army for my young friend and which they refused. I now felt every day a serious illness approaching. The fatal disease of India (Liver complaint) attacked me, entirely resulting from my overstrained exertions in suppressing this awful fire.

A Curtailed Memoir of the incidents and occurrences in the life of John Surman Carden, vice admiral, written by himself, 1850. (Now first printed and edited by C. Atkinson) 1912, pp. 193-197.

Farewell to Bombay.

PRINCE KARAGEORGEWITCH.

Bombay, towering above the sea in a golden glory—the tall towers and minarets standing out in sharp outline against the sky, splendid in colour and glow. Far away Malabar Hill and a white speck—the Towers of Silence; Elephanta, like a transparent gem, reflected in the aquamarine-coloured water.

A rosy light flooded the whole scene with fiery radiance, and then suddenly, with no twilight, darkness blotted out the shape of things, drowning all in purple haze; and there, where India had vanished, a white mist rose from the ocean that mirrored the stars.

Enchanted India, page 305.

NOTES ON THE AUTHORS QUOTED.

Aberigh-Mackay, George

(1848-1881).

This brilliant humorist is best known by his *nom-de-plume* of " Sir Ali Baba," under which he wrote his famous book, *Twenty-one days in India*, which consists of a series of sketches of Indian life and society, which first appeared in *Vanity Fair* in 1878-79. But Aberigh-Mackay was not only a keen humorist and satirist, but wrote also several serious works, which, though now forgotten, deserve to be still read. One of these was a " Hand-book of Hindustan " which he wrote in 1875 on the occasion of the late King Edward VII's visit to this country as Prince of Wales, for the use of English visitors to India who flocked in great numbers at the time. Our extracts are taken from this excellent Hand-book which, besides containing some very good writing, gives concise and readable information on such subjects as Sport, British Administration, and the Native States. Aberigh-Mackay was the son of a Scotch missionary in Bengal and belonged to the Education Department of the United Provinces. He gave much attention to the education of young native princes and was for several years the head of the Rajkumar College at Indore.

Aitken, Edward Hamilton

(1851-1909).

This distinguished author wrote under the well-known *nom-de-plume* of "Eha" formed by his initials, several works which have obtained a high place in Ango-Indian literature. He was a graduate of the Bombay university and for several years taught Latin in Deccan College, Poona. Later he entered the Customs Department and rose to be Collector of Customs, Karachi. He was the son of a Scotch missionary who worked in the Bombay Presidency with Dr. Wilson (1804-1875) and others. *Tribes on my Frontier* which appeared in the "Times of India" and in book form a little later, first revealed his powers as a light and very clever writer and a close observer of Indian natural history. This was followed by others in the same vein at intervals till his death in Scotland shortly after his retirement from this country. He was for some time a useful member of the Bombay Municipal Corporation.

Philip Anderson

(1816-1857).

This antiquary belonged to the Bombay Ecclesiastical Establishment, being for several years a Chaplain at Colaba. Anderson was the first to make a to special study of the antiquities and history of our city as well as of the early English intercourse with Western India. He wrote on the latter subject a book in 1854, which is still very useful because it is based on his study of the manuscript records at the Government Secretariat at Bombay. He was editor of the *Bombay Quarterty Review*, a very able literary periodical which did not survive his death in 1857. His "English in Western India" after being first published in Bombay in 1854 was reprinted two years later in England by Messrs. Smith & Elder. In this work he brought his subject to the end of the seventeenth century. It was his intention to treat of the eighteenth century in another volume, and he wrote several articles about it in his "Review" which would have formed a part of this volume; but his premature death put a stop to further progress.

Arnold, Sir Edwin

(1832-1904).

This famous journalist and poet began his career in the Bombay Education Department nearly sixty years ago. Though he left Bombay and India after only a stay of five years, this country had a strong fascination for him and has inspired most of his poetry, especially the famous *Light of Asia.* He revisited India a quarter of a century after he had left it in 1861, and recorded his impressions in a striking book from which we have quoted. It originally appeared in the *Daily Telegraph* with which paper he was intimately connected for a long time as leader writer and then as editor.

Blavatsky, Helena Petrovna

(1831-1891).

This celebrated founder of the Theosophical Society had a most romantic career and was an intrepid traveller in several lands. The work from which we have quoted is made up of letters written in 1879 to a Russian paper called the *Messenger* under the editorship of the famous Russian journalist M. Katkoff, (1818-1887). She was then on a prolonged visit to India in connection with the well known Society she had established a few years previously in America. Her impressions of Bombay are very interesting and couched in very striking language.

Buist, Dr. George

(1805-1860).

A well-known Anglo-Indian journalist who was for 18 years (1839-59) editor of the *Bombay Times,* which later became the *Times of India.* He not only made his mark as a very able and independent journalist but won renown also as a scientist, especially as a meteorologist and geologist. He also took great interest in our city of Bombay of which he wrote a somewhat fragmentary guide, chiefly scientific, on which he was long engaged. Towards the end of his career he severed his connection with the *Bombay Times* and also with our city, and settled at Allahabad as Superintendent of the Government Press there; but he died shortly afterwards at Calcutta during a brief visit to that city.

Buckingham, James Silk

(1786-1855).

This noted journalist of the early nineteenth century, who founded in 1828 the well known literary paper, the *Athenæum*, first came to India in 1815 landing at Bombay, the life and society of which he has described in his *Autobiography* published soon after his death in 1855. He afterwards went to Calcutta, where as an independent journalist he soon came into collision with the Company's authorities, who deported him to Europe under the rig old Press regulations then in force. He entered the Reformed Parliament in 1832, and both there as well as in the press he ceaselessly urged his grievances against the Company till a few years before his death he succeeded in obtaining a pension from the latter by way of compensation. He was also a noted traveller, and his books of travel were interesting. When he came to Bombay in 1815 he had passed through Egypt, Asia Minor, Arabia and other less known lands of his time, and he recounted some of his interesting travelling experiences before the Bombay Literary society founded ten years previously by Sir James Mackintosh.

Baker, Sir Samuel

(1821-1893).

This distinguished traveller and explorer is best remembered as the discoverer of the Albert Nyanza, one of the two great lakes which are the principal feeders of the Nile. He was in the service of the Khedive of Egypt for several years and did much to suppress slave-trade, an account of which he published in a work entitled *Ismailia*, a new name which he bestowed, in honour of the Khedive Ismail, on the country formerly known as Gondokoro, on its annexation to Egypt. He visited India seven times between 1879 and 1892 and took a close personal interest in the administration and defence of this great dependency. It was during his visit to this country during the cold weather of 1888, that he wrote the remarkable article in the *Fortnightly Review* from which we have given his striking description of Bombay. This article contains his mature reflections on the Indian Empire and especially on its Frontier-policy, which he considered too strictly defensive and inactive. He favoured a bold forward policy. He was also a keen sportsman and the big game of India had great attractions for him.

Burton, Isabel Lady

(1831-1896).

The wife of the famous traveller and linguist, Sir Richard Burton (1821-1890), was in some ways as remarkable a woman as the husband was as a man. She came to Bombay in February 1876 with her husband, and our extracts are taken from the elaborate journals that she kept then and that are printed in W. H. Wilkins' biography of her published by Hutchinson in 1897. Her descriptions of Matheran, Mahableshwar, Hyderabad, and above all, of Goa, which had particular attractions for her as an ardent Catholic, on account of its containing the shrine of St. Francis Xavier, the Apostle of India, are very vivid.

Brown, Robert

(1822-1864).

This philanthrophist was a partner of Ewart Lyon & Co., from 1845 to 1856, during which eleven years he was in Bombay. He was well-known for his earnest Christian spirit, and he devoted his life here to doing practical good amongst his fellows. A rare little book called *Passages in the Life of an Indian Merchant*, published in 1867, by Nisbet, containing extracts from his journal and letters, gives an excellent insight into the noble character of this truly remarkable Christian merchant. This book, compiled by his sister, contains also the extracts we have given, descriptive of Bombay and its surroundings two generations ago. An illness which affected his chest made him retire from Bombay at the early age of thirty-four. He survived eight years longer and died an early death in 1864. Brown was of extraordinary height being six feet seven. When he was sixteen, his sister tells us, "he had a rheumatic fever and on recovery his figure grew to the extraordinary height of six feet seven inches rendering him a 'marked' man in after life."

Lady Brassey

(*d.* 1887).

The first wife of the present Lord Brassey (*b.* 1836) whom she married in 1860, and mother of Lady Willingdon, is known all over the world by her books, which have obtained immense popularity, describing the various voyages of the yacht "Sunbeam" which has come to be inseparably associated with her name. Her first voyage was undertaken in company with her husband in 1876 round the world, and her account of it, which she was induced to publish two years later, met at once with a very flattering reception from the public which surprised no one more than herself. As Lord Brassey says in his brief but very touching memoir that he wrote for his children immediately after her sad death at sea off the coast of northern Queensland in the *Sunbeam*, "the favourable reception of the first book was wholly unexpected by the writer: she awoke and found herself famous." During the next nine or ten years she published some more *Sunbeam* books, till her *Last Voyage* undertaken in 1887 was published posthumously from her journal and notes. During this voyage she came to India and stayed in Bombay while we were celebrating the Golden Jubilee of Queen Victoria in February 1887, of which she has given a vivid account from which we have taken an extract. Her health, which had been excellent in Northern India, fell away after leaving Bombay, and in Borneo she was attacked by malarial fever which recurred on the north coast of Australia where she died on 14 September 1887.

Lady Brassey had a singularly charitable disposition, and she took part in several philanthropic movements, chief amongst which was the St. John's Ambulance Association in which she interested herself most zealously. She took up ambulance work at a time when it was not in fashion as it is now, because she sincerely believed it to be a good cause worthy of all her efforts. During her last voyage she tried to interest people in this cause wherever she went; and while she was in Bombay, Lord Reay, the Governor, called at her instance a meeting of influential citizens in order to revive some interest, as she says, in the rather languishing local branch of this very useful institution.

Birdwood, Sir George

(*b.* 1832).

This distinguished Anglo-Indian passed only some fourteen years of his long life in Bombay, and retired at the early age of thirty-six owing to ill health; but his enthusiasm for our city has all along been boundless. One of the ways in which he has shown this enthusiasm is by writing and speaking about Bombay and its surroundings in striking and eloquent terms whenever he has an opportunity. His article in *The Times* on the burst of the monsoon from which we have given an extract is really remarkable for its singular beauty of style and close observation of nature. It has remained all these years almost unknown, chiefly because it appeared anonymously, like nearly all the articles in the great London paper, and because it was not reprinted in book form. Indeed nearly all of Sir George's writings lie scattered in various newspapers and journals and are not easily accessible to the public though many of them are of permanent value.*

---

*As these sheets are passing through the press a volume of selections from these writings has appeared (Philip Lee-Warner, London, 1915), and the article on the Monsoon has rightly the place of honour in it.

On Bombay he has written largely during the past half century, and even now though he has entered upon his ninth decade, he still hardly ever allows an opportunity of writing about the city, which was the scene of his early labours in this country, pass by unutilised. He may be said to have been one of the founders of "New Bombay" in Sir Bartle Frere's days. Many improvements in our city in those days can be traced directly or indirectly to him and his influence with the high authorities. He designed the Victoria Gardens and took a lead in founding the Victoria and Albert Museum close by; but it is strange that there should be nothing in the Gardens to commemorate the fact. There is, however, a bronze bust of him in the University Library, the tribute of his Bombay admirers.

Caine, William S.

(1842-1903).

This English politician who took a keen interest in India and its affairs, is best remembered for his zeal in the cause of temperance in this country to which he came several times. He wrote *Picturesque India* published by Messrs. Routledge in 1890, which is a sort of tourist's guide-book and does justice within its limits to the various cities and other objects of interest in India. He was a severe critic of the ways of Indian Administration and was a member of the Royal commission on Indian Expenditure which was appointed twenty-one years ago to suggest means of reducing the costliness of the Indian Administrative system.

Caunter, John Hobart

(1794-1851).

This author of the well-known "Romance of Indian History" began his career as a soldier in India, and was in Bombay and Western India at the beginning of the second decade of the last century. But he was disgusted with oriental life and returning home he entered the Church. The remainder of his life he passed as an Anglican clergyman. His rather voluminous works are like his career divided between India and theology. His *Oriental Annual*, a series of sketches and scenes in India, issued for several years from 1834, was once very popular. The volumes contained beautiful engravings of Indian scenes and buildings from the drawings of the famous painter William Daniell (*d.* 1837), who had passed several years in India with his uncle Thomas, Daniell (1749-1840), for pictorial purposes. The descriptive accounts in the volumes were written by Caunter. As Caunter had himself been in India and wielded a good pen, these accounts which embrace nearly all the ancient and famous cities and other places in India, are very readable and vivid. His descriptions of Bombay and the Elephanta and Kanheri Caves, from which we have quoted, are particularly striking.

Campbell, Sir James

(1847-1903).

An eminent Bombay Civilian, whose labours extending nearly over a generation on the organisation and compilation of the Gazetteer of our Presidency will be long remembered. The long extract we have given is taken from one of the many useful red-letter chapters as they are called, which are published decennially in the Administration Reports of this Presidency. This minute pen picture of the panorama of Bombay lies buried in a huge folio and is not generally known. We hope that in the form in which it is presented here, it will be widely read and appreciated. His "Bombay Gazetteer" is an extensive and very painstaking work in 35 distinct parts, the last of which appeared in 1901, a year after his retirement from Bombay. This great work, however, did not include a Gazetteer of Bombay City, though in three thick parts of its twenty-sixth volume are embodied extracts from Government Records, which are very useful as materials for Bombay history up till the beginning of the nineteenth century. This want was supplied six years after Campbell's death by Mr. S. M. Edwardes, who gave us in three volumes a work worthy at once of the City and of the high reputation deservedly enjoyed by the series of Gazetteers of this Presidency in which it appeared and which it fitly closed. Campbell's research work for the Gazetteer was recognised by his own University of Glasgow which conferred on him an honorary doctorate, and he also got a K.C.I.E. from the Government towards the close of his active career mainly for these literary labours.

Crane, Walter

(*b.* 1845).

This well known painter and book illustrator came to India in the cold weather of 1906-07 and published his book of impressions obtained during his Indian tour soon after. The book is illustrated with excellent sketches by the author who shows himself no less clever with the pen than with the pencil. Mr. Crane shows himself very sympathetic towards the people of this country, as was to be expected from one who was very friendly with the young Indian reformers in England.

Craik, Sir Henry

(*b.* 1846).

This eminent Scotch educationist has for a long time been in the Education Department at Whitehall. He has latterly been in Parliament also. In 1907-8 he made a tour of India, writing about it in the *Scotsman*. His impressions were so favourably received that they were at once published in a book (London, Macmillan) which is of great value as containing the ripe reflections of a penetrating observer. Sir Henry is an accomplished author and has written on literature and history. Some thirty years ago he edited an excellent series of little manuals by various writers on the rights and responsibilities of the English Citizen, himself contributing to it a volume on the "State and Education."

Crowe, Sir Joseph

(1825-1896).

A distinguished diplomatist, who in early life spent a few years in Bombay as a journalist and also as a teacher in the local School of Arts. A little before his death he published a volume of reminiscences of his varied and long career, and his recollections of Bombay life and society in the late fifties of the last century form not the least interesting portion of it. His literary partnership with Cavalcaselle in producing the famous "History of Italian Painting" is well known.

Cunha, Dr. Gerson da

(1842-1900).

This distinguished Orientalist had settled in Bombay from Goa, and was for long a well-known figure in literary and scientific circles in our city. He was particularly interested in the antiquities of Bassein, Bombay and other places during the period of Portuguese ascendancy. At the beginning of his career he wrote a valuable book on Bassein and Chaul. At the close of it he was engaged on a work on our city, which was published posthumously, called

The Origin of Bombay. This book owing to the circumstances of its production is ill arranged and not well digested, but contains good materials, especially for the Protuguese period of the history of Bombay which is so little known. Da Cunha who was by profession a physician, was also an expert numismatist.

Crawford, Arthur Travers

1835-1911.

No English official of the past generation knew Bombay so intimately as Arthur Crawford and no one had the real good of the city at heart more than he. He had very large opportunities during his eventful Municipal Commissionership nearly fifty years ago, and he utilised them to the full, beautifying the city and doing good to it in numberless ways in spite of the bitter opposition of its citizens. He was a man with grand ideas looking far ahead into the future and anticipating in those early days the city's position at the present time. All his ideas and schemes were not of course carried out in the sixties of the last century owing to financial considerations. But if they had been, our work in the twentieth century would have been simplified considerably. He had forseen the great progress which our city has made and would fain have provided for a Greater Bombay such as the present generation is engaged in building, had he had his own way unhampered. But it must be said that the resources of the city in his time were narrow and he far outran them. He never stooped to count the cost of his improvements and was lavish in expenditure. So the civic finances were hopelessly deranged and the bitter outcry from the citizens drove him from his post and most of his plans were abandoned. Crawford later fell on evil days, and had to leave the Bombay Civil Service in gloom almost at the end of his long career and after having risen almost to the top. In the last part of his long life he came to Bombay again and had the great satisfaction of seeing with his own eyes the immense progress of the city along the lines he had foreseen in his younger days. After leaving the service in 1889, he turned author and wrote some very good books based on his personal knowledge of this country and intimate acquaintance with its people. His *Reminiscences of an Indian Police Official*, from which we have quoted, is indeed a remarkable book, and the acquaintance which it reveals with the seamy side of Indian life in our presidency and city is almost unrivalled.

Del Mar, Walter

(*b.* 1862).

This retired American Banker and son of a well-known economical writer has travelled a good deal, and published several books of Eastern travel and impressions. He came to India in 1904 and wrote his *India of To-day* from which our extract is taken.

Douglas, James

1826-1904.

This well-known local antiquary, who did much by his writings, spread over nearly a quarter of a century, to stir up zeal in the present generation for old Bombay history and antiquities, was by profession not a man of letters at all, but a broker doing exchange business for thirty years in our city. He remained in Bombay till he was well past his seventy-fifth year and went home to Scotland only to die. He contributed his articles chiefly to our two local papers, and collected them at first in two pleasant little volumes called *Book of Bombay* (published by the "Bombay Gazette" in 1883) and *Round About Bombay* (1886). In 1893 he expanded these two books into two large volumes, *Bombay and Western*

India, by which it was his ambition to be known to posterity. But though the book has merits, not the least of which is that of stirring up the enthusiasm of its readers, it has some grave defects which stand in the way of its being recognised as a work of permanent historical importance and value. One of the chief of these is that he rarely, if ever, verified his references. He quotes his authorities loosely from memory which, however tenacious, betrays him into many misstatements, and it is rare to find among his sparse foot-notes a book referred to by volume and page. In 1900 he published a supplementary volume called *Glimpses of Old Bombay*, containing some more of his pleasant chatty articles, which are by no means confined to old Bombay but range from Alexander the great and Herodotus and Pliny to the Crusades and Albuquerque and Aquaviva. One of these latter miscellaneous papers, "Ostia to Ozein, A.D. 68," is however the best thing Douglas ever wrote, being distinguished alike by a fine imaginativeness and vivacity.

Dufferin, The Marquess of

1826-1902.

'This well-known Viceroy of India from 1884 to 1888 was in the diplomatic service and the only administrative post that he had filled before coming to India was that of Governor-General of Canada. However in spite of his lack of previous administrative experience, he proved a highly successful and popular Viceroy. His chief work was the annexation of Burma, a country which had long continued to trouble us. This annexation was at first unpopular with the Indians, who severely criticised it as an additional burden on the revenues of this country, as Burma for some years did not pay its way. But time has justified Lord Dufferin's wise step, and the new province not only pays its way now, but every year gives a handsome surplus to the Imperial treasury and is an undoubted source of strength to the empire, besides getting rid forever of a very troublesome and semi-savage independent neighbour. Lord Dufferin had brilliant literary gifts, inherited no doubt partly from his great-grandfather, Sheridan. His mother also was a brilliant literary lady. He wrote only a couple of books, but his brilliancy also appears in his letters one of which we have quoted, and many of them have been included in the late Sir Alfred Lyall's life of him (published by John Murray) that appeared four years after his death. Lady Dufferin, who accompained her husband to India, published in *Our Viceregal Life in India* a very vivacious account of the lighter side of the lives of rulers of this country.

Edwardes, Stephen Meredyth

(*b.* 1873).

This prominent Bombay Civilian and man of letters, has continued Sir James Campbell's labours on the *Bombay Gazetteer* and given us in 1909 in three volumes a long needed Gazetteer of our City which had not been included in its 35 big tomes. He has also published a sketch of the rise and growth of Bombay, and an excellent series of papers describing phases of life in our city and its neighbourhood. The latter were contributed to the *Times of India* and afterwards separately published in a volume, from which we have made our extracts. The former first appeared in 1901 as the historical part of the Report of the Census of Bombay City which he wrote as Census Commissioner. This historical part was so thoroughly done by him that his successor ten years later during the Census of 1911, Dr. J. Turner, needed not to do it again. He is since 1910 Commissioner of Police of the city, with whose past as well as present he is so intimately acquainted.

Elphinstone, Mountstuart

1779-1859.

This well-known Governor of Bombay from 1819 to 1827, though he passed nearly the whole of his active career in our Presidency was a Bengal Civilian and had originally spent a few years in that Presidency. He made his mark very early at the Mahratha court of the Peshwa at Poona, where he was posted, and was present at the battles of Assaye and Argaum, Wellington's great Indian victories, and witnessed the shattering of the power of the Mahratha Confederacy. He again went to Poona, after a few years, as Resident at the last Peshwa's court. He spent seven laborious years in watching and checkmating the tortuous policy of Baji Rao II and his anti-British advisers. At last Baji Rao was obliged to declare himself in his true colours, and make open war against the English. The battle of Kirkee in 1817 put an end to his rule, and the honours of the battle belonged to Elphinstone, though he was a civilian. The Peshwa's territories were annexed, and Elphinstone after spending some time in the work of 'settling' them, was appointed Governor of Bombay at the unusual age of forty.

His rule, prolonged for eight years, was marked by consolidation of territory, and by amelioration of the condition of the people. His efforts for the education of the people under him were very zealous, and he has the great credit of laying the foundation of the system of public instruction in this Presidency which has been productive of great good to the Indians, who showed their gratitude on his departure by large voluntary contributions towards the establishment of the College called after his name. He left Bombay for Europe in 1827 and though he was then under fifty and though he lived for over thirty years afterwards, he declined many high and very responsible posts that were offered to him. He twice declined the Governor-Generalship of India, besides the permanent Under-Secretaryship of the Board of Control and a special mission to Canada.

Elphinstone is well-known also as the author of several important books, and his history of India has long been a standard work on the Mohammadan period which it mainly treats of. He was also a good letter-writer as appears from the intimate letters that he wrote to friends, especially those to Edward Strachey, the father of the late Sir Richard and Sir John Strachey. The letter we have given describing his impressions of Bombay life and society on the threshold of his Governorship here, was addressed to his relative John Adam, another brilliant Bengal civilian who rose to be member of the Supreme Council in the same year in which Elphinstone got the Bombay Governorship and also acted as Governor-General for several months in 1823 at the early age of forty-four. These letters as well as a very interesting journal that he kept for a good part of his life were published in 1884 by Sir Edward Colebrooke in his biography of Elphinstone (published by John Murray).

Elwood, Mrs. Anne

This writer came to Bombay in July 1826 by the Overland Route through Egypt and the Red Sea and was the first lady to travel by this route. Of this journey overland from England to India she published an account in two volumes in 1830. She was in Bombay and the neighbouring places for nearly two years and her account of the city and other places in Western India is very elaborate. On her return voyage to Europe she followed the old route by the Cape of Good Hope. Mrs. Elwood afterwards wrote another book called "Memoirs of the Literary Ladies of England." She was the daughter of Edward Curteis of Windmill Hill, Sussex, and was married to Col. Elwood. The account of her overland journey to India is written in the form of letters addressed to her sister Mrs. Elphinstone.

Fraser, Lovat

This brilliant Anglo-Indian journalist was ten years in Bombay first as assistant editor and then as editor of the *Times of India*, and during all this time he came to know our city intimately. After his retirement in 1907, he wrote his *India under Lord Curzon*, which is generally accepted as a worthy record of a great Indian administration. Bombay, naturally, is often mentioned in Mr. Fraser's book and his account of the Plague in our city, from which we have quoted, is valuable as well as vivid. He wields a powerful pen and is still writing about Indian affairs in *the Times* and other leading papers. He is at present engaged upon the biography of a great Bombay citizen, the late Mr. Jamsetji Tata.

Falkland, Amelia Viscountess

1803-1858.

This lively lady was the daughter of William IV. and Mrs. Jordan. She married Viscount Falkland, (a descendant of the famous Falkland of the time of the Great Rebellion), who was Governor of Bombay from 1848 to 1853. She came out with her husband and took keen interest in her surroundings in this city and presidency. She kept a Journal from which she published selections on her return to Europe in 1857 under the somewhat cryptic title of Chow-Chow. She herself explains it as follows:—"The Pedlers in India carry their wares from village in boxes and baskets; among the latter, there is always one called the Chow-Chow basket, in which there is every variety of merchandize. The word Chow-Chow means 'Odds and Ends,' and in offering my Chow-Chow basket to the public, I venture to hope that something, however trifling, may be found in it, suited to the taste of everyone." The book contains vivid accounts of her experiences here of the various classes of people with whom she came in contact, of the manners and customs of Indians and many other interesting things besides. She was an admirer of Nature and her descriptions of the natural scenery of places like Poona, Mahableshwar etc. are striking. She mixed with the Indians freely and came to know their sentiments and opinions somewhat intimately. Her sketches of Bombay, of which we have given some specimens, are life-like as well as lively. The book is well worth reprinting. Lady Falkland died shortly after the publication of her book.

Forjett, Charles

1810-1890.

A well-known Commissioner of Police in our city two generations ago. His knowledge of Indians and his command over their languages was so perfect that he passed easily as an Indian himself in their midst whenever he chose. At the crisis of the Mutiny his intimate knowledge of Indians as well as his marvellous sources of gathering information were of great use to our city, in as much as they averted a serious Sepoy outbreak here. He has himself told the story in a book published twenty years later from which we have given extracts. It is pleasant to recall that the citizens of Bombay appreciated his great services on his retirement in 1864 in a substantial manner by presenting him with a purse of over a lakh of rupees.

Forrest, L. R. Windham

A well-known member of the Anglo-Indian mercantile community of our city twenty years ago. He was a partner in the firm of Messrs. Killick Nixon, and was for several years Chairman of the Bombay Chamber of Commerce. He was also member of the local Legislative Council. He took a great interest in developing the resources of Gujarat and under his guidance his firm undertook the work, very beneficent for commerce, of commencing to build feeder-railways in that province. The Tapti Valley Railway, running through a very fertile country and connecting the Bombay Baroda with the Great Indian Peninsula Railway, owes its construction mainly to his enterprise. Our city where he resided for over thirty years and to develop whose commerce he had worked hard, he knew intimately and on his retirement he read a paper before the Royal Society of Arts in 1901 which gives in short compass an outline of the history and present position of Bombay.

Fortescue, The Hon. John

(*b.* 1859).

This eminent writer is better known as the historian of the British army than by any books on India. But as Librarian at Windsor Castle he came out to this country in the suite of the King and Queen during their visit in 1911-12 and wrote a narrative of the Royal Tour (published by Messrs. Macmillan). This book though not very striking is a useful short account of this epoch-marking event. He is a son of the late Earl Fortescue.

Frere, Sir Bartle

1815-1884.

One of our greatest Governors and one to whom the city of Bombay especially owes much. He belonged to the Bombay Civil Service, and was the last member of that Service so far to rise to the post of ruler of the presidency. Modern Bombay owes its rise mainly to him. The Town walls, which were so long felt to be a hindrance, were finally pulled down under him and the site thus released was utilised for erecting splendid mercantile and other useful buildings. The city was vastly improved in several other directions also and he gave us our first Municipality. The first years of his governorship coincided with the period of phenomenal prosperity which Bombay enjoyed owing to the enormous rise in the price of cotton consequent on the Civil War in America. This vast and sudden influx of wealth led to extravagant projects, and wild speculation raged unchecked for a time. Then came the crash and numberless people were ruined. The great wealth that had turned the heads of most of its people suddenly disappeared. Frere was blamed by many at the time for not having checked the spirit of speculation in time. The last two years of his rule were those of gloom and reaction. But making allowance for his mistakes, it must be said that he did much to soften the blow which staggered Bombay in 1865. He left Bombay in 1867. He came once more to our city eight years later as the *cicerone* of the late King Edward when he visited India as Prince of Wales in 1875-76. When Frere's term as Governor was over all the communities and the various representative bodies of our city presented him with farewell addresses to mark their sense of his great services, and he delivered many important speeches in answering these addresses. We have given some characteristic extracts from these speeches, which along with others were collected in a volume with an introduction by that eminent Indian, the late Mr. Justice Ranade (1842-1901).

Forbes, Alexander Kinloch

1821-1865.

This distinguished Bombay civilian who died at Poona an early death was a Judge of our High Court and Vice-Chancellor of our University. Throughout his career here he devoted all his leisure to the early history of the Province of Gujarat where he mostly served. He acquired great command over old Gujarati, the language in which most of his materials were composed. In 1856 when he was only thirty-five he brought out the results of his historical labours in his *Ras-Mala* or Hindu Annals of Gujarat in two volumes, a work of great labour and value which does for its subject what Tod's *Rajasthan* has done for Rajputana. Unfortunately it is not so well known and appreciated as it deserves, though its merits both literary and historical are great. Forbes though an antiquary was no Dryasdust; he had fine imagination and an excellent style.

He took great interest in architecture and his descriptions of old cities like Anhilwada and Champanir and their ruins are well worth reading.

Graham, Maria

1785-1842.

This lady is better known in the literary world as Lady Callcott, the author of the widely read "Little Arthur's History of England." She was the daughter of Admiral George Dundas. In 1809 she married Captain Thomas Graham of the Royal Navy and spent the next year in India travelling through the country. Whilst in Bombay she was the guest of Sir James Mackintosh who was then Recorder here. She published two books on her return to England in 1811 descriptive of her Indian travels. The first was called "Journal of a Residence in India" which was later translated into French. Her second book was called "Letters on India" and was published in 1814. Both these books contain much that is interesting about this country and its peoples. Captain Graham having died in 1822 she married in 1827 Sir Augustus Callcott (1779-1844) a well-known landscape painter. As Lady Callcott she wrote many successful children's books of which the best remembered now is "Little Arthur's History of England" first published in 1835. Besides India she travelled in several other countries such as Brazil and Chili and wrote books about them.

Grant-Duff, Sir Mountstuart Elphinstone

1829-1906.

This distinguished English politician became Governor of Madras from 1881 to 1886. He had been previously connected with Indian administration as Under-Secretary of State for this country when the eighth Duke of Argyll (1823-1900) was Indian Secretary in Gladstone's first Administration of 1868-74. Some months after that great Administration was dissolved by the defeat of the Liberals at the polls in 1874, Grant Duff visited India to see personally the country for whose government he was responsible in the House of Commons for the preceding six years. The impressions of this Indian tour were first printed in a Review, and afterwards appeared in book form. Grant Duff was passionately fond of botany, and his "Notes of an Indian Journey" are full of information and observation on the flora of this country. Though he was officially connected with the southern Presidency as its Governor, he had an hereditary interest in our province. His father knew the

Mahrathas intimately and wrote their history in an authoritative work. His god-father was the famous Governor of Bombay, Mountstuart Elphinstone (1779-1859) whose name he bore. During the latter part of his life he published his voluminous "Notes from a Diary," a work useful to the future historian of the state of society in Victorian times.

Grindlay, Robert Melville

The founder of the well-known firm of Anglo-Indian agents and bankers, Grindlay Groom and Co., was at first in the service of the East India Company from which he retired with the rank of Captain. Being fond of sketching and drawing, he had made a large collection of drawings of scenery and buildings whilst in this country. In 1830 he published a selection from his own as well as other artists' Indian pictures, under the title of "Scenery Costumes and Architecture, chiefly on the Western side of India," which was well received and several times reprinted, the last being in 1892. This magnificent work consists of thirty-six large plates of which no less than twelve are devoted to Bombay, Elephanta and the neighbouring places. The plates are accompanied by descriptive letterpress which contain several good passages.

Mrs. Guthrie

This charming writer was the wife of an officer in the Bombay Presidency and came to Bombay about forty years ago. She had already travelled in Russia and written a book called "Through Russia." She lived for some years in this country and wrote two books about it. Her first book "My year in an Indian Fort" describes her life in Belgaum where she was stationed for a year. The preliminary part of the book is devoted to the outward voyage and to Bombay, and her account of the sights and scenes in our city is very lively as may be judged from the extracts we have given. The other book, "Life in Western India," published in 1881 is devoted to various places like Bijapur, Dharwar, Sholapur, Hyderabad where duty took her husband. The delightful hill-station of Mahableshwar is well described at length in the first volume. In both these works Mrs. Guthrie weaves into her narrative much of the folklore and legends that she heard at various places, and there are also in the volumes several bits of natural scenery excellently described.

Hall, Basil

1788-1844.

This well-known traveller and author was the son of Sir James Hall (1761-1832) a noted geologist. He was a captain in the Royal navy and served in various countries. He visited China in Lord Amherst's embassy and on the way he had an interview at St. Helena with Napoleon, who had known his father, Sir James Hall, when a boy at school at Brienne. Basil Hall was in Bombay in 1812 with his frigate, and in 1814 he became Captain of the Victor sloop which was then building at Bombay and which he took to England in the following year. He visited later several countries about which he wrote various books. But his reputation mainly rests on his "Fragments of Voyages and Travels" which appeared in three series in three successive years from 1831. These contain many interesting personal experiences of the author gained in several countries and imparted in a good literary style. Whilst in Bombay he was charmed with every thing and his accounts as given in the second series of this work are very enthusiastic. Two years before his death his mind unfortunately gave way and he died in an asylum.

Harris, Lord

(*b.* 1851).

Governor of Bombay from 1890 to 1895. His term of office was marked by the great encouragement given to sport amongst Indians, especially cricket. Lord Harris was himself a great cricketer and did much to promote his favourite game here, especially among Parsis. On his return to England he read a paper on Bombay before the Society of Arts which shows his great love and enthusiasm for our city. Lord Harris came again to our city during the Royal Visit in the cold weather of 1911-12. His connection with India is hereditary, his father having been Governor of Madras sixty years ago during the Mutiny; and his great-grandfather was the famous conqueror of Tipu, the great Duke of Wellington then serving under him.

Hübner, Baron Joseph von

1811-1892.

An eminent Austrian diplomatist and man of letters. He was also a great traveller. In 1883 he travelled through the British Empire, visiting India and the Colonies. He wrote an account of this tour in 1885 from which we have taken a part abcut what he saw in Bombay.

In this excellent work von Hübner does full justice to England's work in India, and it is well worth close attention, coming as it does from a foreign statesman of his wide experience and high position. He was Austrian ambassador at various European Courts including those of Paris and Rome. He was also a well known author and an earlier account that he wrote in 1871 of a tour round the world, which however did not include India, was translated into several European languages. He also wrote an excellent history of Pope Sixtus V. from the Catholic point of view.

Hunter, Sir William Wilson

1840-1900.

This distinguished Anglo-Indian, historian and statistician was at the head of the Statistical Department of the Government of India and planned the series of Gazetteers for the various provinces of this country, compiled by a whole host of district officers intimately acquainted with the places about which they wrote. He himself took under his special care the Gazetteer of the whole country of which he published the first edition in 1881 in nine volumes and the second five years later in fourteen volumes. He, however, died just before the third edition was decided by Lord

Curzon's Government to be undertaken. The article on Bombay in the second edition of his *Imperial Gazetteer* from which we have quoted gives an excellent compact account of our City. He also wrote the article on Bombay in the ninth edition of the *Encyclopædia Britannica.* He was also a voluminous writer on Anglo-Indian history and biography, and edited the well-known series of short biographical and historical monographs called "Rulers of India." Towards the close of his busy literary life he began to publish a great history of British India which would have run to five or six large volumes; but his death at the age of sixty put a stop to what would have been his *magnum opus.* It proceeded to only a couple of volumes.

Von Koeningsmarck, Count Hans

This distinguished military officer on the General Staff of the German Army came to India in the cold weather of 1905-06, and wrote on his return his impressions of India and the British Administration here, which were published in Germany where they were very favourably received. In 1910 this German book "Dü Englanden in Indien" was translated into English and became very popular. The Count had previously twice visited the country in the early nineties, so his knowledge of India cannot be said to be very limited. He showed great powers of accurate observation and also marked literary ability. His judgment of the English work in India is very favourable and he praises without stint the high purpose and lofty aims with which he saw the officials here inspired. This was all the more remarkable as coming from a foreigner and especially, a German. The Count's description of Bombay is striking both on account of its enthusiasm and literary power. The book "A German Staff Officer in India" (Kegan Paul) is gracefully dedicated to Lady Blood, the wife of General Sir Bindon Blood and daughter of the late Sir Auckland Colvin, as a token of the Count's homage to the English-woman in India.

Karageorgevitch, Prince Bojidar

This Prince of the reigning family of Servia came to India in 1897, when we celebrated the Diamond Jubilee of Queen Victoria and also when Plague had only recently entered the country. *Enchanted India* (Harpers) as he calls his book of Indian travel is remarkable for its striking and picturesque descriptions of the cities and sights of this country. The passages that we have given will give some idea of the Prince's great gift of conveying the impressions made by Indian sights and scenes in striking language.

Lamington, Lord

(*b.* 1860).

Governor of Bombay from 1903 to 1907. He was another of the retired rulers of this Presidency who was invited by the Society of Arts to read a paper on his reminiscences of life here. He had previously discoursed before the same Society on his travels in Indo-China. He is very fond of travel, and since he left Bombay seven years ago has been twice to Persia. He was also Governor of the Colony of Queensland in Australia before he came to Bombay as its Governor. Popular among all classes in Bombay, his premature departure was regretted when owing to domestic circumstances he had to give up his office before his term of five years was over. He is the son of a great friend of Disraeli, Baillie-Cochrane first Baron Lamington, who was a well-known writer and whose book *In the Days of the Dandies* had a great vogue once.

Lee-Warner, Sir William

1846-1914.

This brilliant Anglo-Indian official and writer knew our city thoroughly as he passed almost his whole Indian career in the Secretariat here; and long residence did not cool the enthusiasm he had at first felt for it. The fine passage we have quoted about Bombay and its glorious scenery from a lecture that he gave almost towards the close of his residence in this city is proof of the spell that Bombay had cast round him. After his retirement from the Bombay Civil Service nearly twenty years ago, he published some noteworthy books, especially a biography of the Marquess of Dalhousie in which that much-maligned ruler has at last had full justice done to him after nearly half a century of misunderstanding at the hands of posterity. Sir William died only very recently, a little after his retirement from the India Council which he had served either as Political Secretary or member for seventeen years after leaving India.

Low, Sidney

(*b.* 1857).

This able journalist came to India in 1905-06, as special correspondent of the London

Standard, with which paper he has been closely connected for a series of years, during the first tour in India of His present Majesty as Prince of Wales. This book *A Vision of India* (1906, Smith Elder) does not merely give an account of the Royal Tour, but also attempts to give the reader an idea of the conditions of life and society prevailing in the country. He tries to convey to the reader his impressions not only of the sights he saw but of the machinery of British Administration and its manifold results. He mixed with officials as well as non-officials, and the views that he expresses strike one as those of a man of wide learning and close observation. His powers of picturesque narration and vivid description of the sights that he saw are also remarkable.

He is also the author of the "Governance of England" a very able work on the English constitution in its practical working; and of the final volume treating of the reign of Victoria in Dr. William Hunt's "Political History of England." He edited thirty years ago with the late Prof. Pulling a valuable historical work of reference called "The Dictionary of English History," a book still in wide use.

Lytton, Lord

1831-1891.

Viceroy of India from 1876 to 1880. He came to India like another Viceroy, Lord Dufferin, from the diplomatic service, and like Lord Dufferin too, who had previously declined the Governorship of Bombay, he had declined the Governorship of Madras. His rule in India was eventful and marked not only by the Afghan War but by wide-spread famine and popular discontent. Queen Victoria was proclaimed Empress of India with great pomp and circumstance in a grand Darbar at Delhi, the precursor of the grander Darbars of our days. He was a favourite with that good Queen with whom he corresponded freely, and the letter giving his impressions of Bombay on first arrival, from which we have quoted, will give some idea of his powers as a letter writer. Many of his letters to friends were published in 1906 by his accomplished daughter, Lady Betty Balfour, who had previously written an account of his Indian Viceroyalty. Lord Lytton was a very good writer, and his speeches and despatches had literary finish. He wrote also poetry and some of his poems like "The Ring of Amasis," and "King Poppy," are well-known. He was made an Earl for his work in India, and on being sent later to Paris as British Ambassador he became very popular with Frenchmen.

Mackintosh, Sir James

1765-1832.

This famous English writer and politician came to Bombay in 1804, as Judge of the Recorder's Court, established here six years before. The first Recorder, Sir William Syer, had succumbed here to the Indian climate and Mackintosh came here with some hesitation; but he stayed here for nearly eight years returning home to take part in English politics for over twenty years thereafter. He had previously applied unsuccessfully for the post of Advocate-General of Bengal, but he got the higher judicial post at Bombay which also carried with it a knighthood. He had came to India with the same object as Macaulay in the following generation, namely, to obtain a competency for life from his Indian savings which would enable him to take an independent part in politics at home. While Macaulay, who had great admiration for him, achieved that object remaining for only about half the period of Mackintosh, the latter somehow missed his, and failed to take the high position in the political life of his time which his parts undoubtedly deserved. Nor did he, like Macaulay, make his mark in literature by a great work. A certain weakness of character and infirmity of purpose are responsible for this double failure. He had planned on a great scale a history of the

English Revolution of 1688, and though he worked at it off and on for twenty years and more, he left it only a fragment when he died.

When he was in Bombay he read immensely taking little part in society, and Government House at Parel, which Governor Duncan kindly laid at his disposal for residence at first, and then "Tarala" his subsequent house at Mazagon, never harboured so erudite an inmate before or since. But he seems to have read his whole time away at Bombay doing very little substantial literary work. While Macaulay wrote some of his best essays in Calcutta, Mackintosh, who was also an *Edinburgh* Reviewer, did nothing of the kind whilst at Bombay. One great thing, however, he did whilst here, and that was to found the Bombay Literary Society which under a changed name still exists and has in the course of its long existence done much for the archæology and philology of Western India. Through this Society Mackintosh influenced several young Anglo-Indians to investigate and write about the antiquities and history of India. Mackintosh whilst here kept a journal which was subsequently published in his biography by his son and from this we have taken our extracts.

Maclean,. James Mackenzie

1835-1906

A distinguished Bombay citizen and journalist, who after his retirement from our city in 1880, took an active part in English politics and was a member of Parliament for many years. Whilst in Bombay he was not only editor of the *Bombay Gazette* for a long time, but also a prominent member of our Municipal Corporation. He took a large part in obtaining the present municipal constitution for our City, which owes to him too its proud motto *Urbs prima in Indis.* His *Guide to Bombay*, originally published in 1875 in connection with the visit to India of the late King Edward VII as Prince of Wales, occupied for nearly a quarter of a century a unique place as a compact and trustworthy handbook to our city useful alike for the tourist and the permanent resident. It was republished annually with occasional revisions till fifteen years ago when it was allowed to go out of print.

When the Riots of 1874 broke out, and the Mahomedans of Bombay rose against the Parsis and wrecked their fire-temples, Maclean took up the cause of the latter, and did much to obtain justice for them by his articles and reports in his paper. He was an eye-witness of most of the scenes of lawlessness then enacted in the city, and his accounts were considered the best at the time. His writings in the *Bombay Gazette* on the subject were collected and reprinted in a pamphlet which had a wide sale. Our extract about an episode during these riots which attracted much attention at the time is taken from this pamphlet.

Macleod, Norman

1812-1872.

This eloquent and popular Scotch preacher came to India at the end of 1867. He was sent to this country to inquire into the condition of the Church of Scotland Missions. His interest in India had been first aroused early in life by the Marchioness of Hastings, widow of the famous Governor-General of India, who presented him with his first living, that of Loudoun in Ayrshire in 1838. Ever since those early days of intercourse with the noble widow, he had taken deep interest in Indian affairs and history, and latterly he took an active part in the management of India Missions. So that when he was selected along with Dr. Watson of Dundee by the General Assembly of 1867 to go to India and after personal enquiries on the spot to report on Missions there, he undertook the journey with alacrity, though his medical advisers had assured him that his going out to India would entail almost certain death.

In Bombay and wherever else he went, he was received most cordially by all classes of the people. He was Chaplain to Queen Victoria and one of her favourite preachers in Scotland. This official position had something to do with his reception, but apart from this his attractive personality and intense sincerity would have ensured him a hearty welcome everywhere. Sir Arthur Helps has called him the greatest and most convincing preacher he had ever heard, and in India too people crowded to hear him preach or speak. He spent only three months in the country, but the impressions that he gathered in such a short time were remarkable for their accuracy and fairness. He came to Bombay just in time to be present at the great St. Andrew's dinner of 1867. He went about everywhere and saw everything. His impressions and reminiscences of Bombay and other Indian cities he contributed to *Good Words*, a magazine which he edited and which became in his hands one of the greatest successes of the time in periodical literature. These articles were re-published with additions and alterations in 1869 in a book called "Peeps at the Far East" which had great vogue at the time and deserves to be read still, as it has an inner depth and a philosophical value beyond that of a mere record of travel. Our extracts will, we hope, show the great value of the book. There is not much about missions in it, the main object for which he came here; but that is because he embodied his investigations on that subject in a separate official Missionary Report. The year after his return from India he was chosen Moderator of the General Assembly and in his official address he dealt largely with his Indian experiences. He survived his return from the Indian tour only four years and died in June 1872.

Mayo, Lord

1822-1872.

This popular but unfortunate Viceroy of India, from 1869 to 1872, came to Bombay, in the latter part of December, 1868, on his way to Calcutta to assume the Viceroyalty from Lord Lawrence. He had been appointed to his high office by Disraeli when his first administration was already tottering. It was at Bombay that Mayo heard of the fall of Disraeli and the advent of the Liberals under Gladstone. While he was in England there had been a violent outcry against his appointment on the score of his want of experience of Indian affairs. So he might well have been doubtful, when he landed in Bombay and saw our city, about his further journey to Calcutta to assume office. But Gladstone and the Liberal Ministry confirmed their predecessors' nomination. During the ten days that he spent in our city he discussed most of the local problems and was specially interested in our Municipal affairs which were then under Arthur Crawford, our great Municipal Commissioner. He visited the Vehar Water Works, at that time our only works of the kind and saw the docks. These too were very small affairs indeed compared to the extensive docks that we have now come to possess. Still Mayo was much impressed with all that he saw and called Bombay the finest site for commerce in the world. He was destined never to come again to Bombay for his departure at the end of his term of office, He was assassinated in the midst of his beneficent career three years later by a fanatic Afghan in the Andamans when he had not yet completed his fiftieth year. Sir William Hunter, who was then a rising official, published his biography three years later, in which he gives Mayo's diary from which we have extracted, and other personal materials.

Moor, Edward

1771-1848.

The well-known author of the *Hindoo Pantheon* was in the military service of the East India Company and employed mostly in the South. The last six years, 1799-1805, of his stay in India he spent in Bombay, where he was employed as garrison store-keeper or Commissory-General. He retired in 1805 when he was only thirty-four. He was of an observing studious nature and had while in this country made the Hindoo religion his special study. He had gathered extensive materials for this and made a large collection of Indian images, pictures and the like. Five years after leaving India he published his great work on Hindoo Mythology and religion in which he utilised the materials he had collected in this country. This work as well as another smaller book called "Oriental Fragments" which he published in 1834, contain several passages giving interesting reminiscences of his residence in Bombay and other Indian places. Our extract from the former work, *Hindoo Pantheon*, about the Hindoo sacred place at Malabar Point illustrates this. The year before he left Bombay, he was among those learned Anglo-Indians who helped Mackintosh to found the Literary Society of Bombay. His valuable collection of Indian images was lately exhibited by his grandson at the Indian Court of the Festival of Empire.

Mrs. Postans

This lively writer of two generations ago was the author of several books about Bombay and Western India which were popular in her days. She was married twice, first to Capt. Postans and then to a missionary named Young, and came in close contact with Indian life and society in this city as well as Surat and other places. Her book on Bombay from which our extracts have been made, is a good record of the city at the beginning of Queen Victoria's reign, and may be read with profit for the sake of comparison with the progress since made. Her *Moslem Noble*, which she published in 1857 under her second name of Mrs. Young, is a good picture of high class Mahomedan life at Surat from within as it were, and contains other interesting matter besides.

Perry, Sir Erskine

1806-1882.

Once the Chief Justice of the Supreme Court at Bombay, Perry is much better known as a lawyer than as a man of letters. His *Bird's-eye View of India* is well worth reading still, though it appeared sixty years ago. It contains a journal kept during one of his long tours in India and gives several first hand impressions which are worth reading. He wrote also a very interesting book of gleanings of Indian social life from his judge's note-book. After his retirement from Bombay in 1852, he was long known in England for his strong and persistent advocacy of the cause of Indians first in Parliament and then in the Council of India. During his sojourn in Bombay from 1839 to 1852, he took great interest in the education of the natives of this city and was President of the old Board of Education which gave place a little after his retirement to the Department of Public Instruction.

Price, David

1762-1835.

Like Major Moor with whom, while in India, he had contracted a life-long friendship, David Price was in the army of the East India Company and employed against Tipu in Mysore and the South. He began his career in this city and was off and on in Bombay, Poona, Surat and other places in Western India during his Indian career extending from 1782 to 1805. He was Judge Advocate of the Bombay army in 1795 and the following years. With his friend Moor he retired early from the service in 1805, and like him too he spent his retirement in literary ease writing several important works. He too a little before his retirement took part in founding the Bombay Literary Society. The subject of his special studies was Mahomedan History.

Prinsep, Valentine Cameron

1838-1904.

This distinguished English artist belonged to the well known Anglo-Indian family of the Prinseps who have been for several generations in the Indian Civil Service. He himself like his father and brother was intended for the same service and actually was for some time at Haileybury; but having decidedly an artistic bent he chose to pursue an artistic career, in which he achieved a marked success. Being born on Valentine's Day at Calcutta, where his father then was in the Supreme Council, he was called Valentine, and this was contracted into Val, and he was known generally as Val Prinsep. He was the pupil with Sir Edward Poynter and Whistler of the famous painter G. F. Watts (1817-1904). He was an intimate friend of Millais, Burne-Jones, and other celebrated Victorian painters. In October 1876 he received from Lord Lytton a commission to paint a picture for the Indian Government of the coming Imperial Assemblage at Delhi to be given as a present to Her Majesty Queen Victoria on the occasion of her assumption of the title of Empress of India. This picture necessitated a long tour of nearly a year, as he had to be present not only at the Darbar but had also later on to visit the Native Courts in order to portray from life in his picture the various and numerous Native Princes that attended that grand function. This picture was finished in

1879 and was exhibited at the Royal Academy in the following year. It hangs now at Buckingham Palace. He afterwards published an account of his tour for his Durbar picture in a book called *Imperial India: An Artist's Journals.* (1879, Chapman and Hall). This book like Rousselet's deals almost exclusively with Native India, as he visited only the Courts of the principal Native Princes. Prinsep relates his experiences in a bright humorous way. He executed several commissions for the Native Princes and his portraits hang in several Native Courts in India.

Ramsay, Balcarres D. Wardlaw

A grandson of the 23rd Earl of Crawford and Balcarres, Col. Ramsay was well connected with the aristocracy of England and obtained several coveted posts. He served in India twice: he passed through the Indian Mutiny, and some thirteen years earlier he came out to Bombay on the personal staff of the Governor, Sir George Arthur (1784-1854). Towards the close of his career he published his "Rough Recollections of Military Service and Society" (1882, 2 vols., Blackwood) which are very pleasant reading and contain many good anecdotes. His recollections of Bombay as he saw it in 1844-45, are very interesting as Ramsay went about with his eyes open. He was afterwards on the staff of the Governor-General, Lord Hardinge, (1785-1856).

———

Reed, Dr. Stanley

(*b.* 1872).

This distinguished Anglo-Indian journalist is editor of the *Times of India* since 1907. His connection with this paper began ten years earlier, and he was its Special Correspondent on important occasions like the great Famine of 1900-01, the tour of the Prince and Princess of Wales in India, 1905-06, the Amir of Afghanistan's visit, 1907, etc. His account of the Prince's tour of 1905 was so well written and highly appreciated that it rendered unnecessary the official narrative whose publication was dropped in its favour. He also represented his paper when six years later the King and Queen visited India again. His narrative of this memorable Royal visit attracted considerable attention, and was well received when it appeared, like its predecessor, in a sumptuous volume. From both these books our extracts are taken. Much of what relates to Bombay in the volume on the Royal Visit is from the pen of Mr. S. T Sheppard, Assistant Editor of the *Times of India*, who has made Bombay history and topography his special subject, as appears from the preface of Dr. Reed, who says: "I am indebted to my colleague, Mr. S. T. Sheppard, for much valuable assistance. He wrote a considerable part of the Bombay chapter, etc."

Dr. Reed represented the press of Western India at the Imperial Press Conference held in London in 1909, and the University of Glasgow conferred its Doctorate on him on the occasion. A predecessor of his in the editorship of the *Times of India*, the well-known Dr. Buist (1805-1860) had been similarly honoured by a Scotch University two generations earlier.

Rees, Sir John

(*b.* 1854).

A distinguished Anglo-Indian writer, who after a career in the Madras Civil Service from 1875-1901, has entered English politics, and become Member of Parliament. While in India he was Private Secretary to three successive Governors of Madras, and wrote an excellent account of the tours of one of them, the late Lord Connemara (1827-1902), from which our extract is taken. The quotation in this extract (*p.* 4 *supra*) is from Tennyson's well-known lines on Milton beginning 'O Mighty-mouth'd inventor of harmonies!' (Poetical Works, Globe ed., p. 243).

Rousselet, Louis

A French artist who spent six years, 1864-69, in India on a picturesque tour like Daniell and some other Englishmen before him, studying the architectural monuments and other works of art in this country. He was particularly interested in the India of the Native Princes and he visited their Courts, not caring so much for the parts under the British rule. He was received by these Native Princes with great honour, and every facility was given him of prosecuting his artistic studies. During the years he was in India the name of France stood high in the world, and though he had come in no official capacity from his country, the Native States received him everywhere as a distinguished visitor belonging to a great nation. He afterwards published an elaborate book of his Indian experiences and impressions which also appeared in an English edition in 1876. This book was beautifully illustrated with the author's striking engravings especially of the architectural remains. The book naturally contains little about British India; still Bombay has a good many pages, as Louis Rousselet started on his long Indian tour from our city in which he stayed for several months in 1864, visiting Elephanta and Kanheri Caves and other places of interest. His long account of Bombay, its peoples and sights, is lively and entertaining, as may be seen from our extracts.

Steel, Flora Annie

(*b.* 1847).

A noted novelist and writer on India, this lady has achieved a name in Anglo-Indian literature second only to that of Mr. Rudyard Kipling. The wife of a Bengal Civilian serving in the Punjab from 1862 to 1889, she was with him for twenty years in this country, and was herself officially employed as an Inspectress of Schools in the Land of the Five Rivers whose people she came to know intimately. Of her several novels the most noteworthy are "On the Face of the Waters," a powerful tale of the Indian Mutiny, and "The Potter's Thumb," a remarkable story of Anglo-Indian and Indian life. Mrs. Steel wrote the letterpress for one of Mr. Mortimer Menpes' books of coloured illustrations on India in Messrs. Black's delightful series of "Colour Books," and our extract is taken from thence.

Steevens, George Warrington

1869-1900.

This brilliant journalist came to India only a year before his untimely death, and wrote as the result the most brilliant of his books, *In India* (Blackwood, 1899). He came with Lord Curzon when the latter assumed the Viceroyalty.

at the beginning of 1899, and remained some months traversing the country, and the impressions that he gathered of life and society as well as administration, he has put in this remarkable book which is wonderfully accurate, besides being thoroughly readable. Steevens had the gift of insight combined with that of vivid and telling description, which together make his book really remarkable.

After his return from India, Steevens went to South Africa as war correspondent of the *Daily Mail*, and was subsequently besieged in Ladysmith, where unfortunately he died of enteric fever on the 15th of January 1900. His correspondence during the Boer War and the Siege of Ladysmith was afterwards published posthumously. He also wrote during his short career four or five other books describing America, Egypt, the Sudan, etc., which were made up of his brilliant special correspondence for the *Daily Mail*.

Sydenham, Lord

(*b.* 1848).

Governor of Bombay from 1907 to 1913. The term of the administration of Sir George Clarke, as he was known whilst in Bombay, was eventful in itself, and the Royal Visit to our city that fell during it, may also be said to have distinguished it much. To the rapid growth and expansion of Bombay that has been going on for years past he devoted special care and attention, drawing up elaborate projects for the improvement and extension of our city. Education and popular unrest also engaged him largely. His rule was on the whole successful and he was popular with several classes of Indians. He was made a Baron shortly before he left Bombay for his vigorous and successful administration. Lord Sydenham is a practiced writer and has written more than half a dozen books. His special subject is Imperial defence, on which he is considered an authority and for which he had visited various outlying parts of the Empire before coming to Bombay.

Temple, Sir Richard

1826-1902.

This well-known Anglo-Indian Civilian was for three years, 1877-1880, at the close of his brilliant Indian career, Governor of Bombay. Like other rulers he too was charmed with Bombay and is enthusiastic in his references to our city in his various works, especially his autobiography called "Story of my Life" published in 1896 from which our extracts are taken. Sir Richard besides being an administrator of great note, was also a voluminous writer on India, many of whose provinces he had known intimately and administered ably. He had the reputation of being acquainted personally with the nooks and corners of our presidency more than any of his predecessors, and the experience thus gained he utilised not only in his minutes here as governor but also in his books later on.

West, Sir Raymond

1832-1912.

A well-known Bombay Civilian of the last generation and educationist. He was Judge of the Bombay High Court for many years and closed his career as Member of Council retiring in 1892. With the Bombay University he was intimately connected as its Vice-Chancellor for a series of years. His annual Convocation addresses in the latter capacity were models of learning and academic eloquence. He was also an ardent encourager of research and learning whilst in Bombay. As a lawyer his reputation was high and his work on Hindu Law in collaboration with Dr. Bühler (1837-1898) is authoritative.

NOTE ON THE WRITERS OF ACCOUNTS OF BOMBAY.

The earliest account of Bombay under the English hitherto quoted is that of Fryer written in 1675 only six or seven years after the Island passed into British hands. But a still earlier account was unearthed by the late Sir Henry Yule and published a little before his death in 1889, among other unpublished materials in his very valuable edition of the Diary of Sir William Hedges for the Hakluyt Society. This was written by **Sir Streynsham Master** (1640-1724) who was one of the four leading servants of the East India Company who had been selected in 1668 to go to Bombay from Surat and take over the Island from the King's officers when Charles II had determined to transfer it to the Company, thinking it useless and expensive. Master had first come to Surat as a lad of sixteen in 1656 in company with his uncle, George Oxenden, who later became President of the Surat Factory and was the first Company's Governor of Bombay, dying a few months after his appointment in July 1669. Oxenden has been completely forgotten long ago, though he has a splendid mausoleum at Surat. So also is Master, who had left no trace of his connection with Bombay before the fortunate discovery of this account among the family papers by a descendant who communicated it to Yule. He is remembered now, if remembered at all, for his later connection with Madras, where he became chief of the Factory in 1678 and built the Church which has the distinction of being the first English Church in India. Owing to grave differences with his employers he returned to England in 1681, and took a prominent part in the affairs of their rival, the New East India Company, of which he became one of the Directors.

Yule's edition of *Hedges' Diary*, which mostly refers to Bengal, is not a very likely place for finding an account of Bombay, and consequently I have hardly ever seen it referred to or used by writers about our Island. I called attention to it in 1900 in the *Times of India*, where it was quoted in its entirety. In the present book it takes its proper place as leading all the early accounts of this Island given in the section specially devoted to them. Valuable and detailed as is Fryer's account, yet Master's has an authority which the latter cannot claim. Fryer was a traveller, a globe-trotter, though a very intelligent one, and new to the country; while Master had been sixteen years in India at the time of writing his description and must have known the Island pretty intimately as he was one of the Commissioners, as said above, for receiving it on behalf of the Company from the King's officers. Till the official account written by Master's chief; the well-known Gerald Aungier, turns up some day at the India Office Library or elsewhere, this account is not likely to lose its great importance.

John Fryer (1650-1733) was a physician who, soon after taking his M.B. degree at Cambridge in 1671, embarked on a lengthened tour in India and Persia, undertaken in the interests of the East India Company, which lasted for ten years from 1672 till 1682. He was in Bombay in 1674 and his account, from which we have quoted, is contained in a letter dated from Surat, 15th January 1675. This and the other letters which form his well known book *A New Account of East India and Persia* were not published till 1698. He could not easily be persuaded to give an account of his wanderings to the world, but at length piqued at the frequent appearance of translations of foreign, especially French, books of travel in which English industry and enterprise in India were decried, and annoyed by numerous private enquiries about his experiences, he came out with the handsome folio which has saved his name from oblivion, and which has been quoted so often for these two centuries. The book besides narrating his experiences of the various parts of India and Persia he passed through, in an interesting and often amusing manner, contains curious particulars respecting the natural history and medicines of these countries. Fryer took his M.D. on returing from his tour in 1683 and was elected a Fellow of the Royal Society a year before the appearance of his book, which fully testified to both his medical and scientific attainments. It was somewhat strange that Fryer's book, considering its great interest and value, should not have been reprinted till a few years ago, when Mr. W. Crookes brought out for the Hakluyt Society his scholarly edition. The late Mr. Talboys Wheeler (1824-1897), the historical writer, had indeed reprinted the Indian part in the Calcutta *Englishman* more than forty years ago, but the volume in which the articles were collected soon went out of print. Philip Anderson (1816-1857) in his excellent historical account of the English in Bombay and Western India in the seventeenth century, published in 1854, in our city, has summarised Fryer so deftly that we have given it also.

Ovington who came sixteen years after Fryer, published his book, *A Voyage to Suratt in the year 1689*, two years earlier in 1696. He was a Chaplain in the Royal Navy and remained for several years on the coasts of India; and he has left behind in this book, beside his account of Bombay and Elephanta, a detailed description of Surat and its cosmopolitan population, for Surat was in his days pretty much what Bombay is at present, representing so many castes and creeds.

A quarter of a century later came another Chaplain, **Richard Cobbe,** a learned and pious man, who left his mark here during the few years that he resided in this settlement by stirring religious enthusiasm and thereby promoting the erection of our venerable Cathedral, not indeed so styled at the time, but as he modestly calls it, "the Bombay Church." But he held peculiar views about his office and duties as chaplain, and coming into collision with the Council, he had to retire abruptly in 1719. He survived for half a century and published so late as 1766 a rare little volume giving an account of the Bombay Church in whose erection he had taken a large and enthusiastic part. In this he prints a letter addressed to the Bishop of London, soon after his arrival here in 1715, in which he gives him a short account of Bombay which we have quoted from this scarce book. The Bishop, it seems, had asked him, on parting, to interest himself in the place and send him some account of the island and the state of religion. The letter was in answer to this request and though it does not say much has still some interest.

Alexander Hamilton (? 1658-1732) whose account is as well known as that of Fryer, was a sea captain, who, after gaining some maritime experience in Europe and the West Indies, came out to the East Indies in 1688 and did not return to Europe till 1723, visiting during those thirty-five years almost every port from Jeddah to Amoy. He was in Bombay often and knew it intimately. But he was what was called an "interloper," following a life of commercial adventure, and as such had a strong prejudice against the East India Company with which his book is strongly tinged. His *New Account of the East Indies* was published in 1727 and went through a second edition in 1744. Though it has not been reprinted since in separate form, it is well known owing to long extracts given by both Pinkerton and Kerr in their general collections of voyages and travels published in the early part of the last century. Of this work of Capt. Hamilton, a very competent authority, Sir John Laughton, speaks in these high terms: "In the charm of its naive simplicity, perfect honesty, with some similarity of subject in its account of the manners and history of people little known, it offers a closer parallel to the history of Herodotus than perhaps any other in modern literature." (Dict. of Nat. Biog., Vol. VIII, p. 1017. 2nd ed.)

Edward Ives (? 1720-1786) was a surgeon in the navy who came to Bombay in 1754 on board the 'Kent,' the ship bearing the flag of Admiral Watson (1714-1757) as commander-in-chief in the East Indies, and remained in the Indian seas till the Admiral's death in Aug. 1757, when he resigned his appointment and returned to England overland by way of Persia and Asia Minor. In 1773 Ives published his experiences in India and of his overland journey homewards in a quarto volume entitled "A Voyage from England to India in 1754 and an Historical Narrative of the Operations of the Squadron and Army in India under the command of Vice-Admiral Watson and Col. Clive in

1755-57," which is important on account of his personal intimacy with Watson and of his presence at many of the transactions described.

Carsten Niebuhr (1733-1815) the father of the famous historian of Rome, Barthold Niebuhr (1776-1831) came to Bombay in the course of his scientific tour in Arabia and India in 1761-1767, undertaken at the expense of the Danish Government, and stayed here for fourteen months from Oct. 1763 to Dec. 1764, and wrote a well-known account which is often referred to. This appeared in his *Voyage en Arabie* which was published in two volumes in 1774-78, and contains his experiences of that long and interesting tour in the course of which he visited Egypt, Arabia, India, Persia and Palestine. At Bombay he was well received and made several lasting friendships with Englishmen on the Island. He also learned English here, and endeavoured to obtain information about the Parsis and Hindus which he utilised in his work, which was translated in an abridged form from the original French into English. Niebuhr was a native of Hanover, and educated at the Gottingen University, from which he passed to Copenhagen and entered Danish service in which he passed his life. His more famous son, born at Copenhagen, began life in the service of Denmark, but soon entered that of Prussia and distinguished himself as a diplomatist and still more as a historian. As a young man he studied at Edinburgh for a year and was, as he himself says, received as one of the family in the house of a venerable man, Francis Scott of Harden, whose friendship had been formed by his father while in Bombay.

John Henry Grose, (fl. 1750-1783) younger brother of the well-known antiquary Francis Grose, (1731-1791), came out to Bombay in 1750 as a Civil Servant of the East India Company and on his return published in 1757 in a single volume an account of his experiences. This volume gives a good account of Eastern manners and customs then little known, and was said to have been compiled from Grose's notes by John Cleland (1709-1789), who had himself been in Bombay as servant of the Company for several years. (For Cleland's career in Bombay and other matters, the curious may refer to an article by me in the *Athenæum*, December, 1905). A second edition appeared in 1766, enlarged in two volumes, and a third followed in 1772. The first edition was translated into French in 1758. The work has been made the basis of many popular accounts.

James Forbes (1749-1819) was another of the Company's Bombay Civilians who wrote a widely known account of our Island after a long residence here. He came to Bombay as a Civil Servant in 1766 and remained in the service till 1783, serving in various places in Gujarat like Broach, Dhabhoi, etc. During these seventeen years he had imbibed a genuine love for the country and its inhabitants as well as amassed a large collection of sketches and notes on the flora, fauna, manners, religions, and archæology of India. These he utilised as materials for his great work *Oriental Memoirs*, which he published in four large quarto volumes between 1813 and 1815. This work has now for a century deservedly held a very high place in Anglo-Indian literature. Its marked characteristic is the genuine love for the country and sympathy for its inhabitants that it shows by the side of its intimate arquaintance with their sentiments and prejudices. Count de Montalembert, (1810-1870), the famous French orator and historian was his daughter's son and was brought up with great care in his early days by him. For his grandson's eventual use when he should come to the age of discretion, Forbes prepared an enlarged manuscript edition of the *Memoirs*, expanding the four volumes to forty-two by inserting copies of his original sketches, letters, verses and numerous other additions; but Montalembert took no interest in the East and consequently neglected these manuscript treasures, which, however, are preserved by the family at Oscott College.

Forbes had retired from Bombay on a comfortable competency and spent thirty-five years of retirement in learned ease and occasional travel. Whilst travelling in France during the peace of Amiens, he was detained prisoner with all other British subjects by Napoleon when he broke that peace in 1803. He was, however, after some time allowed to return to England in the middle of 1804, and he published two years later his "Letters from France," which contain an interesting account of his captivity. His only daughter who had married Marc de Montalembert, a member of an old French noble family, whom the Revolution had driven to England, published in 1834 an abridgement of the "Oriental Memoirs" in two octavos, which brought the splendid but unwieldy work into a form more adapted for easy handling. It is somewhat strange that in these days of reprints nobody should have thought of republishing in a popular form Forbes' most interesting and diverting volumes. If Englishmen in India were to read these Memoirs at the outset of their career here, they could not fail to imbibe at least some of the author's love for the land and sympathy for its peoples.

Of the two anonymous accounts quoted, that of 1724 is from an exceedingly rare little volume kindly placed at my disposal by Mr. S. T. Sheppard, of the *Times of India*, an enthusiastic collector of *Bombayana*. This book is specially important for an account of the Portuguese cession of the Island to the English and the documents relating thereto. The other book, published in 1781, is attributed to Samuel Pechel in Halkett and Laing's "Anomymous Literature." He is supposed to be a Civil Servant, but I have been unable to trace him in the official lists given in Sir G. Forrest's old Bombay Secretariat Papers. The book is almost entirely devoted to a narrative of the first Mahratha War (1778-1781) then drawing to a close.

It has been thought fit to close this section with Walter Hamilton's account, as his bulky book, *Description of Hindustan*, may be said to have begun the age of Indian Gazetteers. Indeed he called the second edition of the book published in 1828 by this title. From that point forward the accounts multiply fast and the books quoted in the other sections will give a clue to them.